DEVELOPING A THESIS AND A WORKING OUTLINE

WRITING YOUR FIRST DRAFT

REVISING YOUR PAPER

PREPARING YOUR FINAL COPY

The Bedford Guide
to the Research Process

SECOND EDITION

The Bedford Guide to the Research Process

Jean Johnson

University of Maryland at College Park

Bedford Books *of* **St. Martin's Press**

Boston

For Mark, Eric, and Hilary

For Bedford Books
Publisher: Charles H. Christensen
Associate Publisher: Joan E. Feinberg
Managing Editor: Elizabeth M. Schaaf
Developmental Editors: Stephen A. Scipione and Ellen M. Kuhl
Production Editor: Tara L. Masih
Copyeditor: Barbara Flanagan
Cover Design: Richard Emery Design, Inc.
Cover Art: Tom Hughes

Library of Congress Catalog Card Number: 90–71611

For information, write: St. Martin's Press, Inc.
175 Fifth Avenue, New York, NY 10010

Editorial Offices: Bedford Books *of* St. Martin's Press
29 Winchester Street, Boston, MA 02116

ISBN: 0–312–03466–0

Acknowledgments

Stephen Barrett, M.D., from "Commercial Hair Analysis: Science or Scam?" in *JAMA: The Journal of the American Medical Association* 254.8 (August 23/30, 1985): 1042, 1044. Copyright © 1985, American Medical Association. Reprinted by permission of *JAMA: The Journal of the American Medical Association*.

Stephen Vincent Benet, from *Western Star* copyright page. *Western Star* by Stephen Vincent Benet. Holt, Rinehart and Winston, Inc. Copyright 1943 by Rosemary Carr Benet. Copyright renewed © 1971 by Rachel Benet Lewis, Thomas C. Benet, and Stephanie Benet Mahin. Reprinted by permission of Brandt & Brandt Literary Agents, Inc.

Bibliographic Index, "Falklands Islands War" entry. *Bibliographic Index*, 1989. Copyright © 1989 by The H. W. Wilson Company. Material reproduced with permission of the publisher.

Book Review Digest, "Drinka, George Frederick" entry. *Book Review Digest*, 1985. Copyright © 1985 by The H. W. Wilson Company. Material reproduced with permission of the publisher.

Books in Print, 1990–1991, from "Duke Ellington" entry in the Subject Guide. Copyright © 1990 by Reed Publishing (U.S.A.) Inc. Reprinted by permission of R. R. Bowker/Martindale-Hubbell.

Acknowledgments and copyrights are continued at the back of the book on pages 395–396, which constitute an extension of the copyright page.

Preface

The Bedford Guide to the Research Process, Second Edition, helps students recognize their natural curiosity and desire to learn and apply these motivating forces to more sophisticated forms of research. My goal has been to provide information that students need about the research process while encouraging them to educate themselves and to make their own choices with confidence.

Organization

Like its predecessor, this second edition serves students in two ways: as a step-by-step guide to the research process for a course in which a research paper is assigned and as a reference for writing papers both in college and after graduation. Chapter 1 provides help with choosing a topic—for some students the hardest part of writing a research paper. Chapter 2 assists students in planning the paper and designing a search strategy. Chapters 3, 4, and 5 present detailed guidelines for collecting information from library sources as well as from questionnaires, interviews, oral history, and court documents. Students are also shown how to keep accurate notes and records—on paper or on a computer—as well as how to paraphrase, summarize, quote, and document sources in their papers while avoiding plagiarism.

The principles and practice of re-searching and outlining are discussed in Chapter 6. Then, to emphasize that more than one draft is needed in writing a research paper and that each draft serves a special rhetorical purpose, students are guided through three writing stages: the first draft (Chapter 7), the revising process (Chapter 8), and preparation of the final copy (Chapter 9). Optional or auxiliary parts of a paper—such as illustrations, table of contents, and abstracts—are discussed and illustrated.

Chapters 10, 11, and 12 explain the guidelines of the three major systems for documenting, formatting, and using in-text parenthetical citation: the MLA or author/page system, used primarily in the humanities; the APA or author/date system, favored by writers in the social sciences; and the number system, used by writers in the sciences.

(For those who prefer to use footnotes or endnotes, Appendix 2 contains guidelines for using the *Chicago Manual of Style* format.) These final chapters include four annotated student papers from different academic disciplines to illustrate the three systems.

Features Retained and Strengthened

The features that instructors and students appreciated in the first edition such as the step-by-step procedures, the optional search log, the end-of-chapter exercises, and the examples of student writing from many disciplines, have been retained and, I believe, improved. The inclusion of actual student experiences encourages students to see themselves as explorers in an engaging and worthwhile human activity, not as mere computers receiving, storing, and repeating information at the command of a teacher. Furthermore, students writing in various disciplines—from engineering, biology, sociology, psychology, or computer science to history, arts, music, or literature—will find student examples at every stage in their process, providing them with a sense of how others have worked in their field.

The annotated list of references in Appendix 1, a cross-curricular feature that many instructors found to be one of the most helpful parts of the first edition, has been expanded to include more subject areas and greater coverage of databases. Appendix 3 has been revised and expanded to direct advanced students to style manuals in twenty-eight disciplines.

New Features

In response to suggestions from those who used the first edition and developments in the fields of research and composition, I have introduced several new features.

Computer-aided Research and Writing. More and more students have computers available at school and at home. For many students, "writing" has come to mean composing on the computer. Libraries are using computers to store their information and also to make it available to students. Therefore, advice on using computers has been added to each chapter so that, if students wish, they will be able to integrate automated research and writing resources into each stage of their writing and research process. Chapter 3 includes a list of the commonly used databases in each discipline, along with the types of format available for each and a summary of the subject matter covered. So many databases are now available in a variety of formats—online, on CD-ROM, and in print—that the choice can be confusing; this edition explains the advantages and disadvantages of each.

Critical Thinking and Rhetorical Argument. Because critical thinking is necessary at each stage of the research process, many new student examples are included to demonstrate thinking skills and logical argumentation. In addition, Chapter 6 provides guidelines for analyzing and evaluating a paper's argument or thesis according to the model set forth by Stephen Toulmin in *The Uses of Argument.* A new research paper in Chapter 10 employs the techniques of rhetorical argument as it explores a current controversial subject, the repatriation of Native American artifacts and remains.

Collaborative Learning. The classroom provides an opportunity for students to help each other. To facilitate such learning, I have added peer review exercises to every chapter where they are appropriate.

Acknowledgments

I have many to thank for the improvements in this new edition. For their thoughtful comments on the first edition and the first draft, I thank reviewers Brian Kennedy, Cedarville College; Charles Elwert, University of Illinois; and Tom Recchio, University of Connecticut.

For taking the time to answer a questionnaire on how the book worked in their classrooms, I am very grateful to Gary Acton, Eastern Montana College; Lori A. Alfe, Rock Valley College; Katya Amato, Portland State University; Charles Beall, San Diego State University; Sheila Bender, Shoreline Community College; Edel A. Berberi, Southwestern Michigan College; M. F. Bertelt, Brainerd Community College; James Bowen, Southwestern Oregon Community College; Brenda Jo Breuggeman, University of Louisville; Margaret Brofman, Mira Costa College; Julie Colish, University of Michigan at Flint; Uel Combs, West Chester University; Patricia Derby, Chabot College; Lesa Dill, Western Kentucky University; Richard Dennis Finn, San Diego State University; Charles Fisher, Aims Community College; Susan Frantz, La Roche College; Lawrence B. Fuller, Bloomsburg University; Katherine A. Glowes, Sierra College; Della Carden Gravson, University of California at Irvine; John Hagaman, Western Kentucky University; Roy Higginson, Iowa State University; Patricia J. Hoovler, El Camino College; Laurie L. Hoskin, University of Michigan at Flint; Caroline A. Julyan, Northeast Missouri State University; Linda Micheli, Bentley College; Scott Orme, Spokane Community College; Anne M. Ousterhout of Michigan State University; Ruth J. Pauli, University of Maryland at College Park; Kathleen G. Rousseau, West Virginia University; Joseph L. Sanders, Lakeland Community College; Leslie Vitale, Oakland University; Robert Vuturo, Kansas City Kansas Community College; Hazel G. Warlaumont, University of California at Irvine; Allen D. Widerburg, Clackamas Community

College; D. C. Woodcox, Northeast Missouri State University; and Ann Woodlief, Virginia Commonwealth University.

Without the help of knowledgeable librarians, I could not have included the information on the library that is one of the central features of this book. Judy Solberg of the University of Maryland at College Park provided the research for the expanded annotated reference list in Appendix 1. My thanks also to Em Claire Knowles, Daphne Harrington, and Candy Schwartz of the Simmons College Graduate School of Library and Information Science for their careful and perceptive reviews of the chapters on the use of computers in searching. Librarians Ed Adams, Pat Herron, John King, Robert Merikangas, and Ann Masnik at the University of Maryland were unfailingly patient in answering my many questions. Thanks also to John Dorsey of the Boston Public Library for his help in providing reference materials. For guidance on library databases, I often turned to William B. Katz's *Introduction to Reference Work* (New York: McGraw-Hill, 1987).

I remain grateful to those who helped shape the first edition: Donald McQuade, University of California, Berkeley; Shirley Morahan, Northeast Missouri State University; Walter Minot, Gannon University; Michael Flanigan, University of Oklahoma; Margaret Gooch, Tufts University; David Bloch, University of Texas at Austin; Melinda Kramer, Purdue University; Kenneth Morrison; Alan Johnson; Michael Williamson, Indiana University of Pennsylvania; Michael Gustin, University of California, Los Angeles; Hilary Johnson; Betty Day; Gail Sonneman, Marge Posner, and the other reference librarians at the Fenwick Library, George Mason University.

My gratitude goes to all of those at Bedford Books who attended so competently to the many details connected with publication. Once again my special thanks to Charles Christensen, whose idea this was from the beginning, and Joan Feinberg, whose advice and support were always helpful. I am grateful to have been able to work with Stephen A. Scipione, who saw the possibilities for improvements in this edition and whose encouragement and good humor sustained me throughout the project. Others at Bedford Books whose expert assistance were invaluable include Ellen Kuhl, who coordinated much of the process; Beth Castrodale, who attended to many of the editorial details; Barbara Flanagan, whose careful editing makes this book more accurate and much easier to read; and Tara L. Masih, who patiently guided the manuscript into print.

While I have been teaching my students about research, they have been teaching me. I want to thank especially Kenneth Bogart, Marisa Colli, Melinda Godwin, David Kuijt, and Justin Lev-Tov, who allowed me to use parts of their work in this second edition. My thanks, too, to my friend and colleague Mary Scheltema for suggestions based on her students' use of the first edition.

Contents

PART III   Writing Papers Across the Curriculum: Documentation Systems   *237*

10   Writing a Paper in the Humanities: The Author/Page Style   *239*

The Bedford Guide
to the Research Process

PART I

Searching

INTRODUCTION

Research: Searching, Re-Searching, and Writing

Why We Do Research

"Searching," "exploring," "discovering"—we associate these words with excitement and pleasure, and for good reasons. We like the idea of uncovering what has been hidden, of turning the unknown into the known, whether we are exploring our inner space, like Plato or Freud, or the space beyond us, like Christopher Columbus or Sir Edmund Hillary. Then, after we have made our discoveries, we like to tell others about them. Our choice of medium can be anything from film or newspapers to novels or poems. One of the most common media—and the one you will be mastering—is the research paper.

Why do we search? Searching seems to be a result of our natural curiosity, our desire to find answers to problems, our urge to question what others have told us, or perhaps just our need to know more about the unknown. We want to know how to cure polio or how to get a job; we want to know how things work—how plants grow or how the human mind functions. But we may not have a specific goal. We may just want to collect information—to find out what is inside the earth, what is on the moon, or how children behave at the age of two. Collecting such information and analyzing it may lead to questions about it and to further searches.

Sometimes we search to find answers to controversial social questions. As members of a community, we may find our beliefs in conflict with those of others. Should abortion be legal? Should criminals be executed? How much should we be taxed? Answering such questions requires that we check the validity of our assumptions, inform ourselves adequately about the subject, and analyze the information thoughtfully. It requires that we think creatively and critically—and not become just passive receptors of someone else's obvious or popular conclusions.

Whatever our motivation is, when we search for information we must think creatively and critically during the whole process. We must first choose a subject that will yield information likely to be valuable to ourselves or to others. Then we must find and evaluate the most reliable sources, using or rejecting the information we find. Next we must analyze that information to find its meaning, and finally we must weigh its value and implications.

With the research paper, as with all exploration, the search is as important as the telling, but when a search is compelling and absorbing for the searcher, there is an almost equally compelling urge to tell or write about it. And not simply to tell about it, but to tell it so well that the reader or listener can participate in the experience and learn as well as the writer what the search resulted in. The more interested you are in your project, the better chance you have of producing an interesting paper. There are other benefits besides this tangible result. Because you direct your own search, you will gain knowledge that is important to you, that can even change your life—as, in varying degrees, all learning does.

One student, Iori Miller, discovered in doing his research paper an area of knowledge that he wanted to continue to explore professionally. When the research paper was assigned, Miller considered plants as a possible subject. At first, he thought he would concentrate on ferns— he had always admired the different kinds of ferns in the woods near his home and thought he would like to find out more about them. While looking for information about them, he came across a book on cacti and became fascinated by them. He began reading books about cacti and enrolled in a botany course. The following year he became a student assistant in the botany lab and eventually went on to do graduate work in botany.

As Miller's search shows, a search like this has no predictable pattern and no predictable results; if they were predictable, there would be no point in undertaking the search. Henry David Thoreau (1817–1862), whom we remember as the author of *Walden*, chose a large subject for his search—he wanted to discover the meaning of life. He decided to live alone in a cabin in the woods to collect his information. Later, in *Walden*, he explained his purpose:

> I went to the woods because I wished to live deliberately. . . . I wanted to drive life into a corner, and reduce it to its lowest terms, and, if it proved to be mean, why then to get the whole and genuine meanness of it, and publish its meanness to the world; or if it were sublime, to know it by experience, and be able to give a true account of it.

Notice that Thoreau's purpose was not only to gather information for himself. He also wanted to "publish" it "to the world"; he wanted to "give a true account of it." During his two years at Walden Pond, Thoreau kept a journal in which he recorded his observations of the animals, the people, the lake, the trees, and the sky and the thoughts that these observations inspired. In his journal, he recorded in dated entries his observations and thoughts as he experienced them. These were his data, his raw material. Natural events, in other words, were the books in which Thoreau did his research on life.

> I start a sparrow from her three eggs in the grass, where she had settled for the night. The earliest corn is beginning to show its tassels now, and I scent it as I walk—its peculiar dry scent. . . . I smell the huckleberry bushes. I hear a human voice—some laborer singing after his day's toil. . . . The air is remarkably still and unobjectionable on the hilltop, and the whole world below is covered as with a gossamer of moonlight. It is just about as yellow as a blanket.

Seven years after he left Walden Pond, he published *Walden*, in which he selected parts of his journal and reordered them topically under such headlines as "Reading," "Sounds," "Visitors," and "The Pond in Winter." This type of organization allowed him to focus on the aspects of his experience that had the most meaning for him and to explain what that meaning was. The observations in his journal, when reviewed, gave new meaning to his subject—the sparrow instructed Thoreau in his subject, life.

> The first sparrow of spring! The year beginning with younger hope than ever! . . . the symbol of perpetual youth, the grass-blade, like a long green ribbon, streams from the sod into the summer. . . . So our human life but dies down to its root, and still puts forth its green blade to eternity.

Charles Darwin (1809–1882), an amateur naturalist from England, set out in 1831 on a five-year voyage around the world on HMS *Beagle*. Like Thoreau, he kept a journal recording his observations of natural life in minute detail. His *Journal of Researches into the Geology and Natural History of the Various Countries Visited by HMS Beagle, 1832–36* was published after he returned. From the notes in his journal he developed a theory on the formation of coral reefs and a theory of evolution by natural selection. The latter revolutionary theory he explained in *On the Origin of Species*, published in 1859.

Each of these kinds of writing—the journal and the book created from it—has its own organizational form; each has its own value.

Like Thoreau's observations in *Walden* and Darwin's in his *Origin of Species*, what you discover while researching and writing this paper may be important not only to you but also to someone else. Peter DeGress, a student, did a study to find out whether solar energy would be a practical source of heat for his uncle's house. After finding out the costs of installation and computing the savings, he concluded that only solar hot-water heating would save his uncle money. He then drew plans for such a system and presented his results to his uncle as well as to the class.

The aunt of Rhonda Martin, another student, wondered whether a soldier with a name similar to hers who was mentioned in books on the Civil War was a relative. Martin decided to find out. She did much of her research in the genealogical section of the Library of Congress in Washington, D.C. (she happened to live nearby), and she also made a trip to a town in Maryland to look at court documents from the Civil War. She discovered that the soldier was indeed a relative, and she was able to find out a good deal more about where he had lived and worked than the family had known before. Martin's aunt paid her a small amount for her report.

Courtenay Coogan heard her microbiology instructor refer to a little-known organism, *Pseudomonas pseudomallei*, that was causing a hard-to-detect and usually fatal disease in Vietnam veterans. She wanted to find out what research had been conducted on this organism and to determine whether anything could be done to diagnose the disease more accurately. She was able to report to her classmates on the growing danger of this disease and the steps that can be taken to prevent it.

Joan Keller, also a student, examined different types of word processors to see which would be best for her office to buy. Because a word processing system for an office is expensive, she had to do her research carefully and thoroughly. She visited computer stores and talked to sales people to learn the prices and features of computers; she interviewed managers of companies who had purchased computer systems to find out actual time and money benefits as well as their ease of operation and repair records. Through her research she was able to help her company make a decision that would increase staff efficiency as well as save money.

How We Do Research

Searching: Finding Answers to Your Questions

The first stage in writing a paper—searching or exploring—is an activity you began very early in life, probably shortly after you were born. By the age of two you were in high gear, trying to find out everything you could about your world. "The love of the chase is an inherent delight in man—a relic of an instinctive passion," wrote Darwin as he looked back at his journey on the *Beagle*. A two-year-old is probably the preeminent human explorer, akin in many ways to the likes of Darwin or Thoreau. Watch a two-year-old on his or her own for fifteen minutes, and you'll get some idea of the single-mindedness, determination, and zest that distinguish the successful researcher. Because of these characteristics, the two-year-old will learn at an astonishingly rapid rate. Later, other search-and-find activities begin to interest us—games of hide-and-seek and treasure hunts. In school we continue our search for information with the help of others. As we get older, we may search for special kinds of seashells, antiques, or buried treasure. As professionals we continue to search: as archaeologists we seek evidence of past civilizations; as ornithologists we look for rare birds; as immunologists we try to find the cure for a disease; as business managers we search for ways to improve a product or service; as lawyers we examine records for pertinent cases. In fact, we often define ourselves or our interests according to the area in which we choose to search.

The search is as important to the searcher as is the written account. Without the interest in the search itself, the product will be of little value or interest either to the researcher or to others. For the true searcher, the product, like the extent of the search, is unpredictable, at least at the beginning. Thoreau's goal was not to write *Walden*; Darwin was not planning to write *On the Origin of Species*. They searched and observed and kept journals. Students, on the other hand, may know they will be writing a report, but what they don't know is the exact *content* of their report.

Choosing Your Topic.   As you begin to choose the subject you will explore, you should be asking yourself not only "What *subject* do I want to explore?" but also "What subject do *I* want to be an explorer of?" You ask these questions because your result will be not only an additional paper but also an addition to your personal store of knowledge— each helps to define you as a person.

Chances are you already have your subject in mind—that is, in your mind. You just haven't uncovered it yet or decided which to choose of the many subjects you have in mind. Take some time to listen to the questions you are asking yourself daily about the subjects you are studying or about what is going on around you. Thoreau asked himself, "What is life?" Darwin asked, "What animals and plants exist in other parts of the world?" Peter DeGress asked, "Can my uncle heat his home with solar energy?"

Finding Sources.   Two of the benefits of writing this paper will be discovering new information and, more important, new ways of finding information. As you begin, you may think first of the process often used by beginning researchers in finding information: going to the library, looking in the *Readers' Guide* and the library catalog, checking out a few books, photocopying a few articles, and then beginning to write. In doing this paper you will learn how to expand this process. No matter what size your community is, you have many sources available to you. Libraries provide books, articles, pamphlets, computer data-bases, microfilms, videotapes, records, and often other resources. You can probably find experts on your subject on your campus or in your town. For some types of historical research, interviews with people who have had relevant experience may be the best source. The local court-house or statehouse has documents available to the public; museums store documents and artifacts. The dedicated researcher, in other words, looks under the stones that others merely walk around.

Collecting Information.   When you select for your search one of the many subjects you are interested in, you have your first direction—the first clue in your search. The thoroughness of your search determines the amount of information you have to work with and thus, to a large extent, the quality of your paper. Peter DeGress had to find out the cost of solar space-heating systems and solar water-heating systems. He had to analyze the structure of his uncle's house and family's needs to see how these matched up with available systems. To determine savings, he had to learn about costs of other fuels and returns on other possible in-vestments of the money that would be spent on the heating system. Then he had to compute the effects of these expenditures and savings on his uncle's tax liabilities. Some of this information he could collect directly: as an engineering major, he could study the structure of his uncle's house and take the necessary measurements. For some infor-mation he had to rely on other people: he had to read books, pam-phlets, and periodicals and make judgments about the reliability of his materials, such as how accurate a pamphlet put out by a manufacturer was or whether an article by a consumer affairs group would be more reliable. And for a technological subject like this, the information had to be up to date; a book published in 1971 was not likely to be of much value. As he collected his information, he recorded it on cards or drew diagrams.

The research paper often requires you to be more an observer of events than a participant in them. You will probably be getting most of your information from the work and experiences of others—experts who may have spent years studying, observing, and examining the same things you want to know about. You'll find this information in books or articles or through interviews. However, you may find that making your own observations or conducting your own experiments is more rewarding or appropriate. Whatever your method of research, your collecting of information will be *purposeful* and *directed*—you'll want to find out more about a specific subject or answer a specific question.

Keeping Records.   In previous papers you've written, you assimi-lated the information you gathered through your senses or perhaps by listening to others and then re-searched it (found what was significant in it) and wrote it down. Even if you were only recording your experience, you were ordering and selecting and therefore giving significance to some part of your experience rather than another. So the main difference between those papers and your research paper will be the gathering of your information and the documentation of your sources in your writing.

Recording Two Kinds of Information: Keeping a Search Log and Taking Notes. Since you will probably be using more than your own experience as a source of information, you must learn new techniques for gathering and storing information. You won't be able to rely on your memory to store everything you learn; you'll have to write it down as you go along. And because you will be learning a process as you gather data, you will be collecting two kinds of information: *what you do* and *what you find.* To keep track of both, you'll need to keep two kinds of records.

First, you'll be keeping a record of what you do—where you go, what kinds of sources you discover, whom you interview, and so on—in a *search log* (much as the captain of a ship keeps a log) so that you will know where you have been and what you still have to do. You can buy a small notebook for this or use a part of your loose-leaf binder. Some of you may want to use a computer or a word processor. Jot down in a notebook what you do, and then record it later in a file in your computer. Besides summarizing what you have done each day, you can put down your thoughts and feelings about your project as well as your questions or problems. It's so much easier and faster to write on a computer that you're likely to write more if you use one. Talking to yourself on a computer about your project can help you understand more clearly what you are doing and where you are going. Besides, if you misplace your notebook, you'll still have a record.

This record can also be helpful when you do research in the future. Although logs or journals are commonly used to record various kinds of data, including personal experience, and are meant for a limited audience, they are sometimes interesting enough to be published (as were Darwin's and parts of Thoreau's) because often the story of the search is as exciting as what is found. When scientists Francis Crick and James Watson discovered the structure of DNA, they explained *what they found* in a scientific article, ''Molecular Structure of Nucleic Acids'' (1953), in the journal *Nature.* In 1968 James Watson published *The Double Helix,* an account of their search written for the general public that became a best seller. So *what you do* can be as interesting as *what you find.* If you enjoy the search, you will more likely enjoy writing about what you find and thus write an interesting paper. You will probably be ''publishing'' only the results of your search, though you may share parts of your search log with your classmates as you go along.

Second, what you find—the information you discover—will go on note cards or separate pieces of paper so you can organize that information for easy use when you begin to write your research paper. It may be even more efficient, however, to put this information into the computer immediately. Several computer programs are available to help you put your information on "cards" in the computer, which will then sort them for you. For more information on how to take notes on cards and on the computer, see Chapter 4.

Re-Searching: The Search for Meaning

The mere collecting and recording of information is only the first stage. *Re-searching* is looking back over that information and making sense of it, seeing how it fits together and how it links up with what you already know. The two-year-old is searching (exploring); she gathers and stores information but doesn't find the meaning in it as an adult would. In other words, *search* plus *re-search* equals *research*.

Of course, you have gone through this process many times. You research when you look for the scores of your favorite baseball team (the searching stage) and then analyze why they played so poorly or so well (the re-searching stage). You use the process when you plan a trip: in the searching stage you decide what route to follow, what supplies to bring, how much time to allot; and in the re-searching stage you decide whether you have the time or the money to go. Or you might decide to buy a new television. As part of your searching stage you would read the ads in the newspaper, ask a friend whether he likes his new set, and perhaps read an article in *Consumer Reports*. Then you would re-search it; you would put all this information together with what you already have observed about televisions and make your decision.

Writing the Research Paper

Exchanging Information. Writing down the results of your findings is naturally the next step in this process. You're finding out all along—both as you research and as you write—what significance your information has for you and what conclusions you've reached, and you're putting them in a form that will make them available to others. There's a generosity about bothering to write down the results of your search, just as there is a generosity about orally sharing your information and thoughts. Personal relations are enhanced by giving and receiving information. (Peter DeGress gave his results to his uncle, Rhonda Martin gave hers to her aunt, and Joan Keller shared hers with her office staff; all of them shared their information with other members of their class.) Communities of interest (scientific, academic, agricultural, political, religious, and sports, for example) are built and maintained through this sharing of information.

Collaborative Writing. Besides exchanging with your classmates the information you've gathered, you might want to assist one another in all parts of the process—in effect becoming collaborators on your projects. If you do, the writing classroom, where you have the opportunity to exchange information and ideas, can also serve as a writing workshop. You have an opportunity presented to you that may not occur again: it's not easy to assemble outside the classroom a group of people with similar goals who will meet regularly for several weeks to concentrate on writing.

To be a helpful member of this group you don't have to be an expert on writing (your instructor is), but you can act as a surrogate or intermediary audience for your classmates; each of you can provide reactions and feedback to one another at all points of the research and writing process. You might also be able to provide information and sources to each other. When everyone in the class is aware of the topics of the other class members, the class becomes a network of searchers that can report back relevant information found in their daily reading of newspapers, magazines, and books.

There are many other ways you can collaborate. As you go through the process outlined in this book, you will find exercises suggested for working in groups that will help you to give and receive help in writing.

The Writing Process. Of course, you already know from writing other papers that writing a paper is not just a simple matter of sitting down one night, recording what you know, and handing it in the next day. First you need a written plan—an outline—to organize the information you have collected so that it is logical and understandable. When you sit down to write, an outline will save you time because you won't have to decide what to write next. In your first draft you need only fill in the structure of your outline with details that further shape and make meaning out of your materials. Most people need (1) a second draft to refine the organization and to check the effectiveness of paragraphs, sentences, and words and (2) a final draft to check the documentation of sources and to solve problems of punctuation, grammar, spelling, and the like. Some parts may have to be rewritten more than three times. Starting early and following a carefully planned schedule will make it possible for you to write a good paper and meet your deadline.

The Importance of Abundance. Start thinking now of providing more than you need at each stage of your research process. Abundance—even overabundance—is part of nature's back-up system, and you can benefit from it too. Start with a list of more subjects to choose from than you need for your paper. Collect more information than you think you can use. Write more drafts than you plan to. And, if you can possibly manage it, plan to spend more time than you think it may take you to complete the project.

Even when it comes to using paper, be generous. Using both sides of sheets and cards without leaving margins may save you some money, but it will cost you a lot of time. Instead, leave plenty of space so that you can add material if you want to, and write on only one side of the paper or card. Smaller amounts of information on more cards or pieces of paper will also make sorting and organizing much easier.

Building overabundance into your process means that you must be willing to discard what you don't need. (Place your discarded paper in one of the receptacles for recycling now available on most campuses.) Producing more than you need will save you time in the long run and make your product better because it will give you choices. In case something does not work—a subject, source, piece of information, sentence, paragraph—you will have a back-up. Space missions operate on this theory. When people are launched into space, they carry extra equipment with them. So as you begin your exploration, plan for leftovers. You'll end up with a better paper and save time as well.

CHAPTER 1

Choosing Your Topic

Choosing a topic is often regarded as something that is done only at term paper or essay writing time. But we are choosing topics to explore every day. We may explore something as mundane as the taste of a new kind of cheese or as exciting as a mountain. And we're not only choosing topics, we're also rejecting many that we would like to investigate because we don't have time or they aren't important enough.

Choosing a topic is not a single one-time act, like picking a carton of milk off the shelf. Choosing a topic is more of an evolutionary process that coincides with the beginning of your search. There's a bit of a catch-22 feeling at first: you can't begin your search until you have a topic, but you can't decide on a topic until you've done some research. You need to find out

1. what the scope of the subject is;
2. what information is available;
3. whether you can get the information in the required time;
4. whether the time required to explore the subject adequately and write your results corresponds to the time you have.

In the early stages of your search, your topic and your information direct each other: your topic tells you where to find your information (for example, in books, from people, or by observation), and your information helps shape your topic or perhaps leads you to abandon one topic and choose another. Because it's important to have a clearly defined topic as soon as possible, it is a good idea to begin your search as early as you can.

Before you can decide on a specific *topic* for your paper, you will probably want to explore one or more *subjects*, or general areas of study.

13

These subjects interest you because of what you have read or heard or because of what has happened to you or to someone you know. Of course, the intensity of your interest will vary from one subject to another. Now is the time to look at some of those overlooked subjects. Although your choice of subject for a research paper will depend on other things besides your interest in it, interest is certainly the main criterion and the one to consider first. The intensity of your desire to know more about your subject will keep you searching even when obstacles arise— when information seems hard to find, when you are busy with other things, and when the necessary time doesn't seem to be there. The first step in writing a good research paper, then, is to recall some of the subjects that attract you and to choose the most suitable for this occasion.

"But what if I'm assigned a subject to write on?" you may be asking. "Then I can't write about what *I'm* interested in." Yes, usually you can. You need to find the part of that subject that relates to something you are interested in. Let's say that in an American history course, your instructor asks you to write a paper on Custer's last stand—the Battle of the Little Bighorn. Before you say that this subject doesn't appeal to you, ask yourself questions about the event that relate to other interests of yours until you find an aspect of it that you think you might like to explore. If you are taking a course in which this subject is relevant, you probably already have some information about it. Questions like the following might occur to you: Was it Custer's fault that the battle was lost? Was he a good military strategist? What was Custer's ability to command men? What was the role of the Battle of the Little Bighorn in settling the West? What is known about Custer's personal life? What fictional treatments have there been of Custer? What films have been made about this battle or about Custer? How does this battle fit into the general policy of dealing with the Indians? After asking yourself questions like these you might come up with the following topics:

> Custer's military strategy
> The role of the Battle of the Little Bighorn in settling the West
> The effect of the battle on relations with the Indians
> The treatment of Custer in films
> The treatment of Custer in fiction

Because any subject can be treated from so many angles, the steps outlined in the following pages for helping you find a subject that intrigues you can be adapted to your own use, even if you are starting with someone else's initial selection.

As you follow the steps given in this chapter, you'll notice that you begin not with choosing a single topic for your paper but with choosing a number of *general subjects* from which you can derive a more specific and manageable topic. Having more possibilities than you need will help you find a better topic. The steps outlined in the following pages are designed to help you find a subject that you will enjoy exploring and writing about and that will result in a paper you and others will enjoy reading. Record the results in your search log, where you will be able to refer to them as a guide as you go through the process of deciding on a topic.

Making a List of Subjects

Set aside an hour or more, sit down at your computer or go to a quiet place with your notebook, and let your mind range over the subjects that interest you. To aid your exploration and direct your thinking, use categories such as experiences, course work, and hobbies. Give your entry a title and a date, say "Subjects for research paper—September 28." Write down the categories you've chosen and under each category record your thoughts about it and possible related subjects.

Writing on the Computer.   Using a computer may help you to write more, and writing more than you need can be helpful at this stage. The ideas that come to you first are not always the best; besides, the more you write, the more choices you'll have. As you're writing your **thoughts**, try darkening the monitor so you won't focus on what is on the screen; you don't want to be thinking about spelling or grammar right now. Then, as you write down the **subjects**, try using boldface, so that you can easily pick them out later. Print out the results when you've finished.

Don't hurry this step. You are not trying to come up with a final topic; you are trying to find out what interests you and get your ideas down. If some subjects are too broad, you may reduce them to specific topics later—you'll be given suggestions for this. Just let your mind wander freely as you contemplate each one of these areas. Here are some examples:

Experiences: What experiences of yours (or someone close to you) have raised questions in your mind that you couldn't answer?

Thoughts: "I had a friend who was an alcoholic. I wonder why. I wonder if he could have been helped."

Possible subjects: The causes and control of alcoholism. How friends can help an alcoholic.

School subjects: What subjects have you studied that you wish you had time to learn more about?

Thoughts: "My psych teacher mentioned gestalt psychology. It sounded interesting, but what is it?"

Possible subjects: The origins of gestalt psychology. The role of gestalt psychology in mental therapy.

Hobbies: What do you like to do in your spare time? Which of these would you like to find out more about?

Thoughts: "I planted a few tomatoes last year, but I'd like to have more plants next year—a small garden maybe. Do I have enough space? Do I have enough sunlight? What would I plant? What plants grow well together? Would I use chemical fertilizers?"

Possible subjects: Planting a small garden. Chemical fertilizers versus organic gardening.

Reading and television: What television programs have you seen that made you want to learn more? What books, newspapers, or magazine articles have you read that made you want to learn more about a subject?

Thoughts: "I saw a television program on the mind. My grandmother has Alzheimer's disease. I wonder what this means and whether there is a cure. . . . I've been watching a series of programs on China—about Buddhism and Confucianism, about the Chinese use of acupuncture, about the practice of tai chi and other martial arts to keep fit. I've always wanted to know more about China."

Possible subjects: Alzheimer's disease. How to keep the brain from aging. The use of acupuncture in modern China. The practice of tai chi and how it keeps your body healthy.

Current controversial issues: What social or ethical problems have you discussed recently with your friends? What are some current issues that you haven't been able to make up your mind about?

Thoughts: "The use of drugs is certainly a problem that seems to be getting out of hand. Should the use of drugs be made legal? What would be the consequence of legalization? Should employees be tested for drugs? Should certain groups be tested? It's confusing."

Possible subjects: Legalization of drugs. Mandatory drug testing in the workplace. Mandatory drug testing of college students.

Now that you've started your list, add to it as possible subjects occur to you. With the added awareness your search has already given you, you'll find that your list will increase.

Choosing Possible Topics

Reread your list carefully, putting a check mark beside the subjects that seem most interesting to you. Then reread those you have checked. Pick two that appeal to you most and make each into a sentence beginning "I want to know more about. . . ." Then complete the following exploratory sentences for each.

1. I already know that _____.
2. I want to find out who _____.
3. I want to find out what _____.
4. I want to find out where _____.
5. I want to find out when _____.
6. I want to find out why _____.
7. I want to find out how _____.

Write these sentences in your search log. Here is an example.

Subject sentence: I want to know more about flying saucers.

Exploratory sentences:

I already know
that a lot of people say they have seen them.
that the air force says they don't exist.
that there are a lot of theories about what they are.

I want to find out
why the air force thinks they don't exist.
why there weren't any reported for a long time until recent sightings.
where they have been seen.
how they are propelled.
who has reported seeing them.
how reliable these people are.

After writing down your sentences, you should revise your subject sentence so that it more accurately reflects what you want to find out. Begin this time with "I want to know. . . ."

Revised subject sentence: I want to know whether flying saucers exist.

At this point, try rephrasing the sentence as a question to focus your topic further. "I want to know whether flying saucers exist" may become "Do flying saucers exist?" And "I want to find out why the air force thinks they don't exist" may become "Why does the air force think there are no flying saucers?" These sentences make it clear that you are looking for answers to questions and that your paper will give the answers.

Your question "Do flying saucers exist?" now supplies you with a topic—"The existence of flying saucers." The subheadings relating to their existence (such as "why the air force thinks they don't exist") will now become more important and a subheading such as "how they are propelled" will be less important, though it may still be included in your search.

The Controlling Idea or Thesis Statement

After you have done some of your research, you might be able to compose a sentence about the existence of flying saucers, such as "Flying saucers do not exist," "Yes, there are flying saucers," or "The existence of flying saucers cannot be proved or disproved." Such a statement will help you further focus your search. Although now you may probably not yet be able to arrive at the controlling idea that directs your writing stage, you should be alert at each step to the possibility of making your topic more specific. As with other stages, you will find yourself engaged in a back-and-forth process: as you look further into your subject you will be able to define it better; as you define it better you will be able to direct your search more economically. With a controversial topic like flying saucers, you may not feel you can compose a thesis statement (a sentence that summarizes your paper) until you have collected most of your information. Of course, even as you are writing, you are continuing to focus your topic; focusing is something to be aware of through each stage. (For more information on composing a controlling statement, see Chapter 6.)

Critical Thinking

Now is a good time to use your critical abilities to analyze your subject. What aspects of your subject have you failed to consider? What assumptions have you made in choosing your subject that may need to be checked for their validity?

Student Alice Denton chose as her subject the deterioration of the family in the United States. She wanted to know why the family has deteriorated and what the effects of this deterioration have been. In her "I already know" statements she wrote that the extended family was the norm in the nineteenth and early twentieth centuries; grandparents, aunts, and uncles were around for support. Then came the nuclear family with only father, mother, and children. Now, she wrote, the divorce rate is up; there are more single-parent families and families with stepparents. Drug use and crime rates are up.

First Denton had to identify the assumptions she had made. What she claimed to "know" were really beliefs that she held without knowing whether they were true. After rereading her statements and discussing them with her classmates, she realized that she had made the following assumptions without careful examination:

1. *Families have gotten smaller and their composition has changed.* However, she did not have any data to show that this was so. In fact, one of her classmates pointed out that his great-grandparents had immigrated to this country around 1900. They were a nuclear family that in later generations became an extended family; their family became larger, not smaller. It seemed likely that many families had had that experience.

2. *The family has deteriorated because its size and composition have changed.* First she had assumed that the quality of family life had declined and then that the size and composition of the family were related to the quality of family life. But she had no evidence that either of these was so. She also needed to define what she meant by *deterioration.*

3. *The deterioration of the family is responsible for social ills such as drug use and crime.* She realized that she had no proof that social ills were related to family composition. They might be, but there could be other reasons for social problems as well.

Denton decided to do more preliminary research on the family before making these or any other assumptions. She needed to find answers to the following questions:

1. What are the composition and size of the average family, and what changes have occurred in family structure over the last century?
2. What are the criteria for determining the quality of family life?
3. What is the judgment of expert sociologists about the quality of family life: do they believe that that quality has changed over the years? Why?

In fact, examining her assumptions now became the central part of Denton's research.

Dealing with Special Problems

Maybe you know so little about your subject that you have trouble completing your explanatory sentences. Or maybe your mind refuses to get itself in gear and comes up with blanks instead of overflowing with ideas. Here are three ways of solving these problems. If one doesn't work, try the others or try all three, using the same subject.

1. *Look up your subject in a general reference source.* You can use the *Encyclopaedia Britannica*, the *Encyclopedia Americana*, or an encyclopedia that specializes in one area of knowledge. (General and special encyclopedias and other reference works are discussed in Chapter 3.) One student heard ''gestalt therapy'' referred to in psychology class as a recent development in psychotherapy and decided she would like to look into the possibility of using this therapy as a research subject. The reference librarian directed her to the *International Encyclopedia of Psychiatry, Psychology, Psychoanalysis, and Neurology.* Under ''Gestalt Therapy'' she found a three-page article explaining the origins of the theory, the philosophy behind it, and its use in therapy. As she read the article, she realized that the techniques used in therapy were what interested her most. They were explained in the following paragraph.

There are several forms which a Gestalt experiment might take (Polster and Polster, 1973). One is the enactment of some important part of the patient's life. Dramatizing a memory or a dreaded encounter provides a stage for inventive action, unhampered by some of the limits, appropriate or not, that the patient might otherwise set for himself or herself during the actual event. It is also a way to explore unfamiliar aspects of the self, as in dramatizing oneself as bully or savior. Directed behavior encourages the patient to expand disregarded behavior or to try out new behaviors as, for example, speaking without qualifications, saying yes more often, and an infinite range of other therapeutically relevant behaviors. By actually performing these behaviors the individual's customary personal boundaries are extended. Fantasy, another form of the Gestalt experiment, is also a means for extending and amplifying feelings about central events in the patient's life. The fantasy is the individual's technique par excellence for representation of an otherwise unavailable world. Once this world is readmitted and assimilated in the supportive framework of the therapy session, the necessity to shun circumstances where these feelings may be provoked is diminished and the patient's confidence is enhanced for successfully traversing dangerous emotional territory. Dreamwork, one form of fantasy, received especially great attention from Perls, particularly in his demonstrations (Perls, 1969, 1973). Pervading the Gestalt view of dreams is the belief that the dreamer has cast himself or herself into each of the elements in his or her dream. These castout parts of the self must be actively reowned and assimilated as relevant ingredients in the patient's experience. Sometimes this involves communication between missing elements in the patient's own personality; some quality of himself or herself which he or she has spurned and projected and which has to be reclaimed. Sometimes the dream reveals a missing or distorted contact which has left the patient with unfinished business with another person.

After rereading this paragraph, she made a list of the techniques that might be used in a therapy session: *dramatization, directed behavior, fantasy,* and *dreamwork.* She thought that she might not have time to find out about all of these, so she chose the last one. Her topic became "How dreams are used in gestalt therapy." As a result of reading the article, she had not only a topic but also a framework in which to place that topic: she knew a little about the history and the philosophy of the movement, and she had a general idea about the techniques used. In addition, a bibliography at the end of the article (Figure 1.1) gave her some sources with which to start her search.

This knowledge from her preliminary research gave her flexibility; she was able to expand or redirect her topic in response to the information that she had found. Although she decided to concentrate on dream techniques, she might have chosen any of the other techniques that

FIGURE 1.1   Sample Bibliography

BIBLIOGRAPHY

PERLS, F. S. *Ego, hunger and aggression.* London: George Allen and Unwin, 1947.

PERLS, F. S. *Gestalt therapy verbatim.* Lafayette, Calif.: Real People, 1969.

PERLS, F. S. *In and out of the garbage pail.* Lafayette, Calif.: Real People, 1969.

PERLS, F. *The Gestalt approach and eye witness to therapy.* Palo Alto, Calif.: Science and Behavior Books, 1973.

PERLS, F. S.; HEFFERLINE, R. F.; and GOODMAN, P. *Gestalt therapy.* New York: Julian, 1951.

POLSTER, E. and POLSTER, M. *Gestalt therapy integrated.* New York: Brunner/Mazel, 1973.

FIGURE 1.2   Search Log Entry

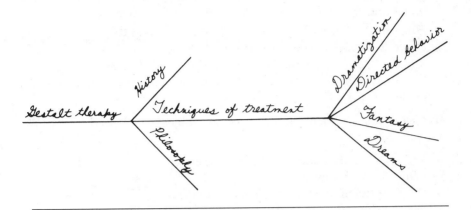

looked interesting. She might also have included a brief summary of the history and philosophy of the theory at the beginning of her paper. With this map of her subject, she began her search with confidence. She had a clear sense of direction with flexibility enough to adapt to whatever other information she might find. In her search log she recorded a map of her mental journey so far (see Figure 1.2).

2. *Use special categories to help you analyze your subject.* We are all familiar with the physical habits we've developed—getting up at the same time, eating the same foods, and so on. We are not always so aware of our mental habits. Our minds get caught in the same daily grooves. A characteristic of the good researcher is the ability to see things in a different way. The following exercise helps stimulate your thinking processes by looking at a subject from various points of view. You don't have to be a scientist to find a use in thinking about a subject from a scientific point of view. Just thinking about a subject this way may suggest something completely different to you because it will help you break down your traditional thinking habits and improve your mental agility. Try applying these exploratory categories—personal or psychological, sociological, political, historical, scientific, and any others you wish to include—to any of your subjects. The following examples illustrate how to use such categories to stimulate new ways of thinking.

Subject: Dropping the bomb on Hiroshima

Personal: Who were the people in the airplane that dropped the bomb? What was their reaction? How do they feel about it now? How do the Japanese who survived the attack feel toward the United States?

Sociological: What were the effects on the people of Japan? Did it have an impact on the social structure?

Political: What were the short- and long-term political repercussions in the United States? How did it affect relations between the United States and Japan after the war? Was the attack justified?

Historical: What was the historical significance of this event? What effect did it have on Japanese history?

Scientific: Was there any scientific value in this act? How was the bomb developed? What medical treatment were victims of the attack given?

Trying to answer such questions on this subject might lead to the following topics.

The effect on the people who flew in the plane of dropping the bomb
Why the bomb should not have been dropped
Why President Truman made the right decision
The development of nuclear arms in the future

3. *Try talking to your computer.* Some computer programs (often called "prewriting" or "preinvention programs") prompt your thinking with questions about the purpose of your topic or your reasons for selecting it. Your computer may even answer you on the screen. If you don't have a special program, try talking to yourself and writing the conversation on the computer.

"Why can't I come up with a topic I like?"
"Because I've got two or three good topics and I can't make up my mind which one to settle on."
"Well, why not?"
"Maybe if I had more time. That's not really it. I like one but I don't know if the teacher would like it. But it would be popular with my classmates."
"But why don't you pick the one *you* want to find out about? And what is it about this topic that makes you want to choose it?"

Keep going. Press yourself to say what's on your mind. Talk about the pros and cons of the topics you're considering.

If you are a visually oriented person, try using a graphics program. Draw a group of balloons on the screen with a subject in each or an aspect of your subject in each. Puncture the ones you don't like. Add to the ones you like. Or use the shape of a tree with branches. Finally, perhaps you see your subject as a series of events—a kind of story—or as parts of a process. Then create a flow chart, a series of connected boxes or circles, each containing an aspect of your subject that comes to mind. Let them branch out to make mini–flow charts.

Some people—even those who have never used a computer before—feel that a computer allows them more freedom to play with an idea than a pen or pencil does.

Choosing a Topic

Choose one of your two topics as the subject in which you will do your research, using your own interest or the approval of your instructor as your guide. Keep your second subject in reserve. When you start a search, you are embarking on the unknown, or at least on what is largely unknown to you—that is the nature of the activity. You must do some planning on the basis of what you know and what others have told you, but until you get there, you don't know whether your plans will work. Therefore, you need both a first-choice topic to begin your search with as well as a back-up topic.

Turn to your back-up topic if the answer to any of the following questions about your first-choice topic is yes.

1. *Is your topic so new that little has been written on it?*

Topics aimed at exploring recent technical developments, newly discovered diseases, or new solutions to old medical problems often prove frustrating because of the lack of information available.

2. *Can the answer to your main question be found only in a single source?*

Instead of writing a research paper, you would end up paraphrasing or summarizing a book or an article. Such a problem often arises with a process topic that may be covered in a manual (''How to Set Up a Salt Water Aquarium'') or with a general historical topic that may be adequately summarized in a good encyclopedia (''Events Leading Up to the Revolutionary War''). Historical subjects that are more limited or that have produced different points of view may work better (for example, ''How Pennsylvania Came to Enter the Revolution'' or ''The Importance of French Assistance in the Revolutionary War'').

3. *Are you unable to find the information you need in your library?*

4. *Is the information you need contained in highly technical journals written in language you don't understand?*

Translating these articles would take you too much time (for example, articles from the *IEEE Transactions of Quantum Electronics*).

5. *Could it take you more time than you have to find the information you need?*

You might, for example, have to write to a government agency that cannot promise you a reply in time. Or you might have to get your materials through interlibrary loan. You can avoid the latter problem by checking your library for sources as soon as possible, and if interlibrary borrowing is necessary, finding out how long it will take to get the publication you want.

Sometimes you can anticipate these problems before you choose a topic. Your instructor, who has had more experience than you, can also be helpful. But sometimes it is impossible to know what your problems are until you start your search. Kathy Matthews, in a narrative she wrote explaining her research process, tells what happened to her.

> The hardest part of the research paper for me was getting the right topic. I had several criteria to meet: (1) the topic had to be approved by my history teacher; (2) it had to be large enough so that I could write a ten- to fifteen-page paper on it; and (3) it had to be interesting enough to help get me through several otherwise tedious weeks of research. After making lists of subjects I was interested in, I finally settled on ''The Effects of Agent Orange on Vietnam Veterans.'' I figured that periodicals and government documents would be my chief sources of information.
>
> What I didn't know until I started my search was that the campus library had very few government documents. I discovered that all of the military documents on defoliation are still classified and unavailable to civilians. A few newspaper articles had been written, but they seemed to have the same problems I did—little solid information. Fortunately I had a second choice—''The Uses and Abuses of the Artificial Heart (Jarvik 7).'' This topic, though I had to get my information primarily from newspapers and periodicals, worked out successfully.

After you begin your search and complete your preliminary bibliography (see suggestions given in Chapter 3), you should be firmly committed to your topic. To turn back later than that would make it difficult for you to finish your paper on time.

EXERCISES

1. **FOR YOUR SEARCH LOG**
   a. Record the subject you have chosen to search.
   b. Identify and list the assumptions you made as you selected your subject. Leave several spaces between each.
   c. After each assumption, write down the information you have that makes it true.

   You may want to ask your classmates to help you locate and examine these assumptions.

2. **FOR PEER RESPONSE**   Choose one of your subject sentences and read it, along with your exploratory sentences, to a group of your classmates. Read your sentences slowly and clearly to give your listeners time to think about them. Then ask your listeners the following questions.
   a. Do you think there are other parts of this subject that would be interesting to explore?

b. What do you know about this subject that might help me?

c. Where do you think I might get more information?

Write down the answers in your search log.

3. **FOR PEER RESPONSE**   Read part of a recent daily newspaper or newsmagazine. (Members of your class may agree to read the same selections.) As you read, make a list of any interesting research subjects that the articles suggest to you. Choose five subjects, read them to your classmates, and discuss their possibilities as subjects for research.

C H A P T E R   2

Planning Your Search

Creating a Search Strategy

Now that you have chosen a topic, you will want to plan your search, much as you would plan a trip. You'll need an itinerary or search strategy showing where you will go, what you will do, and in what order you will undertake the search. Such a strategy will ensure that you conduct your search in the most effective and efficient way possible. Of course, your plans are always subject to change as you learn more about your subject and about the sources available. Like every explorer you may have to change directions. You may find new areas to explore; you may find that some places you had planned to go no longer interest you. Although you need a firm plan to follow, you also need to be ready to alter that plan when new information requires it. So before you begin your search complete the following tasks.

1. Make a timetable.
2. Compose a preliminary outline.
3. Adjust the scope of your project.
4. List possible sources of information.
5. Develop a search strategy.
6. Assemble your materials.

Record the timetable, outline, and list of information sources in your search log. The rest of this chapter provides suggestions to help you.

Making a Timetable

A timetable will help you allocate enough time to each part of your project so that you meet your deadlines and end up with a good paper.

As you make your estimates, take into consideration your writing habits, the amount of time you will be able to spend on the paper, and the recommendations given here (which are based on an average of about two working hours a day). Although it is difficult to make such a plan—it is especially hard to judge how much time to set aside for gathering your information—you need to set up the framework and then revise it as circumstances require.

Divide your work into the following stages: (1) searching, (2) re-searching, (3) writing, (4) revising, and (5) typing the final copy (each of these is discussed in a separate chapter). Estimate how long it will take you to do each part, starting with the due date and working your way back to the present. You will thus allot time first to those tasks whose required time is easiest to estimate and leave the remaining time for searching, the most difficult stage to predict. Such a timetable will be most effective if you work a few hours each day or each week instead of concentrating on your project for a week or two and then neglecting it for a few weeks. If you don't maintain continuity, you will have to re-think your project each time you start to work on it.

1. The searching stage (see Chapters 3, 4, and 5) is the most difficult to estimate at the beginning because you don't know yet what you need to find, what you will find, and where you need to go to find it. Will you be conducting interviews? You will need to arrange them. Will you be administering a questionnaire? You will have to design and admin- ister it. Because the time required for this stage is so unpredictable, it's a good idea to start your search as soon as possible. The first step will be to compile a preliminary list of sources; then you will need to find out whether the sources are available. You should make these determi- nations as soon as possible—within a few days of beginning your search. If all goes well, you can proceed with your search. On the other hand, if you decide that your topic will not work, you will have time to change it. The recommended minimum time for searching (assuming you can spend six hours a week) is one month, more if you have it.

2. At the next stage, re-searching (see Chapter 6), you will have completed your searching and will now be organizing your material, writing a detailed and accurate outline, and developing or revising your controlling idea. Recommended minimum time is six to eight hours, divided between two days.

3. The third stage is writing the first draft (see Chapter 7). Most people like to write the first draft of a ten- to fifteen-page paper at one or two sittings. If your paper is shorter or longer, adjust your time ac- cordingly. Try to reserve two consecutive days for this work—four or five hours a day. The recommended minimum time for this process is ten hours divided between two days.

4. Revising (see Chapters 8 and 9) is the stage in which you will have to make a judgment about your writing habits. Some people revise as

they write the first draft; most people write two or three drafts before the final draft. Leave time in between your drafts for "incubation" and for doing other classwork. Two weeks is the recommended minimum time.

5. Typing the final copy (see Chapters 10, 11, and 12) is the final stage. Your answers to these questions will help you estimate the time required for this step: Will you type the final copy? How good a typist are you? If you have someone type it for you, how far in advance must you give the person the final draft? If you are using your college's computer system, can you arrange for computer and printer time when you want it? Will other papers be due at the same time? When are final exams scheduled? Allow time, too, for proofreading and photocopying. The recommended minimum time is three days for a ten- to fifteen-page paper. Adjust your schedule to fit the length of your paper.

Adapt these suggestions to fit your own needs and count back from the time your paper is due to get specific dates. Mark these dates on your calendar. Here is a typical schedule for an assignment received early in the semester.

Searching: February 15 to March 22
    By February 22, complete preliminary list of sources and make final decision on choice of topic.
    February 23 to March 22, conduct search.
Re-searching: March 23 to April 1.
Writing: April 2 to April 15.
Incubation: April 16 to April 19.
Revising: April 20 to April 30.
Typing: April 30 to May 1.
Proofreading, correcting, and photocopying: May 2.
Paper due: May 3.

If your paper must be completed in a shorter time, you should scale down this timetable to suit your needs. Here's a suggested shortened timetable of about a month. To finish a paper in this length of time, you may have to spend more time each day and on weekends.

Searching: April 1 to April 14.
Re-searching: April 15 to April 18.
Writing: April 19 to April 25.
Incubation: April 26.
Revising: April 27 to April 30.
Typing final copy: May 1 to May 2.
Proofreading, correcting, and photocopying: May 2.
Paper Due: May 3.

If you are working within a quarterly system, use the following timetable as a guide.

Searching: March 27 to May 19.
Re-searching: May 20 to May 25.
Writing: May 26 to June 8.
Incubation: June 9.
Revising: June 10 to June 17.
Typing final copy: June 18 to June 19.
Proofreading, correcting, and photocopying: June 20 to June 21.
Paper due: June 22.

Composing a Preliminary Outline

Reread the exploratory sentences you have written in your notebook or your computer file. By grouping them and rearranging them, make a brief outline to help you organize your search. If your subject is "Do flying saucers (UFOs) exist?" you might have the following exploratory sentences.

I already know
that a lot of people say they have seen them.
that the air force says they don't exist.
that there are a lot of theories about what they are.

I want to find out
why the air force thinks they don't exist.
why there weren't any reported for a long time until recent
    sightings.
where they have been seen.
how they are propelled.
who has reported seeing them.
how reliable these people are.

The first step in organizing these headings is to group them. They seem to fall into two main groups: information about sightings of flying saucers and investigations by the air force. The headings for these two groups could be "Sightings of UFOs" and "Investigations by the air force." It might occur to you that there may have been other investigations, perhaps by newspaper reporters, so you abbreviate your heading: "Investigations." By arranging your subheadings under these main headings, you produce the following list. You may use either the traditional outline numbering system or, because the list is relatively short, just leave out numbers and letters and indent the subheadings.

    [I.] Sightings of UFOs
        [A.] Who has reported seeing them and how reliable they are
        [B.] Where and when they have been seen
        [C.] What they look like and how they seem to be propelled
        [D.] Where they come from—theories of those who have seen
            them

[II.] Investigations
    [A.] Air force investigations and conclusions
    [B.] Newspaper investigations and conclusions
    [C.] Possible other investigations

Adjusting the Scope of Your Subject

Once you have divided your subject this way, you can usually limit it by dropping one or more of the headings or subheadings according to what you find as you begin your search. You might discover, for example, that certain data are limited or nonexistent, or that it takes so long to gather the information on one of your important points that you begin to run out of time. If your topic is flying saucers, for instance, you might need to write to the air force for information about its investigations or you might want to conduct interviews—both of which efforts are time-consuming—so perhaps you would decide to concentrate your time and energy on these sources instead of newspaper investigations. You should also add to your outline as you discover topics you weren't aware of. For example, you might discover that the sighting of UFOs is not a contemporary phenomenon and that similar stories have been told throughout history.

Possible Sources of Information

Make a list in your search log of all the places where you think you might find information on your subject. From what you know about your subject, you should have some general ideas about where you will find most of your information. Joe Collins, who decided to evaluate gas-saving devices for cars, knew that he was going to get most of his information from examining and testing the devices himself. In addition, he had seen at least one article on such devices and thought there might be more. Margaret Little, in researching the effects of caffeine, realized that she would not be able to do her own experiments on the subject and would have to rely on reports from original researchers. She guessed she would find her information primarily in periodicals and perhaps books.

Here are some sources that have been successfully used by student researchers. You will find items on this list that don't apply to your subject or you may know of other places where you can get the information you need. You cannot, of course, be completely sure what sources will be helpful until you try them. See Chapter 3 for details on how to use the library.

Library sources:
General reference works (encyclopedias, biographical sources, indexes, dictionaries, handbooks)

Specific books on the subject
Periodicals (journals, magazines, newspapers, newsletters)
Government documents
Pamphlets and brochures
Computer databases
Films
Recordings
Videotapes
Reference librarians

See Chapter 5 for details on the following sources:

Other sources:
Lectures (public or academic)
Museums
Television and radio programs
Interviews
Letters
Questionnaires
Personal observations, tests, or experiments

The list for a paper on UFOs might look like this:

Library sources:
Encyclopedias
Indexes
Periodicals, newspapers
Specific books on the subject
Government documents (for air force studies)
Reference librarians

Other sources:
Television and radio programs

The Computer as a Search Tool.   Most topics can be researched in print or microform sources, but computer searching has advantages that will probably result in increasing use of this research tool. Perhaps the greatest benefit is saving time. In a few minutes, you can search through the equivalent of many volumes of print sources. In addition, more and more libraries, especially small ones, are subscribing to computer services instead of, or in addition to, print sources.

Some narrowly defined topics require a computer search. For example, because databases can be searched with many more terms, you might use such a search to find sources on adult education programs for immigrants. Such a narrowly defined topic would be difficult to search in printed indexes with their limited terminology and cross-references.

Another advantage of computer searching is that because databases are constantly updated, recent information is more likely to be available on them than in print indexes. A computer search provides current information on such subjects as recent political events, new scientific discoveries, or contemporary literary criticism. The printed version of the *Readers' Guide,* for example, is updated semimonthly for six months of the year and monthly for the other six months. In addition, it takes some time to get the information printed and mailed. But the information from the *Readers' Guide* on a computer database is available as soon as it's loaded into the computer.

Many college libraries now provide the option of computer searches on CD-ROM (compact disc–read only memory) as well as online (via a connection to a large computer containing many databases). If your library subscribes to a service that provides databases on CD-ROM, you can check out the disc that is likely to contain the information you want, insert it in a small computer in the reference room, read the information on the monitor, and probably print it out if you wish. In some libraries the CD-ROMs are locked into the computers; you'll be directed to the one with the database you want. Most libraries provide access to CD-ROM databases without cost; however, you may be charged a fee for online searching.

If you have a home computer, consider using it not only for word processing but also for searching. With your own personal computer and a modem (plus an access fee), you can search databases without going to the library. If you still want to use the library to find your sources, you have the option of recording your data on your computer. Instead of putting your information on cards or paper, file it on disks using almost any number of key words and phrases (the program SuperFile, for example, will allow you to file information under 250 different keywords). When your search is completed, you can use any of the keywords to locate the information you have gathered and then print it out in any order you wish. Of course, you have to be able to bring sources and computer together, and if you're working in the library you may not be able to do this. However, you can check out most books and photocopy most articles, so consider trying this method of storing and retrieving information.

Developing a Search Strategy

After you complete your list, decide what order you will use in exploring these sources. Devise a strategy that will take into consideration the needs of your topic, the materials available, and the requirements of the assignment. Estimate how long each step in your search will take—whether you will have to make advance appointments or request material by mail, for example, and how important to your project such information would be. Of course, you will have only a rough idea at the beginning of your search of what your sources might be. As your search progresses, you will revise your strategy to fit your experience. The reordered list for a paper on UFOs might look like this:

1. Encyclopedias
2. Government documents (These are an important source that might take some time to obtain.)
3. Television and radio programs (These may be of questionable importance, and they would take time to find and review.)
4. Indexes
5. Specific books on the subject
6. Reference librarians (This source might be consulted earlier if you encounter difficulty.)

A researcher relying primarily on personal observation might have quite a different set of priorities. Marian Glass, writing on the image of the elderly on television, expected to gather her information for her paper from watching television programs. Written sources would be secondary. Her ordered list looked like this:

1. Television programs (These are an ongoing source.)
2. Lectures (Her psychology professor had devoted part of a lecture to the way different age groups are portrayed on TV; she would reread her notes.)
3. Interviews (She would call immediately to see whether she could get an interview with the local newspaper's reviewer of TV programs. For a discussion of interviewing, see Chapter 5.)
4. Indexes, periodicals
5. Pamphlets (These might contain recent studies of television programs.)
6. Books (These were the least likely to be useful because the information in them was probably outdated.)

Assembling Your Materials

As you do your research, you acquire two kinds of learning: knowledge about a subject you're interested in and knowledge about a process—how to search for, find, record, and organize information from your observation and from outside sources. Because you won't be able to contain all of this information in your head, you'll need to keep the following records: (1) the data from your sources, written on cards, on specially prepared paper, or on your computer; (2) an account of the process you use, recorded in your search log.

Taking some time now to decide what materials to use and buying them if necessary will make your work easier and save you time later. Here are some items to consider.

Writing Implements.　Writing on a computer is much faster than handwriting and the copy is easier to read. You may be able to use a computer in the library or even bring a lap-top computer in. If not, take your books out of the library and photocopy or get printouts of journal articles. Then take your notes. (Do not, however, use photocopying as a substitute for note taking—it's only an intermediate step.) If you must handwrite your notes, use pen, not pencil, because pencil smudges easily and is generally more difficult to read.

Writing Materials.　If you use a computer, you need to buy only computer paper for everything—for note taking as well as for writing your paper. Most writers, however, will probably take some notes on paper. Cards are easy to carry and easy to sort later; use 4-by-6-inch or 5-by-8-inch cards for notes (3-by-5-inch cards are useful for recording your sources). You might choose to take notes in small notebooks the size of note cards. Finally you might use ordinary 8 ½ -by-11-inch notebook paper divided evenly into two or three horizontal sections. When you're ready to write your paper, cut the pieces apart and rearrange them. (How to record information on these cards is discussed and illustrated in Chapters 4 and 5.)

Planning for Efficiency.　The important thing is to use the most efficient materials available, unless you have an unlimited amount of time to spend on your project. With the proper software, notes on a computer can be inserted directly into your paper. Some programs make it possible to divide the screen so that you can read a note and type it or parts of it into your draft at the same time. With note cards, you can write one piece of information on each card and then order them according to your outline before you begin writing your paper. Cards are easier to arrange and more durable than paper.

The following hints will make your work more efficient and will save you time and money in the long run.

1. *Do not take notes on random scraps of paper.* This may result in lost material or too many items on a page.
2. *Do not write your notes continuously in a notebook.* If you write your notes under headings you will have less difficulty organizing them later.
3. *Do not write on both sides of your paper.* If you use only one side you will be able to look at all of your notes at once.
4. *Do not use photocopying as a substitute for taking notes.* Note taking is an important part of thinking critically about your material. Photocopy only when you don't have time to read the material in the library or when you are storing your information in a home computer.

EXERCISES

1. On the basis of entries in your search log, write a two- or three-page paper for your instructor based on the following information.

   a. The topic of your research paper.
   b. Why you chose this subject.
   c. What you already know about this subject.
   d. What you plan to find out about this subject.

2. **FOR PEER RESPONSE**   Read your paper to your classmates and ask them whether there are other aspects of your subject that interest them and that might interest you. They may also have suggestions about sources of information.

CHAPTER 3

Compiling Your Working Bibliography

Where to Start Looking

There is no single best place to start a search for information. You can start by interviewing someone who knows about your subject, by gathering information through observation, by distributing a questionnaire, or by going to the library to extract information from others' thoughts and experiences. Two considerations are important in deciding where to start: you want to get some general information about your subject so that you have a framework within which to operate, and you want to give priority to those types of information that take more time to obtain. Each of the following students started searching in a different place.

Bob Larkin, who wanted to study the culture of the Mayan Indians, began his search in an encylopedia to see what was generally known about the Indians and to get some bibliographic leads. Judy Farnsworth, who planned to investigate learning disabilities in children, went first to the psychology teacher who had mentioned the subject in class and talked further with him about specific areas she might study. Besides some good advice on how to go about her project, she obtained a list of helpful books on the subject. Moira Jones wanted to examine the disposal of hazardous wastes, so she decided to visit a company engaged in that business. John Exley, whose subject was the use of steroids by college athletes and who wanted to send a questionnaire to college coaches, concluded that he had better design and send his questionnaire as quickly as possible to have the returns back in time to include them in his paper.

What You Can Find in the Library

For many students, the library is the best place to start a search, and compiling a *working bibliography*—making a list of possible information sources—is the first step. In addition to printed information (including books, journals, newspapers, and pamphlets), your library may have films, records, and videotapes. Some libraries have paintings, photographs, and collections of private papers. Printed matter is often accessible on microforms—either microfiche (a film sheet that usually reduces the size of the material contained on it) or microfilm (35-mm film rolls). Computer services may be available to help you find printed information. To aid you in finding your way, many libraries offer tours, both guided and unguided, and most have a directory or map. Taking advantage of these services will save you time in the long run.

The information given here about libraries applies primarily to academic or other research libraries. Most public libraries will not have all of the specialized indexes, dictionaries, and professional journals that are in a small college library. However, they sometimes have books of general interest that college libraries would not have, so you may want to look in both types.

Making a List of Sources

Before you begin to read and take notes in the library, you should compile a list of possible sources—your working bibliography. It will change as you begin to read; you may drop some sources that are not relevant and add others that are suggested by your reading.

The information given in this chapter will provide a guide for most of the information sources in the library. The detailed discussions of each group of sources will help you decide which of them apply to your project and which you can omit.

As you locate your sources, keep three kinds of records: (1) a record of the sources you have found, (2) an account of where you went and what you did, and (3) notes on your reading for use in your paper.

Recording Bibliographic Information

Record identifying information about books, periodicals, pamphlets, and other sources that are potentially useful on 3-by-5-inch cards, on specially prepared paper in your notebook, or in a file in your computer. This list will be your working bibliography. (See Figure 3.1 for examples from a working bibliography.) Because the list will

FIGURE 3.1 Selections from a Working Bibliography (APA Style)

Bakal, A. (1987, January). Saccharin functionality and safety. <u>Food</u>
<u>Technology</u>, pp. 116-117.

Department of Health, Education, and Welfare. (1975). <u>Sweeteners:</u>
<u>Issues and uncertainties</u>. Washington, DC: National Academy
of Sciences.

Jacobson, M. (1988, February 19). Fake food, real problems. <u>The New</u>
<u>York Times</u>, p. A35.

Mazur, R. (1983). Aspartame. <u>Encyclopedia of Chemical Technology</u>
(3rd ed.).

Schiffman, S. S., Buckley, C. E., Sampson, H. A., Massey, E. W., Bara-
niuk, J. N., Follett, J. V., & Warwick, Z. S. (1987). Aspartame
and susceptibility to headache. <u>New England Journal of Medicine</u>,
<u>317</u>, 1181-1185.

contain only those sources in which substantive information for your paper is found, it won't include titles of indexes (the *Readers' Guide*, for example). However, it may include indexes containing abstracts (such as *Psychological Abstracts*) if you plan to use the information contained in the abstracts. The list will also include those encyclopedias or dictionaries that provide you with enough information to use in your paper. Encyclopedias and dictionaries used only for background reading or for bibliographic leads are usually not listed in a bibliography. Record useful information from an encyclopedia or from indexes on 4-by-6-inch or 5-by-8-inch note cards or in your computer. (See Chapter 4 for more suggestions on taking notes.)

Make sure you put down all of the bibliographic information about your sources that you will need later for full, scholarly documentation of your paper. You might want to decide now which of the three main documentation systems you will be using (see Chapters 10, 11, and 12) so that you can record the data on your bibliography cards in the appropriate order. However, although each system orders the bibliographic data in a slightly different way and uses different styles of punctuation, all systems require the following information.

Books.   Record the copy call number, author(s), title and subtitle, editor, translator, edition, volume number of book or total volumes in the book, name of the series, place of publication, publisher, and date. You will find this information on the title and copyright pages. Copy the facts down exactly as you find them. If only the author and title are given, put those on a card and fill in the other details when you look up the book in the card catalog. (See ''Finding Information in the Library Catalog,'' p. 43.)

Articles.   For articles in periodicals, record the author(s), title of article, name of periodical, volume number (omit for popular magazines), date or issue, and page numbers. Add a note indicating where you found this reference. If you found it in an index, give the name of the index— you might want to return to the same index for further references.

It may be tempting to list books and articles on a sheet of paper at this early stage, but it's best to put every work on a separate card, even if you don't know yet whether you will use it. Then when you actually find the work, you can add extra information that might help you, such as details from the table of contents, titles of relevant chapters, a summary of the abstract, or the fact that it has a bibliography. That way if you decide not to use a work, you'll know why. Eventually, of course, you will arrange the cards in the order in which you record them in your list of citations at the end of your paper.

Recording the Bibliography on a Computer.   If you locate your sources in a print index, you can put them on cards and transfer them to your computer file later. If you're using a computer database—either online or on CD-ROM (see p. 49)—the computer may have an at-

FIGURE 3.2   Bibliography Cards (MLA Style)

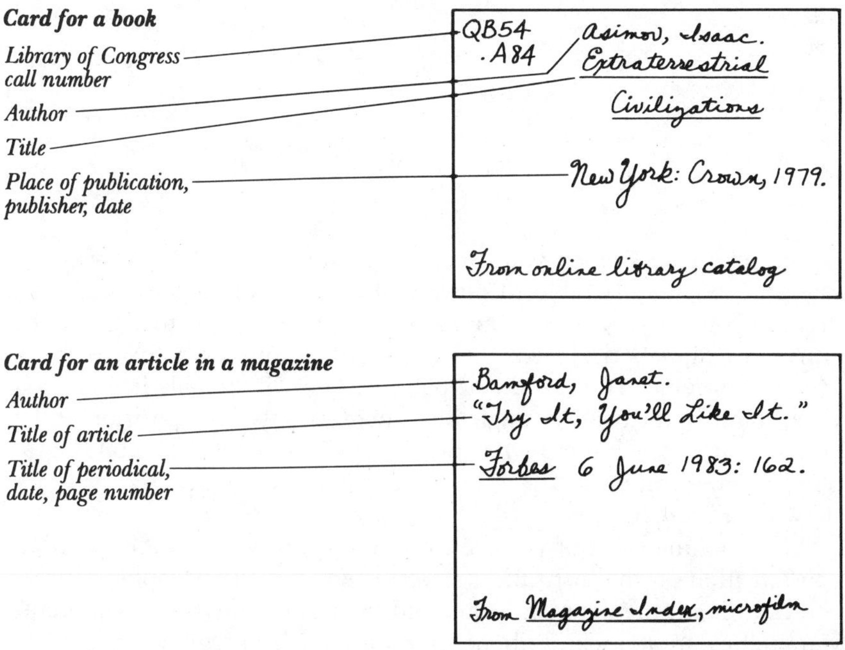

Card for a book

Library of Congress call number

Author

Title

Place of publication, publisher, date

> QB54
> .A84   Asimov, Isaac.
> Extraterrestrial
> Civilizations
> New York: Crown, 1979.
>
> From online library catalog

Card for an article in a magazine

Author

Title of article

Title of periodical, date, page number

> Bamford, Janet.
> "Try It, You'll Like It."
> Forbes 6 June 1983: 162.
>
> From Magazine Index, microfilm

(continued)

Card for a book with an editor

> PQ4835 Pirandello, Luigi. *Naked*
> .I7a27 *Masks: Five Plays.*
> Ed. Eric Bentley.
> New York: Dutton, 1952.
>
> Listed in *Americana*, 1988 ed.
> Has 5-page bibliography.
>   print

Card for part of a book

> P588 Kazin, Alfred.
> .K3 "A Lover and His Guilty
> Land." *An American*
> *Procession.* New York:
> Knopf, 1984. 63-80.
> Listed in *Essay and Gen. Lit. Index.*
>   print

Card for an article in a journal

> Trilling, Lionel.
> "A Speech on Robert Frost:
> A Cultural Episode."
> *Partisan Review* 26 (1959):
> 445-52. Rpt in Cox 151-58.
>
> From *MLA International*
> *Bibliography*, vol. IV, 1989.
>   print

tached printer on which you can print a copy of sources you want to save; or you may be able to download the information to your own disk. As you add to your list, your computer may be able to arrange the entries in alphabetical order. Check your computer software for a SORT command. If it has this capability, you will be able later, if you wish, to move the list as a single document into its final position at the end of your paper. Figure 3.1 shows excerpts from a working bibliography kept in a computer file. The main types of bibliography cards are shown in Figure 3.2.

After making a list of your sources, record in your search log what you did, that is, the institution(s) you used, the bibliographic sources you examined, the date you examined them, and any other comments you might want to include about your search. (See Figure 3.3.)

FIGURE 3.3   Search Log Entry

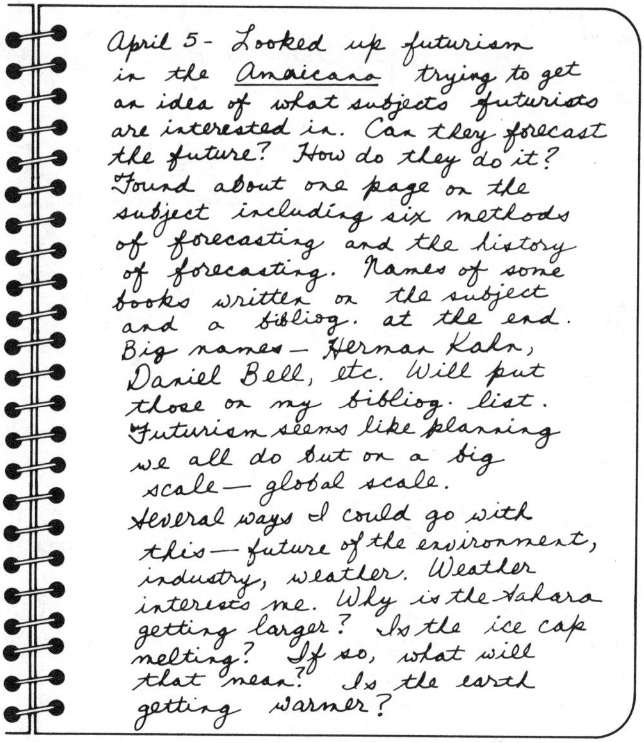

April 5 - Looked up futurism in the _Americana_ trying to get an idea of what subjects futurists are interested in. Can they forecast the future? How do they do it? Found about one page on the subject including six methods of forecasting and the history of forecasting. Names of some books written on the subject and a bibliog. at the end. Big names — Herman Kahn, Daniel Bell, etc. Will put those on my bibliog. list. Futurism seems like planning we all do but on a big scale — global scale. Several ways I could go with this — future of the environment, industry, weather. Weather interests me. Why is the Sahara getting larger? Is the ice cap melting? If so, what will that mean? Is the earth getting warmer?

Finally, record any information you think you may use and photocopy articles for later reading. Although you will probably take most of your notes later as you read books, articles, and other sources, you may find some information worth recording through your exploratory reading in encyclopedias (see Figure 3.4). (For suggestions on taking notes and for further models of note cards, see Chapter 4.)

Beginning Your Library Search

Most libraries contain the following areas: (1) a place where the _library catalog_ is stored, either on cards (the card catalog) or on a computer (the online catalog); (2) a _reference_ section containing encyclopedias, indexes, computer terminals, and other materials that cannot be taken from the library; (3) a _periodicals_ area or room that includes microfilm machines for viewing stored texts; (4) a section called the _stacks_ where books that can be taken out are shelved; and (5) an _audiovisual_ section where

FIGURE 3.4   Brief Exploratory Entry from an Encyclopedia

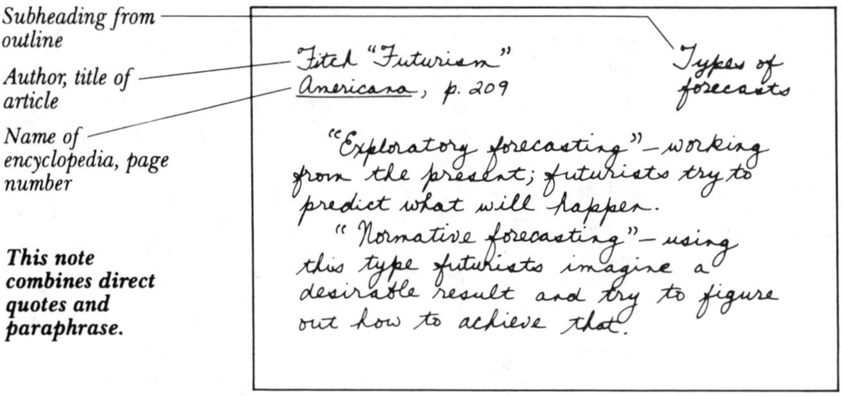

Subheading from outline

Author, title of article

Name of encyclopedia, page number

This note combines direct quotes and paraphrase.

Filed "Futurism"
Americana, p. 209

Types of forecasts

"Exploratory forecasting" — working from the present; futurists try to predict what will happen.
"Normative forecasting" — using this type futurists imagine a desirable result and try to figure out how to achieve that.

audiotapes and videotapes are stored. In addition, some libraries have rooms for storing special collections such as government documents, music, and maps.

Although you can begin your search in any of these areas, the library catalog is a logical place to start because the call numbers of all the books in the library, including those in the reference section, are recorded there (although sometimes a library catalog may not contain recent acquisitions, and special collections are often recorded in a separate catalog). In some libraries the catalog also contains the names of periodicals and nonprint media sources. So if you're looking for the names of indexes, dictionaries, or encyclopedias in the reference room, you should be able to find them listed in the catalog, along with their location. Of course, the catalog will also list the titles and location of books stored in the stacks.

From the catalog, you can go to the stacks and find your books or to the reference room to locate periodicals. You would continue your search in the reference room if you need general information on your subject (which you would find in encyclopedias, handbooks, or dictionaries) and if you need current information (which you would find in periodicals). Although you may be more accustomed to using books, periodicals are much more up to date.

As you gain more experience in library research, you will find yourself going back and forth between the reference section and the library catalog to find sources. Through encyclopedia articles you may find relevant book titles, which you will want to look up in the library catalog; in books you may find references to periodical articles, which may be in the reference room.

A Typical Library Search

Although each person's search strategy is different, the typical library search proceeds in this order:

1. To the *library catalog*, to find the titles and location of encyclopedias, indexes, and books.
2. To the *reference section*, to find articles in encyclopedias and titles of relevant articles in indexes.
3. To the *periodical room*, to locate and read the articles in print or on microform.
4. To the *stacks*, to locate books.
5. To *special collections*, to locate government documents and non-print sources.

The sections that follow in this chapter will help you compile a working bibliography by guiding you through the catalog and the reference room. Although you'll find here most of the information you'll need for your search, you may be unable to locate something on your own or be uncertain at some point how to proceed. Consult the reference librarian in such a situation.

Finding Information in the Library Catalog

Each book in the library is given a unique call number so that it can be easily distinguished from all other books. This call number appears on the book and on the pertinent cards in the card catalog or in entries in the online catalog. Two classification systems, Dewey decimal and Library of Congress, are in common use.

Dewey Decimal System

This system classifies books by using numbers and decimal points. All information is divided into the following ten groups:

000–099	General Works	600–699	Technology
100–199	Philosophy		(Applied Sciences)
200–299	Religion	700–799	The Arts
300–399	Social Sciences	800–899	Literature
400–499	Language	900–999	History
500–599	Pure Science		

Each of these classes is further divided into groups of ten, each of these groups into more subdivisions, and so on. Decimal points are added to increase the number of subdivisions. Here are the ten main subdivisions of Technology:

600	Technology (Applied Sciences)	650	Management
		660	Chemical Technology
610	Medical Sciences	670	Manufactures
620	Engineering	680	Miscellaneous Manufactures
630	Agriculture		
640	Home Economics	690	Buildings

Under a specific number and its divisions (for example, 610.73, which includes books about nursing) is a combination of letters and numbers that represents the individual book's author and title. Ronald Philip Preston's *The Dilemmas of Care* has been classified this way:

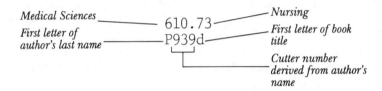

Library of Congress System

This system was developed to make even more categories possible than are allowed under the Dewey decimal system. Instead of the ten basic divisions of knowledge of the Dewey system, the Library of Congress system maintains twenty basic divisions corresponding to the letters of the alphabet (I, O, W, X, and Y are omitted, and E and F are both reserved for American history):

A	General Works	K	Law
B	Philosophy, Psychology, Religion	L	Education
		M	Music
C	History and Auxiliary Sciences	N	Fine Arts
		P	Language and Literature
D	History and Topography (except North and South America)	Q	Science
		R	Medicine
		S	Agriculture
E–F	History: North and South America	T	Technology
		U	Military Science
G	Geography and Anthropology	V	Naval Science
		Z	Bibliography and Library Science
H	Social Sciences		
J	Political Science		

An additional letter subdivides these divisions. Medicine, for example, is divided into the following categories:

R	Medicine (General)	RL	Dermatology
RA	Public Aspects of Medicine	RM	Therapeutics
RB	Pathology	RS	Pharmacy and Materia
RC	Internal Medicine		Medica
RD	Surgery	RT	Nursing
RE	Ophthalmology	RV	Botanic, Thomsonian,
RF	Otorhinolaryngology		and Eclectic Medicine
RG	Gynecology and Obstetrics	RX	Homeopathy
RJ	Pediatrics	RZ	Other Systems of
RK	Dentistry		Medicine

Other letters and numbers that follow the decimal point provide further subdivisions. Here is the call number for *Rehabilitation Medicine* by Howard A. Rusk:

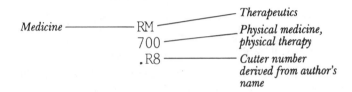

Library of Congress Subject Headings

Most college and university libraries use the Library of Congress classification system for cataloging their books and for arranging the contents of both the online and the library catalogs. They may also use the index system of the Library of Congress to organize their library catalogs. Therefore, you may save yourself some time if you consult the *Library of Congress Subject Headings (LCSH)*, usually located near the library catalog, before you begin your search to find out whether the words you have used to identify your subject are the same terms that the library has used to identify it. For example, if your subject is "solar power," you will not find books under that subject in the library catalog. If you have looked first in the *LCSH*, you will know that instead of "solar power," the Library of Congress uses the heading "Solar energy":

Solar power
USE Solar energy

Under "Solar energy" in the *LCSH*, you will find other subject headings that might be helpful (see Figure 3.5). The front pages of the *LCSH* contain a complete list of symbols and abbreviations. (In the 1989 edition of the *LCSH* the symbols, abbreviations, and some of the headings used in previous editions have been changed.)

FIGURE 3.5   Entry from the *Library of Congress Subject Headings*

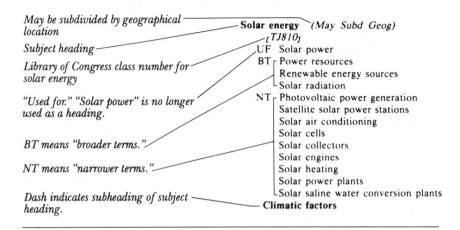

The Library Catalog

The library catalog—which may be either a card catalog or an online (computerized) catalog—is usually located on the first floor.

The Card Catalog.   Card catalogs consist of alphabetically arranged 3-by-5-inch cards in catalog drawers. Many card catalogs are divided into two sections, with cards organized by author and title in one section and by subject in another. A book in such a system will have three or more cards filed for it: an author card, a title card, and one or more subject cards. (Figure 3.6 shows a subject card for "solar energy.") If you are looking for indexes, dictionaries, or bibliographies in your subject, you will find the titles on cards filed under the subject heading with an appropriate subdivision. Figure 3.7 shows a subject card for "solar energy" with a "Bibliography" subheading.

The Online Catalog.   The online catalog stores information about the library's holdings in a large computer, which you can access at a terminal consisting of a keyboard and a screen monitor. A printer may be connected to the terminal. After you turn on the computer at a terminal, a message will appear on the screen asking you to choose whether you want to search by author, title, or subject. You may see several screens, each containing more specific information about your author, title, or subject and requiring some response from you. Finally a screen will appear providing the same information a card catalog does: the call number, complete title, name of author, publication data, and subjects under which the title is filed. In addition, it will usually show whether or not the book has been checked out. (Online library catalogs have varied methods of organization. Check the directions for operating the online catalog in your library.)

FIGURE 3.6   A Library of Congress Subject Card with Subject
Subdivision

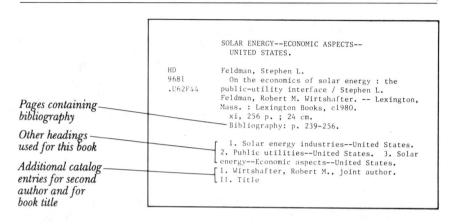

Pages containing bibliography

Other headings used for this book

Additional catalog entries for second author and for book title

FIGURE 3.7   A Library of Congress Subject Card with a Bibliography
Subdivision

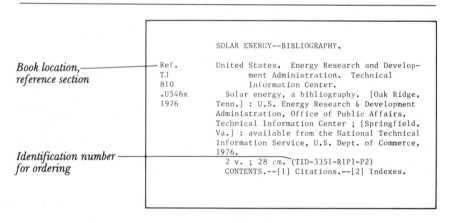

Book location, reference section

Identification number for ordering

An online catalog has several advantages over a card catalog. First, it is updated as soon as a book is cataloged; you don't have to wait for someone to file the cards. It also saves time—you can do all of your searching in one place by putting commands into the computer. In addition, the online catalog may allow you to search by using key words (other than *LCSH* headings) or by combining terms. (Ask your reference librarian whether your library catalog has this capability.) Finally, if the terminal is connected to a printer, you can get a printed copy of citations you wish to keep. With some systems you may even be able to download information onto your own disk.

You can use the online catalog to find the subject heading your library uses for your subject if you have the title of one book in your subject area. Look up the title of that book in the online catalog, and the screen will show the headings under which that book and books like it are classified.

You can also use the online catalog to locate indexes in your subject. Here are some suggestions:

1. First find the title of an index in your subject area. (A list of indexes appears in Appendix I in this book.) Perform a title search in the catalog to get the call number and location of the index. (You may also be able to find index titles in the serials list along with other periodical publications. See p. 70.)
2. Search the catalog using your subject heading. The indexes will appear after the subject with the subheadings ''periodicals—indexes.'' For example: ''Biology—periodicals—indexes.''

When you are finished searching in the library catalog, you will probably have a list of indexes and other reference books to find in the reference room along with a list of books to find in the stacks.

Finding Information in the Reference Area

The reference room is a good place to continue your search. As you enter the room, check to see if the library has a display rack containing handouts. College libraries often prepare lists of the commonly used sources in specific disciplinary areas as well as lists of index titles with their library call numbers and lists of automated reference sources organized by subject. Such lists can be timesavers because the library has completed the first steps of your research for you.

The following list shows the materials usually available in a library's reference room. Consulting the sources in the order presented here—from general to more specific—works best for most search projects, but you can adapt this list to your own needs.

1. Encyclopedias: general encyclopedias, such as the *Encyclopedia Americana*, or a specific encyclopedia, such as the *Encyclopedia of Philosophy*, or both
2. General sources of bibliographic information
3. Biographical indexes
4. Periodical indexes
5. Periodical file or serials list for the library you're using
6. Dictionaries
7. Pamphlets
8. Indexes to government documents
9. Handbooks and directories

If, for example, your topic is "The Role of the Ku Klux Klan during the Civil Rights Movement," you might compile this list of sources to consult, in order, in the reference area:

Encyclopedia Americana
Essay and General Literature Index
New York Times Index
Social Sciences Index
Sociological Abstracts
Serials list or periodical file
A Dictionary of Politics
Congressional Record

All of these will probably be available in print in the reference room. Most of them will also be available on computer databases.

Computer-Aided Searching

For years, scholars have searched through volumes of printed indexes in the library to find sources of information; then they have located the books or periodicals elsewhere in the library and have copied down with pen or pencil the information they have found. But now you will find alternatives in your library. Now at a computer terminal either connected by a telephone line to a large mainframe computer or equipped with a CD-ROM reader, you can search several years of a periodical index or a group of book titles. Or you can search the texts of some books themselves—encyclopedias, for example—to find information on the subjects you're interested in. If you're connected to a large enough storage system you may be able to search all of these at one time and even get the references or the texts themselves printed out.

Databases. A database is a collection of information accessible by computer. There are hundreds of databases. The bibliographic databases—those containing indexes and abstracts—are the ones most used in college libraries now. However, more and more reference works, such as encyclopedias and dictionaries, are being stored in databases and will become available.

Searching on CD-ROM Discs. Many of the same databases available online are now stored on a laser disc called a CD-ROM (compact disc–read only memory). These discs are sometimes kept at the desk by the librarian who will loan you one for use in the library. In some cases, the disc is preinstalled in the computer, although you may still have to sign up to use it. You can slip the disc into a microcomputer just as you would place a disc in your home CD player. After following the on-screen directions, a list of references—or pages of text—will appear on the screen. You can print any of these on a connected printer, or you can download the information onto your own disk. In most libraries you will not have to pay anything; the library subscribes to CD-ROM databases in much the same way it subscribes to printed indexes. The vendor provides updated discs at intervals of one to three months. Information on CD-ROM is usually not as current as information online; but for most research projects, it is adequate.

The computer printout in Figure 3.8 shows an excerpt from the PsycLIT database, available on CD-ROM. With this database the searcher can use natural language as well as the descriptors suggested in the *Thesaurus of Psychological Index Terms*. The searcher here entered the terms "agoraphobia," "treatment," and "etiology"; that is, all three terms had to be found in the title or the abstract in order for the article to be cited. The more terms one uses, the narrower the search will be. In this case, only three articles were found.

Searching Online. At a computer terminal connected by a telephone line to a large mainframe computer, you can search several years

FIGURE 3.8   Printout from a CD-ROM Search

```
                        Vendor or        Database      Database is on      Dates of journals
Number of articles      distributor                    2 discs             included
in which each term
is found             SilverPlatter 1.6       PsycLIT Disc 2 (1/83 - 9/90)
                     -----------------------------------------------------------------
Number of articles   No.    Records  Request
using all three
terms                1:       821     AGORAPHOBIA                          Indicates second
                     2:     40239     TREATMENT                            record out of 30
                     3:      4776     ETIOLOGY
Title of article     4:        30     AGORAPHOBIA and TREATMENT and ETIOLOGY
Author               -----------------------------------------------------------------
Institution                                                              2 of 30
Journal              TI: Agoraphobia: A review of research and treatment.   Year of publication
                     AU: Miranda,-David; Doctor,-Ronald-M.
                     IN: California State U, Northridge, US
Page numbers         JN: Phobia-Practice-and-Research-Journal; 1989 Spr-Sum Vol 2(1);
                     37-55
Language of          IS: 08949565—ISSN: International                      Volume and issue
publication          LA: English       Standard Serial Number   Date of issue   number
                     PY: 1989
Publication year     AB: Discusses agoraphobia etiology, onset, and demographic
                     characteristics of sufferers. The exact nature of agoraphobia is
Abstract: a short    the subject of controversy. A nontechnical approach is used to
summary of the       promote understanding of the disputes and consensuses that have
article              occurred in the past 20 yrs. A description of various treatments
                     and outcomes is included. Cognitive and educational treatment
                     components are delineated and advantages of group therapy are
Key phrase           discussed. (PsycLIT Database Copyright 1990 American
                     Psychological Assn, all rights reserved)
Descriptors          KP: etiology & treatment of agoraphobia; literature review
                     DE: ETIOLOGY-; AGORAPHOBIA-; TREATMENT-; LITERATURE-REVIEW
Population           CC: 3210; 3300; 32; 33
describing           PO: Human           Classification code
this entry           UD: 9005
                     AN: 77-12443        Volume of Psychological Abstracts and abstract number
Update code          JC: 3319            Journal code
```

of periodical titles, book titles, or authors, or even full texts of several volumes of books (encyclopedias, for example)—all at the same time. In addition, you can get the references printed out for you. Full texts of articles from journals to which your library does not subscribe can be especially valuable.

Libraries usually charge a fee for this service, from $5 to $100 for a list of references, based on the computer time required, the database searched, and the time of day (searching during daytime business hours is more expensive). You may have to sign up in advance because a librarian may have to conduct the search or at least assist you. You may be asked to meet with the librarian or to fill out a questionnaire to help the librarian determine the best subject terms or "descriptors" to use. Then the librarian will usually log on for you and perform the search. In a few minutes you will receive your printed list of references. To cut down on the expense, you may be able to have them printed offline and mailed to you. For the full text of referenced works to be mailed to you, you will probably have to wait several days. Full-text copies provided online can cost several hundred dollars.

Frequently Used Databases. Most college students will find that their research falls into one of the following subject areas: business, government and politics, humanities, law, life sciences, physical sciences, and social sciences. Listed on the following pages are some of the most frequently used databases on college campuses for these subject areas. Also included are some multidisciplinary databases; these can be helpful if you have a subject that crosses disciplinary boundaries—if, for example, you want to explore the legal implications of a scientific or medical process. In addition, InfoTrac, a CD-ROM system, which provides access to several databases, is reviewed.

All of the databases listed here are on CD-ROM except NEXIS, LEXIS, and Dow Jones News/Retrieval, which are only online because their primary value lies in providing up-to-date information. Even though online searching can be expensive, those databases are listed here because some college libraries offer students access to them free of charge. In these cases, students may conduct their own searches at computer stations that provide direct access to mainframe computers.

Each database is listed with its CD-ROM title. Its availability online or in print is given, along with its title in those formats.

BUSINESS

ABI/INFORM ON DISC. (Online: ABI/INFORM; no print version) Indexes such subjects as personnel management, operations research, organizational behavior, public relations, advertising, and communications. The full text of some of the journal articles is provided in *Business Periodicals Ondisc*.

Business Periodicals Ondisc (BPO). This database indexes and provides full-text printouts of articles in 300 of the 800 journals indexed in ABI/INFORM.

DOW JONES NEWS/RETRIEVAL. Provides access to financial and general information on corporations and industries. News is taken from the *Wall Street Journal* and *Barron's* as well as from the Dow Jones newswire.

GOVERNMENT AND POLITICS

CONGRESSIONAL MASTERFILE I. (Online: CIS; print: *CIS/Index to Publications of the U.S. Congress*) Indexes Congressional and Senate hearings from 1833 to 1969 and printed material from committees from 1830 to 1969.

CONGRESSIONAL MASTERFILE II. (Online: CIS; print: *CIS/Index to Publications of the U.S. Congress*) Provides bibliographic access to congressional publications. Microfiche copies of documents are available.

PAIS (Public Affairs Information Service). (Online: PAIS International Bulletin; print: *PAIS Bulletin* and *PAIS Foreign Language Index*) Indexes information in books, pamphlets, government publications, periodicals, and conference proceedings related to the social sciences and government; its coverage is worldwide.

HUMANITIES

ART INDEX. (Online: ART INDEX; print: *Art Index*) Indexes museum bulletins and yearbooks as well as articles from periodicals in archaeology, architecture, art history, city planning, crafts, films, graphic arts, industrial design, interior design, landscape architecture, and photography.

ERIC (Educational Resources Information Center). (Online: ERIC; print: *Resources in Education* and *Current Index to Journals in Education*) Provides abstracts of educational research and technical reports and indexes more than 700 education journals. The full text of the references is available on microfiche.

MLA INTERNATIONAL BIBLIOGRAPHY. (Online: MLA BIBLIOGRAPHY; print: *MLA International Bibliography of Books and Articles on the Modern Languages and Literatures*) Indexes journals, books, and dissertations on linguistics, modern languages, literature, and folklore. It's one of the major indexes for the humanities.

LAW

CONGRESSIONAL MASTERFILE II. (See "Government and Politics")

LEXIS. (Online only) Provides the complete text of cases heard in the U.S. Supreme Court, state supreme courts, and courts of appeals; also covers the *Federal Register, Code of Federal Regulations, U.S. Code*, and *American Law Reports*, as well as some law reviews.

LIFE SCIENCES

BIOLOGICAL ABSTRACTS. (Online: BIOSIS Previews [Bio-Sciences Information Services Previews]; print: *Biological Abstracts* and *Biological Abstracts/RRM* [Reports, Reviews, and Meetings]) Surveys more than 800 periodicals, books, and monographs and provides information on many scientific subjects, including biology, biochemistry, medicine, and ecology.

General Science Index (GSI). (Online: GENERAL SCIENCE INDEX; print: *General Science Index*) Covers journals in most branches of science.

MEDLINE. (Online: MEDLARS; print: *Index Medicus, Index to Dental Literature*, and *International Nursing Index*) One of the databases is MEDLARS, a family of databases provided by the National Library of Medicine, Bethesda, Maryland. MEDLINE indexes and abstracts literature about health and medicine from around the world. The National Library of Medicine recently developed GRATEFUL MED, a software program that provides easy access to most of its databases, including MEDLINE. With this software, which costs about $30, you need only a modem attached to an IBM (or compatible) computer or a Macintosh to have access to the largest medical library in the world. The service may be especially worthwhile if you have a long research project or several projects in the health field. Because GRATEFUL MED allows you to record the results of a search offline, the average search costs only about $3. If your library does not offer MEDLINE, the personal computer access may be worth considering.

PHYSICAL SCIENCES

Applied Science and Technology Index (AST). (Online: AST; print: *Applied Science and Technology Index*) Indexes such subjects as aeronautics and space science, chemistry, computer science, electronics, geology, mathematics, physics, and engineering.

General Science Index. (See "Life Sciences")

Science Citation Index (SCI CD). (Online: SciSearch; print: *Science Citation Index*) Searches using title key words and cited references. Subjects in the applied and pure sciences are included.

SOCIAL SCIENCES

ERIC. See "Humanities."

PAIS. See "Government and Politics."

PsycLIT. (Online: PsycINFO; print: *Psychological Abstracts*) Indexes 1,300 psychology and related journals in twenty-seven languages from fifty countries. Although used primarily by researchers in psychology, PsycLIT can be used for searching other subjects with a psychological component. For example, if you are interested in the effects of space travel on humans, you might want to look here for the psychological aspects.

MULTIDISCIPLINARY DATABASES

NEXIS. (Online only) Indexes major American newspapers such as the *New York Times*, the *Washington Post*, the *Wall Street Journal*, the *Christian Science Monitor*, and the *Los Angeles Times*, as well as numerous regional newspapers. Also indexed are wire services (including the Soviet Press Service, the Associated Press, United Press International, and Reuters) and more than 100 periodicals including such popular magazines as *Time, Sports Illustrated,* and *Consumer Reports,* and a number of business and technical journals. You can search in just one newspaper or in all periodicals and newspapers at the same time. This service is very helpful in finding out what is going on elsewhere in the world.

NewsBank. Indexes articles from more than 500 U.S. newspapers in current events, business, biographies, film, theater, television, literature, and fine arts. NewsBank is useful for getting local news reports in such areas as politics, environmental problems, and economic trends.

PAIS. See ''Government and Politics.''

InfoTrac. A CD-ROM system from IAC (Information Access Corporation) that searches the past three years of more than 1,000 periodicals at once. InfoTrac compiles its CD-ROMs from its numerous online databases such as the *General Periodicals Index*, which includes the *Magazine Index* and the *Business Index*; the *National Newspaper Index*, which provides access to the *New York Times*, the *Wall Street Journal*, the *Washington Post*, the *Christian Science Monitor*, and the *Los Angeles Times*; and the *Government Publications Index*, which includes publications of the legislative and executive branches of the government and which can be searched by subject, author, and issuing agency.

InfoTrac is popular at college libraries because it is easy to use and because a large number of documents can be searched on it. The disc is preinstalled in a microcomputer that can be accessed from up to four work stations (computer terminals with printers). All you have to do is sit down at the terminal, follow the clearly labeled keyboard and the helpful chart next to it, and sit back and watch as perhaps several dozen references emerge from the printer. (You can also select and print individual references.)

It is tempting to make InfoTrac your only source, but it has limitations. InfoTrac's databases are oriented toward business subjects, and they draw heavily on popular magazines rather than on professional journals. Check the list of periodicals covered (type "LIST PUB") to make sure the journals you want to consult are there.

Choosing the Best Format.   Because many indexes are available in the library in more than one format, you can often choose whether to use an index on CD-ROM, online, or in print. Here are the main advantages and disadvantages of each format.

CD-ROM

Advantages: Access is easy, although you may have to sign up in advance; instructions are provided onscreen; use is free to the user; the information can be printed out; information is sufficiently current for most projects; there is a wide choice of indexes.

Disadvantages: Not all indexes are available in this format yet, though more are continually being added; information is usually not as current as that available online, though it is usually more current than in print; small libraries may have a limited selection of databases.

Best Use: Good for most undergraduate research projects in libraries with a variety of databases.

ONLINE

Advantages: It usually provides more up-to-date information than other formats; many databases can be searched in a short time; the information can be printed out; its use may be less frustrating if the librarian does the search for you; there is a wide choice of databases and therefore more information is likely to be available.

Disadvantages: A fee is usually charged, sometimes more than $100; because help from the librarian is usually needed, an appointment and waiting period may be required; online searching may not be available in smaller libraries; full-text printing may be delayed if it's done offline and mailed.

Best use: Good for extensive research projects, for projects requiring very current information, and for in-depth search of narrow or complicated subjects.

PRINT

Advantages: More indexes, especially the less traditional ones, may be available in this form than in any other; all libraries have some print indexes; there is no cost to the user; they allow random browsing; they're easier for the inexperienced searcher to use.

Disadvantages: It takes much more time to search through several volumes of different print indexes than either computer index format; printed indexes are much less current; sources have to be copied by hand or photocopied.

Best use: Print is the only choice in libraries without computer-assisted facilities; print is useful for a broad search and for searching that requires only a few sources. Best choice for a quick search for a single item.

As CD-ROM technology is improved, as more databases become available in that format, and as more libraries purchase CD-ROM terminals, you can expect to do more of your searching using this format. Because of the expense and inconvenience of the online search, libraries are likely to become more inclined to provide databases on CD-ROM. And although the CD-ROM discs in your library probably have only textual or numerical information now, in the future they will probably store illustrated information as well.

Budget and space restrictions will probably cause libraries to limit print indexes to those that are not available in databases and those that are frequently consulted for short searches.

The following reference books are some of the most frequently consulted printed sources in the library. Their availability online or on CD-ROM is also noted.

Encyclopedias

General Encyclopedias.   Unless your subject is an event or discovery that occurred very recently, the best place for you to start may be a general encyclopedia, in which you might discover facets of your subject that you hadn't thought of. Such discoveries may lead you to expand or narrow your search or to change direction. An encyclopedia article also shows you how your specific topic fits within the framework of the subject as a whole. General encyclopedias attempt to give summaries of knowledge about everything—an impossible task, of course—and in order to make this knowledge easily accessible, most of them are organized alphabetically. Finally, most encyclopedia articles conclude with helpful bibliographies. Be sure to check the publication date of the encyclopedia if your topic requires recent information.

The *New Encyclopaedia Britannica* (1989, 32 vols., new printing yearly), which contains the *Micropaedia: Ready Reference* (vols. 1–12), the *Macropaedia: Knowledge in Depth* (vols. 13–29), the *Propaedia: Outline of Knowledge* (1 vol.), and the Index (2 vols.), has attempted to counteract the fragmentation that occurs with alphabetical organization of subjects. The *Propaedia* is a volume-length outline of subjects discussed in the *Micropaedia* and *Macropaedia* in which the editors try to show the interrelatedness of all knowledge. They divide all knowledge into ten areas (such as "Matter and Energy," "The Earth," and "Human Society") and explain in an introductory essay, "A Circle of Learning," their belief that knowledge is circular, not linear. A table of contents at the beginning of the volume directs you to the part of the outline in the

Propaedia in which you can find the subject you are interested in. After each section of the outline, you are referred to relevant articles in the *Micropaedia* and *Macropaedia*.

There are no articles in the *Propaedia* except for introductory essays to each of the ten sections. Browsing in this volume might help you to determine the part of a subject you would like to research and also give you valuable perspective—a framework for your research. For example, if you're interested in the theater but aren't sure what aspect of theater to study, you could look under "Part Six, Art." Under "Section 622. Theatre," you would find a detailed outline followed by a list of articles given in the *Micropaedia* and *Macropaedia*. See Figure 3.9 for an excerpt from this outline and Figure 3.10 for a list of subject headings on this subject to be found in the *Macropaedia* and *Micropaedia*. In addition, the *Propaedia* contains a directory of the full names and professional affiliations of the authors of articles in the *Micropaedia* and *Macropaedia* (in the latter volumes authors are identified only by their initials).

The *Micropaedia* contains short articles that summarize a subject and refer you to related articles in the *Macropaedia*. The *Macropaedia* contains longer signed articles on broader subjects with bibliographies at the end. You will find more on a specific subject in the *Micropaedia*, but in the *Macropaedia* that subject is discussed in a larger context—perhaps in several different articles. For example, if your subject were the Italian

FIGURE 3.9 Part of the Outline for "Theatre" in the *Propaedia*

c. Kinds defined by their system of production; *e.g.*, single-performance productions, repertory systems, stock companies, touring companies

d. Kinds defined by the controlling artist; *e.g.*, actor-dominated productions, dramatist-controlled productions, productions controlled by a nonperforming director

e. Kinds defined by their style: general aesthetic style; styles of particular countries, historical periods, and playwrights

f. Kinds defined by the lack of a unified dramatic structure
 i. Circuses and carnivals
 ii. Pageants, parades, and related forms
 iii. Popular entertainments: music hall, variety, and burlesque productions; nightclub shows; cabaret; musical comedy and revue

Section and outline   g. Kinds defined by the cultural character of their audience: primitive, folk, and popular
reference elsewhere ——— theatre
in the <u>Propaedia</u>   [see 611.B.3.]

2. Methods of theatrical production

C. Elements of theatrical production

 1. The production area: theatre buildings, stages, auditoriums
 a. Theatre as place: kinds and uses of theatre buildings, stages, and auditoriums
 b. The historical development of theatres in Western and non-Western cultures

 2. Staging and stage design: the arrangement of words, dance, music, costumes, makeup, lighting, sound, and properties for theatrical effect

D. The history of theatre

 1. Western theatre

 2. Non-Western theatre
 [see 613]

FIGURE 3.10   Subject Headings in the *Macropaedia* and the *Micropaedia*

Suggested reading in the *Encyclopædia Britannica*:

MACROPAEDIA: Major articles dealing with the theatre

African Arts	Oceanic Arts	Southeast Asian Arts
American Indians	Pageantry and	Theatre, The Art of the
Central Asian Arts	Spectacle	Theatre, The History of Western
East Asian Arts	Popular Arts	Theatrical Production
Folk Arts	South Asian Arts	

MICROPAEDIA: Selected entries of reference information

General subjects

dramatic conventions	Stanislavsky	*popular dramatic*
and techniques:	method	*entertainment:*
agon	stock company	burlesque show
alienation effect	summer theatre	cabaret
lazzo	theatre	carnival
soliloquy	theatre-in-the-round	circus
elements of theatrical	theatrical	conjuring
production:	production	Fasching
acting	*movements and*	ice show
actor-manager	*tendencies:*	masque
system	Absurd, Theatre	mime and
chorus	of the	pantomime
courtyard	biomechanics	minstrel show
theatre	Cruelty, Theatre of	music hall and
directing	environmental	variety
hanamichi	theatre	pageant
open stage	Fact, Theatre of	revue
proscenium	little theatre	shell game
régisseur	Living Newspaper	son et lumière
repertory theatre	Open Theatre	vaudeville
skene	theatricalism	Wild West show

---

novelist and playwright Luigi Pirandello, you could look him up in the
Index, where you would see references to articles in the *Micropaedia* and
Macropaedia (see Figure 3.11).

If you looked up the reference following his name, you would find in
the *Micropaedia* (vol. 9), a summary of his life and professional accom-
plishments along with a bibliography. Under the first subheading you
would find an article in the *Micropaedia* about his association with a

FIGURE 3.11   *Encyclopaedia Britannica* Index entry

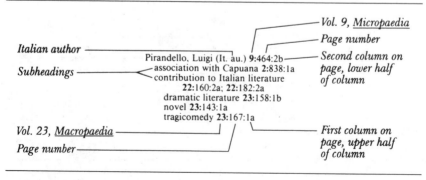

contemporary novelist, Capuana. The second subheading, "contribution to," introduces articles in both the *Micropaedia* and *Macropaedia* on Pirandello's contribution to Italian literature in general and on his specific contributions to Italian theater, novel, and tragicomedy.

The *Encyclopedia Americana* (30 vols., new printing yearly) contains an index volume, which is helpful if you haven't used the same terminology as the *Americana* has for your subject. This encyclopedia is known for its attention to North American affairs and to scientific and technical subjects; in recent editions it has expanded its coverage of international subjects as well. The editors consult with school curriculum designers and make an attempt to keep up with the current needs of American students, a goal that may account for the relatively large amount of space given to biographies. The final paragraph and the bibliography of the *Americana*'s discussion on Pirandello are illustrated in Figure 3.12.

Examples of a bibliography card and a note card derived from an encyclopedia article are shown in Figures 3.13 and 3.14. In Figure 3.14, notice that the volume and page numbers aren't given; these are unnecessary for notes from encyclopedias that are organized alphabetically. Significant words in Figure 3.14 are enclosed in quotation marks.

The *New Columbia Encyclopedia* is an excellent one-volume work providing concise articles in most academic areas. It is a good choice if you want a short summary of a subject along with a brief bibliography. The entry on Pirandello gives a brief account of his life, names his main novels and plays, and lists four authors who have written about him.

You may want to consult more than one of these encyclopedias, depending on your purpose: the *New Encyclopaedia Britannica*, for establishing the interrelationships of your subject with other areas of knowl-

FIGURE 3.12   Last Paragraph and Bibliography from the Pirandello Entry in the *Encyclopedia Americana*

A few of Pirandello's contemporaries failed to understand the subtlety of his thought and technique and tended to dismiss his theater as a clever hoax. Most serious critics, however, expressed great admiration for it and valued highly his contribution, despite a recurrent weakness in his dramatic structure. Commentators in Italy engaged in controversies concerning the validity of Pirandello's ideas, but even those who accused him of excessive "cerebral" qualities granted him a high place as a theatrical innovator, ". . . an artist at the center of our time."

THOMAS W. BISHOP
Author of "Pirandello and the French Theater"

Bibliography

Bentley, Eric, *The Pirandello Commentaries* (Northwestern Univ. Press 1986).
Bishop, Thomas W., *Pirandello and the French Theater* (1960; N.Y. Univ. Press 1970).
Paolucci, Anne, *Pirandello's Theater: The Recovery of the Modern Stage for Dramatic Art* (Southern Ill. Univ. Press 1974).
Sogliuzzo, A. Richard, *Luigi Pirandello, Director: The Playwright in the Theatre* (Scarecrow 1982).
Vittorini, Domenico, *The Drama of Luigi Pirandello*, 2d ed. (1959; reprint, Russell & Russell 1969).

FIGURE 3.13 Bibliography Card for an Encyclopedia Article

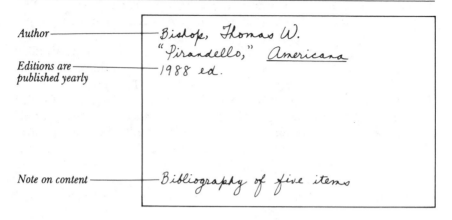

FIGURE 3.14 Note Card for an Encyclopedia Article

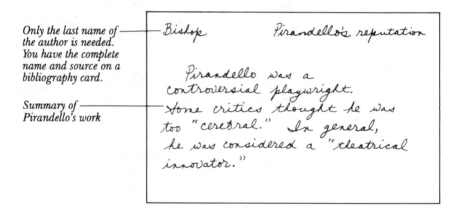

edge; the *Americana* for science and technology, American studies, and biographies; and the *New Columbia Encyclopedia* for a brief introduction to your subject.

Specialized Encyclopedias. An encyclopedia dealing only with your subject, such as the *Encyclopedia of Educational Research* or the *Encyclopedia of Anthropology,* may give you specific information unavailable in other, more general encyclopedias. For instance, if you want to know about the religion of the Hittites, who lived about 1000 B.C., consult the *Encyclopedia of Religion and Ethics*, which contains an extensive discussion along with a bibliography. Other specialized encyclopedias and reference books are listed in Appendix 1.

General Sources of Bibliographic Information

You may be looking for a bibliography on your subject to give you a start in your research; if you are, look in an index of bibliographies—a bibliography of bibliographies. Here are some of the most commonly used general bibliographic guides (for indexes and bibliographies on specific subjects refer to Appendix 1 of this book).

Bibliographic Index: A Cumulative Bibliography of Bibliographies is published quarterly with a yearly cumulative index. It cites not only periodical articles that contain bibliographies but also books with substantial bibliographic information and separately published bibliographies. By looking up either a subject or an author, you will find sources that contain bibliographies. Figure 3.15 shows a sample entry under the major heading "Falkland Islands War" and tells you where you can obtain a list of sources on that subject.

Published in London, the *Guide to Reference Material* by A. J. Walford (4th ed., 3 vols.), is a source for international bibliographies with a British emphasis. Bibliographies for science and technology are listed in Volume 1 (1980), those for social and historical sciences, philosophy, and religion in Volume 2 (1982), "generalia," language and literature, and the arts in Volume 3 (1987). As the example in Figure 3.16 shows, Walford's annotations are thorough. Walford's *Concise Guide to Reference Material* (1981, 1 vol.) covers all subjects.

FIGURE 3.15   Entry from the *Bibliographic Index*

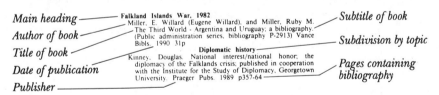

FIGURE 3.16   Entry from Walford's *Guide to Reference Material*, Volume 3, *Generalia, Language and Literature, the Arts*

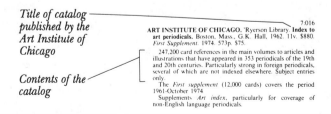

Trade Bibliographies and Bibliographies of Books

Books in Print (with new editions yearly) is a multivolume index of the books currently available for sale by book agents in the United States. (It is also available online and on CD-ROM.) If an important source book on your topic is not on the library shelf or has been ordered but not yet cataloged, *Books in Print* will supply you with complete bibliographic information, including publisher's name and address. Books are classified by subject, title, and author. The subject listing for Duke Ellington, shown in Figure 3.17, contains four recent books about him. Other bibliographic guides are the *Cumulative Book Index* and the *National Union Catalog* for books available in the United States. All three guides are available online, on CD-ROM, and in print.

Ulrich's International Periodicals Directory (3 vols. in print; also available online and on CD-ROM), published annually, can answer many questions you may have about periodicals related to your topic. The main section, "Classified List of Serials," contains periodicals arranged by subject; the "Title Index" lists periodicals by title with a cross-reference to the main section. Use *Ulrich's* if you do not know the titles of periodicals in your subject area or if you know the titles but don't know where they are indexed. For each periodical listed, *Ulrich's* provides such information as the first year of publication, the publisher or sponsor, where it is indexed, and whether it is available online or on CD-ROM. It even gives telex and fax numbers if they are available. *Ulrich's* provides the notation "Refereed Serial" for periodicals (usually professional journals) whose articles are evaluated by peer reviewers before acceptance. The example in Figure 3.18 shows some of the other information this valuable reference book provides.

FIGURE 3.17 Entry from Subject Index to *Books in Print*

Subject heading ——	**ELLINGTON, DUKE, 1899-1974**
	Collier, James L. Duke Ellington. LC 86-33309. (Illus.). 340p. 1987. 19.95 (ISBN 0-19-503770-7). Oxford U Pr.
Asterisk indicates first appearance in <u>*Books in Print.*</u>	*Didion, Joan & Fusco, Peter. Robert Graham: The Duke Ellington Memorial in Progress. LC 81-23629. (Illus.). 108p. (Orig.). 1982. pap. 16.00x. LA Co Art Mus.
	Gammond, Peter, ed. Duke Ellington: His Life & Music. LC 77-1927. (The Roots of Jazz Ser.). 1977. Repr. of 1958 ed. lib. bdg. 29.50 (ISBN 0-306-70874-4). Da Capo.
Book has library binding.	King, Coretta S., intro. by. Duke Ellington: Bandleader & Composer. (Black Americans of Achievement Ser.). (Illus.). 112p. (YA) (gr. 7-12). PLB 16.95 (200417). Know Unltd.
Author of introduction	

International Standard Book Number
Publication date
Original text, not a reprint
Book is one of a series.
Title
Subtitle
Price
Publisher

FIGURE 3.18   Entry from *Ulrich's International Periodicals Directory*

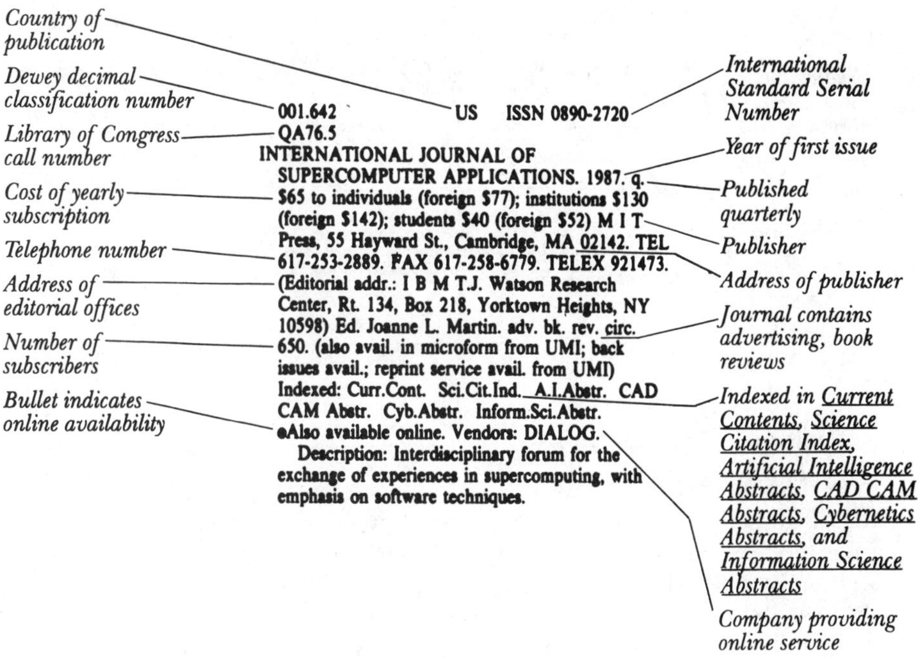

Country of publication

Dewey decimal classification number

Library of Congress call number

Cost of yearly subscription

Telephone number

Address of editorial offices

Number of subscribers

Bullet indicates online availability

001.642   US   ISSN 0890-2720
QA76.5
INTERNATIONAL JOURNAL OF
SUPERCOMPUTER APPLICATIONS. 1987. q.
$65 to individuals (foreign $77); institutions $130
(foreign $142); students $40 (foreign $52) M I T
Press, 55 Hayward St., Cambridge, MA 02142. TEL
617-253-2889. FAX 617-258-6779. TELEX 921473.
(Editorial addr.: I B M T.J. Watson Research
Center, Rt. 134, Box 218, Yorktown Heights, NY
10598) Ed. Joanne L. Martin. adv. bk. rev. circ.
650. (also avail. in microform from UMI; back
issues avail.; reprint service avail. from UMI)
Indexed in: Curr.Cont. Sci.Cit.Ind. A.I.Abstr. CAD
CAM Abstr. Cyb.Abstr. Inform.Sci.Abstr.
•Also available online. Vendors: DIALOG.
   Description: Interdisciplinary forum for the
exchange of experiences in supercomputing, with
emphasis on software techniques.

International Standard Serial Number

Year of first issue

Published quarterly

Publisher

Address of publisher

Journal contains advertising, book reviews

Indexed in Current Contents, Science Citation Index, Artificial Intelligence Abstracts, CAD CAM Abstracts, Cybernetics Abstracts, and Information Science Abstracts

Company providing online service

Paperbound Books in Print, organized by author, title, and subject, lists books available in paperback editions or in both paperbound and hardcover copies. The *Essay and General Literature Index* (from 1900, issued three times a year with a yearly cumulative volume) contains citations to essays and parts of books in the humanities that are generally not listed in other indexes. Material is indexed by author, subject, and sometimes title. Figure 3.19 gives an example.

Biographical Indexes

The *Biography Index* is a good source if you want to know more about the history of the person you are studying. It will refer you to material in American periodicals and books about famous people from all over the world—from basketball players (''Abdul-Jabbar, Kareem'') to authors (''Zola, Émile''). An additional index of names by profession and occupation is given in the back, referring you to entries in the alphabetical listings. For other sources of biographical information, see the annotated list in Appendix 1.

FIGURE 3.19   Entry from the *Essay and General Literature Index*

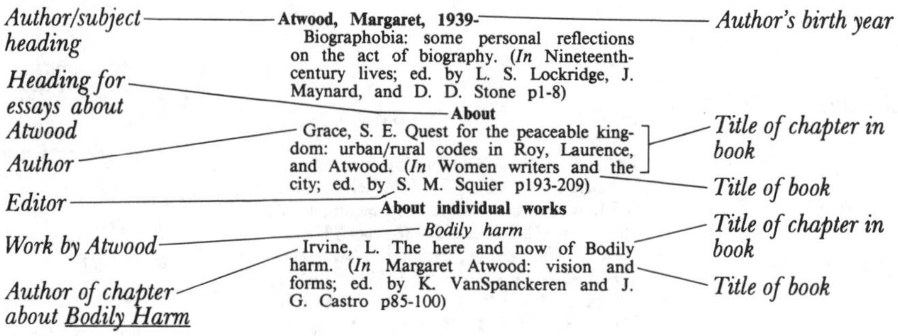

Author/subject heading — **Atwood, Margaret, 1939-** — Author's birth year
Biographobia: some personal reflections on the act of biography. (*In* Nineteenth-century lives; ed. by L. S. Lockridge, J. Maynard, and D. D. Stone p1-8)

Heading for essays about Atwood — **About**

Author — Grace, S. E. Quest for the peaceable kingdom: urban/rural codes in Roy, Laurence, and Atwood. (*In* Women writers and the city; ed. by S. M. Squier p193-209) — Title of chapter in book — Title of book

Editor — **About individual works**

Work by Atwood — *Bodily harm* — Title of chapter in book
Irvine, L. The here and now of Bodily harm. (*In* Margaret Atwood: vision and forms; ed. by K. VanSpanckeren and J. G. Castro p85-100) — Title of book

Author of chapter about *Bodily Harm*

Periodical Indexes

Periodicals are publications that appear at regular intervals; journals, magazines, newspapers, and newsletters are all periodicals. *Journal* is the term usually used to refer to a periodical that contains articles written by and for professionals in the field (*Journal of American Folklore*, *American Mathematical Monthly*). A *magazine* is a periodical containing articles on popular subjects not necessarily written by experts (*Vogue*, *Time*). The term *serials* is often used by libraries to refer to publications that appear in successive parts, often at irregular intervals, and that may be issued by organizations and research institutions. *Serials* is also used generically to refer to all of these publications; for example, the serials list in a library's reference room includes journals, magazines, and serials.

Articles in periodicals are indexed in print, in microform, online, or on a CD-ROM, with the subjects, titles, and authors organized alphabetically. To decide whether you want to look in a magazine or a journal for your information, consider the differences between the two. Journals are usually published by nonprofit professional organizations or academic institutions; before being accepted, an article is usually approved by a panel of experts. The professional status or brief biography of the author that is usually given is a further clue to a journal article's authoritativeness, and the articles are fully and professionally documented. Magazine articles are designed to help sell a particular magazine; their quality and reliability vary, from those in the respected *New Yorker* and *Harper's* to the primarily entertaining, as in *Vogue* or *Life*. However, they are much easier to understand because they're not written for the expert. In addition, they may contain more up-to-date information than articles in journals, which, because of their high professional quality and the time limitations of noncommercial publishing, are often slower to produce.

Before consulting a periodical index in print, check the explanatory material in the front of the book to learn the abbreviations for citing the information you need, such as volume and page numbers, date, and the periodicals that the index includes.

Magazine Indexes. The *Readers' Guide to Periodical Literature,* also on-line and on CD-ROM, indexes about 200 magazines from 1900 to the present, including *Newsweek, The New Yorker, Rolling Stone,* and *Scientific American.* The semimonthly supplements make it possible to find up-to-date articles on many subjects. Bound cumulative volumes are issued for each year, and some libraries may have back issues available on microfilm or as bound volumes. Articles are indexed by subject and author. There is a book review section at the end of each volume; movie reviews are indexed under "Motion picture reviews—Single Works." The *Readers' Guide* uses subheadings to group related articles under the main subject. In Figure 3.20, for example, the subject "Small business" is divided by topic and by subtopic. In addition, places in the United States are listed by state. Figure 3.21 shows an author entry.

Magazine Index, available in many libraries online or in microform, covers a greater number of popular magazines—more than 400—than the *Readers' Guide,* including, for example, more computer magazines,

FIGURE 3.20 Subject Entry from the *Readers' Guide to Periodical Literature*

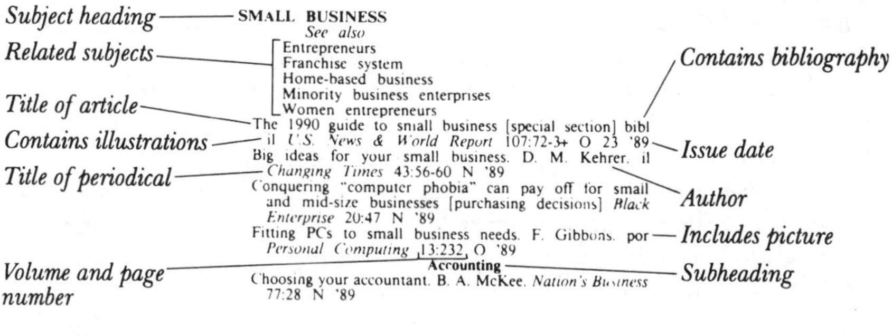

FIGURE 3.21 Author Entry from the *Readers' Guide to Periodical Literature*

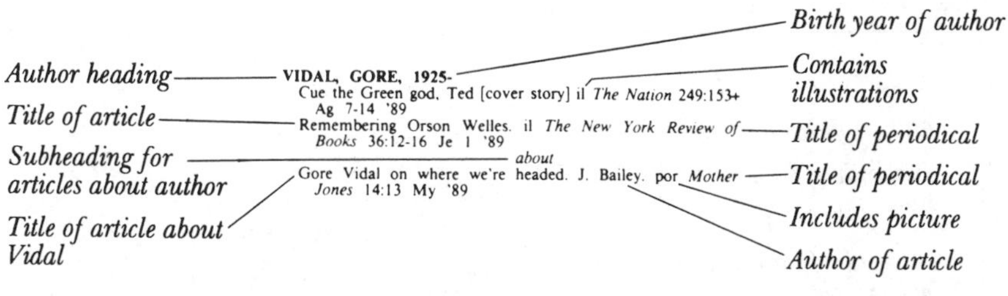

such as *PC Magazine* and *PC Week*. *Magazine Index* indexes by title, subject, and also product and brand name.

Journal Indexes. In professional journals you can often find articles on your subject written by experts for other experts. Such articles are likely to be more detailed and more authoritative than those in a popular magazine. The disadvantage is that technical terms unfamiliar to the layperson are often used. If, for example, you want to find out the latest developments in heart transplants, you may have to learn the meanings of unfamiliar medical terms. If you need to look up only a few words, you'll probably find the article useful. But if the article requires an extensive background that you don't have, you'll probably be more successful with magazines aimed at a less specialized audience. Many professional journals, however, present few problems to the college student. Here are five of the most commonly used print indexes to professional journals.

The *Humanities Index* (April 1974–) is published yearly with quarterly updates; it is also available online and on CD-ROM. It indexes by author and subject 345 periodicals on art, drama, literature, history, philosophy, music, film, and folklore. For information before 1974, see the *International Index* (1907–1965) and the *Social Sciences and Humanities Index* (1965–1974), both of which were superseded by the *Humanities Index*. As Figure 3.22 shows, the format of the entries in the *Humanities Index* is similar to that in the *Readers' Guide.*

The *MLA International Bibliography of Books and Articles on the Modern Languages and Literatures* (1921–), also online and on CD-ROM, changed its format in 1981, going from three volumes to five and adding a subject index. Now Volumes I and II cover national literatures; III, linguistics; IV, general literature; and V, folklore. The five volumes are issued and bound yearly in one volume and are subtitled *Classified Listings with Author Index*. A second annual volume is the *Subject Index*. To find entries in the *Classified Listings*, look either in the *Subject Index* (organized alphabetically) or in the *Classified Listings*, finding first the appropriate section or national literature, then the time period of your subject (for example, the nineteenth century), and finally the author (if your subject is a writer) listed alphabetically. Figure 3.23 shows the ref-

FIGURE 3.22 Entry from the *Humanities Index*

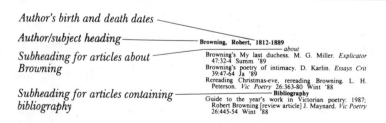

Author's birth and death dates

Author/subject heading

Subheading for articles about Browning

Subheading for articles containing bibliography

Browning, Robert, 1812-1889
——— *about*
Browning's My last duchess. M. G. Miller. *Explicator* 47:32-4 Summ '89
Browning's poetry of intimacy. D. Karlin. *Essays Crit* 39:47-64 Ja '89
Rereading Christmas-eve, rereading Browning. L. H. Peterson. *Vic Poetry* 26:363-80 Wint '88
——— **Bibliography**
Guide to the year's work in Victorian poetry; 1987; Robert Browning [review article] J. Maynard. *Vic Poetry* 26:445-54 Wint '88

erences you will find if you look up ''Feminist theory'' in the *Subject Index*.

Each volume in the classified section is numbered with roman numerals (I–IV) and each entry with arabic numerals. Figure 3.24 presents the entry you would find if you looked up the reference to Brecht in Volume II, number 6455 in the *Classified Listings* (Figure 3.23).

The *Public Affairs Information Service Bulletin (PAIS)*(1915–), in print, indexes 1,400 worldwide publications in six languages in such subjects as economics, political science, business, law, finance, education, and social work using the *Readers' Guide* index entry format. *PAIS* is published semimonthly, with cumulative volumes issued four times a year and bound volumes annually; it is also available online and on CD-ROM.

The *Social Sciences Index* (April 1974–) consists of yearly volumes updated quarterly and contains guides to about 250 English-language periodicals on sociology, psychology, environmental affairs, economics, political science, geography, and anthropology. Like *PAIS*, it uses the *Readers' Guide* citation format. (From 1907 to 1965, this index was called the *International Index* and from 1965 to 1974, the *Social Sciences and Humanities Index*.)

FIGURE 3.23 Entry from the *Subject Index, MLA International Bibliography*

Main subject heading

Primary subheading   **FEMINIST THEORY**
                                General literature. Theater.
Secondary   Role of *Verfremdung* ; gestus; historicity in theater theory of Brecht, Bertolt;
subheadings   relationship to gender; sexual difference in FEMINIST THEORY. Feminist
                                approach. IV:939 (II:6455).
Listed in vol. IV of   **German literature. 1900-1999.**
Classified Listings,   Brecht, Bertolt. Role of *Verfremdung* ; gestus; historicity in theater theory; rela-
citation number 939   tionship to gender; sexual difference in FEMINIST THEORY. Feminist ap-
(also in vol. II,   proach. II:6455 (IV:939).
no. 6455)

FIGURE 3.24 Entry from the *Classified Listings*, Volume II, *MLA International Bibliography*

Title of article

Author

Citation number — [**6479**] Caldwell, Ellen C. "Poststructuring Brecht: Pluralism and Propaganda in
Title of periodical — *Galileo* ." *CIBS,*. 1988 Apr.; 17(2): 38-47. [†Treatment of pluralism; relationship to
                        propaganda.]
Volume and issue number, page number

Dagger denotes heading used as subject descriptor (see Figure 3.23)

Citation Indexes.   Three citation indexes have a special type of organization in print that enables you to quickly build a network of authoritative sources on your subject.

The *Social Sciences Citation Index* (1972–), also available online and on CD-ROM, is useful for subjects in the social, behavioral, and related sciences such as urban planning and development. The print version is divided into four parts: Citation, Source, Permuterm Subject, and Corporate. Any of these may be used to begin a search, but the most usual place to begin is the Citation Index. Perhaps you have the name of an authority in your field from an encyclopedia article or one of your textbooks. For example, if you look up the name of B. F. Skinner, a psychologist, in the Citation Index, you will find the names of other writers who have cited this authority and who are probably writing about the same subjects (see Figure 3.25). This list can help you build a bibliography of experts in your subject area.

Let's say that after looking up Skinner in the Citation Index you decide to look up Wearden, who cites Skinner's 1931 article in the *Journal of General Psychology*. When you look up Wearden in the Source Index, you find that his reference to Skinner occurred in Wearden's review of

FIGURE 3.25   Entry from the Citation Index, *Social Sciences Citation Index*

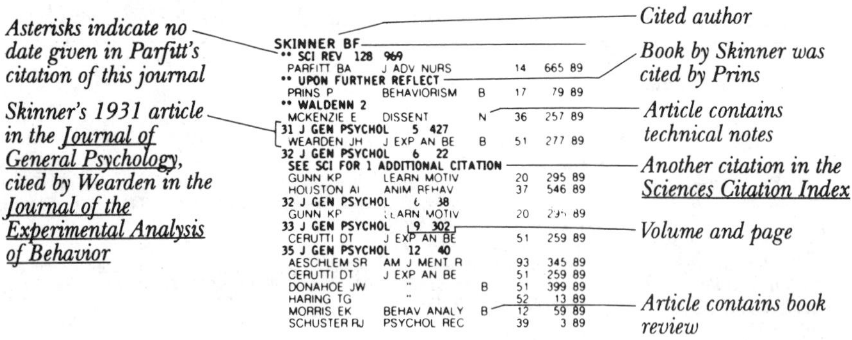

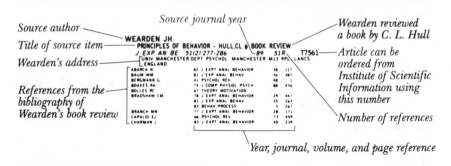

FIGURE 3.26   Entry from the Source Index, *Social Sciences Citation Index*

a book *Principles of Behavior* by C. L. Hull (see Figure 3.26). You also find the names of other authors referred to by Wearden in his review. You can look up any of these authors as well as other authors who cite Skinner. Following these steps you can quickly build a bibliography of experts in your subject area.

The Permuterm Subject Index enables you to search a subject by pairing significant related words from titles of articles. If you are interested in drug use by adolescents, this index will provide authors who have written on the subject (Figure 3.27). For publication details, look up these authors in the Citation Index.

The Corporate Index can be especially valuable for college students. It arranges items in the Source Index geographically. Thus you can find out what articles have been published by authors affiliated with organizations in your city or state; or you can find out what is being published by authors in other countries. Locations in the United States are alphabetized by state. If you would like to find out recent articles published by writers in Wellesley, for example, you would look under the state, Massachusetts, and then under the city. Figure 3.28 shows references to journals containing articles by authors affiliated with two colleges in Wellesley—Babson and Wellesley. For further information on these authors, you would look them up in the Source Index.

FIGURE 3.27 Entry from the Permuterm Subject Index, *Social Sciences Citation Index*

FIGURE 3.28 Entry from the Corporate Index, *Social Sciences Citation Index*

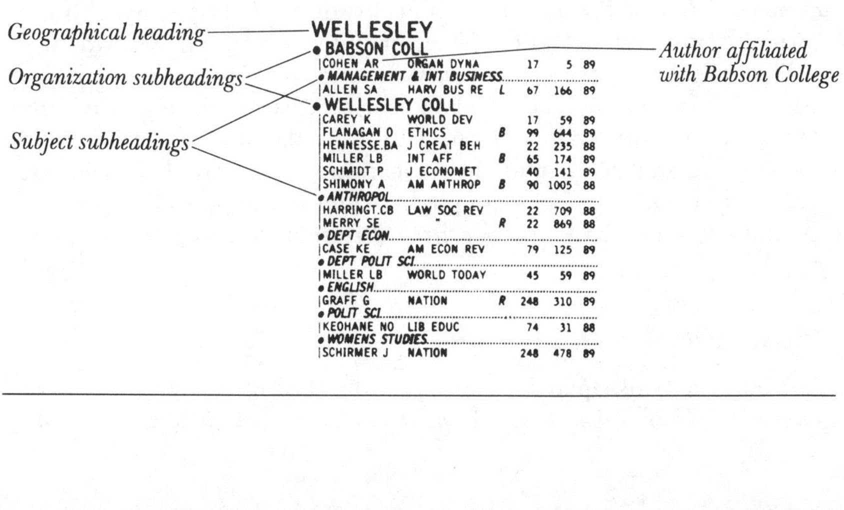

If you do not know the location of an organization, you can find it in the index of this volume; all organizations and institutions in the index are listed alphabetically along with their locations.

The *Science Citation Index* (1961–), also available online, and on CD-ROM), and the *Arts & Humanities Citation Index* (1977–), available online, can be used in the same way as the *Social Sciences Citation Index* to build up a network of sources. If your library does not carry an article referred to in one of these citation indexes that you believe to be important to your study, you can order it from the publisher, the Institute for Scientific Information. You will have to pay for this service, but delivery is prompt.

You can save time by searching these citation indexes online or on CD-ROM because you do not have to handle several different volumes to follow up a citation. Your library may offer this service.

Indexes for Specific Disciplines.   Indexes for journals in specific disciplines are listed and annotated in Appendix 1. Look in one of these specialized indexes—such as the *Music Index* or the *Index Medicus*—if your topic is highly technical or if you have trouble finding references in the general indexes.

Newspaper Indexes.   Newspapers provide current accounts of subjects as well as contemporary views of historical events. The following newspapers publish their own indexes (items are indexed by subject only): the *Christian Science Monitor, Los Angeles Times, New York Times, Wall Street Journal, Washington Post,* and London *Times.* The *National Newspaper Index* (available online, on CD-ROM, and on microfilm) is a guide to articles in the *Christian Science Monitor, Los Angeles Times, New York Times, Wall Street Journal,* and *Washington Post.* Each index covers two and a half years, and the *Index* is updated frequently; old films are on microfiche. The *National Newspaper Index* is also available online as part of the database *NewSearch* and on CD-ROM through InfoTrac (see "Frequently Used Databases" above).

Periodical File or Serials List.   This list of periodicals—which may be available in print, on microfiche, or online—will tell you whether your library has the periodicals you want and, if so, where they are located. It lists in alphabetical order the periodicals the library owns, the beginning and ending dates of acquisition by the library, the physical form they are stored in, and their location. If call numbers are not given, the journals are shelved alphabetically in the periodical section of the library. Figure 3.29 shows three different locations for periodicals.

Dictionaries

The massive book open on a stand or low shelf in the reference area is probably *Webster's Third New International Dictionary of the English Lan-*

FIGURE 3.29 Entry from a Periodical File

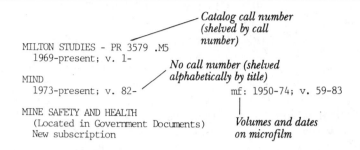

MILTON STUDIES - PR 3579 .M5
1969-present; v. 1-

MIND
1973-present; v. 82-

MINE SAFETY AND HEALTH
(Located in Government Documents)
New subscription

Catalog call number (shelved by call number)

No call number (shelved alphabetically by title)

mf: 1950-74; v. 59-83

Volumes and dates on microfilm

guage (1981). If it looks well worn, it is probably the earlier 1961 edition. This unabridged dictionary contains more words than any other American dictionary. It covers "the current vocabulary of standard written and spoken English" and is especially good for pronunciation and usage.

If the way a word has been used over the years is important in your search, see the *Oxford English Dictionary* (13 vols., also online and on CD-ROM). Known as the *OED*, this dictionary illustrates the history of each word it defines by giving quotations in historical order beginning with the first known usage. Supplements keep the *OED* up to date. Figure 3.30 shows the changing meanings of the word *educate*. One of its uses in the early seventeenth century—to rear children and animals by supplying their physical needs—is now obsolete. But it's interesting to notice that Shakespeare's use of the word as early as 1588

FIGURE 3.30 Entry from the *Oxford English Dictionary*, Second Edition

educate ('ɛdjʊkeɪt), *v.* [f. L. *ēducāt-* ppl. stem of *ēducāre* to rear, bring up (children, young animals), related to *ēdūcere* to lead forth (see EDUCE), which is sometimes used nearly in the same sense.] *trans.* or *absol.*

† **1.** To rear, bring up (children, animals) by supply of food and attention to physical wants. *Obs.*

1607 TOPSELL *Four-f. Beasts* 229 The Epirotan & Sicilian horses are not to be despised, if they were well bred & educated. **1651** WITTIE tr. *Primrose's Pop. Err.* 292 A boy of a good habit of body, with large veines, well and freely educated. **1690** [see EDUCATED]. **1818** [see 2].

2. To bring up (young persons) from childhood, so as to form (their) habits, manners, intellectual and physical aptitudes.

1618 BOLTON *Florus* I. i. 3 Himselfe delighting in the Rivers and Mountaines, among which he had beene educated. **1818** CRUISE *Digest* VI. 336 A devise..to the intent that with the profits he should educate his daughter. **1839** tr. *Lamartine's Trav. East* 168/1 The principal amongst them [Greeks] have their children educated in Hungary. **1875** JOWETT *Plato* (ed. 2) V. 40 The youth of a people should be educated in forms and strains of virtue.

b. To instruct, provide schooling for (young persons).

1588 SHAKS. *L.L.L.* v. i. 84 Do you not educate youth at the Charg-house on the top of the Mountaine? **1863** MARY HOWITT tr. *F. Bremer's Greece* I. i. 13 It has educated, and

it educates to this day, a great portion of the Athenian female youth of all classes. **1863** A. TYLOR *Educ. & Manuf.* 40 It costs 8*d.* per week to educate a child.

3. To train (any person) so as to develop the intellectual and moral powers generally.

1849 KINGSLEY *Lett.* (1878) I. 198 In my eyes the question is not what to teach, but how to Educate. **1875** JOWETT *Plato* (ed. 2) V. 120 Elder men, if they want to educate others, should begin by educating themselves. **1886** *Pall Mall G.* 10 July 4/2 Our artists are not educated at all, they are only trained.

4. To train, discipline (a person, a class of persons, a particular mental or physical faculty or organ), so as to develop some special aptitude, taste, or disposition. *Const. to*, also *inf.*

1841-4 EMERSON *Ess. Hist.* Wks. (Bohn) I. 11 And the habit of supplying his own needs educates the body to wonderful performances. **1847** —— *Repr. Men.* v. *Shaks.* ibid. I. 359 Our ears are educated to music by his rhythm. **1867** DISRAELI in *Scotsman* 30 Oct., I had to prepare the mind of the country, and to educate,—if not too arrogant to use such a phrase,—our party. *Mod.* He is educating himself to eat tomatoes.

b. To train (animals).

1850 LANG *Wand. India* 2 No horses, except those educated in India, would crawl into these holes cut out of the earth and rock. **1856** KANE *Arct. Expl.* I. xxix. 389 The dogs of Smith's Sound are educated more thoroughly than any of their more southern brethren.

was much the same as our use of it is today. After listing a word, the *OED* gives the pronunciation, part of speech, derivation, and grammatical use. Each numbered section provides a meaning of the word followed by the date, author, title of work, and quotation illustrating the word.

The word you want may be in a special dictionary, such as the *McGraw-Hill Dictionary of Scientific and Technical Terms*. Some dictionaries, such as the *Dictionary of Symbols* by J. E. Cirlot, are much like encyclopedias, with extended entries on a single subject. To find the dictionary best for you, consult *Dictionaries, Encyclopedias, and Other Word-Related Books* (2 vols.), edited by Annie M. Brewer.

Pamphlets

The library's pamphlet file contains uncataloged printed material. This material varies in size from pamphlets of a few pages to small paperbound books of a hundred or more pages published by local government agencies, business firms, or special interest groups. Most libraries store pamphlets or serial publications in file drawers, commonly known as vertical files. Contents of the files are usually arranged alphabetically according to subject.

To discover whether pamphlets have been published on your subject, consult the *Vertical File Index: A Subject and Title Index to Selected Pamphlet Materials*, published monthly with a cumulative subject index issued quarterly. Besides pamphlets it lists charts, posters, and maps for classroom use. This index gives the name of the pamphlet, the source, and the cost so that you can order the pamphlet directly if your library doesn't own the item. Most entries also include a brief annotation. It's a good idea to order pamphlets as soon as possible because the length of time it takes to receive them is unpredictable. Figure 3.31 shows one of the many kinds of pamphlets you might find through this source.

FIGURE 3.31   Entry from the *Vertical File Index*

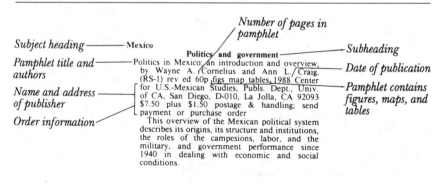

Indexes to Government Documents

If the subject of your search pertains to history, government, or law, federal government documents can provide interesting firsthand reports of committee findings, bills passed, and much other information about what goes on in Congress and elsewhere in the government. Many college libraries are repositories for government documents (a library must have at least 15,000 titles in its catalog to qualify as a repository). One repository in each state (a regional repository) receives all government documents; other repositories (selective repositories) choose the documents they wish to receive. Selective repositories may obtain any document they do not have from the nearest regional repository. Although some government documents can be checked out of the library, most do not circulate, and they may be stored in either print or microform. Small collections of government documents might be kept in the reference area, but large collections will probably be located in their own room or department.

Libraries with large collections of government documents usually do not list them in the library catalog and therefore do not use the classification systems used for other material. (Libraries with limited numbers of government documents may, however, integrate them into their regular cataloging system.) Instead, government documents in repository libraries are assigned a SuDoc (Superintendent of Documents) number that looks like this: Y 10.2:W29/2. Consult the librarian for indexes to the documents and their location. Here are the chief indexes.

The *Monthly Catalog of U.S. Government Publications,* issued by the Government Printing Office online and on CD-ROM (as *GPO and Government Documents Catalog*), describes all of the publications sent to repository libraries. The contents are indexed in the back of the catalog by author, title, subject, series, stock number, and title key word. These cumulative indexes are issued semiannually and annually. Documents published before 1971 are indexed somewhat differently and may best be located in two commercial publications: the *Cumulative Subject Index to the Monthly Catalog, 1900–1971* (15 vols.), by William W. Buchanan and Edna M. Kanely, and the *Decennial Cumulative Personal Author Index* (3 vols.), edited by Edward Przebienda, covering the years 1941 to 1970. As the title indicates, you can locate information in the Buchanan–Kanely index by looking up a subject; you can also find some authors by looking up "Addresses, Lectures," where speakers' names are listed in alphabetical order. Przebienda indexes material only by author.

The *CIS/Index to Publications of the United States Congress*, online and on CD-ROM as *Congressional and Masterfile I* and *Congressional Masterfile II*, is issued monthly in two parts—Abstracts and Indexes—with quarterly and annual cumulative volumes. Items are indexed by subject, name, title, document number, and committee chairman. To find in-

FIGURE 3.32   Abstract Entry from the *CIS/Index to Publications of the United States Congress*

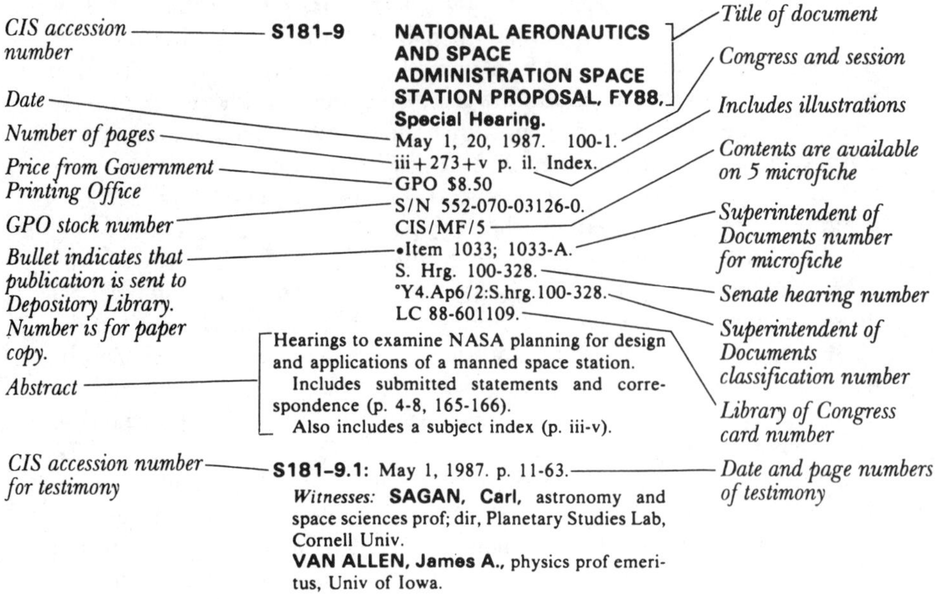

CIS accession number ——— **S181-9**   NATIONAL AERONAUTICS AND SPACE ADMINISTRATION SPACE STATION PROPOSAL, FY88, Special Hearing. — *Title of document*

Congress and session

Date — May 1, 20, 1987.   100-1. — *Includes illustrations*

Number of pages — iii+273+v p. il. Index. — *Contents are available on 5 microfiche*

Price from Government Printing Office — GPO $8.50

GPO stock number — S/N 552-070-03126-0.

CIS/MF/5 — *Superintendent of Documents number for microfiche*

Bullet indicates that publication is sent to Depository Library. Number is for paper copy. — •Item 1033; 1033-A.   S. Hrg. 100-328. — *Senate hearing number*

°Y4.Ap6/2:S.hrg.100-328. — *Superintendent of Documents classification number*

LC 88-601109. — *Library of Congress card number*

Abstract — Hearings to examine NASA planning for design and applications of a manned space station. Includes submitted statements and correspondence (p. 4-8, 165-166). Also includes a subject index (p. iii-v).

CIS accession number for testimony — **S181-9.1:** May 1, 1987. p. 11-63. — *Date and page numbers of testimony*

Witnesses: **SAGAN, Carl,** astronomy and space sciences prof; dir, Planetary Studies Lab, Cornell Univ.
VAN ALLEN, James A., physics prof emeritus, Univ of Iowa.

formation in this volume, look up your subject in the Index and find the number of the document you want; then find the abstract in the Abstracts volume of the *CIS/Index*. Figure 3.32 presents a sample abstract entry from the *CIS/Index*.

The *American Statistics Index* (*ASI*) is a guide to government publications containing statistical information. It follows the same format as the *CIS/Index*.

The *Congressional Record*, a daily record of proceedings in the House and Senate, is usually shelved in the reference room or in the government documents section. Published daily, the *Congressional Record* is indexed biweekly, with a yearly bound cumulative issue. Material is indexed by author and subject. It is available on microfilm from 1873.

Interlibrary Loans

If you find that some of the most promising articles or books are not available in your library, your reference librarian may be able to get them through interlibrary loan. A computer network, such as OCLC (Online Computer Library Center), which links the catalogs of subscribing libraries, may be able to assist you in finding a library that has the source you want. If you want a book, arrangements may be made to borrow it for you. You may also arrange for photocopies of periodical articles to be sent to you, for which you will probably pay a small fee. Before you ask for such a service, however, determine the relevance of your article by reading an abstract of it in an index of abstracts if one.is available for your subject. You will find indexes of abstracts along with other indexes in Appendix 1. Although OCLC, with more than 300 subscribers from academic and nonacademic libraries, is the largest of these networks, other online networks are available to libraries that want to participate, including RLIN (Research Libraries Information Network), a network of large academic research libraries such as Cornell, Harvard, Stanford, and the University of California; WLN (Washington Library Network), a network of Pacific Northwest libraries; and UTLAS (University of Toronto Library Automation System), a Canadian libraries system.

Before you leave the reference room, take a few minutes to review your records. You should have a list of possible sources on cards or note paper and, in your search log, a record of where you went and what you did, including names of indexes you searched.

Taking Stock

You are now ready to find the periodicals that have the articles you want and to locate the books you need on the library's shelves. Help in evaluating these sources and taking notes will be given in Chapter 4, but before you begin that process, it would be wise for you to answer the questions Where am I? Where have I been? Where am I going?

As you followed the steps in compiling your bibliography, you were constantly finding references to related subjects. Beginning with the encyclopedia, you were given a number of directions to take. When you looked through the indexes, you found more possibilities. Again as you searched the library catalog, you were presented with subject headings from which to choose. By this time you had to make a number of choices of direction; some of those decisions you made consciously, others unconsciously. Now, before you begin to locate your sources, review your progress and note where you are headed.

Widening or Narrowing?

First review your original outline or list of subtopics and add possibilities you may have found in encyclopedias, indexes, periodical listings, and the catalog. Then choose from this expanded list the subtopics you want to cover. In deciding which ones to include, consider their relevance to your main topic, your interests, and the time and sources available to you. The list you make now will guide you as you look up and examine your sources. Use the subtopics from your outline as headings for your note cards.

Focusing a Topic

A subject—any subject—is a little like a Fourth of July sparkler: it gives off sparks or light in all directions. Sometimes when you're starting to investigate a subject, these sparks seem to be multiplying at an uncontrollable rate. Marvin Kohl started to write a paper on pornography. He wanted to know answers to these questions: What is pornography? Is it harmful? Should anything be done about it? He went first to the *Encyclopaedia Britannica*'s *Micropaedia* where he found, besides a brief definition, two reasons for laws against pornography: it corrupts morals and it causes crime. In the *Macropaedia* he found a discussion of the following subjects: censorship, laws against pornography and obscenity, a history of such laws, laws in other countries, and book banning. He then looked up his subject in the *Encyclopedia Americana* and found that this source concentrated on American obscenity laws and referred to congressional hearings. To keep track of all these ideas and others that were occurring to him, he drew a diagram (Figure 3.33) to show how one subject suggested another. From this diagram he selected the topics he was most interested in: laws passed in the United States and elsewhere and the effects of pornography.

FIGURE 3.33   Focusing a Topic

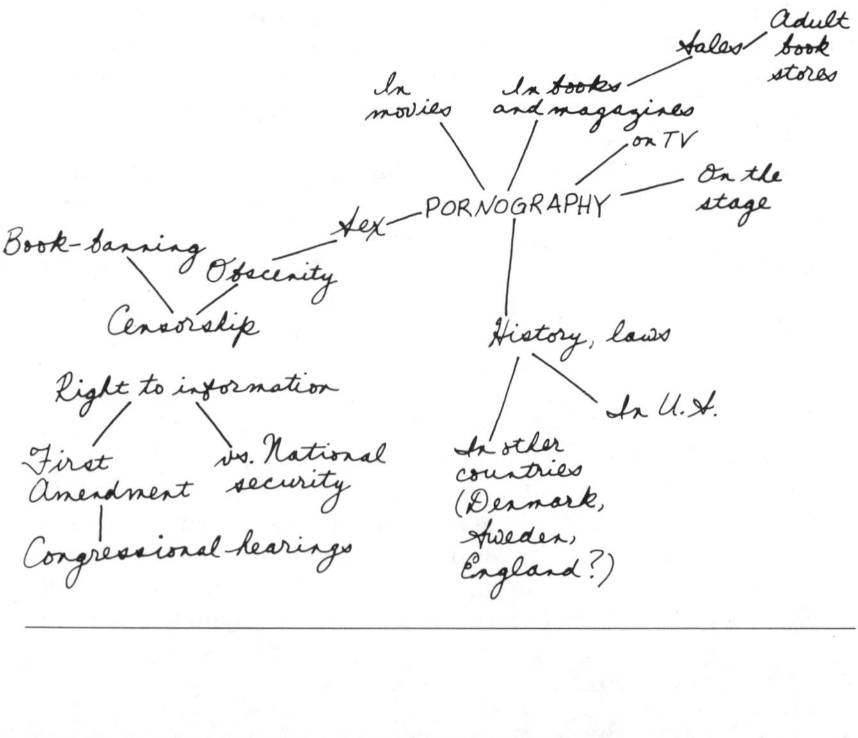

His next step was to search the *Encyclopedia of Psychology*, where he found an article that referred to reports of the Commission on Obscenity and Pornography. In the *Readers' Guide* he spotted a reference to an article that attacked pornography on the grounds of violation of women's rights. Next the reference librarian recommended the *Encyclopedia of Crime and Justice,* which, as it turned out, was an excellent suggestion because the article on pornography discussed the two aspects of the subject he was mainly interested in—behavioral and legal. It was a lengthy article with a long bibliography. On the basis of this article, he decided to concentrate on photographic pornography. Kohl was now ready to compose a working title and a preliminary outline.

The Social Effects of Photographic Pornography

Possible bad effects (to be verified or disproven)
    Involves the exploitation of children
    Leads to the exploitation of women
    Causes increase in crime
    Results in moral corruption
Possible good effects (to be verified or refuted)
    Can be used in sex education and treatment programs
    Helps in preventing some crimes
Laws relating to pornography
    Legalization of pornography in Denmark
    Laws against pornography in the United States

He next read over his outline to make sure that the topics and subtopics were listed in the order of most to least important. On review, Kohl thought he might have trouble covering all these topics in the time available; but he decided that if necessary, he could drop "Laws relating to pornography" and still produce a paper with a valid argument.

Refer to the following summary of steps in assessing your position and deciding which direction to take.

1. List all the possible subtopics you might cover.
2. Choose the ones you want to include in your search.
3. Reexamine your purpose and restate your topic.
4. Rewrite your list of subtopics according to your revised topic to make a working outline; that is, put the subtopics in logical order and group them under headings to demonstrate their relationships.

This kind of decision making is, as you have found, a continual part of your search. Searching, or exploring, always means going into unknown territory. It means setting out on a Lewis and Clark expedition with some general guidelines and an idea of the ground to be covered but also with the need to constantly reassess your strategy and direction.

Keeping a Search Log: Student Examples

Be sure to record in your search log what you did. Such a record will make it possible for you to resume your search quickly even if you have to stop for other assignments for a few days. The following students' accounts of their searches were written on the basis of records kept in their search logs.

Michelle Stigliano's Bibliographic Search.   Michelle Stigliano's account of the beginning of her search on "The Treatment of Anorexia Nervosa" shows how the focus of a topic can change; she gradually realized how she wanted to shape her topic as she looked at the subject listings in the card (or library) catalog, consulted indexes to periodicals, and browsed in books. Notice that in her case it helped to work back and forth between the reference area and the card catalog.

I started my search with the card catalog. Looking in the subject headings section under "Anorexia nervosa," I found three possible sources of information: *The Golden Cage, Psychosomatic Families,* and *Eating, Sleeping, and Sexuality.* At the end of the cards on anorexia, a card read "see: DIET, HUNGER." Looking up "Diet," I found many cards with that heading. After picking out several possibilities I came to the last card, which said:

DIET
see also:
GASTRONOMY
NUTRITION
COOKERY
FOOD
MENUS
DEFICIENCY DISEASES
FOOD HABITS
SCHOOL CHILDREN—FOOD
BEVERAGES

The items on this card were leading me away from my original subject, so I decided to look in the indexes and abstracts and come back to the card catalog later. I checked through the library's list of indexes and abstracts and picked three that would probably list sources relevant to my topic: *Abridged Index Medicus, Bibliography of the History of Medicine,* and *Nutrition Studies Abstracts.* Copying the references for all the articles became tedious, but as I read the titles I realized that I was not really sure whether I wanted to evaluate the treatments of anorexia or go into the personality characteristics of the victims and their families. So instead of continuing through the lists of periodicals and writing down every possible source, I decided it would make more sense to stop and do some browsing through the books I had selected to determine which topic I wanted to pursue.

Looking at the table of contents in *The Golden Cage* by Hilde Bruch, I found myself most interested in Chapter 4, "How It Starts," and after reading it I realized I had found the area I wanted to concentrate on—how it starts. I went back to the periodicals and was able to pick out the ones that would help me on this topic.

Vaurice Starks's Bibliographic Search.   Vaurice Starks's search for a working bibliography on her topic, "The Hazards of Smoking to the Smoker and to Others," went smoothly at the beginning. Here is her account.

When I went to the library to begin my search, I wasn't sure where to start. There were so many possibilities—the card catalog, indexes, and encyclopedias. I decided to start with the card catalog.

I pulled out the drawer labeled "Smithsonian I–Social." I slowly flipped through the cards, pausing when I got to "Smoking." There were several book titles relating specifically to my subject; two of these were Harold Diehl, *Tobacco and Your Health: The Smoking Controversy,* and Ruth Winter, *The Scientific Case against Smoking.* Some titles didn't indicate a relationship to my subject, but when I read the details of the contents on the card, I thought they might be useful (for example, *The Stop-smoking Book for Teens* by Curtis Casewit). There was a summary on the card that said, "Examines the physical and psychological implications of smoking cigarettes."

In order to keep track of the books I wanted to look up, I listed them on index cards. I found this convenient because I could put together all the cards for books located on the same floor. I checked the location of the books and took the elevator to the second floor. It took me quite a while to find books because some of them were misshelved. I ended up finding five out of the seven books I wanted. When I went down to the circulation desk to see if the other two were checked out, I was told that they would be returned in two weeks. I filled out a reserve form and the librarian said she would notify me when the books came in. By this time I was tired so I went home.

The next day I went to the orientation session given by the librarian for our class. I found out that the library has indexes and abstracts on just about everything. I was accustomed to using only the *Readers' Guide to Periodical Literature.* After Judy, the librarian, showed us examples of index entries on slides, she directed us to a table where she had arranged indexes and periodicals on our various topics. I asked her what indexes would be helpful for me and she showed me *Pollution Abstracts* and the *Public Affairs Information Service Bulletin (PAIS).* (Later on my own I found the *Index to Nursing and Allied Health Literature* and looked up my topic in it and also in the *Readers' Guide.*) I found a number of articles about smoking. At first I had trouble translating some of the code numbers in the indexes, but Judy showed me that 67: 7–8, M'81 meant volume 67, pages 7 and 8 in the March 1981 issue.

After deciding which of these articles were pertinent to my topic, I wrote them down on index cards too. Besides the name of the article, I wrote down who wrote it, the name of the periodical, the volume, the page numbers, and the date. I also included a brief summary of what the article was about when this was given in the index or collection of abstracts. Then I went off to see if the periodicals I wanted were in the library. I found the titles listed in alphabetical order on microfiche, which I had placed in a machine that magnified them. The library had all the magazines I was looking for. I was lucky.

Starks still had some focusing to do, but this took place later. As she read her materials, she realized that, because she did not smoke, she was more interested in the hazards to "passive smokers"—those who are in physical proximity to smokers—and concentrated on the dangers to them.

EXERCISES

1. Make a list of other sources that Michelle Stigliano and Vaurice Starks might have used.
2. Write a two- or three-page essay in which you state the subject of your search and discuss the following points: why you chose your subject; what the most difficult parts of your search have been so far; what you have learned about a library search that you didn't know before; and how the search for this paper has been different from other library searches you have done.
3. To begin your library search, find the following sources in your college library and record them either in a memo to your instructor, on your computer, or on note cards to keep with the rest of your bibliography cards.

   a. The title of an article on your subject either in a college-level general encyclopedia such as the *Encyclopaedia Britannica* (see pp. 56–60) or in an encyclopedia in your specific subject area (see Appendix 1, Section III, for titles). Record the author (you may have to look this up in the encyclopedia index), the title of the article, the name of the encyclopedia, and the year of publication (see p. 60 for format).

   b. The title of an article listed in a general index (see Appendix 1, under General Sources, for titles of general indexes). Record the author, title of the article, title of the periodical, the date (or volume and year), and page numbers. Also note the title of the index and the format (online, CD-ROM, microfilm, or print). Record as you did the encyclopedia entry.

   c. The title of an article found in an index in your specific subject area (for names of these indexes, see Appendix 1, Section III). Record as you did the previous entry.

4. **FOR YOUR SEARCH LOG** Using the notes in your search log, write a narrative account of your search up to this point. Use the straightforward approach of Stigliano or Starks. Or make a list in your search log of all the metaphors for searching that occur to you, such as exploring a cave, climbing a mountain, going to the moon, snorkeling. Then write an account of your library search using one of

those metaphors as a framework. Attach a copy of your working bibliography and a brief working outline.

5. **FOR PEER RESPONSE** In groups of three or four, read the papers written for Exercise 1 to each other. After hearing each paper, make a note on your paper or elsewhere of the ideas you might want to try. As a group, pick three or four that seem most useful; then choose a group member to report to the class in turn with a reporter from each of the other groups.

CHAPTER 4

Recording Information from Library Sources

The Library [is] a wilderness of books. . . . It is necessary to find out exactly what books to read on a given subject. Though there may be a thousand books written upon it, it is only important to read three or four; they will contain all that is essential, and a few pages will show which they are.   —H. D. Thoreau, *A Writer's Journal*

If you have followed the suggestion in the Introduction to build abundance into your search process, you will have perhaps not the thousand books that Thoreau mentions but many more books and articles on your list than you will need or can use. Here are the next steps:

1. Locate your sources in the library.
2. Evaluate your sources and select the most useful and reliable.
3. Take notes on your reading.

Locating Books and Periodicals

Books, unless they are reference books such as encyclopedias, dictionaries, and the like, are shelved in the stacks according to their call numbers. These stacks are open in most college libraries; that is, you may locate books yourself and take them to the checkout desk. (In some large public libraries, you must hand in your book requests and wait for your books to be delivered to you.) An advantage of open stacks is that you may see other books on the subject that interest you while you are looking for the ones on your list. To simplify your search for books, arrange your bibliography cards in order according to the classification system used by your library. If your library uses the Library of Congress classification system, put all of your PF cards together, your QPs, and so forth, then arrange them in alphabetical order, according to library practice.

Bound volumes of periodicals may be located in a separate room or in the book stacks by call number (see Chapter 3). You may want to photocopy short articles from them to read later (be sure to record complete publication data on these copies so that you can identify them). Microforms may also be stored separately, along with the machines for using them; some of these machines may print copies of the microforms.

Once you have located your sources, you are ready to evaluate, read, and take notes. Skillful reading and note taking are crucial to the writing of a good research paper.

Evaluating Your Sources

As you evaluate your working bibliography you will find out which sources will be the most useful and reliable for your paper. You have probably already begun this process by noticing the copyright date (if currency is important to you), by paying special attention to authors who have been recommended, and by reading abstracts of books and articles. The evaluation process, which, like other parts of searching, is continuous, is especially useful at this stage, when you have assembled your bibliography and are about to begin reading. The following suggestions will help to eliminate those sources that are not worth your time to read.

Some sources may be of limited value to you, others so unreliable as to be misleading and deceptive, and the value of still others may be hard to determine until you begin to read them. But you should keep in mind that the integrity of your paper depends to a great extent on the reliability or authenticity of your sources. If your subject is controversial, you will want to make sure that you use unbiased sources or, at least, that you are aware of their biases. Although all standards of reliability are relative and subject to error, the *copyright date, author, periodical* in which an article appears, *recommendations and reviews*, and *content* provide you with the information necessary to make a reasonable judgment. Although you may not be able to judge the content adequately until you start reading, you can learn about it to some extent beforehand. If you evaluate your sources according to the following guidelines, you will be able to begin your reading and note taking with reliable and useful sources.

Copyright Date

The publication, or copyright, date of a book or article is important for any research project. In the sciences, for instance, researchers build on the information of their predecessors because knowledge in these subjects is increasing at a rate that produces obsolescence almost over- night. For a paper on the uses of artificial satellites, for example, most sources more than five years old are of limited value; new uses for sat- ellites in communications and new reports from satellites used as ob- servatories are reported almost daily. In the social sciences, too, the date may be crucial: a study on the methods of achieving school inte- gration should look at contemporary data; currently, instead of busing, many school districts are integrating through the use of magnet schools. Although sources in the humanities tend to age more slowly than those in the sciences, new information or new documents some- times emerge that make old sources obsolete. For example, a study fo- cusing on Virginia Woolf's later writing would be limited without an examination of the latest volume of her diaries, parts of which are be- ing issued at irregular intervals.

You will usually find the publication date on the copyright page (the page following the title page) or sometimes on the title page itself. The number of dates may be confusing, but the significant date, the one you would use in your bibliography, is the latest copyright date, which is the date of the last revision. Additional printings do not necessarily indicate changes in the text—only new *editions* acquire new copyright dates. Figure 4.1 shows examples of copyright dates from two different publications.

Once in a while you may come across a book that does not give a publication date. In that case, check the library catalog; a copyright date may be given on the card or in the entry for the book. (The abbre- viation *c* before a date in a catalog entry means "copyright.")

FIGURE 4.1   Sample Copyright Dates

Latest copyright date

Symbol for copyright, Universal Copyright Convention

Copyright © 1960, 1966, 1967, 1968, 1969, 1973, 1975, 1978, 1981 by the Trustees of the Merton Legacy Trust
Copyright © 1959, 1961, 1963, 1964, 1965, 1981 by The Abbey of Gethsemani, Inc.
Copyright 1953 by Our Lady of Gethsemani Monastery

All rights reserved. Except for brief passages quoted in a newspaper, magazine, radio, or television review, no part of this book may be reproduced in any form or by any means, electronic or mechanical, including photocopying and recording, or by any information stor- age and retrieval system, without permission in writing from the Publisher.

Date of last revision

Reprinting dates; no changes made in text

PUBLISHED, JUNE, 1943
SECOND PRINTING, DECEMBER, 1958
THIRD PRINTING, APRIL, 1961

Author

The status, experience, and professional position of an author are clues to the reliability of the writing. You may learn about an author's background in such sources as *Who's Who in America* (there are similar books for other countries). Those in academic disciplines and professions may be found in the appropriate subject volume of the *Who's Who* series, which includes American history, arts and literature, commerce and industry, economics, electronics, engineering, finance and industry, government, law, music, nursing, opera, politics, religion, technology, and theater. For biographies of writers, consult *Contemporary Authors* (updated volumes appear regularly) and the *Directory of American Scholars*. Credentials of scientists can be checked in *Modern Scientists and Engineers* and *American Men and Women of Science*. All these sources are usually shelved in the reference area.

You can also tell something about the professional status of writers by how often they are mentioned by other experts. For example, if your subject is in the social sciences, see the *Social Sciences Citation Index* for names of other writers who have cited the author of a book or article on your list (Chapter 3 describes this index in detail). Although these citations are not recommendations in themselves, their appearance in professional sources is some indication of the author's importance. As you proceed with your reading, watch for references to other writers; then look up these names in the index that applies to their discipline (the *MLA Bibliography*, for example, if they are writing on literary subjects) and study their publishing record.

Professional Journals

Articles in professional journals are usually more trustworthy than those in widely circulating magazines. Published by professional associations or by academic institutions, they are approved for publication by specialists in a field and are written for an audience knowledgeable in that field. As a result, such articles are usually well documented and carefully reasoned. However, articles in some commercially published magazines and newspapers, though they are not as formally documented as those in scholarly journals, can also supply bibliographic information and can be equally reliable.

Every periodical possesses its own point of view to attract its audience. If you use an article that discusses only one side of an issue, you should at least be aware of that bias and try to find other points of view. Moreover, whatever the bias of an article, you should always judge the writing by the presentation of facts and the conclusions based on them. *Magazines for Libraries* evaluates both journals and magazines and explains the kinds of articles most often published by them as well as any detectable biases. It also gives the circulation size, which may indicate

FIGURE 4.2 Reviews from *Magazines for Libraries*

The Nation. 1865. w. $21. Blair Clark. Nation Co., 333 Ave. of the Americas, New York, N.Y. 10014. Illus., index, adv. Circ: 30,000. Sample. Vol. ends: June & Dec. Microform: UMI. *Indexed:* PAIS, RG. *Bk. rev:* 4, 1,500 words, signed. *Aud:* Hs, Ga, Ac.

No liberal magazine in America is better known than this, other than its sometimes look-alike cousin *The New Republic.* Contributors include almost all major liberal figures from Ralph Nader and Robert Sherrill to the late Martin Luther King, Jr. The articles are concerned with foreign affairs, local and national politics, disarmament, education, law, etc. There are excellent regular reviews of books, theatre, films, and the arts. There is some advertising, but the magazine depends almost entirely upon subscriptions.

National Review; a journal of fact and opinion. 1955. bi-w. $15. William F. Buckley, Jr. William A. Rusher, 150 E. 35th St., New York, N.Y. 10016. Illus., index, adv. Circ: 110,000. Sample. Vol. ends: Dec. 31. Microform: UMI.

Indexed: RG. *Bk. rev:* 5–8, 800 words, notes, signed. *Aud:* Hs, Ga, Ac.

The intellectual voice of conservatism in America, this is the outspoken critic of most liberal or progressive ideas. In coverage and scope it is somewhat similar to *The New Republic* and *The Nation.* Here the analogy ends. First and foremost, it is the child of William Buckley, its controversial editor who has brought a degree of respectability to the conservative school. He blasts both reactionary right and progressive left with a telling wit and a style that is sometimes flippant, sometimes penetrating, but always readable. All contributors represent a depth of thought and opinion that brings out the respectable aspects of the conservative cause. It must be noted that the conservatives have yet to produce as many major journals as their liberal counterparts, but the emergence of publications such as *Conservative Digest* and *The Alternative* indicates that this lack may be remedied in the future. *National Review,* however, always will be a major voice of conservatism, and because of its intellectual approach should be in every library, from senior high school to academic. (C.W.)

a limited audience. See Figure 4.2 for reviews of two magazines with different political views.

Also be on guard against bias by reading the masthead of a magazine or periodical (usually found on the same page as the table of contents) to see who publishes it. Many lobbying organizations, such as the Sierra Club or the National Rifle Association, issue their own publications in which the point of view of their organization is promoted.

Recommendations and Reviews

You may also determine the reliability of a book or article by the source that recommended the material to you. College faculty, librarians, and others knowledgeable about your subject are dependable sources. Bibliographies in printed sources, such as encyclopedias or books by known professionals, are usually reliable. The presence of a book or periodical in a college library may also recommend it because such material is often chosen by instructors in the field or by librarians who have studied reviews. However, some books of doubtful validity do make their way into college libraries, so double-checking may be necessary.

Book Review Digest provides excerpts from book reviews by professionals writing in about 200 periodicals such as *Commentary*, the *New York Review of Books*, and *Science* as well as in scholarly journals such as the *American Journal of Sociology* and *Modern Language Journal.* The reviews cited have appeared in at least two periodicals and within eighteen months of a book's publication. Although you may not find it necessary to look up a review of every book you find on your subject, you might want to research further a book that deals with a controversial subject or that is central to your paper. Figure 4.3 presents excerpts from reviews of a book on the history of neurosis from *Book Review Digest.*

If you do not find the work you are looking for in *Book Review Digest,* you might try *Book Review Index,* which indexes almost 450 publica-

FIGURE 4.3 Reviews from *Book Review Digest*

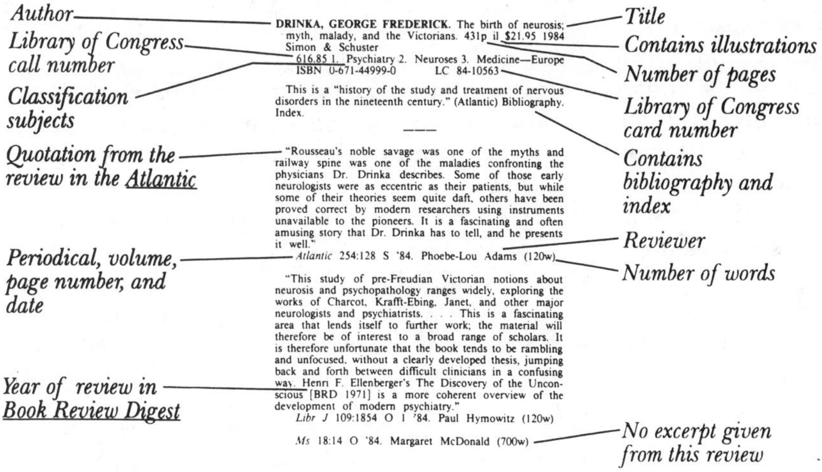

Author — DRINKA, GEORGE FREDERICK. The birth of neurosis; — Title
Library of Congress — myth, malady, and the Victorians. 431p_il $21.95 1984 — Contains illustrations
call number — Simon & Schuster — 616.85 1. Psychiatry 2. Neuroses 3. Medicine—Europe — Number of pages
ISBN 0-671-44999-0   LC 84-10563 —
Classification — This is a "history of the study and treatment of nervous — Library of Congress
subjects — disorders in the nineteenth century." (Atlantic) Bibliography. — card number
Index.

Quotation from the — "Rousseau's noble savage was one of the myths and — Contains
review in the *Atlantic* — railway spine was one of the maladies confronting the — bibliography and
physicians Dr. Drinka describes. Some of those early — index
neurologists were as eccentric as their patients, but while
some of their theories seem quite daft, others have been
proved correct by modern researchers using instruments
unavailable to the pioneers. It is a fascinating and often
amusing story that Dr. Drinka has to tell, and he presents
it well." — Reviewer
Periodical, volume, — Atlantic 254:128 S '84. Phoebe-Lou Adams (120w) — Number of words
page number, and — "This study of pre-Freudian Victorian notions about
date — neurosis and psychopathology ranges widely, exploring the
works of Charcot, Krafft-Ebing, Janet, and other major
neurologists and psychiatrists. . . . This is a fascinating
area that lends itself to further work; the material will
therefore be of interest to a broad range of scholars. It
is therefore unfortunate that the book tends to be rambling
and unfocused, without a clearly developed thesis, jumping
back and forth between difficult clinicians in a confusing
Year of review in — way. Henri F. Ellenberger's The Discovery of the Uncon-
Book Review Digest — scious [BRD 1971] is a more coherent overview of the
development of modern psychiatry."
Libr J 109:1854 O 1 '84. Paul Hymowitz (120w)

Ms 18:14 O '84. Margaret McDonald (700w) — No excerpt given
from this review

tions, from the *Atlantic* and the *New York Times* to scholarly journals such as the *Journal of Asian Studies* and the *American Historical Review*. Because the *Index* functions only as a referral, you must look up the original review in the source cited. Two other helpful works that index reviews are the *Index to Book Reviews in the Humanities* and the *Index to Book Reviews in the Social Sciences*.

Choice, an American Library Association monthly publication used by many librarians and faculty to evaluate books for academic libraries, is another good source for checking the reliability of your sources. Unlike *Book Review Digest* or *Book Review Index*, *Choice* contains complete, short reviews by experts as well as bibliographic essays that discuss books written on a subject of current interest; these essays are indexed in *Library Literature*. Figure 4.4 provides an example.

FIGURE 4.4 Review from *Choice*

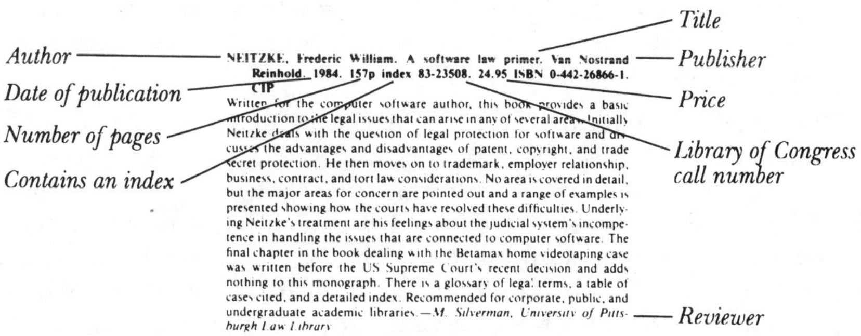

Title
Author — NEITZKE, Frederic William. A software law primer. Van Nostrand — Publisher
Reinhold. 1984. 157p index 83-23508. 24.95 ISBN 0-442-26866-1.
Date of publication — CIP — Price
Written for the computer software author, this book provides a basic
introduction to the legal issues that can arise in any of several areas. Initially
Number of pages — Neitzke deals with the question of legal protection for software and discusses the advantages and disadvantages of patent, copyright, and trade
secret protection. He then moves on to trademark, employer relationship, — Library of Congress
Contains an index — business, contract, and tort law considerations. No area is covered in detail, — call number
but the major areas for concern are pointed out and a range of examples is
presented showing how the courts have resolved these difficulties. Underlying Neitzke's treatment are his feelings about the judicial system's incompe-
tence in handling the issues that are connected to computer software. The
final chapter in the book dealing with the Betamax home videotaping case
was written before the US Supreme Court's recent decision and adds
nothing to this monograph. There is a glossary of legal terms, a table of
cases cited, and a detailed index. Recommended for corporate, public, and
undergraduate academic libraries. —M. Silverman, University of Pitts- — Reviewer
burgh Law Library

Content

The most important indication of the reliability of an article or book is, of course, its content. Primary sources are usually more valuable than secondary sources. They may be either firsthand accounts (autobiographies and eyewitness reports); original research based on questionnaires, interviews, observations, personal experiences, or experiments; or poems, novels, plays, and other original creations of an author. However, secondary sources—articles, books, speeches, and so on—derived from primary sources are also important; in fact, an expert's commentary on primary sources is sometimes more valuable to a nonexpert than information gained through primary research. For a college writer, a combination of these two kinds of sources is desirable. Use the following questions to help you evaluate the content of a source.

1. *If information is gathered through original research, are the problem and the search strategy or method clearly stated?*

A scientific article detailing an experiment usually follows a four-part format: an introduction stating the problem and reviewing previous work on the subject, an explanation of methods and materials including how the research was conducted, a description of the results, and a discussion or conclusion analyzing those results. The methods and materials section provides the details that make evaluation possible. Figure 4.5, from an article in the *Journal of the American Medical Association*, shows how such details are explained. The problem being investigated is whether commercial hair analysis is a scientific process. From the methods section, readers can judge whether the writers selected their samples carefully and evaluated their statistics fairly.

In *Consumer Reports*, aimed at a more general audience than the *Journal of the American Medical Association*, the experiments are less formal in presentation, but they contain similar information. Notice that in the excerpt (Figure 4.6) the purpose of the study, methodology, results, and discussion of the results are all given.

2. *If the information you find in a book or article is based on someone else's original research or experience, are the sources and method of research explained well enough to validate the findings? Or are the secondary sources authoritative enough to be convincing without further explanation?*

The article "Whose Brain Is It, Anyway?" by David Holzman in the *Washington Post Magazine* (Feb. 12, 1984) shows the strengths and weaknesses of a popular source. Holzman claims that the "triune brain theory" of Paul MacLean, once "used to explain the evolution of the human brain" by such authorities as Carl Sagan, is now being questioned. The validation used by Holzman is given in part in the following sentence: "Of more than 25 brain scientists interviewed about

FIGURE 4.5   Methods Section of a Scientific Article

METHODS
Laboratory Communications

Each of the laboratories in this study was contacted by a "doctor" interested in doing hair analysis on his patients. All responded with instructions for submitting specimens, and most included literature on the supposed value of the test. Additional viewpoints were gathered from articles and advertisements in chiropractic journals and health food industry trade publications.

Preparation of Hair Samples

The specimens consisted of shoulder-length hair from two apparently healthy 17-year-old girls. The hairs varied in length up to about 15 cm. One sample weighed 60 g, while the other weighed 36 g. Each was rinsed 20 times in tap water, allowed to dry, cut into 1- to 2-cm lengths, and mixed thoroughly so that hair from different locations would be selected for inclusion into each laboratory specimen. Twenty-six specimens of 0.5 to 2.0 g each were then prepared from each hair sample according to instructions from each laboratory; some were measured into envelopes, some were measured using a teaspoon, and others were prepared with a balance card supplied by the laboratory.

One sample per subject was sent to each laboratory, under an assumed name, and this process was repeated using different names about three weeks later, so that 52 reports were obtained. Each report presented mineral levels in parts per million or milligrams per 100 g, and indicated in some way whether these values were "low," "normal," or "high" compared with the laboratory's standards. Tables 2 and 3 summarize the values for each mineral. The Figure illustrates portions of the reports from five laboratories.

Statistical Analysis

The degree of concordance between matched pairs for each mineral in the four samples sent to each laboratory was assessed using Cohen's κ, a standard coefficient of agreement.[7] A κ value of 1.00 would signify perfect agreement. A value of .75 or more is usually regarded as a high level of agreement; .41 to .74, moderate agreement; and .40 or less, low agreement. The 13 laboratories scored as follows: laboratory A, .70; laboratory B, .42; laboratory C, .24; laboratory D, .40; laboratory E, .73; laboratory F, .83; laboratory G, .28; laboratory H, .83; laboratory I, −.06; laboratory J, .66; laboratory K, .78; laboratory L, .62; laboratory M, .90.

MacLean's triune brain, only a few say they subscribe to the view and all but one of these say it is accurate in only a general sense." Only two of these scientists are quoted and named. Nor does Holzman explain how the brain scientists were chosen or how representative and reliable they are. However, the audience for this article probably is interested only in the ideas discussed and does not want to read and evaluate the methodology. They are willing to trust the *Washington Post Magazine*, the author, who is identified as "a Washington science writer," and the author's logic. An article like this cannot be dismissed, but it needs corroboration by other sources if it is to be cited as evidence.

3. *Is consideration given to both sides of a controversial subject? If not, can you find another source that supplies the opposing point of view?*

Of course, it is impossible to find completely unbiased sources. All of us have our own ways of looking at events because of our past experi-

FIGURE 4.6   Extract from *Consumer Reports*

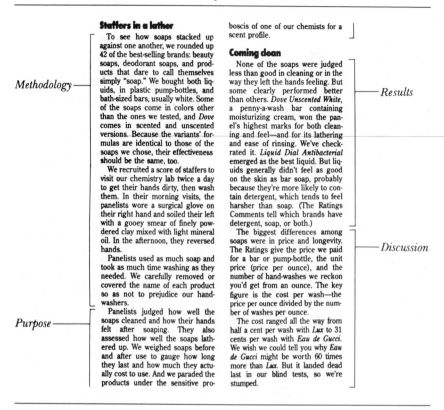

Methodology

Staffers in a lather

To see how soaps stacked up against one another, we rounded up 42 of the best-selling brands: beauty soaps, deodorant soaps, and products that dare to call themselves simply "soap." We bought both liquids, in plastic pump-bottles, and bath-sized bars, usually white. Some of the soaps come in colors other than the ones we tested, and *Dove* comes in scented and unscented versions. Because the variants' formulas are identical to those of the soaps we chose, their effectiveness should be the same, too.

We recruited a score of staffers to visit our chemistry lab twice a day to get their hands dirty, then wash them. In their morning visits, the panelists wore a surgical glove on their right hand and soiled their left with a gooey smear of finely powdered clay mixed with light mineral oil. In the afternoon, they reversed hands.

Panelists used as much soap and took as much time washing as they needed. We carefully removed or covered the name of each product so as not to prejudice our hand-washers.

Purpose

Panelists judged how well the soaps cleaned and how their hands felt after soaping. They also assessed how well the soaps lathered up. We weighed soaps before and after use to gauge how long they last and how much they actually cost to use. And we paraded the products under the sensitive proboscis of one of our chemists for a scent profile.

Coming clean

None of the soaps were judged less than good in cleaning or in the way they left the hands feeling. But some clearly performed better than others. *Dove Unscented White*, a penny-a-wash bar containing moisturizing cream, won the panel's highest marks for both cleaning and feel—and for its lathering and ease of rinsing. We've checkrated it. *Liquid Dial Antibacterial* emerged as the best liquid. But liquids generally didn't feel as good on the skin as bar soap, probably because they're more likely to contain detergent, which tends to feel harsher than soap. (The Ratings Comments tell which brands have detergent, soap, or both.)

Results

The biggest differences among soaps were in price and longevity. The Ratings give the price we paid for a bar or pump-bottle, the unit price (price per ounce), and the number of hand-washes we reckon you'd get from an ounce. The key figure is the cost per wash—the price per ounce divided by the number of washes per ounce.

The cost ranged all the way from half a cent per wash with *Lux* to 31 cents per wash with *Eau de Gucci*. We wish we could tell you why *Eau de Gucci* might be worth 60 times more than *Lux*. But it landed dead last in our blind tests, so we're stumped.

Discussion

ences. Even the objectivity of science has recently come under criticism; for example, see Jackson Albrecht's article "Social Context of Policy Research" in *Sociological Methods & Research* (Feb. 13, 1985) in which he speaks of "the myth of value-free science." Universities, he points out, often have their research funded by government agencies or business firms. Politics often determines what research will be funded within the government. "Researchers," he declares, "carry their values into any study they begin." What is the solution? He urges scientists to "openly [declare] their assumptions and biases, stating the research objectives of the funding agency, investigators, and audience, and describing the location, time, and context of the study." As a student, rather than a professional researcher, you may have difficulty discerning subtle influences of values, but you should be aware of the more obvious ones. It is wise, for example, to carefully examine studies by tobacco companies that describe the effects of tobacco on health. Also remember that you as a researcher and an individual have your own biases and you should recognize them.

4. *Are statistics used accurately and are they interpreted fairly?*

The use of statistics is like the use of other evidence in research: their collection and interpretation is subject to bias. In his book *A Primer of Statistics for Non-Statisticians*, Abraham N. Franzblau warns:

> First and foremost, the consumer [reader of statistics] should beware of statistics with a built-in bias—statistics, in other words, which aim to serve a vested interest. He should look routinely to the source of every statistic offered and carefully scrutinize the purpose for which it was compiled. He should be wary of sales inducements, clouded contexts, partial truths, and slanted findings. . . .
> The consumer of statistics should also beware of large conclusions drawn from small facts. How was the sample selected? Was it large enough? . . . Are the generalizations which are made justifiable?

It's often difficult for the nonexpert to determine whether statistics are being used fairly. Many times, though, plain common sense will come to your aid. Suppose you find in your research the following "evidence": in random interviews a reporter asked five people on the street whether they think the government is handling a current crisis well. The implication in the story is that their views are representative of those of many other people—how many is never stated. But common sense tells you that this is not a fair sample of the beliefs of a whole country or even a small part of it. Experienced poll takers take samples according to tested poll-taking techniques. But even they recognize that they are not likely to be completely accurate in making claims for large groups on the basis of evidence from small groups. Consequently, they allow for margins of error. The figures of a professional, experienced poll taker should be regarded as good evidence, but no sampling is as reliable as a survey of the whole group. Frequently, you will not be able to examine the way statistics were gathered and compiled, so you will have to rely on the credibility or reputation of your source.

5. *Are generalizations based on sufficient evidence?*

You may have heard a claim like this: "Cigarette smoking isn't harmful. My grandfather smoked every day and he lived to be eighty." One person's experience may be considered, but it cannot be used alone as representative of a group. Individual experiences and examples are valuable for making generalizations understandable but not for proving them. In other words, each piece of evidence should be given appropriate weight.

Source Evaluation: Student Examples

The examples that follow demonstrate how three students evaluated their research sources.

George Forte's Source Evaluation.   Because he was writing on a subject that is controversial—Native Americans' rights to their ancestral remains—George Forte had to get the views of reliable experts on both sides of the issue (Native Americans and museum officials) as well as from those who were not directly involved. He was fortunate that the issue had been argued in hearings before Congress, where the committees had selected experts on both sides to testify. The testimony in such hearings is easy to locate in government documents. He also found books on relevant historical and archaeological research published by university presses, and he located articles in magazines (*National Geographic* and *Harper's*) whose information is usually reliable. An editorial in the *New York Times* provided arguments from a reputable neutral source on the side of Native Americans. Finally, he himself evaluated all of the arguments and evidence according to the Toulmin guidelines (see p. 138).

Jean Carroll's Source Evaluation.   In her paper on agoraphobia (Chapter 11)—the abnormal fear of open spaces—Jean Carroll recognized that she had to rely on the credibility of her professional sources because she did not have the expertise to evaluate the validity of the subject matter. The articles in the journals were written by professionals, and she was satisfied that they were reliable. To find out more about the authors, she looked in the *Social Sciences Citation Index*. All the authors were cited in at least six articles. Two, D. W. Goodwin and J. Wolpe, were cited more than thirty times. The only popular source she used was the *Washington Post*, which she knew to be a reputable newspaper, a view that was confirmed in *Magazines for Libraries*. In addition, the information in the *Post* was based on an interview with an agoraphobic, the kind of information that a newspaper handles especially well.

Margaret Little's Source Evaluation.   Margaret Little's paper on the dangers of caffeine consumption (Chapter 12), which reports and analyzes scientific data, required a somewhat different type of validation. It relied to a great extent on statistics concerning the amount of caffeine in various foods and drinks and on observations of people who had used caffeine. Little had to be sure that the tests and experiments carried out with caffeine were carefully conducted. Her statistics were primarily found in three groups of sources: professional journals in psychology, health, and medicine; publications of government and professional organizations, such as the Federation of American Societies for Experimental Biology and the U.S. Department of Health and Human Services; and general interest articles from newspapers and magazines, such as *Newsweek* and *National Geographic*. The newspaper she used—the *New York Times*—was generally well regarded and was rated high in reliability by *Magazines for Libraries*. The first two groups were established professional sources.

Reading

Finding information is a little like searching for gold. First you have to search to find out where the likely places are—you can't dig everywhere—and then you have to dig carefully and thoroughly. When you have finally located sources of information, you need to read efficiently. You can save time by scanning the whole article or book to see whether it is worth reading at all and, if it is, by deciding which parts you want to scan and which you want to read closely. Then you must read carefully the material that you have decided is important and record the relevant material in your notes.

Scanning a Book

To scan a book, look first at the title and subtitle. Of course you have already written down the title, but you may not have noticed the subtitle, which is often more descriptive of the contents. *Wishes, Lies, and Dreams* by Kenneth Koch is a rhythmic and evocative title, but it does not indicate what the book is about as clearly as the subtitle does—*Teaching Children to Write Poetry*. Record both on your bibliography card. Next read the table of contents to discover the scope of the book and to see whether any chapters or parts of chapters deal with your subject. If you are doing a report on the capacity of the human brain, you might look at Carl Sagan's *The Dragons of Eden: Speculations on the Evolution of Human Intelligence*. The table of contents contains three chapter titles referring to the brain:

Introduction · 1

I
The Cosmic Calendar · 11

II
Genes and Brains · 19

III
The Brain and the Chariot · 49

IV
Eden as a Metaphor: The Evolution of Man · 81

V
The Abstractions of Beasts · 105

VI
Tales of Dim Eden · 125

VII
Lovers and Madmen · 153

Consulting the index to a book is another quick, useful way of determining contents. The index to Sagan's book includes this entry:

The table of contents gives you a general idea of what is in a book; the index gives specific citations or references. Be sure to make a note on your bibliography card of the chapter or page numbers that contain useful information. You may want to come back and read them later.

If the book seems to discuss relevant material, read the preface or introduction (some books have both). The preface usually explains the author's reason for writing the book and perhaps its organization or focus. Carl Sagan's preface gives the hypothesis on which his book is based: his belief "that man is descended from some lowly-organized form." The introduction may not be labeled as such; it may be just a part of the first chapter. The introduction prepares readers for the substance of the book by telling them what they need to know in order to understand the book's contents. In Sagan's introduction, preceding the first chapter, he defines his audience ("the interested layman"), states his fundamental premise (that the workings of the brain "are a consequence of its anatomy and physiology, and nothing more"), and explains that he will outline the evolution of human intelligence. After reading such an introduction, you would be able to decide whether you wanted to continue.

In some cases, you might also want to glance at the conclusion, especially if you plan to read a substantial part of the book. Like the introduction, the conclusion may not be labeled; it may be just the last part of the book. In *The Dragons of Eden*, the last chapter, "Knowledge Is Our Destiny," sums up the author's beliefs, forecasts the discovery of extraterrestrial intelligence, and suggests how the brains of extraterrestrial beings might be constructed.

Finally, if the book has a bibliography, note this fact on your bibliography card. Then check the bibliography to see if any of the sources listed seem relevant to your research. If you find any, record them on separate bibliography cards so that you can look at them later.

Scanning an Article

To scan an article, note first the biographical facts about the author, often given at the beginning or sometimes at the end; these facts will help you further evaluate the article. Then read the first paragraph or first page, which usually states the scope and argument or thesis of the article. Finally, you may want to glance at the last paragraph, which usually states the results or conclusions reached. Scanning these elements will give you a kind of map to follow, making it easier to understand the article if you decide to read it closely.

Suppose you are writing a paper on early women poets and you locate an article by Elizabeth A. Nist in *College English*. The first page is reproduced in Figure 4.7.

FIGURE 4.7   Scanning an Article: The First Page

"Men might consider that women were not created to be their slaves or vassals, for as they had not their origin out of his head, (thereby to command him), so it was not out of his foot to be trod upon, but in a (medium) out of his side to be his fellow-feeler, his equal and companion."

When and by whom was this written? It sounds like some turn of the century suffragist, or, with a little more contemporary diction and syntax, it could be a Bible-belt feminist during the ERA campaign of the 1970s. Probably it goes as far back as some pioneer woman in Nebraska or Utah in the 1870s, but, at the very least, surely it was written after 1700, because even Virginia Woolf admits that "nothing is known about women before the eighteenth century and certainly no woman wrote a word of that extraordinary Elizabethan literature when every other man, it seemed, was capable of song or sonnet." The contents of all our anthologies of British literature suport Virginia Woolf's surmises.

But our opening quote did not come from the "modern" women's movement. It was published in 1640 in London in *The Women's Sharpe Revenge . . . Performed by Mary Tattle-well and Ione Hit-him-home, Spinsters*. A little digging shows these pseudonymous co-authors were not alone in their opinions or their talent for forcefully expressing them.

Women wrote and wrote well during the Elizabethan period. A surprising number of manuscripts have been preserved, but they are not readily available to readers and scholars. Most are held in the British Library, private collections, or university rare book collections and can generally be read only on microfilm. Even though a few good anthologies of women's literature have been published in the past ten years,[1] most professors and teachers of literature remain unaware of these works.

1. Three recent anthologies of early women writers are particularly outstanding: Ann Stanford, ed., *The Women Poets in English* (New York: McGraw-Hill, 1972); Mary R. Mahl and Helene Koon, eds., *The Female Spectator: English Women Writers Before 1800* (Bloomington: Indiana University Press and Old Westbury, N.Y.: The Feminist Press, 1977); and Fidelis Morgan, ed., *The Female Wits: Women Playwrights of the Restoration* (London: Virago Press, 1981).

Elizabeth A. Nist teaches at Utah Technical College. She has published essays, stories, and poems in many journals, and a book of her poems, *Now Is My Springtime*, was published in 1974.

College English, Volume 46, Number 7, November 1984

First, at the bottom note the author's credentials; her professional position and publications are given. The first paragraph of the article is a quotation that can be skimmed quite quickly by reading the first line and glancing over the rest, just for a general understanding. The main point comes in the fourth paragraph—particularly in the first sentence. Here the author tells about the good poetry women wrote in the sixteenth century. Finally, a footnote supplies a short bibliography of anthologies of early women writers. If these interest you, enter them on your bibliography cards.

Turning to the end of the article, you notice four concluding paragraphs (Figure 4.8). The first sentence of this group of paragraphs is almost the same as the thesis statement at the beginning: "Women wrote and wrote well during the Elizabethan period." The second paragraph is a summary of the article, the third paragraph comments on the importance of these women, and the last paragraph makes an appeal for equality of women. After reading the introduction and conclusion of this article, you have a good idea of what it is about and what the author's point of view is. If you wish, you can read the rest of the article later.

In scanning, you save time by not reading everything—instead, you read fast to find out where to read slowly and carefully. Try not to be distracted by interesting but irrelevant material unless you are in the early stages of your search and have time to change direction. In addition, do not waste time by reading sources that merely repeat factual

FIGURE 4.8 Scanning an Article: Concluding Paragraphs

It is obvious that Elizabethan women did write, and they wrote well. This essay presents only eleven of the more than fifty women whose work is known. Yet even from these few examples we get a glimpse of the variety and importance of their writings.

They have given us some wonderful lyric poetry that celebrates not only their joys but, even more significantly, expresses their sorrows and their pain. In their prose we not only have firsthand accounts of life at that time, but realistic and practical accounts. We also have the first attempts to create real-life characters and dialogue in English, along with realistic subplots. In drama we have the first play by a women in English, attracting the attention and respect of the other writers of her time.

These writers speak for themselves. Surely a true picture of our cultural heritage cannot be constructed without their contributions, but, despite the fact that all of these works were published in the sixteenth and seventeenth centuries (many in repeated and popular editions), they are virtually unknown by modern scholars.

That no women wrote before 1800 is a myth, and until women like Margaret More Roper, Mary Sidney Herbert, Elizabeth Cary, and Mary Sidney Wroth stand alongside their husbands, brothers, and uncles, the myth will continue. As Mary Tattle-well said, "Men might consider that women were not created to be their slaves or vassals . . . but out of [their] sides to be [their] fellow-feelers, their equals and companions."

information you already have. Of course, you may want to read several accounts of an important or controversial event, such as the assassination of John F. Kennedy, for a variety of viewpoints, but if you are looking for general information on, for example, the Battle of Bunker Hill, an encyclopedia article will give you the necessary facts that other sources would merely duplicate.

Close Reading

Close reading means reading each word and sentence to learn the author's exact meaning. The following suggestions will help you to read efficiently as well as thoroughly.

Reading with a Purpose.   When you locate a chapter, a book, or an article that you want to read completely, read with a clear sense of what you want to find out. To sharpen this sense of purpose, read with certain questions in mind derived from rephrasing parts of your outline: What is agoraphobia? What causes it? Can agoraphobics be helped? You might look for the answer to one question in one article or book and the answer to another question somewhere else. Of course, at the same time be ready to encounter and absorb information that you were not able to anticipate with your questions. Reading for a paper on nutrition, Jeffrey Smerko began to encounter warnings about advertisers' misrepresentations on health food products, so he decided to add a section in his paper on this subject.

Entering the Mind of the Writer.   Withhold judgment until you have enough evidence. When you are reading an article on one side of a question, try to follow the thoughts of the writer to understand how conclusions were reached. If you make up your mind too soon on a controversial subject, you may overlook important information.

Reading for Main Ideas.   With the main idea or purpose of the author in mind, try to associate each paragraph and sentence with this main idea. If you seem to be getting off the track—if an idea does not seem to fit—stop and figure out whether the fault is yours or the writer's.

Defining Technical Terms.   Do not look up a word that you can figure out by the context unless you have plenty of time. Your goal is to keep your concentration intact.

Paraphrasing.   Put key passages or arguments into your own words. This is the test that determines whether you have understood the writer, whether you have made the writer's thoughts part of your own thinking and expanded your own knowledge not only factually but also conceptually. Failure to achieve this understanding usually results in one of the following problems. First, much of what is termed plagiarism (copying another's words and ideas) results not so much from design as from failure to comprehend the original. What you don't understand you can't put into your own words; the alternative then is to use the words of the original writer simply because there are no other words available. When you do not acknowledge the source, you engage in plagiarism. Second, if you use quotations too frequently, your paper becomes a patchwork of other people's words, and the writer's voice—your voice—is not heard.

Taking Notes

Good notes are the bridge between reading and writing; they make it possible for you to retain all of the material you read. But they have a further advantage: with good notes, not only will you have easy access to what you've read, but you will also have begun the writing process. Photocopying is not a substitute for the mental activity that occurs when you take notes. Although it is a convenient device for taking restricted material out of the library so that you can read it later, photocopying really adds an extra step to the process because you will eventually need to take notes from the photocopies. If you attempt the short cut of writing your paper directly from books or photocopied articles, it will be harder for you to write a good paper. The temptation to use the words of the original may eliminate the step of making the ideas part of your own thinking.

Good notes also tell you where you found your information so that documenting your sources later will be easier. Because taking notes is time-consuming and sometimes laborious, it is tempting to think that you will be able to recall the necessary bibliographic information when you need to assemble and record your sources. Try to resist this temptation. You will collect so much information that you will have trouble remembering it all, and it is unlikely that you will always remember the sources.

Before you start to take notes, decide whether you will put them on cards or on your computer (you can, of course, use a combination of the two). In any case, each note should include, besides the information itself, (1) where you got the information and (2) where it fits in your working outline. You need to know *where it came from and where it's going* so that you can put it in your paper in a logical order and give the source.

Taking Notes on Cards

If you're taking notes on cards, follow these guidelines.

1. *Place an abbreviated form of the source at the top of each card on the left.* Key this name to your working bibliography.

2. *Place a heading from your working outline on the top of each card on the right.* This will help you arrange your notes when you write your paper.

3. *Paraphrase or summarize most of your information.* Be sure to enclose in quotation marks any direct quotations you do write down. Add your own reactions to your reading and enclose them in brackets.

4. *Place the page number of the source following the information from that page.* If you are summarizing or paraphrasing, you may be taking information from more than one page, so be sure to give all the relevant pages. If you are quoting, you must be careful to match the quotation with the exact pages. If a quotation extends over more than one page, mark on your card where the page break is. When you are writing your paper, you may want to use only a part of the quotation.

5. *Use only one side of each card.* Because you will write from your cards, you might find it helpful to spread them out and study their contents or write from them without turning them over. If a single note covers more than one side of a card, use another card and number the cards consecutively in the heading.

6. *Put only information that belongs in the same part of your outline on the same card.* Do this even if you write only one or two lines on a card. If your subject, for instance, is the use of solar power for home heating and your source includes information on both design and cost, put the data on different cards so that you can later sort them by subject.

7. *Write with pen if you're not typing.* Pencil is hard to read and it smudges when the cards rub together.

Figure 4.9 illustrates headings for note cards.

FIGURE 4.9 Note Card Headings

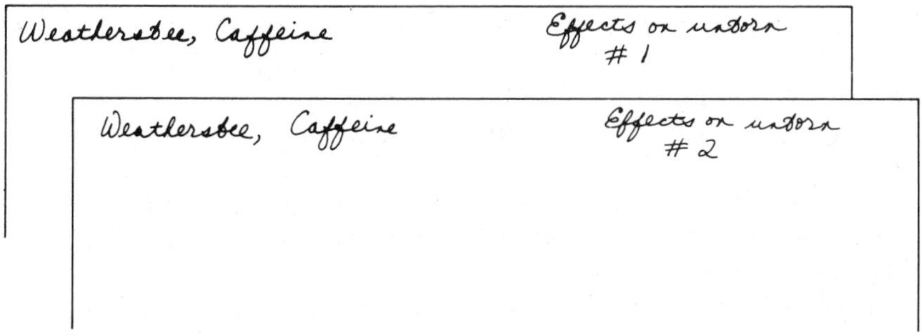

Taking Notes on a Computer

One of the main differences between taking notes on a computer and handwriting your notes is that the computer will order each note as you enter it, if you give it the necessary commands.

Before you begin, decide on a filing system for your information. You might have a different file for each major heading, with headings within this file corresponding to your subheadings. When you want to enter information under your major heading, you will be able to get into the file named for that heading and then find the subheading where your information belongs. Some computer systems allow you to group your files by folder; then the folders could be your major headings. With such a system, it's easier to open parts of your document.

For each note, use guidelines similar to those for taking notes on cards.

1. At the beginning of each note, provide the source and the heading, keyed to your outline.
2. Give page numbers or numbers at the end of each note. For direct quotations, identify page breaks (see guideline 3 for notes on cards).
3. Include in each note only the information that relates to that heading.

Because your notes will be organized by subject as you take them, you'll be able to transfer them easily to your paper. You can retrieve them by opening files corresponding to your headings and subheadings or, within the file, by author, by title, or by word.

When you begin writing, you can print out your notes and read them as you type your paper or, if you have the ability to split your screen, you can read your notes from the computer and type them into your paper without printing them out first.

Recording Your Information

Note taking and close reading are interrelated. You need to read carefully, of course, to take notes; at the same time, note taking is a significant aid to reading with comprehension and retention. It isn't easy, especially at the beginning of your search when you are still defining your topic, to decide what is relevant enough to record on note cards. Instead of being too concerned about what to record, remember the researcher's safety policy: when in doubt, choose abundance and plan to write down much more than it seems you need.

There are three main forms of recording information: paraphrasing, summarizing, and quoting. At first you will probably find yourself quoting quite a bit simply because you are not as familiar with your subject as you will be later. However, you will still save time by summarizing and paraphrasing as much as you can because these represent conversions of someone else's ideas into your own—a step closer to writing your paper. In addition to recording information on your cards, add comments and questions of your own, either on the same card or separately. These comments will also help you integrate your information and make it part of your own thinking. Be sure, though, that you differentiate between what is taken from your sources and what is your own thinking. One way to do this is by putting brackets around your own words or thoughts.

Paraphrase

Paraphase is a kind of translation. If you can paraphrase something, you know you understand it. When you paraphrase, you put the message that appears in someone else's language into your own, but always be sure to credit the actual author in your notes and paper. Paraphrase when you need the details of the original but don't want to use the same words—you want to use your own words so that your paper conveys the sound of your own writing style. Margaret Little, in her paper on caffeine (see Chapter 12), found this sentence in one of her sources: "Although soft drink manufacturers claim that they use caffeine strictly as a flavoring agent, some people are convinced that they add caffeine to their products in a deliberate effort to get children hooked on them." She wrote the paraphrase, as illustrated in Figure 4.10, on her note card. In her paper this note became the following sentence:

> Many consumers believe that soft drink manufacturers add caffeine to their products to cause children to become addicted to the caffeine in them (6).

FIGURE 4.10 Paraphrasing: A Sample Note Card

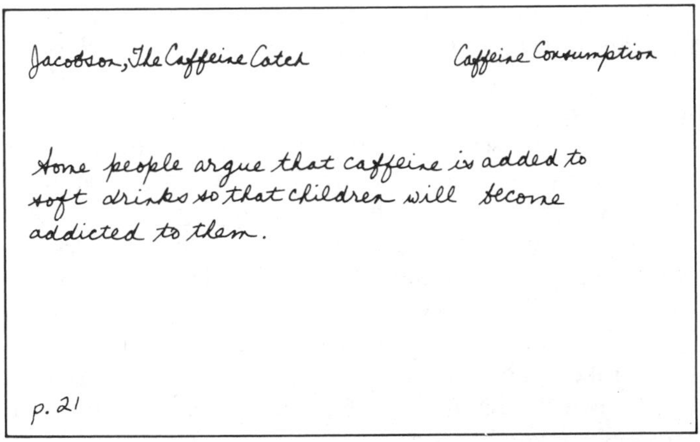

Jacobson, The Caffeine Cated   Caffeine Consumption

Some people argue that caffeine is added to soft drinks so that children will become addicted to them.

p. 21

You might also want to paraphrase when your source is technical or scientific and you know that your audience is unfamiliar with the language it uses. Little's audience was her college writing class, and most of the students were not science majors. In an article in *Medicine and Science in Sports*, she found the following passage:

> Since muscle glycogen depletion is considered responsible, in part, for exhaustion during prolonged exercise, slowing the rate of glycogen utilization should improve endurance performance (5,8,12). It has previously been established that the elevation of plasma FFA [free fatty acids] results in an increased rate of lipid metabolism and a diminished dependence on muscle glycogen in exercising skeletal muscle (5,9,14). In the present study, as in previous investigations, the ingestion of caffeine resulted in a 50 to 100% increase in plasma FFA (1,7,14).

On her note card, Little wrote this paraphrase:

> During exercise tests, the ingestion of caffeine raised the levels of fatty acids in the blood. Since high levels of fatty acids have been shown to slow the rate of carbohydrate depletion, which in turn leads to exhaustion, caffeine seems to help athletes' endurance.

In her paper, this information was reduced to a phrase in the section on the benefits of caffeine:

> In addition, caffeine has been found to enhance the speed and accuracy of those performing physical tasks such as typing (3); it also increases endurance during exercise by reducing carbohydrate oxidation and increasing fat metabolism (20).

Summary

Summarizing takes more concentration than other forms of note taking because you must reduce a long passage (a paragraph, page, or several pages) to a sentence or a few sentences. It requires the ability to generalize—to extract the main ideas from a passage along with any significant details. You can see the difficulty in generalizing when you ask a child to explain a movie she has just seen. She will recount one detail after another without generalizing to show how all the details are related.

To summarize a long piece, first look for the headings, which will announce the topics discussed, and then try to find the main sentence or the main idea in each paragraph. (In newspapers and popular magazines, paragraphs are so short that often they are not built around a central idea or main sentence. You may have to read several paragraphs to detect the general thought that ties them together.) The rest of the paragraph will usually consist of details or elaborations of the central idea. Pick out any of these details that you want to mention in your paper. Take a moment to reflect, to make these ideas and details part of your own thinking, and then write down a summary in your own words of what you have read.

FIGURE 4.11   Underlining Sample

Are you a caffeine addict?

Are you a caffeine addict? The effects of caffeine are extremely variable. While one person may get twitchy and nervous following one cup of brewed coffee, others can drink six, eight, even 10 cups a day without ill effect. In general, most people are able to consume up to 200 milligrams of caffeine a day (see chart), benefiting from the stimulation without apparent harm. An estimated 20 to 30 percent of adult Americans consume 500 to 600 milligrams of caffeine daily (two to three times the "therapeutic" dose) and 10 percent take in more than 1,000 milligrams of caffeine a day.

However, many people, some of whom consume as few as three cups of coffee a day (about 300 milligrams of caffeine), experience symptoms of "caffeinism," the name given to to chronic caffeine intoxication.

The symptoms may include sleep disturbances, headache, tremulousness, jitteriness, anxiety, lightheadedness, irritability, depression, rapid heartbeat, palpitations (skipped heartbeats), rapid breathing, diarrhea, stomach pains, heartburn, frequent urination and muscular tension. The symptoms of caffeinism tend to develop gradually over a period of years and thus are often attributed to many causes other than the correct one. The failure to consider caffeine as a probable cause also often leads to incorrect treatment with drugs and other remedies, rather than attacking the problem directly

by reducing or eliminating caffeine dependence. Taking Valium is not the appropriate long-term solution to caffeine-induced anxiety, nor should sleeping pills be used to eliminate caffeine-caused insomnia.

One way to test how addicted you are to caffeine is to try to stop using it for a day or two. Withdrawal symptoms are common. The first one to occur is usually a headache, which may develop as soon as 18 hours after the last dose of caffeine. The headache typically begins with a sensation of fullness in the head and progresses to a painful throbbing that is made worse by bending over and by exercise. It is relieved by caffeine, including painkillers that contain caffeine (such as Anacin, Excedrin, Empirin and Vanquish), but not by plain aspirin.

Other withdrawal symptoms, some of which mimic the effects of caffeine intoxication, include drowsiness, inability to concentrate, disinclination to work, lethargy, excessive yawning, depression, irritability, nervousness, runny nose and nausea. While the stimulant effects of caffeine are noted within minutes of its consumption, once you stop, it may take several days to clear all caffeine from your system.

Withdrawal symptoms can last for two weeks, and sometimes longer. The discomfort can often be avoided by tapering off caffeine slowly, rather than attempting to quit cold turkey.

If your article or book is photocopied, you can aid your reading and note taking by underlining or highlighting the main points as you read. Figure 4.11 presents an excerpt from the article "Weaning the Body from Dependence on Caffeine" in the *New York Times*, cited by Margaret Little in her paper on caffeine. Because of the heading "Are You a Caffeine Addict?" Little looked for the answer—the signs of caffeine addiction. Working with a photocopy, she underlined the symptoms of caffeinism and some of the details she thought she could use in her report.

Figure 4.12 illustrates how Little summarized the material on her note card. Most of the summary was used in Little's paper; the following passage combines information from this and other note cards:

> Coffee drinkers can detect caffeinism by curbing caffeine intake for 1 to 2 days and checking for the following symptoms: sensations of fullness in the head, drowsiness, euphoria, nausea, excessive yawning, constant runny

FIGURE 4.12   Summarizing: A Sample Note Card

> Brody, N Y Times   Caffeine addiction
>   A lot of coffee drinkers suffer from "caffeinism,"
> or addiction to caffeine. The symptoms are often
> mistakenly diagnosed because they're varied and
> take some time to appear, but you can test yourself
> for caffeinism by not drinking coffee for 1 or 2
> days & checking for sensations of fullness in
> the head, drowsiness, euphoria, nausea,
> excessive yawning, constant runny nose, &
> throbbing headache made worse by bending
> over & exercise.
>
> p. C6

nose, and throbbing headache made worse by bending over and exercising. Withdrawal symptoms can last up to two weeks. A person can alleviate the pain of withdrawal by gradually decreasing caffeine consumption. . . . (16).

You can see that you do not need to use everything you write down; you can combine the material you read into a new piece of writing that is yours. Having a comfortable cushion of extra background material as a basis for your own words will help make your paper distinctively yours.

Quotation

When you quote, you are using the exact words of someone else. However, because one of your purposes in writing a paper is to tell something in your own words, it doesn't make sense to overuse the words of other people. (You don't want to have to title your paper ''A Collection of Quotations on the Use of Solar Energy.'') Therefore, use quotations only when the exact wording is significant or necessary (see Chapter 7 for further suggestions on using and punctuating quotations). On the following occasions, a quotation is the best choice: (1) when you need to say exactly what was said in the original, (2) when the language of the original is metaphorical or highly individualistic, or (3) when the person quoted is an authority on the subject. Sometimes all three conditions apply.

Verbal precision is often important in technical subjects, such as law or medicine. Margaret Little, taking notes on an article by Dr. E. R. Lutz on the effects of caffeine on the human body, quoted some of his words to provide a precise medical description of the symptoms (see Figure 4.13).

FIGURE 4.13   Quoting: A Sample Note Card

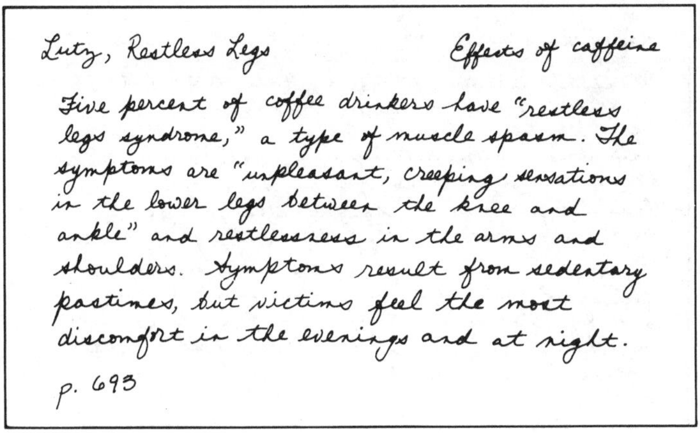

Lutz, Restless Legs   Effects of caffeine

Five percent of coffee drinkers have "restless
legs syndrome," a type of muscle spasm. The
symptoms are "unpleasant, creeping sensations
in the lower legs between the knee and
ankle" and restlessness in the arms and
shoulders. Symptoms result from sedentary
pastimes, but victims feel the most
discomfort in the evenings and at night.

p. 693

Highly individualistic or metaphorical language cannot usually be paraphrased adequately, as in Yogi Berra's statement ''It ain't over till it's over.'' Language that has great emotional appeal or is associated with grand historical moments is also often quoted: ''Give me liberty or give me death'' (Patrick Henry) or Martin Luther King, Jr.'s ''I have a dream'' speech. Poetry or highly metaphorical prose is difficult to paraphrase or summarize. In the following passage from *Moby Dick* by Herman Melville, the metaphors and poetic sounds of the words make it impossible to separate the words from the meaning.

> It was a clear steel-blue day. The firmaments of air and sea were hardly separable in that all-pervading azure; only, the pensive air was transparently pure and soft, with a woman's look, and the robust and man-like sea heaved with long, strong, lingering swells, as Samson's chest in his sleep.

The interest of a quotation may lie in the fact that it was spoken by an authority on the subject or by a well-known person, such as the president of the United States. ''A man paints with his brain and not with his hands'' is an interesting observation, but it has more significance when the reader knows that it was said by Michelangelo.

An authority may be someone with firsthand experience. Jean Carroll wrote down the exact words of a person who had had a phobic attack (see her paper ''The Causes and Treatment of Agoraphobia'' in Chapter 11). Figure 4.14 shows part of what Carroll recorded in her notes.

Personal Comments

Personal Observation.   As you consult your sources, you are consciously or unconsciously making connections between what you have

FIGURE 4.14   Quoting: A Sample Note Card

> Mansfield, Wash. Post   Interview
>
> Mansfield interviewed Marjorie Goff, 64 yrs. old, who
> described her first attack one Saturday in 1946
> in a beauty shop where she regularly had her
> hair done. "I was sitting under the dryer, and
> all of a sudden this feeling swept over me. I'm
> losing my mind, I thought. I'm going crazy.
> My heart started beating fast. My legs felt weak.
> My body trembled. It was the most incredible
> feeling of fear. I wanted to scream, to run
> out of there. I got up with all the pins in
> my hair, slapped a five-dollar bill on the
> counter, and ran all the way home."
> p. 21

read before and what you are reading now. You are analyzing, making judgments, and asking questions. While these thoughts are fresh in your mind and you still remember clearly the readings on which they are based, write them down to use when you are composing your paper. Of course, you might write down brief comments as you record information from your sources, but there may be times when you want to make more lengthy or general observations on your work. Putting these comments on note cards will enable you to order them along with your other cards. As she was reading sources for her paper on agoraphobia (see Chapter 11), Jean Carroll recorded her thoughts, indicating by brackets that they were her own (see Figure 4.15).

FIGURE 4.15   Personal Observation: A Sample Note Card

> Cause of agoraphobia   Mar. 12
> [I haven't been able to find any cause
> yet for agoraphobia. Or, rather, there
> seem to be many theories about the cause.
> Which is right? If they can't find the
> cause, can they find a cure? I'm
> beginning to realize that this is a
> very complicated illness.]

FIGURE 4.16 Descriptive Abstract: A Sample Note Card

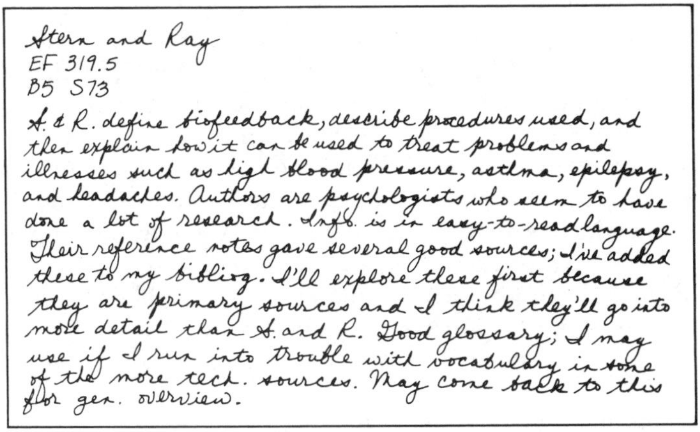

> Stern and Ray
> EF 319.5
> B5 S73
> S. & R. define biofeedback, describe procedures used, and
> then explain how it can be used to treat problems and
> illnesses such as high blood pressure, asthma, epilepsy,
> and headaches. Authors are psychologists who seem to have
> done a lot of research. Info is in easy-to-read language.
> Their reference notes gave several good sources; I've added
> these to my biblig. I'll explore these first because
> they are primary sources and I think they'll go into
> more detail than S. and R. Good glossary; I may
> use if I run into trouble with vocabulary in some
> of the more tech. sources. May come back to this
> for gen. overview.

Descriptive Abstracts.   A descriptive abstract is a personal card that describes or evaluates a source. Instead of summarizing content, you describe what an article or book contains and then perhaps evaluate it. Suppose you find a book early in your search and you aren't sure whether you want to use it. Write a descriptive abstract of the book and file it with your note cards for later reference.

Figure 4.16 presents a descriptive abstract of a book titled *Biofeedback: How to Control Your Body, Improve Your Health, and Increase Your Effectiveness*, by Robert M. Stern and William J. Ray. The writer made the card after reading the preface and the table of contents and after scanning the first chapter, "What Is Biofeedback?" and the reference pages.

As you take notes, write quotations in complete sentences or weave the pertinent lines in with your own words. Make sure, though, to quote your source accurately, including all marks of punctuation (see Chapter 7 for details). If you omit any words, use the marks of ellipsis (. . .). If the ellipsis marks fall at the end of a sentence, you need the three dots of ellipsis plus a period. Any addition of your own within a quotation, such as a comment or mark of punctuation added for clarity, should be enclosed in brackets.

Avoiding Plagiarism

If you take notes carefully and record your sources accurately, you will be able to document your sources when you write your paper. You must give others credit when you use their words or when you paraphrase or summarize their original ideas. Failure to do so is called *pla-*

giarism, which means "literary theft" and may lead to a legal suit if the plagiarized material is published uncredited. In college, plagiarism is also unacceptable. The best way to avoid plagiarism is by converting the ideas of your source into your own words—as summary or paraphrase—as you take notes or, if you quote directly, by making sure that you use quotation marks. Whenever you write down any information from a source, be sure to note where you found it so that you can cite that source in your paper. If someone else's words are on your note cards without identification, you may end up with the same words in your paper, which is unarguably plagiarism. You may also slip into plagiarism by failing to take notes at all and instead trying to write your paper directly from photocopied material or from books. Without the intermediate stage of putting the information into your own words on cards, it is easy to use the words of the original source without realizing it.

But, you might ask, do I have to document every bit of information I put into my paper? Must I have a footnote for every sentence? Because a good bit of what you write will be yours and some of it will be general knowledge, you will not need to document every sentence in your paper, but you must, as a careful researcher, record your sources on your note cards so that you will know to whom to give credit. Suggestions for documenting your paper will be given in Chapter 7.

The preceding sections on paraphrasing and summarizing show how to take notes that do not plagiarize. You will not get into trouble if you make the information part of your own thinking and then put it down in your own words. Trouble arises when you take notes mechanically, without actually understanding what you are writing.

Here are some examples of different types of of plagiarism. The notes are based on the following passage from *The Greek Experience,* by C. M. Bowra.

> **ORIGINAL PASSAGE:** The essence of the heroic outlook is the pursuit of honour through action. The great man is he who, being endowed with superior qualities of body and mind, uses them to the utmost and wins the applause of his fellows because he spares no effort and shirks no risk in his desire to make the most of the gifts and to surpass other men in his exercise of them.

1. *Word-for-word transcription of the entire passage.* Using an exact quotation from a source in your paper without quotation marks and a citation is plagiarism.

2. *A paraphrase using the basic sentence structure of the source with a few of the words or phrases of the note taker substituted for those of the source.* In the following paraphrase, the writer keeps the basic structure of the original and merely changes a few of the words. This is plagiarism.

> **UNACCEPTABLE PARAPHRASE:** The main idea in the heroic outlook is striving to achieve honor by being active. The great man, having the highest

qualities of body and mind, uses them to the greatest extent and is applauded by his comrades because he will pay any price in his desire to make the best of his gifts and to do better than other men in his use of them.

3. A paraphrase using the note taker's sentence structure and many of his or her words but with key words of the author used without quotation marks. The following note uses the note taker's sentence structure but borrows key words and phrases without quotation marks. This also is plagiarism.

> UNACCEPTABLE PARAPHRASE: The Greeks believed that the hero had superior qualities of body and mind. In his desire to make the most of his gifts the great man would spare no effort in his desire to use his gifts in surpassing other men.

The following paraphrases can be integrated into a paper with no danger of plagiarism.

> ACCEPTABLE PARAPHRASE: Heroism to the Greeks meant the demonstration of superiority through great deeds. The Greeks believed that the hero was a man who was superior to other men and who was willing to use his great qualities even if he risked his life doing so. He deserves the praise he gets from his fellowmen.

> ACCEPTABLE PARAPHRASE AND QUOTATION: The Greeks' idea of heroism was "the pursuit of honour through action." The hero has "superior qualities of body and mind" and he will take any risk in order to demonstrate his heroism to his fellowmen.

Of course, in both cases the source must be cited; instead of using a footnote, the writer might give the author's name in the text as part of the introduction to the passage. Notice that single words do not have to be put between quotation marks unless they show an original or distinctive use by the source; the word *superior* as used in the first acceptable paraphrase does not indicate a special use of the word and so no quotation marks are necessary. Notice also that quoted material must be given exactly as it is in the original; in the second example the writer uses the British spelling of *honour*, as in the original.

EXERCISES

1. Write an evaluation of at least three of your sources, including both a book and an article if possible. Explain in detail how you arrived at your evaluation and the sources that guided you.
2. Write an evaluation of one of the authors in your working bibliography; use the suggestions in this chapter.
3. FOR YOUR SEARCH LOG   Record the following in your search log:
   a. The most interesting bit of information you have learned about your subject so far

b. The most frustrating experience you have had so far in your research

c. The most enjoyable part of your research process until now

Exchange your observations with your classmates.

4. **FOR PEER RESPONSE** Photocopy a short article or part of a long article from an encyclopedia or periodical on a subject related to your topic. On note cards, summarize the material on the photocopy in a short paragraph and paraphrase some of it. Intersperse a few words from the original if you wish (being careful to use quotation marks), but the notes should be primarily in your own words. In class, exchange your notes and your photocopy with another class member; then write a comment to the person whose paper you have, answering the following questions.

a. Are the summary and paraphrase accurate?

b. Do they avoid plagiarism?

CHAPTER 5

Gathering Information from Other Sources

Although we often think of research as something that we do only in libraries, we do most of our research outside them. Whether it's going to the moon, exploring caves, finding out about our own city, or just studying our own family tree, we can't limit our search to books. We want to know. We may find diaries, letters, or personal papers that no one else has yet seen, or we may discover information too recent to be in print. We are limited only by our inability to see what is there for us to discover and to figure out how to find it.

You can collect information outside the library by

1. Interviewing
2. Designing and administering questionnaires
3. Recording oral history
4. Reading diaries, letters, and personal papers
5. Examining court and other government records
6. Observing, exploring, and experimenting

Interviewing

The holdings of a library record the experiences and thoughts of people as they have been collected in the past. In interviews you discover people's current thoughts, ideas, and attitudes. You can interview authorities—those who, like college professors, have been purposeful collectors of information—or talk to people about their own beliefs and experiences.

Although there are several kinds of interviews—the employment interview, the doctor-patient interview, the counseling interview, the journalistic interview, and others—you will be conducting an informational or research interview.

Personal Interviews

Personal interviews are usually more productive than telephone interviews or personal letters. Everyone has special information of some kind, and most people enjoy sharing it with others. When you're thinking about people to interview, look first in your home or college community and then widen your net.

Finding People to Interview.   First talk to people in your neighborhood or school. To locate instructors in your subject, consult the college directory, which will tell you the department they are affiliated with. If you want to know about running a business, talk to the small restaurant owner or store owner in your neighborhood. Are you writing a paper about the influence of foreign cars on the American market? Ask the local car dealer for his or her point of view. What does your uncle remember about World War II? What was it like for women when they couldn't vote? The elderly woman who lives down the street or in the nursing home may be able to tell you.

Use the telephone to inquire in your community. The phone book contains names of people and organizations who can help you. Most communities have a chamber of commerce, an association of business-people and merchants that promotes the business interests of a community; chambers of commerce usually publish a membership directory, another useful information source. In the yellow pages, look up "Social Service Organizations" to find phone numbers for groups like the Mental Health Association and the American Heart Association; organizations of ethnic groups, such as the Spanish Community Association, the Polish American Congress, or the Chinese Culture Services Center; political lobbying and information groups, such as the Consumer Product Safety Commission, Common Cause, or National Organization for Women; nonpartisan political information groups, like the League of Women Voters; and educational groups, such as the American Association of University Professors or American Association of University Women. For a partisan point of view, call the local office of your congressional representative or senator and, of course, your local Democratic or Republican party organizations (you can call or write the national headquarters too). For national organizations that might be located in your area, consult the *Encyclopedia of Associations* in the reference room of the library; this source organizes associations alphabetically and geographically and includes social service, educational, hobby, government, scientific, cultural, and many other kinds of groups, both national and international. Whatever your interest, there is likely to be an organization of like-minded people.

Your phone book also has a special section that provides city and county government numbers. See the listings in areas such as environmental management, citizens' information, alcohol and drug programs, community affairs, status of women committees, consumer affairs, and recreation. You might find people at your local newspaper office or radio station, public school system, or police department who would be glad to talk to you. If you are interested in business or management, don't forget that your college or university is also a business, with managers, public relations officials, and others who may be willing to talk to you.

The thought of picking up the phone and calling someone you don't know may be intimidating, but remember that an interview can result in a valuable experience. Stuart Levin, for instance, called a local radio station, explained that he wanted to learn about the career possibilities in broadcasting, and was invited to talk to one of the managers. After a helpful discussion, he was given a tour of the station and invited to sit in on his favorite disk jockey's program.

Making the Appointment. When you reach the person you want to talk to, state your name, the purpose of your call, and the specific information you are seeking: "My name is Steve Gorbush, and I'm a student at Valley State. I'm writing a paper on the New York Stock Exchange, and I wonder if you would have time to answer a few of my questions about it." In arranging a time, be sure to mention the times you will not be able to meet because of classes or other obligations, and then ask the person to set a time convenient for him or her. Indicate how long you need to talk (a half hour is generally sufficient for such an interview) so that your interviewee knows how much time to allow. Be sure to find out the exact location of the interview and any directions that you may need for getting there—you want to arrive on time.

Preparing for the Interview. A good interview requires good preparation. First, clearly define your purpose. What do you want to find out and how do you want to use this information? Review your working outline to see what you need to find out from the person you interview. And do some reading on your subject first—you will better understand the information given to you if you can put it in a context, and you won't waste time asking questions that you can just as well find the answers to in a book or article.

Then write out a list of questions whose answers will serve your purpose. Concentrate on the kinds of questions that can best be answered in an interview, such as questions on current topics like computer security or U.S. policy in the Middle East if that's the person's area of expertise, or questions that can be answered from the interviewee's experience, such as the amount of capital needed to start a small business. Or instead of writing down questions, you may want to jot down subjects to cover. This list will serve as a reminder to you in case the interview begins to stray from your subject. At the same time, though, be prepared to let the interview branch out into areas that perhaps you weren't able to foresee but that might supply valuable information.

Find out as much as you can about the person you are going to interview. If you are interested in the way a lawyer handles *pro bono* or public service cases, try to find out what cases the person you will be interviewing has handled. At the very least, you should know the person's complete name and job title, place of employment, and area of specialization. Decide how you will record the information you obtain. You might take notes during the interview, tape-record the interview, or simply listen and write down your notes later. All three methods have advantages and disadvantages. Writing can distract the speaker and also keep you from concentrating fully on what is being said. Tape-recording can inhibit the speaker even more, but it is more accurate and complete than taking notes. Tape recorders, though, can also fail and leave you with no record at all. If you decide to tape your interview, practice with your machine beforehand so that you can operate it unobtrusively. Also, out of courtesy, ask your interviewee in advance for permission to tape-record.

Although some professional interviewers have trained themselves to listen carefully and memorize what is said, at least in short interviews, most rely on a pen or pencil and a pad of paper. Be sure you take along extra pens. Some interviewers write on note cards, but most professionals find that it is more efficient to transcribe notes onto note cards or a computer after the interview to clarify sketchy notes and weed out irrelevant information. The best procedure is to take notes in your search log and then transfer relevant information to your notes later.

Conducting the Interview. Arrive a few minutes early so that you are calm and relaxed and have a chance to look at your surroundings— they may give you some ideas for questions. A geologist, for example, may have photographs or rock samples decorating his office that would be of interest to you. Questions about these provide an informal, relaxed way to begin the interview. You might also begin with some questions about the background of your interviewee to give both of you time to get used to each other. Assume an attitude that tells your interviewee that you are interested in what he or she has to say. You do not want to act apologetic for taking the interviewee's time, but neither do you want to act as though you are a trial attorney interrogating a witness. Make the interview as conversational as possible, and let your interviewee set the direction as long as he or she does not stray too far from your subject. During pauses, always use your questions as a prompt. If you take notes, take them as unobtrusively as possible, using abbreviations and other means of shorthand when you can. Record the exact words of the speaker when something is said that you would like to quote in your paper. Unless you use a tape recorder, as a courtesy verify direct quotations with your interviewee before you leave. At the end of the time you have both agreed on, thank the person you've been talking with and leave.

Following Up.   As soon as you can, review your notes and add what you didn't have time to write down during the interview. This is also the time to decipher the scribblings that won't be legible the next day. Everything will seem so fresh right after the interview that it is tempting to believe you won't forget what took place, but a few days later, you will have forgotten many details. Transfer relevant information to your note cards or computer as soon as possible. Oral historians and sociologists who conduct interviews generally use tape recorders, but they also write down significant information on note cards as soon as possible after the interview. In addition, they keep a field log or journal in which they record information not included on tape, such as the surroundings, dress and demeanor of the person interviewed, the feelings of the interviewer, and the like. If your purpose is to collect data from the interviewee, such details are irrelevant, but do record them if you think they might be useful.

It's also a good idea to make a bibliography card for your interview because an interview is considered a source and should, in most systems of citation, be recorded in your list of works cited at the end of your paper. Besides the interviewee's name, include his or her position or area of expertise, and the place and date of the interview. You might also want to include a few biographical details.

Finally, within a day or two, write a brief thank-you note to the person who has taken the time to help you.

Ed Kovalcik's Interview with His Professor.   The following account of a personal interview was taken from a student's search log.

> I was sitting at my desk after my computer science class waiting for Professor G. to finish talking to the students crowded around his desk. I had made an appointment at the last class meeting to talk to him after class tonight. I wanted to ask him about the future of computers. What changes did he see coming? Where was the use of computers going? I felt the tension making my body a little stiff, making my heart beat a little faster. Why hadn't I interviewed a friend or relative? Too late to back out now. Then the last student's question was answered and Professor G. came over and sat down near me.
>
> There was a strong feeling of uneasiness in the air. It was my first interview—maybe it was his, too. I started out with some questions about his academic background. He said he had gotten his bachelor's and master's degrees in mathematics from the Polytechnic Institute of Brooklyn and

his Ph.D. from New York University. After a few more questions about his education, the anxiety in my voice and body began to ease and my confidence rose. This isn't too bad after all, I thought.

Knowing that he taught at the university only part-time, I asked him about his full-time job. He explained that he was in charge of research and development at COMSAT (Communications Satellites) Laboratories. "Right now we're working on a communications scheme that allows corporations to send up their information on a time-sharing basis." He continued to explain this process using words like "transducers" and "multiplexers." He was going so fast that I stopped taking notes and waited for him to slow down. He went to the chalkboard and drew a diagram depicting a theory for centralizing radio waves and pointing out the savings that could result for business. When he came back to his desk I began to question him about the future of computers—the subject I was most interested in. "Well, I believe that the smaller computers will become more widely used," he said. "And networking minicomputers to do the work of mainframes will save money for business."

I was now on firmer ground. "Networking" and "mainframes" were my language. Computer questions came streaming from my mind and out of my mouth. Among other things, Professor G. told me that ADA, a new computer language developed by the government, would be a popular language in the future. He also said that some of the older languages like FORTRAN and COBOL were holding on stronger than ever because of senior programmers' aversion to change. Furthermore, because most computer programs still in use were written in these outdated languages, the expense of rewriting the programs would be astronomical. "Computer programmers aren't cheap, as they once were thought to be," he pointed out. "It's the hardware that is inexpensive today."

I began to run out of questions and we were running out of time. "Well, I guess that's it. Thank you," I said. "I appreciate your taking the time out of your busy schedule to talk to me." "I enjoyed it," he answered, shaking hands with me.

As I walked back to my dorm, I felt a sense of exhilaration. I had conquered a new experience. I had gotten to know a person through a new medium for me, an interview.

After this interview, Ed Kovalcik made a bibliography card and several note cards (Figure 5.1).

Telephone and Mail Interviews

Telephone and mail interviews are usually more structured than personal interviews because you cannot observe the person's reactions to your questions and adjust your line of questioning accordingly. Of course, on the phone you can tell something from the tone of voice. For a telephone interview, you may not need an appointment. You might, for example, call a professor during her office hours and say, "I wonder if you would have a few minutes to give me your reaction to the Simpson-Mazzoli bill that just passed in the Senate. You mentioned it in class the

FIGURE 5.1 Bibliography Card and Note Card for an Interview

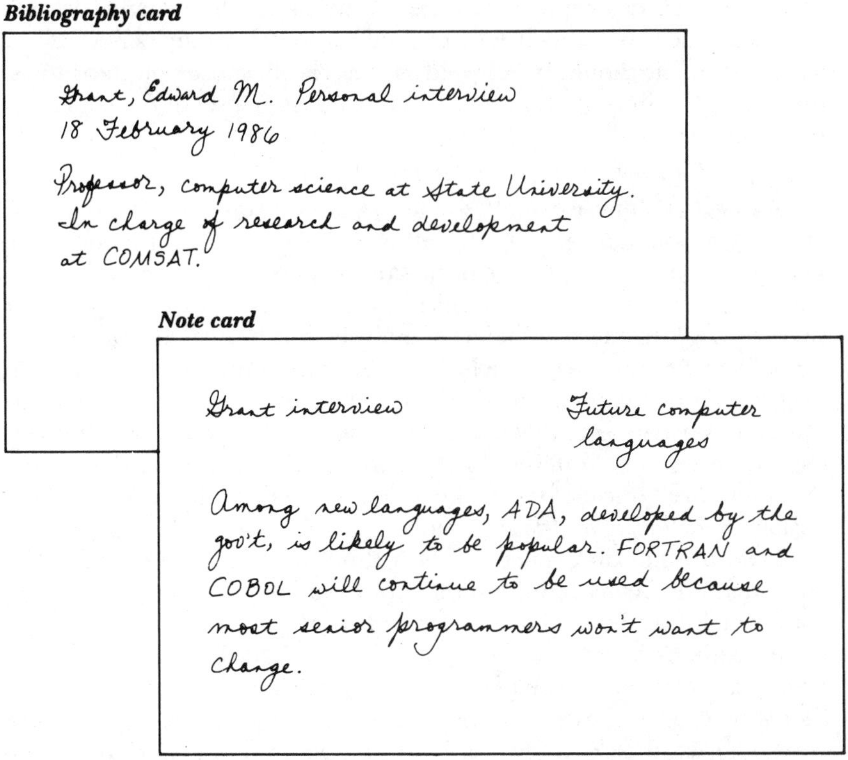

Bibliography card

Grant, Edward M. Personal interview
18 February 1986
Professor, computer science at State University.
In charge of research and development
at COMSAT.

Note card

Grant interview   Future computer
                                   languages

Among new languages, ADA, developed by the
gov't, is likely to be popular. FORTRAN and
COBOL will continue to be used because
most senior programmers won't want to
change.

other day when you were talking about immigration problems." If you
need more than a quick answer to a single question or two, call and make
an appointment, just as you would for a personal interview.

Mail interviews make it possible for you to interview someone in another state or country. They also allow interviewees to answer questions at their own convenience. But they sometimes take more time.
Before you send out a set of questions by mail, you should call the person and ask whether he or she will respond. Then carefully draft your
questions. You may want to send the same questions to several different people. Be sure you explain on the questionnaire or in a covering
letter when you need the answers returned. And enclose a stamped en-
velope with your address on it. Be prepared to telephone or write with
a reminder if your answers are not returned by the deadline.

Surveying. When you interview members of a group (your fellow
students, train engineers, the residents of Smalltown, North Dakota,
or whatever group you want to find out about), you are not usually
trying to acquire knowledge about a subject, such as the best treatment

for leukemia. You would ask experts for that kind of information. Instead, you want to know some of the characteristics, behavior patterns, or attitudes of the group. You might want to know how many cars they own, how they spend their leisure time, or whether they believe physical punishment should be allowed in schools. Because you need to ask the same questions of everyone, you must design a set of questions or a questionnaire.

Polling.   Polling is usually done to develop statistical data about a group. Questionnaires may be self-administered (and distributed by mail or in person), or they can be administered by an interviewer in person or by phone. You should remember that data from polls and surveys are extremely difficult to analyze; it is hazardous for the novice pollster to draw firm conclusions about a group unless everyone in the group is questioned. In fact, it is hazardous for anyone; figures are sometimes used to prove what pollsters want them to prove. However, experts can do an "inferential statistical test" to confirm that results of surveys are typical of the group as a whole. (For details, see Carol A. Saslow, *Basic Research Methods* [Reading, MA: Addison-Wesley, 1982].)

If you are not an expert, the best thing to do is plan and describe your methodology carefully so that your reader has a basis for judging your reliability. For example, suppose that you want to know how many students in your school exercise daily. You do not have time to question everyone, so you decide to take a sample. How many students should you ask? Obviously, the larger the sample, the more reliable your data will be. Still, even a large sample may be faulty if you ask only students going in and out of the gym or studying in the library. Because you want a random sample, you must ensure that every part of the student population is represented. Obtaining a random sample requires that you identify the different groups of the student population according to sex, age, number of courses taken, or other significant characteristics and then sample each of these groups at random. Likewise, you must take your samples at various locations and at different times of the day. Try to think of other ways to make your survey more representative.

Designing a Questionnaire.   When you ask for people's opinions on something, you may have a feeling that you are getting the *truth*, that you are finding out what is really going on in people's minds. But designing a questionnaire that is effective is not easy. If you have never designed a questionnaire before, it would help to do some reading on questionnaire development or to talk to an expert. But if you keep your questionnaire relatively simple and short, you should be able to compose a serviceable one. Before you begin, ask yourself the following questions.

1. *What do I hope to find out from the results of this questionnaire?*

Unless you have a lot of time to spend designing the questions, keep your desired results brief—no more than five items, if possible—and write them down. Use them to focus your questions. Suppose you are doing a survey of health clubs in your area. You might make the following list of what you want to find out: (1) the kind of bodybuilding equipment the clubs have; (2) the exercise facilities they own (swimming pools, tennis courts, and so on); (3) the type of relaxing equipment they have (saunas, steam rooms, and so forth); (4) the kind of instruction that is available and the qualifications of the instructors; and (5) the fees and bonded status of the clubs.

2. *What people will most likely be able to give me the information I need?*

The answers to the questions about health clubs can easily be given by the managers of these clubs; furthermore, much of the information can be verified by a tour of the premises. However, if your questions are different—say you want to find out about the quality of the services offered—the patrons would be able to supply that information better.

3. *What kinds of questions will give me the information I want?*

You can use open-ended questions, two-way questions (those that require choosing one of two alternatives), multiple-choice questions, or questions requiring a specific answer.

Open-ended questions are easy to ask, but they are more difficult to answer as well as to interpret. "What do you think of the registration procedure at the university?" is likely to produce vague answers. The advantage is, of course, that you may get interesting answers you could not anticipate.

Two-way questions are more focused ("Do you prefer objective tests or essay tests?") and you receive quantifiable answers, but they do not leave room for replies that might fall somewhere between the two questions. A person who is asked, "Do you believe abortion should be legal?" might want to respond, "Well, yes and no."

If you think your subject cannot be reduced to only one of two answers, use *multiple-choice questions*. They are easily quantifiable and do not take much time to answer. One kind allows variations of degree ("Abortion should be outlawed. Circle the answer you prefer: Strongly agree, agree somewhat, neither agree nor disagree, disagree somewhat, strongly disagree"). You can have as many alternatives as you wish, although five are the most common.

You can also use multiple-choice questions when you want to find out the extent of the respondents' knowledge (this is the type of multiple-choice question often used in school tests). For instance, you might want to learn how much the students in your school know about foreign affairs or perhaps about U.S. history or geography. Such questions must be carefully thought out so that the answer you want to obtain does not seem obvious. To avoid this problem, provide three or more answers that seem like genuine answers; for example, "In what state did the Wright brothers make the first airplane flight? Ohio, North Carolina, or Alaska." Most respondents would eliminate Alaska immediately, thus leaving only two possible choices. "Ohio" might be a better choice than Alaska because the Wrights lived and worked there. The correct answer, of course, is North Carolina.

Specific questions are the hardest ones to respond to because they require a specific answer: "Who said, 'The only thing we have to fear is fear itself'?" or "How many feet are there in a mile?" If the question deals with behavior rather than knowledge, it might not be as difficult: "How many hours of sleep do you get each night, on the average?"

Be cautious in using questions about behavior that respondents might find threatening. Results from such *unreliable questions* are less reliable because people don't like to admit doing things that others might disapprove of. One way to improve reliability is to use open-ended rather than two-way or multiple-choice questions. The question "How often do you drink beer?" might in some contexts carry the threat of criticism. If given a range, then, the respondent is likely to choose the lowest figure or none at all; in this case it would be better to leave the question open-ended (that is, allow the respondent to name a figure) rather than offer a range. Such a question is also "loaded": it assumes that the behavior exists. Thus it is less threatening than the question "Do you drink beer?" which may sound like an accusation and to which the respondent may be tempted to answer "No." So the question "How often do you drink beer?" asked without a given range, or open-ended, is likely to produce more accurate answers. Another way to improve the accuracy of potentially threatening questions is to ask the respondent about the behavior of others: "Does your roommate smoke? How many cigarettes a day?" Such questions might be a better way to find out about the behavior of members of a group than asking the members directly about themselves.

Although the loading of the question about beer drinking is in the interest of validity, some loaded questions originate in the bias of the questioner and thus are designed to produce biased answers. "Do you believe in supporting the defense of our country by funding the _____ bill?" suggests that a "no" answer would come only from someone unconcerned with national defense or from an unpatriotic citizen. Because few people want to think of themselves as unpatriotic, most of the answers would probably be "Yes."

You can see that the wording of questions is crucial to the validity of a questionnaire. In summary, if you are writing a questionnaire for the first time, it is a good idea to keep it short, word your questions so that you get the information you want, and check your questions for bias. When writing your paper, explain your procedures to your readers;

that is, tell them how many people you questioned, what groups these people belonged to, and the purpose of your questioning as well as the results you obtained. Include a copy of your questionnaire in the body of your paper or in the appendix.

Michelle Morrissey's Telephone Survey. Michelle Morrissey, a student volunteer in a program to teach English as a second language (ESOL), wanted to find out why so many tutors who took the training course either did not tutor or dropped out soon after training. She planned to prepare the results for the Literacy Council of Northern Virginia (LCNV), who trained the tutors, so that they could improve their program. Before she formulated her questions, she read books on preparing questionnaires and consulted with the LCNV staff and with another LCNV volunteer who was a statistician to discover what information they wanted her to gather. Here is part of the introduction to Morrissey's paper.

> After deciding to do a survey, I had to decide what type of survey would suit my purposes best. There are three major types of survey: the direct interview survey, the mail survey, and the telephone survey. The direct interview survey was eliminated because the tutors were too widely dispersed geographically, and the mail survey was unsuitable for such a small survey (300 tutors). The telephone survey, on the other hand, was ideally suited to LCNV needs because it is quick and inexpensive and allows for great flexibility in scheduling interviews. I decided to do a short preliminary survey to find out whom I would be interviewing and to make an appointment for a later call. I then divided this group into three subgroups—active tutors, tutors who have taught but are not teaching now, and trainees who never tutored—then designed a questionnaire for each of these groups. This procedure was time-consuming, but it permitted me to proceed with confidence with the longer interviews because the interviewees knew they were going to be interviewed and had given me a preferred time to call.

Morrissey included in her paper a copy of the short screening questionnaire that she used to identify those she would interview later at length (see Figure 5.2). Figure 5.3 illustrates the questionnaire Morrissey designed for trainees who had never tutored.

After analyzing the results of her questionnaire, Morrissey recommended the following measures: more stringent screening of prospective tutors, the setting up of information sessions before trainees commit themselves, and the establishment of a tutoring center instead of tutoring in homes.

Tape-Recorded Unstructured Interviews

Not all interviews with groups are structured as rigidly as Morrissey's. Studs Terkel in his book *Working* interviewed people to find out

FIGURE 5.2   Screening Questionnaire for a Telephone Survey

```
                    PRELIMINARY SURVEY SAMPLE FORM
                          Michelle Morrissey

Identifying information (already known):
Date and hour of call_____
Name:_____Sex_____
Address:_____Phone_____
Date of training session_____

Questions to ask:
Hello, my name is Michelle Morrissey.  I am calling on behalf of the
Literacy Council of Northern Virginia.  We are doing a survey of ESOL
tutors, and I have a few questions to ask you.
Are you tutoring now?   Yes_____  No_____
If no:  Have you tutored at all since you took your training?
Yes_____  No_____
These are the only questions I am going to ask you now, but I may be
calling you again in a few weeks for more questions.  When is the best
time to reach you?  Weekday evening_____  Saturday daytime_____
Sunday afternoon_____  Anytime_____
Thank you very much.  Good-by.
```

their attitudes toward their jobs. He explains in his book why his interviews were relatively long and unstructured:

> I realized quite early in this adventure that interviews conventionally conducted were meaningless. Conditioned clichés were sure to come. The question-and-answer technique may be of some value in determining favored detergents, tooth-paste, and deodorants, but not in the discovery of men and women.

Because Terkel's interviews were open-ended—without a time limit—he could use a tape recorder effectively. His respondents got used to it with the passage of time and talked as though it weren't there. Terkel's books—*Division Street, Hard Times,* and *Working,* in which he records the edited results of many taped interviews—have been called oral histories. *Oral historiography* or *folklore research* are terms used to refer to the study of the past through the recollections of living people recorded on tape or in questionnaires. Oral historical research has developed rapidly in the past few decades and has its own methodology and theoretical framework. You might want to conduct some interviews of grandparents, aunts, or uncles this way to learn about your family history. Or observe the groups around you—they are living sources of historical information.

FIGURE 5.3 Questionnaire for a Telephone Survey

QUESTIONNAIRE FOR GROUP III

Date of training session_____

Name_____ Phone_____

Hello, my name is Michelle Morrissey. I am calling on behalf of the Literacy
Council. You may remember that I called you earlier. I have a few questions
to ask you. Is this a convenient time? If not, when? _____

Are you a member of LCNV now? Yes____ No____
Are you employed outside your home? Yes____ No____ If yes, PT____ FT____
If yes, are you a teacher or otherwise working in education? Yes____ No____
If not employed, are you retired? ____ staying at home? ____ seeking
    employment? ____
Do you have any preschool children at home? Yes____ No____
    of school age? Yes____ No____

In which age group do you belong? under 35?____ between 35 and 49?_____
    between 50 and 60?____ over sixty?____

Did you take the LCNV training with the intent of tutoring? Yes____ No____

If no, why did you take the training?_____

If yes, why did you change your mind?_____

Would you be interested in tutoring eventually? Yes____ No____

If yes, would you want to attend a refresher course first? Yes____ No____

If yes, would you be interested in tutoring at a center where a group of
    tutors work with many students, either one-to-one or in small groups?
    Yes____ No____

If yes, would you use baby-sitting facilities if offered at the center?
    Yes____ No____

If yes, would you prefer to work there in the morning? ____
    in the afternoon? ____ in the evening? ____

Can you suggest any ways to improve the training? _____

Even though you have not tutored, do you feel the training was useful to
    you in other ways? Yes____ No____

If yes, specify:_____

That's all. Thank you very much for your assistance.

Students have recorded on tape the activities and customs of many
groups, including city bus drivers, tattoo artists, coal miners, palm
readers, neighborhood children, railroad workers, store owners, and
musicians of all kinds. Projects can also be designed by asking a particular group to talk about a specific topic, such as weddings, folk songs,
folk remedies, crafts, recipes, poetry, holiday customs, or rituals (bap-
tisms, marriages, or funerals). Perhaps you can find someone on the
college faculty who has done work in oral history and is willing to talk
to you about a project. Further sources of information are *Folklore: A
Handbook for Study and Research* by J. H. Brunvand (New York: St. Mar-

tin's Press, 1976) and *The Tape-Recorded Interview: A Manual for Field Workers in Folklore and Oral History* by Edward D. Ives (Knoxville: University of Tennessee Press, 1980).

Reading Diaries, Letters, and Other Personal Papers

Many families have writings of various kinds hidden away in boxes in the basement or attic that could provide information about family history. Sometimes personal papers providing local historical information are given to public libraries or local historical societies. Such papers can be used to supplement tape-recorded interviews or used independently like other written sources. One student wrote a biography of her great-grandmother, who married a West Point graduate in 1899 and kept diaries and letters that described in detail her military wedding and her life as an army wife. She wrote of a tour of duty in Idaho when the mines were put under military control after a strike and of her husband's death while riding horseback with the king of Italy. By researching the parallel historical events, the student was able to show how the life of her great-grandmother was part of the history of the United States.

Examining Government Records

State and County Records

It can be fascinating to trace the history of the place where you live. Is there a historic event in your area that you would like to explore, perhaps a flood or a battle? Would you like to find out the history of a town or of a piece of land? Is there a trial or a court case you would like to learn more about? Marit Beecroft was interested in the history of a large park: some of the park had apparently been farmland, whereas other parts of it were preserved as former Indian camping grounds. She found records of land sales and old maps in the county courthouse and traced the history of the area.

Perhaps you would like to learn more about one of your ancestors. State and county records contain large numbers of documents, including census figures, wills, deeds, tax rolls, military rolls, election results, and records of births, deaths, and marriages. Such records can help provide political, social, and economic information about the past as well as about specific persons. (Except for a few records that are sealed, such as adoption records, all court records are open for public examination.) County courthouses store records for their own jurisdictions; a state may maintain a separate archives building for its records.

If you want to examine these records, just go to the office of the clerk of court in the courthouse. Provide the name of the documents you want to see (for example, "land titles" if you are researching a piece of land) and they will be brought to you. If you do not know the name of a document or if you are not sure what areas you want to explore, you can look in the indexes—usually found in the clerk of court's office—to see what information the court has available and for what dates. If you want photocopies to take with you, most courts will provide them, although they tend to cost more than those at your local photocopier.

Federal Records

The National Archives.   Do you like adventure? Do you like to explore the unexplored? discover the unexpected? If so, searching in the Archives may be for you. Billions of pages of "permanently valuable" national records are stored in the National Archives Building in Washington, D.C., in eleven regional Archives branches, and in the nine presidential libraries. These buildings contain documents—some bound, some loose in boxes—that record life in the United States over the past two centuries, and if you are over sixteen, you can look at them. Besides documents, the Archives contain photographs, maps and charts, films, and recordings. If your subject has anything to do with diplomatic relations, land or Indian policies, law, foreign or domestic trade, navigation, military history or affairs, immigration, agriculture, transportation, communications, and many other areas, consider the National Archives. Consultants will help you find the information you are looking for, and although they will not do specific research for you, Archives staff members will answer concise requests for information by mail. You will find specific information about Archives holdings in the following publications; these may be ordered from the Government Printing Office, but check at your library first.

Guide to the National Archives of the United States. Available for purchase from the Superintendent of Documents, U.S. Government Printing Office, Washington, D.C. 20402

Select List of Publications of the National Archives and Records Service. Available free from the Publications Sales Branch (NEPS), General Services Administration, Washington, D.C. 20408

If you are not able to visit the National Archives Building in Washington, D.C., you may be near one of the regional branches in Boston, New York, Philadelphia, Chicago, Atlanta, Kansas City, Fort Worth, Denver, San Francisco, Los Angeles, or Seattle.

Although holdings do vary, in general the regional branches contain many documents, including records from the district courts, U.S.

courts of appeals, the Bureau of Indian Affairs, and the Bureau of Customs, and they provide researchers with reading rooms, microfilm reading equipment, and photocopying machines.

Of special value to college students is the collection of documents on microfilm stored in regional branches and available through interlibrary loan. These include some of the most significant government records in subjects such as history, economics, public administration, political science, law, and genealogy. To learn whether information you need has been recorded on microfilm, send for the *Catalog of National Archives Microfilm Publications* from the Publications Sales Branch (NEPS), General Services Administration, Washington, D.C. 20408. Your library may also have this catalog—look in your library catalog or ask your reference librarian.

Recent Government Papers.   Most government files dated before 1960 have been placed in the National Archives. But if the information you want is in government files dated after 1960, you must search in the current files of government agencies. Under the Freedom of Information Act (FOIA) of 1966, most government files are open to the public. To obtain information of this kind, you must write a letter to the Freedom of Information officer affiliated with the government agency that you think holds the files you need and ask for a specific document or information on the subject you are interested in. (If you send your request to the incorrect agency, your letter will usually be forwarded to the correct one.) The more precise you are in specifying the documents you want or their time period, the less time it will take to honor your request. Perhaps you are interested in what the government has done about the problem of acid rain—such papers are probably filed with the Environmental Protection Agency. Or you might be writing a paper on an author who was active in anti-Vietnam demonstrations, like Norman Mailer, and you want to know whether the Federal Bureau of Investigation has a file on him. Write to the FBI and ask for such information under the FOIA. You will get an acknowledgment within ten days; if you don't receive the documents, you will be told the status of your request. Use the same process to retrieve papers from any government agency. If the documents you require have a security classification, the agency must decide whether they can be declassified. If they can be declassified, they will be copied and sent to you. The first one hundred pages are provided to you without cost; for any pages above that number you will be charged ten cents each. The length of time it takes for such a search varies, so place your request early. You can find the addresses of government agencies in the *United States Government Manual,* which your library should own, or in a District of Columbia telephone book.

Rhonda Martin's Records Search.   Rhonda Martin wanted to find out the background of a legendary figure in her family. Three theories existed: he came to America as a Hessian horse soldier during the American Revolution; he was a Virginian in the Virginia militia during the American Revolution; he arrived as a youth in Pennsylvania from Germany in the 1700s. Martin did her research at the Library of Congress, the National Archives, and the Pennsylvania Archives. At the Library of Congress, she read the rolls of Hessian horse soldiers and the passenger ship lists for 1750 to 1770. No one with the name of her ancestor was listed. From the census records in the National Archives, she discovered where a man by that name lived from 1790, when the first census was taken, until his death in 1823; all of the locations were in Pennsylvania. From the research files of the Daughters of the American Revolution, she learned that a man of the same name had fought in Virginia during the American Revolution but that he had never lived in Pennsylvania. She decided to start from the present and work back. In the Pennsylvania Archives (Harrisburg, Pa.), she located deeds (called indentures) showing that he owned land in Greene County and that he sold "seventeen acres and one hundred and thirty-two perch of land" to his son for seventy-one dollars and twenty cents (a perch equals 30¼ square yards). In 1798 he paid $1,300 as his glass tax, the first tax ever levied, based on the number of glass windows in his home. From these and other details, such as names of wife and children, living places, and land purchases, Martin was able to compose a brief biography. He had never lived in Virginia and the names of his wife and children were different from the names of the wife and children of the Virginia militiaman. Thus she was able to trace the ancestry of those living now back to an indentured servant who had come to the United States when he was seventeen and died in 1823; she was able to prove that the last of the hypotheses was correct.

Observing, Exploring, and Experimenting

All of us observe, explore, and experiment and draw conclusions on the basis of our findings; these are daily activities. We observe and count the kinds of birds in our backyards; we explore a park or a neighborhood; we experiment with a new recipe. However, we usually do not keep records and put our conclusions into writing. Students in the social sciences, natural sciences, and psychology may want to do these kinds of research in a systematic way. The usual order is identifying the problem, planning a search strategy, collecting and measuring data, analyzing the results, and drawing conclusions.

In doing this kind of research, first formulate a question you want to answer. Can gold be found by panning in the local streams? Which grocery chain has the lowest prices? How polluted are the local rivers or the air we breathe? How much violence is there in children's TV programs? After deciding on a question to answer, decide on a plan for collecting your information; then collect your data, analyze it, and draw conclusions and perhaps make recommendations. The result is a scientific paper. (You will find further information on writing a scientific paper in Chapter 12.)

Four Students' Use of Alternative Sources

The following student research projects have used some of the strategies discussed in this chapter.

Sandra Sweitzer observed a prison art class, given for the purpose of rehabilitation. Besides observing the members of the class, she interviewed the instructor, the sheriff, and some members of the class. She concluded that the art class had important therapeutic effects on the prisoners; its benefits as a tool for rehabilitation were more difficult to assess. Her paper, in modified form, was published in a local newspaper.

Doris Hill compared prices at three grocery chain stores. She selected ten staple grocery items and checked their prices at these stores periodically for four weeks. She also interviewed patrons at random. After computing her evidence, she discovered much lower average prices at one of the stores. She described the locations and sizes of the stores as well as the varied economic levels of the shoppers in her analysis of the reasons for the difference in prices.

Tom Davis set out to find the location of knapping rocks in his area. *Knapping* is the term used by geologists and anthropologists to refer to the breaking or shaping of rocks. Indians knapped rocks to make implements, but only certain, glasslike rocks can be used in this way. Tom studied geological maps from the army map service and other geological evidence to determine possible locations of glassy stones, such as semiglassy quartzite, and then visited the areas to confirm his findings. Besides semiglassy quartzite, he found miscellaneous materials such as crushed stone, quartzite gravel, glassy quartz crystal and chert, and manmade glass. His paper containing his methodology and conclusions also included a geological map of the knapping rocks in his area.

Mark Olin wanted to know whether the five streams in his county were polluted. He collected water samples, grew cultures in petri dishes, and counted and identified the bacteria. After determining that the levels of the bacteria *E. coli* constituted dangerous pollution, he concluded that two of the streams qualified as polluted. Olin then studied maps to find out the source of the pollution. Besides writing his paper, he sent a letter to the county board summarizing his findings.

All of these projects grew out of the personal interests of these students. They gathered their information carefully and thoroughly, then analyzed it to make it meaningful to them and their readers. If you want to consider publishing your paper, consult Robert A. Day's *How to Write and Publish a Scientific Paper* (Phoenix: Oryx Press, 1988).

EXERCISES

1. Using a tape recorder, interview the oldest member of your family about one of his or her most memorable experiences. Conduct the interview in a professional manner, as a sample of oral history interviewing. Write an account of the interview in your search log; include the preparations you made, the questions you asked, the reactions of your subject to the interview, what you would do differently next time, and what worked well. Using this information, write a short report for your classmates and instructor on interviewing with a tape recorder.

2. Interview an expert in the profession you wish to enter when you graduate. Ask the person what skills are required for such a position and whether he or she has any suggestions about preparing for this profession. Write a short report on the results of your interview and offer it to the career counseling office at your college.

3. **FOR PEER RESPONSE**   Choose a partner from your class and interview each other. Follow the suggestions for interviewing given in this chapter. Your purpose for interviewing will be to find out everything you can about your partner's research project. Take a few minutes to make a list of questions to ask. Make the interview about ten minutes long. After the interview, write down what you have learned. If you have time, check the facts with your partner for accuracy.

4. **FOR PEER RESPONSE**   Design a short questionnaire—four or five questions—to discover the opinions of college students on a topic of current interest. In groups of three, examine the questionnaires of three other students and suggest improvements based on the guidelines in this chapter. After revising your questionnaire in light of the suggestions, survey a sample of the student body. Finally, write a one- or two-page report giving the purpose of your survey, the results, and an analysis of the results.

PART II

Re-Searching and Writing

CHAPTER 6

Re-Searching, Developing a Thesis Statement, and Outlining

Re-Searching: Reviewing Your Information

You collect your information in bits and pieces according to what may be available first or what may turn up first. During this stage, you don't know what shape your paper will take. Then when you have collected all of your material, you can re-search it; that is, review it and shape it, much as a sculptor creates a form out of marble or wood. Although the information you collect may come from someone else, the meaning you make from it is your own.

The Researcher's Questions

The first steps in re-searching are to read over your notes and to ask yourself the following questions:

1. What was my purpose in doing this search?
2. Did I realize my goal or did it change?
3. If my goal changed, what is my purpose now?
4. What did I learn from my search?
5. What conclusions can I draw from this knowledge?

Answering these questions will help you to shape and give meaning to all of the material you have collected. In answering questions 1, 2, and 3, you reassess your purpose and relate it to the answer to question 4, what you have learned. The answer to question 4 is a summary of the information you have collected. In answering question 5 you make a generalization or an inference based on the information you have collected; that is, the evidence leads you to an opinion, a judgment, or an evaluation. Making such generalizations are part of everyday life, so you are familiar with the process. For instance, you decide which is the best car for you to buy after looking at several cars, examining their features, checking the prices, and driving them. Or you study the schedule of courses, look up the requirements, weigh your needs and desires, and determine which courses will best suit your needs.

Florence McMullen, a student in an anthropology class, selected as her topic "Teaching anthropology to elementary school students." She answered the re-searching questions in the following way.

1. My purpose was to observe a group of sixth graders enrolled in a class in cultural anthropology and study the educational procedures.
2. I changed my goal and my topic.
3. Instead of concentrating on educational procedures, I decided to study the cultural values of the students in the class.
4. I learned that these students value the following qualities:

   a. Intellectual achievement
   b. Social equality, especially between males and females. However, some traditional behavior patterns still exist (boys and girls tend to sit in separate groups; girls primp and comb their hair in class; boys are noisier and more active).
   c. Contributions of technology to personal comfort (television sets, hair dryers, microwave ovens, etc.)
   d. Peace or lack of conflict between individuals and groups

5. I concluded that the cultural values of children have changed in significant ways since I was a child.

Writing a Summary Sentence or Thesis Statement

After you have reviewed your information, you should find it easy to write a sentence or two—sometimes called a thesis statement or argument—that summarizes your paper or states what your paper "proves." Composing such a sentence helps you to find meaning in the information you have collected. Although your summary sentence may change as you write your paper, this statement provides an organizing force for you at the beginning: all parts of your paper must uphold or validate this statement. If you find, as you write, that your material is inconsistent with this statement or irrelevant to it, you can either change your statement to include the new information or discard the new material, leaving your original statement intact.

McMullen's summary statement included her answers to the last two questions; it was both a summary of the information she had found and a conclusion that she had drawn from this information: "In the last twenty years, the changing cultural values of children are shown in the following observed characteristics: respect for learning and intellectual achievement, new perceptions of male/female roles, acceptance of material goods as contributing to the quality of life, and a longing for worldwide peace." Notice that she has discarded as a topic the educational procedures used in this class. Consequently, she will not use any notes she has on this subject.

When you begin to write your paper, the answers to the five questions on page 133 form the framework for your paper. The statement of your purpose and your summary statement are the basis for your introduction; the development of your summary statement forms the body of your paper; and the generalizations you make about your material shape your conclusion. With a good idea of what the beginning, middle, and end of your paper will be, you can write confidently and expeditiously.

Although you are not ready to write yet (you still have to order the details that go into the body of your paper), you may be interested in seeing how McMullen used the answers to these questions in her introduction and conclusion. Here is her introduction.

> I observed a group of sixth graders in a suburban public school. Although I intended at first to record and study the educational procedures used, I became interested in the way the children approached their study topic, cultural anthropology. I realized that they were applying their own cultural values in their study of the cultures of past civilizations. Intrigued by their ethnocentric reactions, I decided to study them in the same way they were studying others. By watching them, I was able to define the cultural values of their (our) society and observe how these values seem to have changed since I was in school.

The following excerpt from McMullen's paper shows how the answer to the last questions formed her conclusion.

> From observing these sixth graders, I conclude that children's cultural values have changed since I was the age of these students. For one thing, they seem to value intellectual pursuits more; they were pleased to be in this special class with an advanced curriculum. When I was in elementary school, children tried to hide any intellectual achievements for fear of teasing or other negative reactions from their peers.

The thesis sentence may appear at the beginning of your paper, in the middle, or at the end. Sometimes it is merely implied. Florence McMullen defines her purpose at the beginning ("to define the cultural values'' of the children she observed). Her thesis statement comes at the end ("'children's cultural values have changed''). Here are thesis statements from other students' papers:

> Firefighting must be made safer.
> The polygraph can detect lying in most cases.
> The plate tectonics theory explains how earthquakes occur.

Critical Thinking

As you chose and evaluated your sources, as you took relevant and adequate notes, as you formulated a summary sentence or thesis statement, you were thinking critically. That is, you were if you wanted to reach your goal and write a good paper.

Critical thinking includes the following activities.

1. Reviewing your information as a skeptic
2. Questioning your own assumptions as well as the assumptions of those whose information you are relying on
3. Examining and identifying your own biases
4. Analyzing your information carefully and assessing its validity
5. Making sure that your conclusions clearly follow from your information

The case studies that follow illustrate how two different students incorporated critical thinking into their re-search. Your own process will, of course, be different, depending on your topic and the purpose of your paper.

Two Students' Use of Critical Thinking

Janet Fiore began her search by trying to find out what effects the increased number of women in the workplace has had on the structure of the family. She found that as more and more women began to work, there were more and more divorces and more single-parent families. She first concluded that the increase in the proportion of women working outside the home had led to the breakup of the traditional family. But as she looked more closely at her information and began to examine her assumptions more carefully, she realized that she did not know which of these factors was cause and which was effect. She had assumed that the entrance of more women into the workplace had led to divorce and single-parent families, but she realized that this assumption reflected a bias. It was true that more women had entered the work force; and it was true that divorce had increased. But there was no evidence that women's working caused divorce. In fact, divorce may have caused women to go to work.

After more study, she decided that probably neither of these cause-and-effect relationships was valid; certainly there was no evidence to point conclusively to either. Instead she decided that a number of cultural factors led to the changes in family composition and family life. She changed the focus of her paper to identify these factors.

Jason Taubert discovered that more than 40,000 people die each year in automobile accidents. His goal was to find the most effective and practical device for preventing deaths in automobile accidents. He began with the basic question, How can automobiles be made safer?

According to his sources, a number of safety features have been designed to reduce injuries and fatalities in automobiles: (1) self-activating seat belts now required in all cars; (2) automatic seat belts, which engage as the driver or passenger enters the car; (3) air bags; and (4) specially designed interiors.

Before he evaluated these devices he determined the advantages and disadvantages of each.

1. Self-activating seat belts

   Advantages: When used they dramatically decrease fatalities. They are inexpensive to install, easy to use, and require no maintenance.

   Disadvantage: Many people do not fasten them. However, in states and countries where use is required, use has gone up dramatically and fatality rates have decreased.

2. Automatic seat belts

   Advantages: Their use leads to a decrease in fatalities. They require no time or effort on the part of the driver or passenger.

   Disadvantage: Because they have a latch allowing the person to detach the belt after an accident, they can be used like a self-activating belt. Or the person can choose not to use the belt at all.

3. Air bags

   Advantages: They inflate automatically and immediately on impact. They deflate automatically after use.

   Disadvantages: Air bags are effective in only 50 percent of fatal crashes. They are not effective in rear-end collisions, side impacts, or rollovers. They are not effective if there is a second impact in the same accident because they will have already deflated. They can be ineffective for small children. They are expensive to install. They have to be reinstalled after use.

4. Specially designed interiors

Advantages: Many fatalities would be prevented. No expensive extra equipment would be required—just the redesign of existing equipment.

Disadvantages: They would not be as effective as other devices in accidents at very high speeds or crashes into very hard obstacles such as walls.

It was not easy to decide which of these devices would be the best. But from the data he had, Taubert concluded that installing both automatic seat belts and air bags would be the most effective. The least expensive solution, and probably just as effective, would be to require manufacturers to install automatic seat belts in all cars and to require occupants to use them.

The Toulmin Model for Analyzing Arguments

A system of argument developed by Stephen Toulmin (*An Introduction to Reasoning*, 1984) is helpful in analyzing arguments and testing the validity of conclusions. According to Toulmin, an argument consists of six elements: claim, grounds, warrant, backing, modal qualifier, and rebuttal. This system can be used in analyzing any generalization you make on the basis of evidence you have gathered: your concluding summary sentence or sentences, your thesis statement, and, in fact, any argument made within your paper. The discussion and illustrations given here apply primarily to the main idea or thesis.

Claim. To follow Toulmin's method, first state your *claim*. The claim could also be called your conclusion, argument, proposition, thesis, or recommendation.

The Pueblo Indians developed an advanced system of astronomical observation.

Nightmares can be an indication of a serious psychological disorder.

Grounds. The *grounds* provide the support or evidence for the claim. They may consist of data or the testimony of experts. If the claim is made that radiation can arrest the development of cancer, statistics would be used as grounds.

Warrant. The *warrant* or *warrants* are assumptions or general beliefs that you and your reader share. They confirm the validity of the grounds and may be stated or unstated. For example, the claim might be made that cholesterol can be reduced by lowering the consumption of certain types of fat. The grounds or supports would include data such as the results of tests conducted at the National Institutes of

Health (NIH). The warrants or unstated assumptions of these grounds would be that high cholesterol is harmful and that NIH testing is a reliable source of such data. The writer using these unstated warrants believes that his or her readers would make the same assumptions.

To make assumptions about the reliability of your grounds, you have to be aware of who your readers will be. Besides assuming that the audience will share his or her belief in the reliability of NIH, the writer about cholesterol would have to make an assumption that his or her readers would have some knowledge of the work done at NIH. Warrants applicable to one reader or group of readers may not persuade others. In addition, the necessary warrants can vary from one discipline or writing situation to another. Articles for popular magazines customarily offer less supporting evidence than, say, articles in a scientific journal. (For more information about considering your audience, see pp. 152–54).

Backing. In some cases an additional component of the argument may be required to reinforce the warrant; Toulmin calls this *backing*. You might, for example, give as warrant a source whose reputation for accuracy or reliability is not widely known or accepted. You would then have to give evidence of the source's reliability by citing his or her past experience or connection with a respected institution. Or, if you are providing the results of your own or others' original research as warrants for claims, readers would probably want to know the methodology of the research.

Modal Qualifier. Toulmin recognized that few arguments are absolutely and unequivocally true. A *modal qualifier* acknowledges the variation in the strength of arguments. If a statement is not true for everyone at all times, you may want to limit it by a qualifier such as *most*, *usually*, or *probably*. Polls often qualify their statistics or predictions with a statement such as "Accuracy may vary by plus or minus three points."

Rebuttal. Toulmin's allowance for *rebuttal* recognizes the fact that an argument may have a weakness or questionable aspect. By examining your own argument closely, you may find yourself making a rebuttal or anticipating the rebuttals of your readers. If you were advocating that employers provide child care for their employees' children, some readers might ask, "But shouldn't employees who choose to have children be responsible for their care?" Then you should consider dealing with that question in your paper.

A Sample Analysis of an Argument. According to Toulmin's system, Taubert's conclusion to his paper on automobile safety devices could be analyzed this way:

1. *Claim:* The installation of both automatic seat belts and air bags in cars will provide the best protection against automobile fatalities.
2. *Grounds:* Tests show that these two devices, when properly designed, will save more lives than any other devices.
3. *Warrant: Consumer Reports* (April 1987) has examined recent models of seat belts and air bags and reports that improved designs will raise the usage rate and result in lower mortality rates.
4. *Backing:* Former Secretary of Transportation Elizabeth Dole agreed and ordered that automatic restraints be installed unless mandatory seat belt laws are enacted.
5. *Modal qualifier:* Though all of the currently available devices have drawbacks, the devices recommended will save more lives than any others designed so far.
6. *Rebuttals:* People should be able to choose whether or not to use safety devices. Installing these devices will be expensive and therefore will cause the prices of cars to rise so much that some people will not be able to afford them.

If you carefully analyze your argument this way, you will be able to recognize any flaws before you present it to your readers.

Creative Thinking

Although the term ''creative writing'' is often used to apply only to fiction and poetry, the writing of creative thinkers can be found in every subject area—from architecture to literary criticism—and in all formats—from professional articles to novels and poems. Creative thinkers write political documents, such as the Declaration of Independence or the American Constitution; others record their personal observations and thoughts, as Annie Dillard did in *Pilgrim at Tinker Creek* (1974), or they write fiction, such as Alice Walker's *The Color Purple* (1982). Scientists are often creative writers in areas other than lab reports and scientific articles: Stephen W. Hawking, a theoretical physicist, wrote *A Brief History of Time* (1988) to explain the origin and structure of the universe. Musicians, who usually express their creativity in performing or writing music, also write *about* music: John Cage, innovative composer and musicologist, predicted the development of electronic music in ''The Future of Music: Credo'' (1958. Rpt. in *Silence*, 1961).

These are well-known creative writers and thinkers. But all of us have creative minds; and we can all be creative thinkers and writers. In fact, at times we all are. Creative thinkers go beyond fulfilling the bare requirements of academic or professional life because they have their own goals. They tend to question what is accepted as true; they like to find solutions to unsolved problems. Thinking creatively often means combining in a new way information already known or seeing implications that others have overlooked.

David Kuijt's Creative Thinking and Writing

One student, David Kuijt, whose hobby was collecting playing cards, began his research project by studying the history of playing cards. His search took him back to the fourteenth century, to the period just before Gutenberg developed the printing press with movable type. As he read his sources (the fact that he could read German was helpful), he found some unexpected information: the passion for card playing among the guild members—the working people—all over Europe and the problem of supplying cards to the players virtually forced the invention of a printing press. The first press used wood blocks.

From that point the movable-type press—Gutenberg's press—was an obvious step. Kuijt argued that that step would not have been taken, at least not as soon, if card playing had not been so popular and if the attempts of rulers to ban card playing had been successful. Previous researchers on the history of playing cards had not examined the history of printing, and researchers on the history of printing had rarely looked at the development of playing cards. Kuijt found it ironic that, if his theory is correct, our technological society owes a considerable debt to the passion of workers for card playing. Kuijt plans to submit his research paper as an article to a magazine on playing cards.

Making an Outline

With your thesis statement as a guide and with a clear idea of the general shape of your paper, you can now turn your attention to the body of the paper. The information you have gathered must be organized logically so that it makes sense to both you and your readers.

You have been using a list of topics and subtopics to guide your search. Now that you have all of your information, you can expand this list if you want to. You can even convert it into a formal outline; that is, an outline with a prescribed logical and syntactical form (explained later in this section). Some people prefer to write using a simple list of topics and subtopics, but others prefer the clarification that designing a formal outline provides. Whether you use an expanded list or a formal outline, be prepared to alter it as you write your first draft. Your list or outline is your attempt to impose form on the chaos of material that continually exerts its own power. From this tension between form and raw material, your paper takes shape.

Creating a Formal Outline

A formal outline delineates the parts into which your paper is divided as well as the relationship between those parts. It will serve as a guide during the writing process. Later, placed at the beginning of your paper or used as the basis for a table of contents, it guides the reader.

If you have been using a computer to record your notes, you'll find it to be especially helpful at this stage. With a program that allows a split screen, you can scan your notes on one part of the screen and create your outline on the other. Some programs will number and letter your outline headings automatically. But even an unsophisticated program can be helpful by making it easier to rearrange your headings and subheadings.

At this point you have cards or files labeled according to your working outline. Organizing them is the next task. Your computer notes will already be sorted and placed into files with names corresponding to your outline. If you're using cards, sort them into groups that correspond to the outline headings and read over the notes on the cards. You may find some information that doesn't seem to belong under the existing headings. Jot down or record a brief description (heading) for each of these pieces of information so that it fits into your outline, or discard information that does not belong in your paper. Don't hesitate to discard some information—you can expect to have superfluous material. On the computer you can store such notes in a separate file instead of deleting them so that they are available if you need them later. Now add any new headings to your outline.

In a paper on soil erosion, the following headings and subheadings were part of Joseph Masters's working outline:

> Strategies for erosion control
>   Agronomic strategies
>   Mechanical strategies

As he went through his notes Masters found information on soil management, that he had not found a good place for in his outline. After deciding that it belonged under "Strategies for erosion control," he labeled it and added it to his outline:

> Strategies for erosion control
>   Agronomic strategies
>   Mechanical strategies
>   Soil management

Your next step is to decide on the order of the information under each heading in your working outline; as you do this, you may want to change headings and create more subheadings. To make the process easier, read each file or group of cards carefully and, on a sheet of paper or on the computer, list the specific subject of each note. Then fit these headings into your working outline, changing the wording where necessary and adding subheadings where they fit.

Mavis Olson used a simple working outline as she gathered information for her paper on physical fitness programs in the workplace:

History
Benefits of fitness programs
    Employee benefits
    Employer benefits
Facilities needed
    Space
    Equipment
Setting up a program

After gathering information, she constructed the following summary or thesis sentence and formal outline with additional subheadings.

Summary sentence: Companies should consider developing physical fitness programs for their employees.

   I. Introduction: History of industry-provided recreation
  II. Objectives of employee fitness programs
      A. To benefit employees
          1. By improving mental and physical health
          2. By reducing boredom, absenteeism, and fatigue
          3. By promoting efficiency
      B. To benefit management
          1. By providing recruitment appeal
          2. By improving employee-employer relations
          3. By lowering organizational health costs
 III. Design of facility
      A. Fitness center design
          1. Architectural layout
          2. Order of construction
          3. Estimated costs
      B. Equipment
          1. Types of exercise equipment
          2. Estimated costs
  IV. Conclusion: The future of fitness programs in the workplace

The Logic of an Outline

An outline organizes the material in your paper into logical divisions. As you sort your cards, notice how the material helps you to create an outline at the same time that the outline helps you to shape your material. It is a back-and-forth operation. The logic demanded by the structure of the outline helps you to organize your material and also provides a way to ensure that you haven't omitted anything important.

If you have, you may need to do a little more reading before you begin to write. In outlining the objectives of employee fitness programs, Mavis Olson found that her notes dealt almost completely with employee benefits; she had noted only that management used recreation programs as a recruitment lure. When she constructed her outline containing this information, she saw how unbalanced it was.

> II. Objectives of employee fitness programs
>   A. To benefit employees
>   1. By improving mental and physical health
>   2. By reducing boredom, absenteeism, and fatigue
>   3. By promoting employee efficiency
>   B. To benefit management: by providing recruitment appeal

She had included only one benefit for management. It seemed logical to Olson that management would have to find more benefits to fund such programs. After doing more reading, she found two additional benefits: improving employee-employer relations and lowering organizational health costs.

In making an outline, you not only ensure that you have enough information, you also design an orderly presentation for your paper. It is this logical structure that makes it easier for your reader to understand what you are trying to convey. Implied in the outline structure are these propositions:

1. *All topics at the same level are of equal, or nearly equal, importance.* All headings numbered with roman numerals, for example, constitute the major divisions of the paper and deserve equal emphasis. Joseph Masters's original outline on soil erosion had these divisions:

> I. Water erosion
>   [subheadings]
> II. Wind erosion
>   [subheadings]
> III. Strategies for erosion control
>   A. Agronomic strategies
>   [subheadings]
>   B. Mechanical strategies
>   [subheadings]
>   C. Soil management

As he looked at his notes and outline, he realized that his paper really had two main parts: kinds of erosion (water and wind) and ways of controlling them. To reflect this, he changed his outline by converting two former main headings to subheadings and adding a new main heading to balance "Strategies for erosion control." His outline then looked like this:

I. Types of erosion
   A. Water erosion
   B. Wind erosion
II. Strategies for erosion control
   A. Agronomic strategies
   B. Mechanical strategies
   C. Soil management

2. *Each topic, if divided, is split into at least two parts that, at each level, add up to the whole.* Thus, Mavis Olson's outline shows, under "II," two objectives of employee fitness programs. We can assume that her paper will not contain any other objectives and that no other information will appear under this heading. Note that it is not logical to divide something into one part. If you find that you have only one subtopic under a single heading, no divisions exist and you should combine the topic and subtopic. Olson's outline first began this way:

I. Introduction
   A. History and philosophy of industry-provided recreation

She realized that if "A" were the only subdivision, it must be the main heading, so she combined the two:

I. Introduction: History of industry-provided recreation

Avoid using the labels "Introduction" and "Conclusions"—which mean only "beginning" and "end"—without indicating what they will include. If you use these terms, combine them with a phrase indicating their content, as Olson did.

3. *To reflect the relationship among categories in the outline, headings at the same level should have the same grammatical structure.* For example, all of Olson's categories designated by roman numerals are nouns. The "A" and "B" subheadings under "II" are infinitives and the headings under each of these are prepositional phrases:

II. Objectives of employee fitness programs
   A. To benefit employees
      1. By improving mental and physical health
      2. By reducing boredom, absenteeism, and fatigue
      3. By promoting employee efficiency
   B. To benefit management

     . . . . .

III. Design of facility

     . . . . .

4. *The outline shows an orderly progression.* In Olson's outline, the progression of the main headings seems to be in the chronological order that would be followed in setting up an employee fitness program. Objectives would come first; then facilities would be designed. Her sub-headings use either order of importance (II) or chronological order (III). To check your outline for a logical sequence, write down the major headings in a list to see whether they are of equal importance and whether they are logically arranged. Then look at each group of sub-headings in the same way. Olson had the most difficulty with the order of subheadings under "II. A." Was health more important than efficiency? She decided that from the point of view of the employee it was.

You can see that an outline, besides helping you to organize your paper, helps you clarify the relative importance of its parts. To write an outline, first decide on the major divisions—the main parts into which you intend to divide your paper. After you have decided on your major categories, divide each of them in a similar way. Think arithmetically; make the parts add up to the whole with nothing left over.

The Form of an Outline

Most outlines use alternating numbers and letters along with indentation. Major divisions are indicated by roman numerals; first subdivisions, by capital letters; and second subdivisions, by arabic numerals. Further subdividing is seldom required in papers written for college classes. If you find you need more subheadings, indicate them by small letters, then by arabic numerals in parentheses, and finally by small letters in parentheses. The order should look like this:

I.
  A.
    1.
      a.
        (1)
          (a)

If you glance back at Olson's outline, you'll notice that the period following each roman numeral is aligned; then each subdivision is indented, with all divisions of the same order arranged in a vertical line and with the letter or number of each subdivision directly under the first letter of the first word in the larger category:

I.
II.
III. Design of facility
  A. Fitness center design
    1. Architectural layout
    2. Order of construction
    3. Estimated costs
  B.

Place a period after each number or letter, but do not put a period after the topics in a topic outline. (You would put periods after the sentences in a sentence outline; see the next section.) Capitalize the first letter of the first word of each topic. Such arrangement and punctuation make your outline easier to read and reinforce its logic.

Other Types of Outlines

Sentence Outlines. The most common type of outline is, like Olson's, the topic outline, which uses single words or phrases. Sometimes, however, a *sentence outline* is used to define the categories more precisely. To make a sentence outline, you must have your material very clearly in mind. Although such precision is not always possible before writing, creating such an outline does force you to be clear about what you want to say. As a result, the actual writing of your paper will be much easier. The following sentence outline helped Farah Farhoumand compose a stronger paper.

Topic: The growing problem of child abuse in the United States
Summary sentence: Child abuse is a growing problem with diverse causes and remedies.

   I. Child abuse is increasing in the United States.
      A. Statistics are difficult to analyze because child abuse is defined differently by different experts.
         1. Some experts define it as severe battering.
         2. Others consider it to be any use of physical force that causes physical injury.
         3. Still others define it as mental as well as physical abuse.
      B. Statistics show that child abuse is increasing.
         1. The Department of Health and Human Services reported that child abuse cases doubled during the last two years.
         2. Large cities, where reporting is more accurate, report dramatic increases in child abuse.
         3. Researchers estimate that the number of reported cases is only a fraction of the real number.
  II. Experts differ as to the causes of child abuse.
      A. According to some, the mental and emotional illness of parents causes child abuse.
      B. Others believe that parents' aggression is learned behavior.
      C. Another theory is that child abuse is caused by social, cultural, and economic factors.
      D. A few believe that children with behavioral problems can contribute to their own abuse.

III. Remedies are as varied as the causes.
   A. Recognition of the problem and reporting of cases are essential.
   B. Psychologically disturbed parents should be treated.
   C. Children should be separated from their parents and treated.

Decimal Outlines.   The *decimal outline* is often used in technical writing because it is easily expanded into many subdivisions. Sometimes almost every paragraph is numbered for easier reference. For example, the third edition of the *MLA Handbook for Writers of Research Papers* (1988) uses the decimal system. By citing divisions and subdivisions in the index instead of page numbers, the editors make it easier to locate information. The decimal system also makes it easier to see at a glance the relative importance of a heading. Notice how these systems correspond.

Using numerals and letters	Using decimals
I. First major topic	1.0
A. Major subtopic	1.1
1. Minor subtopic	1.1.1
a. Subsubtopic	1.1.1.1
b. Subsubtopic	1.1.1.2
2. Minor subtopic	1.1.2
B. Major subtopic	1.2
II. Second main topic	2.0

Diana Holford used the decimal system in her paper surveying home computers. Here is part of her outline.

1.0 Qualities of a good home computer system
  1.1 Memory
  1.2 Display
  1.3 Screen format
  1.4 Graphics resolution
  1.5 Printers
    1.5.1 Impact
    1.5.2 Dot matrix
    1.5.3 Laser
  1.6 Keyboard
    1.6.1 Pressure sensitive
    1.6.2 Typewriter
  1.7 Storage
    1.7.1 Floppy disks
    1.7.2 Hard disks

1.8 Software languages
   1.8.1 BASIC
   1.8.2 FORTRAN
   1.8.3 Others
2.0 Six popular computer systems

The Arrangement of Your Notes According to Your Outline

If you add to your outline or if you change its order or wording, be sure that you change the corresponding words or symbols in the upper corner of each note card or in your computer files. Resort and regroup the notes according to the outline. You will then be ready to write your paper easily and efficiently.

EXERCISES

1. **FOR YOUR SEARCH LOG**   Record the answers to the re-searching questions (see page 133) in your search log.

2. **FOR YOUR SEARCH LOG**   Record your thesis statement, argument, or claim (depending on the terminology you or your instructor wishes to use) in your search log. Following Toulmin's method, analyze your claim by giving your grounds and warrants. If you think you need additional support, supply backing. Then, if your argument is still not strong enough, perhaps you need to add a modal qualifier.

3. **FOR PEER RESPONSE**   Divide into groups, preferably of four or five. Using your search logs, take turns reading aloud to the group the answers to the re-searching questions on page 133. Read slowly. After each reader finishes, the other members of the group should write down what they understand to be the reader's purpose and then the group should discuss the reader's purpose. Did everyone understand it? If not, what was the difficulty? Can it be clarified?

4. Ask one of your classmates to examine the analysis of your claim and your grounds and suggest a rebuttal if that seems necessary. Discuss the rebuttal with your classmate. If the rebuttal reveals a weak point in your argument, make the necessary change in your claim or provide more or better grounds and warrants.

Writing Your First Draft

As you conducted your search, you were satisfying your own curiosity. Now, as you write, you will be satisfying your readers' curiosity. You will also be satisfying the desire we all have at times to tell someone else what we have done, thought, or discovered. If you can maintain the enthusiasm you have when you share information with your best friend, you will automatically eliminate many of the problems that arise in writing a research paper.

Preparing to Write

Preliminary Planning

Using a Computer for Writing. By far the most efficient way to compose and rewrite your research papers is to use a computer with word processing software. If you haven't been using a computer up to this point, reconsider the advantages. More and more colleges and universities are providing access to computers in classroom buildings and dormitories. Many require students to have their own personal computers. It is likely that if you work in a business or profession after graduation you will have to enter your written communications on a personal computer; secretaries who transcribe handwriting or take dictation are no longer available in many offices.

If you have never used a computer, you might be thinking, "I have enough to do without having to learn how to operate a computer." It does take time to learn the commands, and you might feel frustrated at times. But some newer systems take less time to master, and in the long run you will save, many times over, the time you spend learning. Taking a short introductory workshop is helpful in getting started on a computer; many colleges offer such instruction without charge.

If you are not familiar with a typewriter or computer keyboard, you can use a computer software program to teach yourself. With a little practice, you will be able to type your manuscripts as fast as or faster than you can write—and your manuscript will be much easier to revise.

Here are some of the specific advantages of using a computer or word processor:

1. Once you set the margins and format, the computer will format and number every page for you.
2. Because changes are so easy to make, first drafts are easier to write. You can correct errors, change words, or revise phrases as you write. As a result, you may find yourself less likely to put off getting started.
3. Revising a completed draft is much easier with a computer. After printing out a copy of your first draft, you can make changes on the paper as you would if you had typed or handwritten it. Then you can call your text to the screen and transfer the changes from the paper to the computer. Suggestions for revising on a computer are given in Chapter 8.
4. A computer can alert you to errors as you type or as you proofread.
5. If you lose or misplace your manuscript, you can easily make another copy.

Materials. For early drafts you can use any opaque paper; an inexpensive grade of computer paper is fine (avoid onionskin or erasable paper; these are difficult to write on and allow printing to show through). Always write on only one side of the paper so you can follow your writing easily from one page to the next. Plan to use plenty of paper. Wide margins (one and a half or two inches) and double- or triple-spacing will give you plenty of room to add words and sentences. Even if you are writing and editing on a computer, you will want wide margins to allow for editing on hard copy.

Place. Do your composing in a place where you can be free of distractions and, if possible, where you can leave your papers and cards arranged, ready to work on them at any time.

Schedule. Review the timetable you constructed as you were planning your search (see Chapter 2). Write down the total time you scheduled for writing and divide it into parts, allowing time for revising and incubating. Take account of your own writing habits: if you revise as you go along, you will take more time on the first draft and probably less time on subsequent drafts. Also use your timetable to help you change any habits that may not benefit your writing. Procrastination often prevents writers from spending as much time as they need on revising. Making a realistic timetable and following it will help you improve your writing procedure and, consequently, your writing.

The following schedule for a ten- to fifteen-page paper provides for three drafts. Your paper may require more. Or you may find that you have two complete drafts with some pages or paragraphs rewritten several times. Make adjustments for your own writing habits. The schedule also includes an incubation period. Many writers have found— perhaps you have too—that their minds work on a problem or a piece of writing even when they aren't giving it their conscious attention. To allow your mind time to do this work is the idea behind scheduling some time for incubation.

> *Writing the first draft:* Focus on getting down all the information you need to make your points clear. Ten to fifteen hours (four or five hours for each writing period).
>
> *Incubation period:* From one to seven days (if you leave your paper for a longer time, you may forget too much).
>
> *Writing the second draft:* Focus on organization and paragraphing. Ten to fifteen hours.
>
> *Incubation period:* Four to twenty-four hours.
>
> *Writing the third draft:* Focus on sentences, words, punctuation, and format. Eight to ten hours.
>
> *Typing the final draft:* Three to five hours.
>
> *Proofreading and photocopying:* Two to four hours.

Try not to rush during the period you have set aside for writing. Writing progresses best when you don't have to feel anxious about finishing; hurried writing is not usually good writing. Of course you will have a deadline to meet. But following your timetable will make it possible for you to have enough time to do your best and meet your deadline too.

Focusing on Your Audience

When you tell a friend about a concert you have attended or a movie you have seen, you use a vocabulary that you know your friend will understand. You include all of the background information your friend needs to understand what you are talking about; you use an organizational plan that will make it easy for your friend to follow your explanation; and you use grammatical structures that make your meaning clear.

All these techniques are part of the process of verbal communication that you use daily, whether you are aware of using them or not. In writing your paper, you will want to be sure that you use these techniques with precision and care. Your friends may be able to ask you for clarification; they may know you well enough to understand you even if you are sometimes vague. But you have to assume when you write your paper that your audience will not have the chance to ask you to explain your meaning. Writing a paper takes more planning and more careful execution than talking or writing to a friend. Still, the same desire to tell, the same eagerness to make it possible for your readers to understand you, and your own interest in and enthusiasm for your subject are the most important prerequisites for writing a good paper, just as they are for communicating in any medium.

The main thing you will have to decide about your audience is how much knowledge they have about your subject. Will they be familiar with the vocabulary? If your topic is "*Pseudomonas pseudomallei* infections in humans" and you are writing for your microbiology class, you will be able to write such a sentence as "The disease is often mistaken for tuberculosis or mycotic lung infections because of the cavitations on the lungs seen in x-rays" without translating the terms. But if you are writing for your English class, you should either put technical or unfamiliar words in a glossary, define them when you use them, or translate the whole sentence into layperson's terms. How do you decide which of these solutions to use? Here are some guidelines, but they are not hard and fast rules.

1. *Include a glossary* if you use more than five technical words frequently in your paper (for more suggestions on composing a glossary, see Chapter 9). Do not use words in your glossary that are just as difficult as the word you are defining. Defining *flagella* as "helical protein appendages that allow bacteria to be motile" is probably not going to help your readers.

2. *Define words in the text or in a footnote* if you have only four or five words unknown to your audience. You can put each definition in parentheses immediately after the word:

> Sheet erosion (a landslide or mudflow) occurs extremely rapidly and results in greater losses of soil than any other type.

You can put the definition into a sentence that becomes an introduction to the subject:

> A computer network can be thought of as a collection of independent computers; it can include systems as simple as two word processors linked together or as complex as a nationwide research system consisting of many computers connected by telephone lines.

Or you can use a content note or footnote:

> A trained analyst examines each photograph for details such as terrain, structures, ground disturbance, discarded material, and signatures.[1]
>
> ———————
>
> [1]The term "signature" is used to denote a particular pattern, shape, tone, or color that consistently indicates the presence of an object or material in an aerial photograph, even though the object itself may be indistinguishable.

3. *Use words that will be understood by your audience and integrate definitions into your writing when necessary.* At this level, you may be somewhat limited in your ability to discuss highly technical subjects. If you are, don't write:

> The disease is often mistaken in x-rays for tuberculosis or mycotic lung infections because of the cavitations on the lungs.

But write:

> The pittings or small depressions in the lungs caused by the disease and seen on x-rays often lead to mistaken diagnoses of tuberculosis or parasitic fungus infections.

Obviously, technical language or a higher vocabulary level usually requires fewer words and is often more precise. Therefore, you want to use the highest level that you think your audience can understand. But avoid using technical language just to impress your readers.

Besides suiting your vocabulary to the level of your readers' understanding, you will also have to consider how much they know about your subject and how much they need to know to understand what you are trying to say.

Establishing Your Own Style and Tone

With your first words you establish a relationship with your readers, much as you do when you introduce yourself personally. The reader gets a sense of you as a person and of the tone you will use in your paper. Your tone may be serious, friendly, humorous, angry, or concerned—just about any emotion or combination of emotions is possible. It's important, though, that you are conscious of the tone you are using and that it fits your subject and the results you want to obtain. Most research papers are serious, but they need not be dull. Whatever your attitude as you write, it will probably assert itself in your writing. A serious but relaxed and friendly attitude usually works well. Humor may work with some subjects, but you have to use it with care; it would not work well, for example, in a paper on the problems of alcoholism or the prevalence of teenage pregnancy.

Sometimes the syntax—the arrangement of words in the sentence—may make your writing hard to understand; write simply, saving complex sentence forms for complex ideas. Notice the following sentences from a paper on the results of environmental impact studies:

> Currently, field tests are being scheduled by the Envionics Corporation to coincide with the receipt of incremental site assessments which will be forwarded from the Environmental Photographic Interpretation Center (EPIC) upon completion.

Fortunately, the writer of this passage realized before she went very far that she was trying too hard to sound authoritative and that the result was unclear writing. By omitting unnecessary use of the passive voice and unneeded words, she composed a much clearer passage:

> The Envionics Corporation will conduct tests for potential hazards as soon as they receive the site assessments now being completed by the Environmental Photographic Interpretation Center (EPIC).

An excessively formal style in which you try to avoid using *I* or *you* can lead to such awkward constructions as the following:

> As has been said, not all of these writers had a political purpose in writing.
>
> As can be seen from Table 2, all cotton grown in the West is now under irrigation.

Instead, you can strengthen your writing by using simple and clear language:

> As I have already pointed out, not all of these writers had a political purpose in writing.
>
> Table 2 shows that all cotton grown in the West is now under irrigation.

Using your own style, and writing clearly will help to give your paper unity and coherence. Unity will be reinforced if you are consistent in the verb tense you use. Use the present tense for routine or customary activities:

> Most pregnant girls *learn* about the agency through referral by a church or other organization. The first contact *is* usually *made* by phone call, during which an interview *is set up*.

Use the present tense, too, for references to what is in print or in law:

> Section 104 of the Copyright Law *prohibits* the public performance, for profit, of copyrighted music without permission of the copyright holder.
>
> Ziswiler *points out* that "conservation" applies to animal species, not to individual animals (100).

But use past tense when you are relating a past event, such as an interview:

> Mrs. Rumford *explained* that the adoptive couple must go through one to three years of intense interviewing and observation before they are accepted or rejected as adoptive parents.

Of course, you will be able to make changes when you revise, but you can save yourself time by writing as simply and clearly as you can from the beginning. Start with a style that you feel comfortable with, and you will be able to give your complete attention to what you say rather than to how you say it.

Writing Your Introduction

The first part of a paper is its introduction, but whether you label it as such depends in part on the discipline in which you are writing. Papers in the humanities following the style of the *Modern Language Association* usually do not use a heading. The *Publication Manual of the American Psychological Association* and the *Handbook for Authors of Papers in American Chemical Society Publications* recommend against using "Introduction" as a heading because the position of the material at the beginning is sufficient. However, "Introduction" is recommended as a heading in the *CBE Style Manual*, published by the Council of Biology Editors.

In the introduction you tell your readers what they need or would like to know about your subject before you begin your specific discussion of it. You might explain your purpose for writing or state the problem you have studied. In writing some papers (especially if you are doing original research), you may want to review published writing on the same subject.

You have already prepared for writing your introduction in Chapter 6 when you answered this question in your search log: "What was my purpose in doing this search?" Here are some other questions you can ask yourself as you think about how to begin your paper:

1. How did I happen to get started on this subject?
2. What would my reader like to know before I explain what I found?
3. What does my reader need to know to understand my paper?
4. What am I trying to prove?
5. What would my reader like to know about this subject?

Include in your introduction the answers to any of these questions that are relevant to your subject. The answer to the first two questions can provide background or a discussion of the problem you are trying to solve. The answer to the third question may be a brief history of the subject or a summary of what has already been written about it. The answer to the fourth question can be your hypothesis or your thesis statement. You can give your thesis statement in the introduction or in the conclusion at the end of the paper.

Beginning with an Anecdote

Lee Atkinson began a paper about life on Mars by explaining how he became interested in his subject. Notice that his story leads into the question that he will answer in his paper.

> One warm summer day after classes, I made it home just in time to see the noon news. "Viking I has landed and is sending pictures back to earth from Mars," the newscaster said, speaking with the usual deep voice of broadcasters. "Here is the first picture sent back. Notice the can-like object to the left. Scientists say it did not come from Viking."
>
> It looked like a beer can and my mind started whirling. Could there be life on Mars?

Beginning with Background

A paper on the treatments of alcoholism began with some historical background on the use of alcohol.

> As a sign of trust and friendship in the early days of civilization, two men would draw their blood and mingle it with each other's. As time passed, alcohol began to be almost as important as blood. It was called "aqua vitae"—"water of life"—partly because it was often safer to drink than water. Trust was established and friendships and agreements were sealed with a cup of wine.
>
> Today alcohol has become a social drink, but for many people social pressures and everyday problems can cause serious drinking problems. These people have a disease called alcoholism. The alcoholic's only hope for recovery is to stop drinking completely. How the alcoholic can do this is the subject of this paper.

Beginning with a Definition

Tom Davis's report resulting from a field exploration for knapping stones began with a definition to help his nonscientific audience—the members of his class—understand his paper. The opening paragraph closed with a statement of the paper's purpose.

> Knapping is the art of making cutting tools by the controlled fracturing of stones. Glassy minerals, such as obsidian, chert, or flint (see glossary, p. iii), are fairly easy to knap because their smooth texture allows us to predict how they will break. A semiglassy mineral, such as quartzite, is much harder to knap because its graininess makes its fractures less predictable. . . . To find the best places for knapping in the area, I first searched the geological literature, including maps, at the U.S. Geological Survey Headquarters Library. After noting the deposits that are either very large or that were said to contain quartzite cobbles, I knapped cobbles at a site in each deposit. This paper describes the locations of major deposits of knappable stones in the area and the compositions of these deposits. By using the

marked map in the appendix, the knapper should be able to locate these sites easily.

Beginning with a Summary

A paper by Maria Sanchez on the problems of health care in the United States began with a question and then stated four answers, which became the four main parts of the paper.

> Why is our health care system failing? Those who advocate a national health insurance law have cited four reasons: (1) there are not enough doctors and medical facilities, and those we have are not well distributed; (2) medical services are fragmented and poorly coordinated; (3) many people cannot afford adequate medical care or insurance; and (4) the cost of medical care is rising.

Beginning with a Review of the Literature

Sometimes a writer may want to start with a brief review of what other writers have written on the subject, as Raj Premchand does in a study of Mark Twain's pessimism.

> Literary critics have made much ado about Mark Twain's pessimism. What caused it and whether it existed from his early years are questions not yet answered conclusively. On the one hand there are those like DeLancey Ferguson who see him as "a born worrier" (184). Henry Seidel Canby goes to some lengths to explain what he calls Twain's neuroticism (252–54). On the other hand, Bernard De Voto traces his problems to a guilt complex fed by family misfortunes for which he blamed himself (301). But the most likely cause of his problem was, I believe, his feeling of shame for having yielded to the materialism of the Gilded Age.

You can see that an introduction can serve a number of purposes: it can define a word that is crucial to the understanding of the paper; it can state why the writer undertook the study; it can state the purpose of the research; it can briefly outline the body of the paper. In short, the introduction tells readers what they need or would like to know before reading the body of the paper; it introduces them to the subject. Choose the kind of introduction that fits your subject and purpose. You might want to try two or three different kinds to see which works best.

Getting Started without a Plan

If, after trying a number of possibilities for getting started, you still have a blank page in front of you, just begin writing anyway. Start talking on paper or on the computer about your topic as if you were talking to a friend. You can rewrite your introduction later. Or take out your notes and begin writing the body of your paper. You may have a better idea of how you want to write your introduction after you have written some or all of the paper itself.

Using Your Outline and a Computer

Sometimes it's hard to begin writing because the idea of having to begin a long paper can be discouraging. By using your outline and a computer you can combine the advantages of writing without a plan and the advantages of some structure. Just call up your outline on the computer and, thinking of each topic in the outline as the heading for a separate paper, begin to write a series of mini-papers. If you expand each heading into a sentence, you will have a thesis sentence for each mini-paper. If your computer has the capability, divide your screen and call up your notes next to your outline and scroll through them as you write. If the computer can't split the screen, write from your printed notes or your note cards.

Continue to expand each part of your topic on the outline screen. If you will be using the APA style (see Chapter 11) or the number style (see Chapter 12) when you write your paper, you can leave the headings in place. Later you can turn them into a table of contents if you use one.

This strategy can help you to avoid procrastination. Set a modest goal of the number of topics you want to cover when you sit down at the computer—one you know you can accomplish. Then write at least that much. If you decide you want to write more, of course you can.

Writing the Body of Your Paper

In the body of your paper, you tell what you have discovered about your subject. If you are conducting an original study or experiment, you explain the methods you used as well as the results you obtained. If you are using secondary sources—information from others' studies and experiments—the body is where you give the information you have found. This is where you present the evidence that makes your thesis statement true.

Using Headings

The use of headings within the body varies among disciplines. Papers in the humanities usually do not use headings within the body. If you have done primary research, such as a scientific experiment or a field study in social research, you would present your findings under at least three headings (the introduction would have no heading): materials and methods, results, and discussion or conclusions. You can use secondary headings that correspond to your outline. If you are writing a technical report, you will use the headings corresponding to topics and subtopics in your outline. A research paper using secondary sources will usually follow the humanities or technical paper format. In organization, these two are similar, following an outline like those discussed in Chapter 6. (Note that papers citing secondary sources can use any of the three documentation systems illustrated in Chapters 10, 11, and 12.)

Developing Coherence and Unity

Following the outline you have designed before writing your paper (see Chapter 6) will help you to write a paper in which all of the parts are connected logically. Each part should clearly follow the one before it. You should set up expectations for your readers—first in your topic and subsequently in each part of your paper—which you then fulfill. Each paragraph is a kind of promise which is fulfilled in the next paragraph; each sentence is a promise fulfilled in the succeeding sentence. This linkage creates the feeling of coherence in your paper. Your introduction has already pointed to what you will discuss or prove in the body of your paper. You must now make sure that you follow through.

The sample introductions given earlier in this chapter alert readers to what will follow. Read your introduction over again and see whether it prepares your readers for what you will write in the body of your paper. As you complete the discussion of each subtopic, stop and see whether it moves smoothly and clearly from the preceding topic or subtopic.

Your outline should also provide unity for your paper. You want to make sure that you don't include irrelevant information. If you deviate from your outline as you write, make sure you have a good reason for doing so—perhaps you have left something out of your outline. You'll have a chance to check your first draft for coherence and unity when you revise your paper (see Chapter 8).

Integrating Sources into Your Text

A transformation takes place as you write your paper. The information on your note cards or on your computer, based on the words of a number of writers and speakers plus any information you have collected through your own observation, becomes a unified paper written in your own style and your own words. The paper becomes your message to your readers about the discoveries you have made during your search. The following suggestions may help you to make this transformation. With your notes arranged according to your topics and subtopics on your note cards or your computer screen, read your notes slowly and carefully, one subtopic at a time. When the material in one group of notes becomes part of your thinking—when it is integrated with the rest of your knowledge and experience—you will be ready to write. Then write as if you were passing the information on to your readers. The words should come from what is now in your own mind rather than from the words in your notes. Write as much as you can without looking at your notes; refer to your notes primarily for exact quotations or statistics or to cite your sources of information.

Keeping Your Readers in Mind

Instead of feeling that you are mechanically filling up pages for an assignment, maintain the sense of direct and active communication with your readers as you write. Your sources can become participants in this discussion of your subject; what they have to say is part of the story you are telling. Think of the way you might tell someone about a conversation you have heard on a subject on which several people have disagreed. You will say something like "John said this, but Jim disagreed because. . . . And Mary didn't agree with either of them. I thought there was some truth in what they all said. . . ." You will want to give a similar sense of a lively discussion on a topic of interest to you and to your readers, as one student, Joan Ostby, did.

For her paper on Hart Crane's poem *The Bridge*, Ostby entitled a part of her outline "Evaluations." She read over her note cards with this heading and thought about them for a few minutes. There was some ambiguity and disagreement among the critical comments. She looked at her own notes and comments on the poem. She reflected on what had been written by critics about the poem and how she felt about it. When her thinking became clear, she sat down and wrote; she first summarized the views of the critics, quoting from some of them, and then gave her own evaluation. Notice how she varies her introductions of authors and their views.

	The reviews of The Bridge are by no means unfavor-
Quotation with source in parentheses.	able; yet most of the critics seem to feel that it was a noble effort that did not quite succeed. It is termed a
Combination of paraphrase and quotation with author introducing the sentence.	"magnificent failure" by some (Horton 142). Allen Tate writes that The Bridge failed because "a great talent is engaged upon the problem of stating a position that is fundamentally incapable of definition." As a symbol, the bridge, he believes, "stands for no well-defined experience" (210). In Hound and Horn he
View by another critic: reference in text.	expresses his disapproval of the romanticism of the poem (132). Howard Moss objects also to the symbol of the bridge because he believes that it remains a static

Page number identifies source for two previous sentences. Reference not needed for each sentence.

symbol--even though Crane tries to activate it. It is, he says, "metaphysical on one hand and mechanical on the other. It rarely achieves balance between fact and vision" (42).

Introduction to paragraph giving Ostby's view. Quotations from the poet being discussed.

Although these criticisms are probably justified, the poem seems to me to fail because it lacks integration. The "bridge" itself is supposed to be a symbol of unity, connecting the past, present, and future. But the poem as a whole does not present that feeling of unity. The poetry is not consistently good, and the transitions between sections are sometimes rough. It

Quotations from the poet being discussed.

does not seem, either, that he has projected the "absolute ideal" "free from my own personality" that was his design.

Although she quotes other critics, Ostby maintains control of the ideas expressed. They are merely aids that she uses to tell readers her own view of the poem. (For detailed information on citing sources, see Acknowledging Your Sources, p. 169.)

Keeping Your Readers Informed

The Ostby excerpt illustrates how to combine paraphrases and quotations and at the same time let readers know when they are getting information from sources and when they are getting the writer's own opinions. It also shows how to cite those sources so that parenthetical citations disturb the writing as little as possible. When you can put the name of the author and even the book or article title in the text, you need only the page number in the citation.

Handling Quotations

When you indicate that you are using someone else's language by putting the words in quotation marks, you must make sure that you quote accurately; the spelling of each word and each mark of punctuation must be just as they are in the original. When you make changes in the original to make it fit your own language and style, you must indicate these changes to your reader. The instructions that follow for using quotations from your reading include suggestions on how to show such changes.

1. *Let your own voice dominate.* To keep your own style and tone you will want to use direct quotations sparingly, and, when you do use them, you'll want to integrate them carefully into your paper. If you have followed the suggestion of paraphrasing and summarizing as you read your sources (see Chapter 4) and if you have read each group of notes before starting to write, you should find it easy to use your own words. However, if you write directly from an article or book, the words of the source may dominate your thoughts and you might write a passage like this:

> "Don't Worry Baby" "became the first pop standard created by Brian Wilson" (Leaf 52). The song was a "staggering, textured tour de force of harmony, dramatic falsetto, and revolving melody. As an expression of teenage yearning and emotional insecurity, it was unsurpassed in the history of rock" (Priess 24).

The voice of the writer in this passage is lost among quotations of little or no significance. There seems to be little purpose in using the words of Leaf; the following paraphrase of the first sentence would work just as well: "'Don't Worry Baby' was Brian Wilson's first pop standard." And the writer does not prepare us for the quotation from Priess nor does she let us know why she is using it. If the writer thought that this was an especially interesting or significant quotation, she could have introduced it this way: "One critic called it 'an expression of teenage yearning and emotional insecurity' and expressed his great enthusiasm for the piece by referring to it as a 'staggering, textured tour de force of harmony, dramatic falsetto, and revolving melody' that was 'unsurpassed in the history of rock.'" This way the passage takes on more of the writer's style, and we hear *her* quoting Priess's words.

2. *Integrate quotations into your paper by introducing the original author.* Work all short quotations into the fabric of your own writing by giving the name of the original author or by identifying the author in some other way, perhaps as an authority. The use of quotation marks is not enough to alert readers to the fact that the words used are not yours. Quotation marks are visual cues, but you need verbal cues as well. Usually, if the words are important enough to be quoted verbatim, the reader wants to know who said them. This passage provides that necessary information:

> Most social learning theorists hold that child abuse is learned behavior. According to Lystad, parents who severely punish their children produce aggressive children who "in turn tend to punish their children more severely" (336).

3. *Integrate quotations by adding words to make the meaning clear or to make the quotations fit grammatically into the rest of the sentence.* Sometimes you will have to omit words of the quotation at the beginning or end or even insert words of your own into the original (see the use of brackets, p. 167). You must make sure, though, that you indicate the changes by punctuation. For example, you can add a word for clarity.

ORIGINAL:

"Orthodoxy, of whatever colour, seems to demand a lifeless, imitative style." (George Orwell, from *Shooting an Elephant and Other Essays*)

WORD ADDED:

"[Political] orthodoxy, of whatever colour, seems to demand a lifeless, imitative style."

Or you might omit words from the beginning of the quotation and change verb tense when necessary.

ORIGINAL:

"And thus, in the days ahead, only the very courageous will be able to take the hard and unpopular decisions necessary for our survival in the struggle with a powerful enemy. . . ." (John F. Kennedy, from *Profiles in Courage*)

INTEGRATED PASSAGE:

Kennedy concluded that "only the very courageous [would] be able to take the hard and unpopular decisions necessary for our survival in the struggle with a powerful enemy. . . ."

4. *Quote only significant or interesting words.* Although the words of someone else intrude on your style, sometimes the words of your source seem the best way to state an idea. Margaret Sharp found these words in her notes; the source was an interview with the manager of an adoption agency.

"Most girls intend to keep their children. It's rare that a girl comes to the agency intending to give up her baby. Those who do are usually older, more mature girls—nineteen or twenty years old. The average age of girls is fifteen years old. Out of 140 cases, we've placed 43 babies."

When the information appeared in her paper, most of the original was paraphrased; only one word was quoted directly.

Associated Catholic Charities took care of 140 young women and their newborn babies last year. Mrs. Rumford explained that most of these "girls"—except for the older ones, the nineteen- or twenty-year-olds—did not have adoption in mind when they came.

It's clear from the context that the word in quotation marks is Mrs. Rumford's. It is the only word that is hers, but the author wanted to report her use of this term to underline the plight of these young women by indicating that they were mere girls. Quoting the whole passage would not have been necessary and would have detracted from the emphasis on one word.

5. *Use long quotations when you want to hear the voice of your source.* The following passage illustrates why you might want to quote a long passage and what the effect is when you do. It also shows how you can prepare your readers for a long quotation. Alice Drake, in her paper on how writers write, wanted to explain how Eudora Welty, the fiction writer, began her writing career. Drake decided that using Welty's writing style would add to the account, so she introduced her and let her tell it in her own words.

> How do great writers start? Is there some sign at the very beginning of what is to come? Eudora Welty, in her biography *One Writer's Beginnings*, described her start this way:
>
>> The earliest story I kept a copy of was, I had thought, sophisticated, for I'd had the inspiration to lay it in Paris. I wrote it on my new typewriter, and its opening sentence was, ''Monsieur Boule inserted a delicate dagger into Mademoiselle's left side and departed with a poised immediacy.'' I'm afraid it was a perfect example of what my father thought ''fiction'' mostly was (85–86).

Punctuating Quotations

To make your quotations effective and easy to understand, punctuate them carefully. In addition, indicate either by quotation marks (for short quotations) or by indentation (for long quotations) whenever you are borrowing words from someone else.

Introducing Quotations

- Use a comma or a colon to introduce a quotation that can stand alone grammatically: a comma for a short quotation and a colon for a long quotation (see pp. 166–67 for illustrations of long quotations).

  ```
  According to one psychologist, "Child abuse is a phenomenon of
  uniform symptoms but of diverse causation" (Gil 347).
  ```

- Do not use any introductory punctuation when you integrate the quotation into your own sentence structure.

  ```
  One psychologist has stated that child abuse "is a phenomenon
  of uniform symptoms but of diverse causation" (Gil 347).
  ```

- Use a colon to introduce a line of poetry or to emphasize a short quotation.

  ```
  A famous soliloquy of Hamlet begins: "To be, or not to be: /
  That is the question."
  ```

Quotation Marks

- Always place quotation marks outside commas or periods.

  ```
  "With me," William Faulkner told the students, "a story usu-
  ally begins with a single idea or memory or mental picture."
  ```

- Place the quotation marks after the quoted material and the period after the citation when you put a citation at the end of a sentence. The citation is considered part of the sentence but not part of the quotation.

    Lincoln Steffens promoted "the Henry George plan for the clos-
    ing up of all the sources of unearned wealth" (Autobiography
    493).

- Always place semicolons and colons outside quotation marks except when they are part of the quotation.

    We meet Lena in the first sentence of Light in August "sitting
    beside the road, watching the wagon mount the hill toward her";
    she had come "all the way from Alabama a-walking."

    Hotchner writes of Hemingway's "superb skill at instruction":
    Hemingway "guided me every step of the way, from when we pull up
    to set the big hook in his mouth to when we bring him in close
    to be taken."

- Place a question mark inside the quotation marks if the quoted material is a question, outside if the quoted material is part of a sentence that is a question. The following quoted material is a question.

    According to Young, aphasics can answer the question "Were you
    drinking tea?" but cannot tell where they live.

    In the next example, the quoted material is not a question; the sentence that contains the quoted material is a question.

    Do you know who said, "That's one small step for a man, one
    giant leap for mankind"?

- Use three ellipsis points in addition to a period when an unfinished quotation ends the sentence. Notice the order: ellipsis points, quotation marks, citation, and period. (For further explanation of ellipsis points, see p. 168.)

    Halberstam calls the study on the bombing of North Vietnam pre-
    pared by the Policy Planning Council "a pure study" that "re-
    flected the genuine expertise of the government . . ." (435).

Long Quotations

- When quoted material is more than four lines long, indent it ten spaces from the left margin if you're using the author/page style; indent it five spaces for the author/date style. Do not use quotation marks. The right margin remains the same as the rest of the text. If your quotation is only one paragraph or part of a paragraph, don't indent the first word more than the rest. The following quotation begins in the middle of one paragraph and follows with an entire paragraph, the first line of which is indented three additional spaces.

> As The Great Gatsby closes, Carraway speculates about Gatsby's death and life:
>
> > I thought of Gatsby's wonder when he first picked out the green light at the end of Daisy's dock. He had come a long way to this blue lawn, and his dream must have seemed so close that he could hardly fail to grasp it. . . .
> >
> > Gatsby believed in the green light, the orgiastic future that year by year recedes before us.

- If a long quotation contains material in quotation marks, enclose that material in double quotation marks.

> In Tillie Olsen's story "I Stand Here Ironing," the narrator describes her attempt to "make up" for not having paid enough attention to her daughter as she was growing up:
>
> > Now when it is too late (as if she would let me hold and comfort her like I do the others) I get up and go to her at once at her moan or restless stirring. "Are you awake, Emily? Can I get you something?"

Single Quotation Marks

- Use single quotation marks to enclose a quotation within a short quotation.

> As Hart points out, "Given a problem and the necessary raw inputs, and 'left alone' to deal with it, our neocortex obligingly will solve it."

Brackets

- When you add clarifying words or phrases to a quotation, enclose them in brackets.

> Hamlin Garland admitted that he abandoned polemics after "the destruction of the People's party and the failure of this novel [A Spoil of Office]."

- Use brackets when you have to add words to make the quotation fit the grammatical structure of your sentence.

  ```
  Cooper held that to "encourage the rich to hold real estate
  [was] not desirable" (The Redskins 8).
  ```

- Use the Latin word *sic*, which means "thus," in brackets to indicate that your quotation or the spelling of a word is accurate, even though it may appear to be incorrect.

  ```
  At the end of Huckleberry Finn, Huck writes that he is going
  "to light out for the Territory" because his Aunt Sally is "go-
  ing to adopt me and sivilize [sic] me."
  ```

If you do not have brackets on your keyboard, leave a space before and after the material you want to bracket and add the brackets later in ink.

Ellipsis Points

- Use three ellipsis points (spaced periods) with a space before and after each point to indicate that you have left out part of a quoted passage.

  ```
  J. Z. Young maintains that "the important feature of brains
  is . . . the information that they carry" (2).
  ```

- When you omit material at the end of a sentence, place the period at the end as you normally would, with no space between it and the last word, and then add the three ellipsis points—a total of four points in all.

  ```
  According to Time magazine, "the persistent growth of euphemism
  in a language represents a danger to thought and action. . . ."
  ```

- When you omit a sentence or more in the middle of a passage, use four periods. Be sure that you have a complete sentence both before and after the ellipsis points.

  ```
  Faulkner explained in an interview at West Point that "every
  experience of the author affects his writing. . . . He has a
  sort of lumber room in his subconscious that all this goes into,
  and none of it is ever lost."
  ```

Poetry

- When you are quoting more than one line of poetry within a sentence, separate the lines with a virgule, or slash, (/) with a space before and after the virgule.

To substantiate his view, he quoted Blake's lines: "We are led
to believe in a lie / When we see <u>with</u> not <u>through</u> the eye."

- If you are quoting more than three lines of poetry, begin your quotation on a new line, ten spaces from the left margin, and double-space as you would any other quotation.

Ogden Nash is recalled for his witty and sometimes philosophical
poetry:

> I think that I shall never see
> A billboard lovely as a tree.
> Indeed, unless the billboards fall
> I'll never see a tree at all.

However, if the lines are unusually long, you may indent them fewer than ten spaces.
- When a poem has unusual spacing or when some of the lines are indented to follow a pattern, follow the spacing of the original.

In the concluding verse of "Invictus," William Ernest Henley
enunciated his philosophy of self-determination:

> It matters not how strait the gate,
> How charged with punishments the scroll,
> I am the master of my fate:
> I am the captain of my soul.

- Indicate the omission of one or more lines of poetry by typing a line of spaced periods in place of the omitted lines.

In his poem "To a Skylark" Shelley addresses the bird as a
being that knows more than humans:

> Teach us, Sprite or Bird,
> What sweet thoughts are thine:
> . . . .
> Teach me half the gladness
> That thy brain must know.

Acknowledging Your Sources

When to Acknowledge Your Sources

You must give credit in your paper for ideas or information that belongs to someone else, whether you quote it, summarize it, or paraphrase it. Explaining where you got your material is part of the information about your subject that belongs in your paper. It gives readers a chance to judge its reliability and accuracy and also makes it possible for them to look up more about the subject if they want to. Failure to give the source is literary theft or plagiarism. (For suggestions on avoiding plagiarism, see pp. 176–78.)

But give citations only when they are necessary. Every footnote or endnote number or parenthetical citation disturbs the flow of your writing to some extent. The following suggestions will help you determine when you should cite your source. Do not cite your source in the following instances:

1. *Do not cite your source when your information is common knowledge.*

```
Mars was the Roman god of war.

Dwight Eisenhower became president in 1953.
```

Although it may be difficult sometimes to identify what is common knowledge, in most cases you should not have trouble. Any date, like the one given in the example, that can be verified in an encyclopedia, newspaper, or almanac need not be documented, even though many people might not remember it.

2. *Do not cite your source when the information is accepted as true by most people.*

```
Alcoholism impairs the functions of the brain, liver, stomach, and

lungs.
```

This kind of information may be harder to identify. You may be gathering information on a subject you know little about and everything is new to you. In doing research for a paper on drugs, you may read that most former heroin addicts are unable to stay away from heroin permanently. Is this common knowledge among doctors and heroin users? When you aren't sure whether it's common knowledge, and when your readers are people at the same level of knowledge as you who might question the validity of your information or wonder where you got it, you should document it.

3. *Do not cite your source when the statements or observations are your own.*

```
No one should be locked into full-time custodial care when alter-

native means of treatment are available.
```

You should always cite your source in the following instances.

1. *Always cite your source when the information is exclusively the idea or discovery of one person or a group of people.* All direct quotations and most paraphrases and summaries of factual information fit this description.

```
As crime rates rise, more prisoners stay longer in prisons that
are already crammed well past their planned capacity (Jenson
1980).
```

The statement that "more prisoners stay longer" in crowded prisons needs to be documented by citing the person who has the figures to back up this information.

```
In 1981 only 8 percent of architects reported using computers; in
1986, 32 percent of architects are expected to be using computers
in their work ("Computers" 20).
```

You should give the source of any figures unless you compiled them.

2. *Always cite your source when your readers might like to find out more about the subject.*

```
In his "Health Care for All Americans" bill, Senator Kennedy pro-
posed the creation of a comprehensive plan to control health care
expenditures (Riegle).
```

3. *Always cite your source when your readers might question the accuracy or authenticity of the information.* Ask yourself whether your readers are likely to ask "Where did you find that?" or "Who said that?"

```
One species of mammal becomes extinct each year (Ziswiler 17).
```

4. *Always cite your source when you use a direct quotation of one word or more.*

```
In his later years Lowell called Rousseau "a monstrous liar" (Let-
ters 466).
```

How to Acknowledge Your Sources

The documentation within your text can be placed in footnotes or within parentheses; the documentation at the end of your paper will be a list called Works Cited, References, Bibliography, or Endnotes. Your choice of documentation style depends either on your subject or on the preference of the person or organization you are writing for. Check with your instructor to find out what style is required for your paper. The style commonly used by writers in the humanities (English, foreign languages, history, and philosophy) is known as the author/page style and is recommended by the Modern Language Association in the *MLA Handbook* (1988). Chapter 10 gives detailed guidelines for using this system as well as two sample papers illustrating its use.

The author/date system is favored by writers in the social sciences, biology, earth sciences, and business and is recommended in the *Publication Manual of the American Psychological Association* (1983). Details for using this system and a sample paper are given in Chapter 11.

A third major documentation style is the number system, preferred by writers in the applied sciences, medical sciences, and engineering and outlined in the *CBE Style Manual,* published by the Council of Biology Editors (1983). The use of this style is explained and a sample paper is provided in Chapter 12.

These three systems—author/page, author/date, and the number system—recommend that documentation information be given in parentheses within the paper and a list of references be placed at the end. The following guidelines give some of the most frequent uses of these systems. You will find details in Chapters 10, 11, and 12.

Writers in disciplines such as fine arts and political science sometimes use footnotes at the bottom of the page or endnotes following the body along with superscript numbers within the text to refer to the notes. You'll find an explanation of this system together with examples in Appendix 2 (the best-known source of guidelines for this system is the *Chicago Manual of Style* [1982]).

A computer can help you keep track of footnotes and endnotes when you use this system. With the necessary program, your computer will place the correct superscript number in your text when you give the command. Then you can type in your note, either in the text or in a special file. When you are ready, the computer will print the note either at the bottom of the page or at the end of your paper. If you rearrange your notes, your computer will renumber them for you.

While you are writing your first draft, be sure to include sources so that you will know where the material came from when you write your final draft. No matter what citation system you use in your final draft, give at least the author and page number of every summary, paraphrase, or quotation as you write your first draft.

Author/Page System (MLA Style). If you use the author/page system of citation, you need to supply the author's last name and the page number of the work, either in your text sentence or in parentheses. Readers who want to know the name of the work and the publication facts can look those up in the list of works cited at the end of your paper. Place the parenthetical citation as near as possible to the information you are documenting, either where a pause occurs or at the end of the sentence.

When should you put the author's name in your text and when should you put it in parentheses? To decide the answer, consider the needs of your readers. Here are some suggestions.

1. *If the name of the author is a significant part of the information you are giving, give the name in your text, leaving only the page number for your citation.*

According to Van Doren (4), early American fiction writers were often charged with corrupting the public morals.

Here the page number is placed after the name of the author instead of after the information given because a pause occurs after the author's name.

2. *When the information you are giving or the point you are making is more important than the author, place the author's name as well as the page number in the parenthetical citation.*

```
The Alliance adopted the free silver plank in its platform of 1887
(Hicks 132).
```

Note that there is no punctuation between the author and page number and that the period marking the end of the sentence comes after the parenthetical citation.

3. *If you have included more than one work by an author in your list of works cited, you will have to include a brief title in your citation.*

```
As early as 1884, both major parties recognized labor in their
platforms (Destler, American Radicalism 141).
```

4. *If you refer in your text to a whole work, you do not need a parenthetical citation.*

```
In My Ántonia, Willa Cather allows the narrator to overshadow the
heroine.
```

5. *When you have a long quotation set off from the rest of the text, place the citation in parentheses two spaces after the punctuation mark at the end of the quotation.* Indent the quotation ten spaces from the left margin.

```
In The Jungle, Upton Sinclair depicted the horrors of slaughter-
houses in passages like this:
        The fertilizer works of Durham's lay away from the rest
        of the plant.  Few visitors ever saw them, and the few
        who did would come out looking like Dante, of whom the
        peasants declared that he had been into hell.  To this
        part of the yards came all the "tankage," and the waste
        products of all sorts; here they dried out the bones--
        and in suffocating cellars where the daylight never came
        you might see men and women and children bending over
        whirling machines and sawing bits of bone into all sorts
        of shapes, breathing their lungs full of the fine dust.
        (129)
```

In the author/page system, you do not put any documentation in footnotes or endnotes. The only notes you might use are content or explanatory notes to explain a point further or to cite other bibliographic sources. If you use these, you would put them at the end of the paper before the Works Cited section. In the text you would place a super-script numeral—like this[1]—to refer your readers to a note at the end of the paper in a section labeled Notes:

[1] See also Schlesinger (717), who points out that Adams was fascinated with politics throughout his career.

Leave one space between the superscript number and the beginning of the note.

Explanatory or content notes are explained further in Chapter 9; you will find other examples of their use in the sample papers in Chapters 10 and 11.

Author/Date System (APA Style).   For those who use the author/date system (writers in the social sciences, biology, business, economics, linguistics, and earth sciences), the date of the information cited, as well as the name of the author, is important and must appear either in your text or in a parenthetical citation. The list of sources appears at the end of the paper arranged in alphabetical order and usually titled References. A few of the most commonly used citations are given here; you'll find others in Chapter 11, along with a sample paper.

As you would want to do with any of these systems, make sure you introduce your source rather than just giving a quotation or paraphrase with a citation at the end.

1. *If you use the author's name as part of your text, place the date in parentheses following the name.*

Wellington's study (1982) clearly showed that . . .

2. *If the date is important enough to be included in the text, you need no citation unless you are using a direct quotation.* (See number 4.)

Wellington's 1982 study showed that . . .

3. *If the author's name is not significant to your point in the sentence, you can put both the author and date in the parenthetical citation.*

At least one authority (Wellington, 1982) has pointed out that . . .

Note the comma between the author's name and the date.

4. *When you quote directly from someone else's work you* **must** *give a page number.* (Some instructors and some publishers prefer that page numbers be given with each citation.) When the author and the quotation are separated, the date is usually given directly after the name of the author, and the page number follows the quotation.

According to Lowe (1979), prison "should be the last alternative" (p. 14).

Note that the abbreviation "p." is used with the page number in this system.

5. *With a quotation of more than forty words, indent the whole passage five spaces from the left margin.* If there are any paragraphs within the passage, indent the first line of each paragraph five more spaces.

Barlow and Seidner (1983) reported the following results:

> The majority of relationship problems are connected with the phobia. This seemed clearly true in the first client where the relationship was basically very strong. . . . Nevertheless, relationship issues improved considerably as phobia improved. This girl was referred for further therapy concerning interpersonal relationships and career choices following treatment.
>
> The second client, on the other hand, came from a severely disturbed family with constant conflict. The mother held the family together by trying to accommodate everybody but was hospitalized occasionally for periods of amnesia lasting several days during times of particularly intense family stress. (p. 525)

Note the location and punctuation of the page number for a long, indented quotation—two spaces after the final period.

Number System. The number system is used by writers in chemistry, physics, mathematics, medicine, and nursing and by some writers in biology. (A few chemistry journals use the author/date system.) With this system, citations start with 1 and are numbered consecutively throughout the paper. Some writers use a page number with the citation: "1, p. 35." If a reference is repeated, its original number is repeated. Items in the list of references at the end of the paper are given in numerical order.

Some writers use a variation of this system: the list of references is numbered in alphabetical order and, consequently, the numbers in the text are not in serial order. For more details on the use of the number system of citation and a sample paper, see Chapter 12.

A citation using the number system appears this way.

Paroxysmal tachycardia occurs more often in young patients with normal hearts (5).

In a variation of the number system, some writers use both the number and the name of the author(s).

Paroxysmal tachycardia occurs more often in young patients with normal hearts (Krupp and Chatton 5).

Avoiding Plagiarism

Plagiarism is the use of others' words or ideas without attribution (see Chapter 4 for suggestions on avoiding plagiarism while taking notes). The use of summaries, paraphrases, and quotations from others without citing the source is plagiarism; using verbatim quotations without enclosing them in quotation marks is also plagiarism.

Plagiarism results from a writer's failure to integrate information from sources into his or her own thinking. Such failure often originates in inadequate paraphrasing and summarizing during the note-taking process; attempts to shorten the process and write directly from sources can also lead to plagiarism. Besides the academic and legal penalties for plagiarism, one of the most unfortunate results is the writer's loss of the pleasure that comes from discovery of knowledge (plagiarism is evidence of the lack of such discovery) and the subsequent pleasure of telling about it.

Plagiarism is usually recognizable because the borrowed material is written in a different style from that of the author of the paper. Sometimes the borrowed material alternates with the writer's words, and distortion and lack of clarity result. Often terms that were explained earlier in the original are not explained in the paper. Writers involved with their audiences do not write this way. But the writer who uses others' writing instead of his or her own is not concerned primarily with communicating to the reader, and most readers can sense this.

Figure 7.1 is an example of plagiarism in the introduction to a paper. You will find it difficult to understand this passage even though it appears in the beginning of the paper, and you will probably lose interest rather quickly. The plagiarized passages are underlined. Although the writer cites a source, his citation is given only at the end of the last sentence. Therefore, a reader has to conclude that everything but the last sentence is the writer's own. Yet it is obvious that to make such sweeping generalizations about large periods of history, the writer would have had to engage in years of research and would need to produce a book-length work to give the details on which they were based. The scope is beyond a student writer at almost any level. Lack of clarity and coherence are the result of stitching together unexplained generalizations from another writer with a few words of the writer's own.

Plagiarism is a rhetorical as well as an ethical problem. It results from interconnected failures in thinking, note taking, and writing. Here are some suggestions for avoiding plagiarism.

1. Make a schedule when you start work on your paper and follow it as closely as possible. When you find yourself rushing to meet a deadline, it is easy to get careless and save time by using someone else's words.

FIGURE 7.1 Plagiarism

ORIGINAL

The long epoch from the Second Awakening to the war with Spain was also a century of great tribulation, an "ordeal of faith" for church-going America. . . .

On the intellectual level the new challenges were of two sorts. First, there was a set of specific problems that had to be faced separately: Darwin unquestionably became the nineteenth century's Newton, and his theory of evolution through natural selection became the century's cardinal idea. . . . Accompanying these specific problems was a second and more general challenge: the rise of positivistic naturalism, the cumulative result of modern methods for acquiring knowledge. In every discipline from physics to biblical criticism, myth and error were being dispelled, and the result of this activity was a world view which raised problems of the most fundamental sort. (Sydney E. Ahlstrom, *A Religious History of the American People* [New Haven: Yale University Press, 1972], pp. 763–64)

PLAGIARIZED VERSION

The long epoch from the Second Awakening of 1785 and the war with Spain in 1898 was a century of tribulation and ordeal for religious Americans. During this period, but most notably between the years 1865–1900, many intellectual clergymen created a new Liberal Theology built on the tenets of Darwinism and positivistic naturalism, while the unlettered population remained staunchly conservative based on the orthodoxy of the Puritans.

The intellectuals dealt with two challenges, each of them separately. First, there was Darwin, who had become by (1865) the Newton of the nineteenth century, whose theory of natural selection had become the century's cardinal idea.

The second was a more general challenge: the rise of positivistic naturalism, or the cumulative result of modern methods for acquiring information. In every discipline from physics to biblical exegesis, myth and error were being dispelled, and the resulting world view raised fundamental problems concerning faith and the deterministic principles held by the church (Ahlstrom 763–64).

---

2. Choose a topic that you want to learn about and will want to tell others about. If you are genuinely interested in your subject you will want to use your own words to explain it.

3. Make sure you understand the materials you are reading; if you don't understand them, don't use them in your paper. If you don't comprehend your information, you will have to use someone else's words to explain it.

4. Take notes only after you have integrated your reading into your

own thinking. Use paraphrasing and summarizing as much as possible to ensure that the material has become your own.

5. Before you write, review your notes carefully and make sure you understand how and where they will fit into your paper. If you don't see the connection between your information and your overall purpose, it will be difficult for you to use your own words.

6. Avoid writing directly from your sources. It's difficult not to use the words you see right before you.

If you follow these guidelines, it's unlikely that you will find yourself plagiarizing. Even more important, you will have the pleasure of writing a paper that you yourself will enjoy reading.

Writing Your Conclusion

The last questions you answered in your search log as you finished your re-searching were, "What did I learn from my search?" and "What conclusions can I draw from this knowledge?" If your research was successful, your learning will have changed your thinking in some way; you will see things differently. In the conclusion to your paper, record how your thinking has changed. You shouldn't have to strain to find out what these changes are. These changes in your thinking are what your readers would like to know. The examples that follow show how the thinking of the writers changed and how that thinking was recorded in their conclusions. A conclusion may be only a sentence or two, or it may be several paragraphs.

Often the conclusion states or re-states (usually in other words) the paper's thesis. Brian Edwards examined the evidence of global warming and concluded:

> The evidence is clear that the global temperature will rise one or two degrees over the next century. If we do not achieve worldwide cooperation to halt this rise, we risk global devastation.

A conclusion may summarize. In her paper "Two Proposals for a National Insurance," Mary Simione summed up the main differences between two proposals. Notice the detailed summation in the first paragraph followed by a more concise one.

> Senator Kennedy's plan would be more inclusive and comprehensive than President Carter's. Senator Kennedy advocated monitoring the quality of every level of health care while President Carter left the quality of the physician's work virtually uncontrolled. Although the initial cost of Senator Kennedy's plan was higher than President Carter's "Catastrophic Coverage" plan, his "Health Care for All Americans" act offered equal and

quality service to the entire population; the Carter plan just provided supplemental care for the poor and elderly.

Senator Kennedy has worked on restructuring the entire health system; President Carter attempted to solve the problems by guaranteeing care for the portion of the population that doesn't receive it now.

Some papers recommend change. In a paper on prison overcrowding, Linda Thornberry concluded:

> Long-term incarceration is necessary only for a very small percentage of incorrigible criminals. Nonviolent offenders, especially those serving two years or less, are prime candidates for alternatives to imprisonment. The alternatives that exist should be used in order to avoid prison overcrowding as well as to increase the chances of rehabilitation.

A conclusion may evaluate and predict. Joe Collins made a study of gas-saving devices and concluded:

> The vast majority of devices being marketed as mileage improvers are frauds. Because most of them don't work, it is hard for legitimate devices to gain public acceptance. Some devices which could improve mileage can't get to market because they can't conform to some government regulations.
>
> Any significant breakthroughs in mileage will probably come from the auto makers because they are the only ones with enough capital to invest in massive research and development programs. But in these times of trouble for them, even they may not have the funds without government assistance.

A conclusion fits the paper that it was written for. It grows naturally out of what came before it. If you find yourself thinking, "I'm supposed to write a conclusion, but I don't know what to say," take some time to reread your paper and think about it. What is it that you want your readers to know above everything else? What is the main idea that you would like your readers to remember? What thoughts would you like to leave them with? Tell them as clearly as possible.

Writing the Title

You may already have a working title, but after you have written your first draft you may be able to decide on the final version. Your summary or thesis sentence can help you in composing a good title, but it contains more than you need in a title; a thesis sentence includes not only your subject but also what you are going to say about that subject. The title, on the other hand, is not a complete sentence—it doesn't usually have a verb; and it gives only the specific subject of your paper, not your conclusions about that subject.

Mavis Olson's summary sentence was "Companies should consider developing physical fitness programs for their employees." She decided on the title "Developing Physical Fitness Programs in the Workplace.'' The following examples show how thesis statements can become titles:

Thesis sentence: Computer crime can be stopped with expensive security programs.

   Title: Solving the Problem of Computer Crime

Thesis sentence: The Gilded Age shows Mark Twain's cynical attitude toward democracy.

   Title: The Gilded Age: Mark's Twain's Comment on Democracy

Thesis sentence: The adoption agency performs an important service for both the mother and the adopting couple.

   Title: The Role of the Adoption Agency

Thesis sentence: The vast majority of devices being marketed as mileage improvers are frauds.

   Title: Getting Taken for a Ride with Gas-Saving Devices

The title can be imaginative, but use humor or cleverness with care.

Writing an Abstract

An abstract or summary is often placed at the beginning of a paper in the social sciences, in the biological and applied sciences, and in engineering and business. There are two kinds of abstracts, each serving a different purpose: the descriptive abstract tells what a paper *does*; the informative abstract tells what a paper *says*. The descriptive abstract describes what the purpose of the paper is and explains how the purpose is achieved. It talks *about* the paper. The informative abstract, on the other hand, is a summary—a condensed version of the paper. Most papers, however, do not have both kinds of abstracts. If you are asked to write an abstract, be sure you understand what kind it is supposed to be.

An abstract may be a few sentences long (the descriptive abstract is usually short) or it may be several paragraphs long. The informative abstract of a ten- to fifteen-page paper is usually about three-quarters of a page long. It may appear on the title page single-spaced (if it's short), on a separate page at the beginning of the paper, or at the end of the paper.

Descriptive Abstracts.   To write a descriptive abstract, read your outline or table of contents carefully and then convert the outline into cohesive sentences. Notice the following descriptive abstract; it *describes* what is in the paper and gives its basic structure.

This paper analyzes the volunteer program at State Museum and relates volunteer tasks to management functions. Specific areas for improvement are proposed. Finally the role of the volunteer coordinator is discussed, and recommendations are made for improving volunteer performance.

Informative Abstracts. The informative abstract usually starts with the thesis statement or a summary and then gives details. It, too, should follow the outline or table of contents, but it gives the content of the paper as well as its structure. The following informative abstract was included in a paper titled "The Uses of Computers in Architectural Design."

Computers are increasingly being used in architectural practices. The initial cost of the equipment can be as much as one-half million dollars or more, but this expense can be amortized in two to six years depending on the expense of the system and its full integration into the business. Before a computer is installed, the buyer often must remodel to find space to install the system. When the system is installed, there will be a temporary slowdown in productivity; however, once it is integrated into the business, the gains will be evident.

Although many architects are choosing to install a computer system in their business merely to keep up with the competition or to impress clients, most investors find that computer-aided design cuts down on repetitive drawings and therefore increases productivity. Because the computer can produce high quality, accurate drawings, it reduces design problems.

Abstracts make it possible for readers to find out what your paper is about without reading the whole paper. Some readers in business and government read only the abstract. Readers of journals may read the abstract of an article to find out whether they want to read all of it. Margaret Little's paper in Chapter 12 has an informative abstract as part of the paper's front matter.

Designing Illustrations

Are you an artist at heart? Do you think putting pictures on paper is one of your talents? Illustrations (also sometimes referred to as visuals, visual aids, graphics, or graphic aids) are a visual form of communication that anyone can use to clarify meaning. What we can "see" we tend to understand better—literally as well as symbolically. Illustrations can take the form of tables, graphs, charts, diagrams, photographs, maps, or drawings. They are most frequently used in papers in the social sciences, in earth and applied sciences, and in engineering, but they can be helpful additions to any paper. Tables and graphs help you explain quantitative information; drawings and diagrams make hard-to-understand ideas and mechanical systems easier to comprehend. If your paper is in history or geography, you can use maps; if literature is your subject, you may want to use photographs, drawings, or tables; if your paper is on a business topic, you may want to use graphs, organization charts, or flow charts. To decide which of these are appropriate for your paper, look for information that can be quantified or visualized.

Tables

Tables present statistics and other information in a readable, understandable way by organizing them into columns and rows. Short, simple tables that can be read as part of the text need not be numbered or titled. Such *informal tables* also need not be framed with ruled lines nor contain internal ruled lines. In her paper on health care, Mary Simione first wrote the following sentences:

> We are paying more for medical care now than we ever have before. As a percentage of the gross national product (GNP), health expenditures grew from 5.25 percent in 1960, to 8.6 percent in 1975, to 9.1 percent in 1980 (Riegle 96).

She decided that the figures in the second sentence could be compared more easily if they were in table form, so she changed her paper to read:

> We are spending more of our gross national product (GNP) for medical care now than ever before, as the following figures show (Riegle 96):
>
> | | |
> |---|---|
> | GNP 1960 | 5.25% |
> | GNP 1975 | 8.60% |
> | GNP 1980 | 9.10% |

Formal tables, like informal tables, compare data by aligning them in columns and rows. However, formal tables are not part of the text, although they should be placed in the text near the passage that refers to them. They are always numbered and titled. In addition, they often contain more statistics and receive more emphasis through the use of horizontal lines and extra space. Formal tables, like other illustrations can share a page with other text or can occupy a separate page. If you design a table, be sure to label all columns, using parallel grammatical structure, and give the source at the bottom of the table.

Perhaps the easiest way to make a formal table if you don't have a computer system with graphics software is to type it in the form you want it. Then using a ruler with a metal edge, draw the lines with pen and dark ink. To make your lines straight, tape your typed copy to a sheet of graph paper and tape them both to a window (unless you have a drafting table with a light underneath). You will be able to see the graph lines and can easily draw the box lines for your table.

FIGURE 7.2 Preparing a Table

TABLE 1.

Cotton Exports of the United States and the USSR*

in Thousands of Bales

Country of Destination	Exporting Country					
	US 1967/68	USSR 1967	US 1972/73	USSR 1972	US 1978/79	USSR 1978
France	154.9	66.4	151.1	202.0	63.6	443.4
Germany, F. R.	104.0	82.1	188.3	49.3	96.3	111.3
Netherlands	37.4	10.1	48.8	3.2	18.0	23.3
United Kingdom	130.9	68.3	92.9	93.2	72.1	90.3

Data from Cotton and World Situation. Economics, Statistics and Cooperative Service. USDA: August 1980.

*U. S. = crop year; USSR = calendar year

If you find yourself in an artistic mood, you might try creating your lines with charting tape, a product sold under such names as Presto Graphic Tapes or Letraset Transfer Rules at office and art supply stores and most college bookstores. As with the ink-lining process, you should place your typed paper over a sheet of graph paper and tape them both to a window to apply the tape. Trim the tape with a razor blade or an X-Acto knife (worth the small investment if you do several tables). The charting tape and transfer rules, which come in different widths and colors, are especially useful with long or complicated tables. Figure 7.2 shows a table that illustrates the bold effect of lines using charting tape or transfer rules.

If you plan to put your table on part of a page in your text, make the table on a separate sheet of paper; then trim the margins to fit the space where it will go and attach it with paper glue or rubber cement. If your table is very large, you may wish to reduce the size on a photocopy machine before inserting it in your paper. When you use charting tape, photocopy the pages and insert the photocopies in your paper. You want your finished paper to be smooth.

Graphs

Graphs (sometimes called charts) have more pictorial appeal than tables. They frequently show movement—trends or cycles. The three main types are bar graphs, line graphs, and circle or pie graphs. Graph paper, available in different sizes and patterns, makes construction of bar and line graphs relatively simple. After plotting your graph on blue-lined graph paper you can photocopy it, and the blue grid marks will not be visible.

Bar graphs enable readers to compare and understand figures quickly and easily. The bars can be drawn vertically or horizontally. In general, vertical bars are used for altitudes and amounts and horizontal bars for distances, but you do not have to be overly concerned about which type to use as long as you label the items in your graph carefully. If you have graphics capability on your computer, be sure to use it. If not, here are a few guidelines for creating bar graphs.

1. Use a scale that shows your data to their best advantage. You may have to experiment a little to find the best increments. Mark the intervals on graph paper, and then draw your bars.
2. You do not need grid lines on the final graph unless the bars would be so far away from the figures that the amounts would be hard to determine. You need only tick lines on the side to indicate the amounts.
3. Draw bars equidistant from each other, with the width of the spaces less than the width of the bars.

The bars on a bar graph can be grouped; see, for example, the multiple-bar graph in Margaret Little's paper, p. 331.

You can also divide the bars in your bar graph, as Susan Titus did in the segmented-bar graph in Figure 7.3. Bar graphs, like other graphs, can be created on a computer. But they can also be produced by hand. For creating contrasting patterns in multiple- and segmented-bar graphs, use shading films, such as Zipatone, which come in a variety of patterns and colors on adhesive sheets. Lay the film lightly on the area you want to cover and cut it with an X-Acto knife, being careful not to cut the paper underneath. Then separate the film from its backing, lay it over the area to cover, and burnish it so that it firmly adheres. Or, to avoid cutting your paper, photocopy your graph; then lay the film lightly on one copy, cut it to fit, transfer it to its place on the original, and burnish it.

This graph was made for a report on soil contamination. In the first two years of gathering samples, no dioxin (polluting substance) was found. Dioxin increased dramatically in the last year (1984). The patterns add interest to the graph and show the contrasts more clearly.

Line graphs show movement or change, usually over a period of time. The independent variable—or the constant measurement, which in the graph in Figure 7.4 is the time interval—is placed horizontally, along the base of the graph, and the dependent variable—the one subject to change—is placed vertically. Use points to mark the amounts; the line connecting these points draws the eye along, creating a visual sensation

FIGURE 7.3   A Segmented-Bar Graph

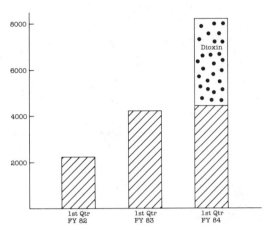

Figure 1. Growth in sample data (in milligrams).

of movement. A line graph can contain two or more lines. For example, Marit Beecroft's graph (Figure 7.4) shows the attendance of all the people in Prince William Park between 1980 and 1990 as a single group only. If the necessary records had been kept by the park service and if she had wanted to show the results, she could have broken down

FIGURE 7.4   A Line Graph

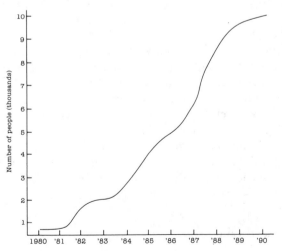

Figure 3. Annual attendance for Prince William Park for the last ten years.

Data from records kept by park rangers.

FIGURE 7.5 Pie Graph Template

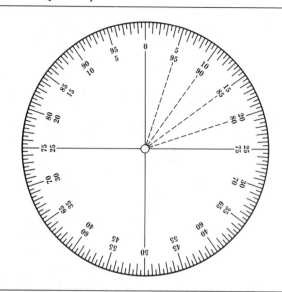

the attendance records into subgroups based on age or any other characteristic. If you use more than one line, you have to distinguish the lines by making them broken, dotted, colored, and so on.

Pie or *circle graphs* are useful if you want to show the relation of parts to a whole. The whole, or 100 percent, is represented by the pie, and each slice is a percentage of the whole. This graph is more limited than the bar graph because it is not effective with more than five or six divisions (you can, however, group several small parts in a single slice and label it ''other'').

To construct a pie graph you will need a compass to draw a circle and a protractor to divide the circumference into segments (3.6 degrees equal 1 percent). Or you can trace Figure 7.5 and use it to find the points on your circumference that correspond to your percentages. Begin at twelve o'clock (at zero on the figure) with the largest segment and proceed around the circle clockwise in descending order of size (unless you have a good reason for using another arrangement, such as maintaining uniformity with related graphs). Label the segments horizontally inside each slice, if there is room. In your labels include percentages and, if desired, the absolute quantity.

Drawings and Diagrams

Even simple drawings can help explain complicated structures and movements. In a paper on the Viking spacecraft, Lee Atkinson included the drawing in Figure 7.6 to show how the moon's gravity was

FIGURE 7.6   A Sample Drawing

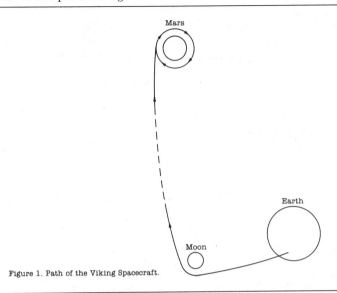

Figure 1. Path of the Viking Spacecraft.

used to direct the spacecraft. The drawing illustrates the route of the spacecraft. First directed toward the moon, the spacecraft was drawn into its gravitational pull, which then directed the craft toward Mars.

Diagrams are more useful than photographs if you want to show only selected details. Peter DeGress drew the diagram shown in Figure 7.7 to demonstrate the placement of a collector in his design for a solar hot-water heating system.

A *flow chart* shows the stages of a process. You can use boxes to enclose the information for each stage, or you can use diagrams or drawings, as you might if you were to show the operation of a machine. The flow chart by Donna Ellis (Figure 7.8) shows the process of developing a telecommunications device, a process she discussed and evaluated in her paper. In making her report, she indicated the steps in the process, starting with "block diagram" and ending with "prototype testing and qualification." The percentages indicate how much time and money has been expended at each stage of the process. When you have completed the circuit design, you are halfway through the process.

Creating Illustrations on the Computer

Computer software is now available to help you create just about any kind of illustration. The computer can be especially helpful in creating the most frequently used types of graphs: bar graphs, line graphs, and pie graphs. If you provide the computer with the percentages and the format, the computer will figure out how long to make the bars in a bar

FIGURE 7.7   A Sample Diagram

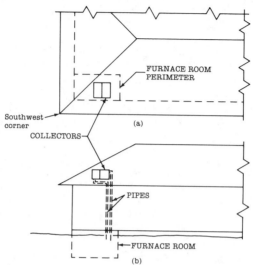

Figure 1. Top (a) and front (b) views of collector placement area.

graph and how to convert percentages into degrees to make a pie graph. It will provide separate shadings or textures. It will draw the lines on a line graph. If your system has color capability, it can even provide you with graphs in color. Figure 7.8 was created on a computer.

As useful as this resource is, the computer operator still has to make the decisions about which kind of graph to use, what order to put the parts in, how to label the parts, and so on. Some software will create standard graphic designs for you. However, use these with care; they may not fit your data.

Making Your Illustrations a Part of Your Text

Think of the illustrations in your paper, not as elements you add as embellishments, but as integral parts of your communication. Introduce and explain your illustrations in your text and then refer your readers to them by number.

U.S. cotton production over the last 45 years shows a continuing shift to the West and Southwest, away from the traditional cotton growing regions of the Delta and the Southeast (see Figure 5, page 3).

FIGURE 7.8 A Flow Chart

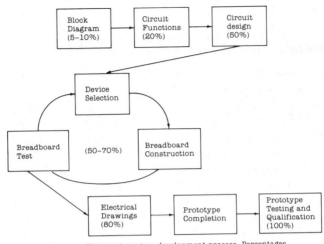

Figure 1.   Electronic system development process. Percentages
indicate the amount of development completed.

Data from P. Korda, RCA Price Operations.

Or make the reference a part of your sentence.

Table 4 shows the dramatic increase in exports of goods from Japan.

If you have three or more illustrations and are using a format with a
table of contents (see Chapter 9), you should have a separate page titled
List of Illustrations in the front matter of your paper, following the table of contents. If all your illustrations are tables, you can title your
page List of Tables; if all are figures, call it List of Figures.

Numbering and Titling Your Illustrations

Illustrations are conventionally classified as either tables or figures.
Number each of these types in a separate series using arabic numerals
(1, 2, 3, and so on). Tables are usually titled at the top. Figures, which
include all other types of illustrations, are usually titled at the bottom
of papers. Give the type of illustration first, then the number and the
title:

Figure 1.   Effects of Energy Sources on Muscle Contraction

The title should clearly describe the contents of your illustration.
Without this guide your readers will have difficulty understanding
what the purpose of the table or figure is. In a paper on evaluating

computers, the title "Comparison of Computers" tells readers little; but "Retail Prices of Eight Popular Personal Computers" gives specific information.

Documenting the Sources of Your Illustrations

Documenting sources of illustrations is more complicated than documenting text sources because illustrations consist of both verbal and visual content. You might, for example, borrow the whole of an illustration or just a part; you might borrow statistics that you then arrange in graphic form; or you might use someone else's drawing but modify it in some way. Consistent and complete guidelines are not always provided in style manuals. The system suggested here is adapted for classroom use from the guidelines formulated by Mary C. Hester, Jacquelyn L. Monday, and John I. Snead in "Documenting Illustrations," *Journal of the Society for Technical Communication*, April 1989.

Placement and Format.   Give your source in parentheses after the title of your illustration. (Some writers prefer to give the source in a separate line below the title or at the bottom of the illustration.) Use the parenthetical documentation system you are using in the text of your paper, unless you are using the number system. If you are using the number system, give an abbreviated form of the source: author, and page number and, if your reference list is not in alphabetical order, give the source number in brackets so your readers can easily locate it:

```
(Data from Kirk, p. 32 [5])
```

Be sure to use the same placement and format throughout your paper.

Guidelines.   The following guidelines provide solutions to the six kinds of documentation needs you are likely to have when you include illustrations in your paper: (1) entirely original illustration, (2) original illustration with borrowed data, (3) photocopy, (4) modified photocopy, (5) copied drawing, and (6) altered drawing. APA documentation style (see Chapter 11) is used in the examples, but you should use the style you use in the rest of your document.

1. ORIGINAL ILLUSTRATION

If the data or verbal information in your illustration is your own and you have created the illustration as well, you need not give any documentation. However, if you like, you can sign your work within the frame of the illustration, or you can credit yourself in the documentation by giving your name or just typing "by the author."

```
Figure 1.  Diagram of Pumping Station (by Timothy McNair).
Figure 1.  Diagram of Pumping Station (by the author).
```

2. ORIGINAL ILLUSTRATION WITH BORROWED DATA

If the data are from another source and you have created the visual framework, write "data from . . ." and give the source.

Figure 1.   Results of Treatment When Patients Control Their Own

Medication for Pain (data from Manson, 1988, p. 24).

3. PHOTOCOPY

If you are using a photocopy without changes, write "reprinted from. . . ."

Figure 1.   The Structure of a Retrovirus (reprinted from Becker,

1986, p. 152).

4. MODIFIED PHOTOCOPY

If you use a photocopy from your source but modify it (if, for example, you photocopy a map but add coloring or shading), write "adapted from. . . ."

Figure 1.   Map of North Carolina Showing Area of Tallulah Falls

Formation (adapted from U.S. Geological Survey, p. 10).

5. HAND-COPIED DRAWING

If you have copied someone else's drawing by hand but have added nothing to it, write "redrawn from. . . ."

Figure 1.   Orbit of Halley's Comet from 1980 to 1988 (redrawn from

Molloy, 1988, p. 42).

6. MODIFIED HAND-COPIED DRAWING

If you have hand-copied a drawing of someone else and have altered it, write "redrawn and adapted from. . . ."

Figure 1.   Highest Known Superconducting Temperatures and the Mate-

rials Used, from 1911 to 1988 (redrawn and adapted from Hanson,

1989, p. 21).

Several kinds of footnote symbols are commonly used in tables and graphs: superscript lowercase leters ([a], [b]), superscript numerals ([1], [2]), and symbols such as asterisks, daggers, and so on. Most style manuals suggest that you use symbols for illustrative material that are different from the ones you use in your text to avoid confusion. Because any symbols you use in your text are likely to be superscript numerals, you would want to use one of the other systems for your table and figure footnotes. The *MLA Handbook* and APA *Manual* recommend superscript lowercase letters; scientific and technical papers show a variety of symbols.

EXERCISES

1. Choosing from the types of introductions given in this chapter, write two different introductions for your paper. Then select the one you like best. Be prepared to explain your choice to your classmates.

2. Write a profile of the person you see as the typical reader of your paper. It should be about a page long and include descriptions of his or her interests, level of education, knowledge of your paper's subject, and any other pertinent information.

3. Make a table from the following information: Maxim Junior College students came last year from three states. But the proportions in the two classes differed. Of first-year students, 28 percent came from North Dakota, 25 percent from South Dakota, and 47 percent from Minnesota. Of second-year students, 17 percent came from North Dakota, 16 percent from South Dakota, and 67 percent from Minnesota.

4. Construct a multiple-bar graph from the information in Exercise 3.

5. Using the information you have collected for your research paper, design a graphic that will explain data more clearly than words do. Look for quantifiable data to make tables and graphs. Look for images that might form the basis of drawings or designs.

6. **FOR PEER RESPONSE**   Using your thesis or summary statement as a source, record in your search log a list of at least three possible titles for your paper. Be thoughtful, but don't avoid putting down whatever comes to mind. These are not your final choices. Discuss your alternatives with other members of your class, perhaps in a group of three or four. Ask for reactions and suggestions for alternatives.

CHAPTER 8

Revising

I have to rewrite everything many, many times just to achieve mediocrity.   —William Gass, novelist

I never reread a text until I have finished the first draft. Otherwise it's too discouraging. Also, when you have the whole thing in front of you for the first time, you've forgotten most of it and see it fresh.
                                                        —Gore Vidal, novelist

I write my first version in longhand (pencil). Then I do a complete revision, also in longhand. . . . Then I type a third draft on yellow paper.
. . . Well, when the yellow draft is finished, I put the manuscript away for a while, a week, a month, sometimes longer. When I take it out again, I read it as coldly as possible, then read it aloud to a friend or two, and decide what changes I want to make and whether or not I want to publish it.   —Truman Capote, novelist and nonfiction writer

I find it easier to discover mistakes or lack of smoothness when I read my paper aloud to myself. That's why I prefer to write and revise my papers when I am all alone. At times I like to read my papers to other people, so I can get an objective opinion about what I have written. It's sometimes easier for another person to hear something wrong than it is for me. When I revise I am constantly crossing out and adding on, so my papers contain a lot of writing in the margins and many arrows.
                                                        —Wendy Cohen, student

Revising is not something that you have to do because you failed to do the first draft properly; it is a natural and necessary part of the writing process. It means revisualizing or reseeing your material. Although the amount of change necessary varies from writer to writer and depends on the nature of the project, sometimes extensive changes are necessary. Figure 8.1, a page from Wendy Cohen's first draft, shows

FIGURE 8.1 Revising the First Draft

Combine with first paragraph on next page

Nearly 600,000 of the nearly 1,000,000 teenage females who become

pregnant each year elect to complete their pregnancies. / Teenage

pregnancy ~~is on the uprise~~ *has been on the rise* since the 1960s and currently ~~results~~ *occurs* in

1/10 of the entire population of teen women each year. ~~These women~~

~~are at high risk of death because of their pregnancy and its com-~~

~~plications than women between 20-35.~~ Adolescents ~~under the age of~~ *15 and older*

14 are in danger from complications related to pregnancy ~~and its~~ *and at higher*

risk of death ~~complications~~ than women between *the ages of* 20-35. ~~Women between 15 and 19~~ *and*

~~die 35 percent more frequently than mothers in their early twenties~~

~~because of complications.~~ *Pregnant* Teenage women ~~who undergo pregnancy~~ *also*

deliver low weight babies twice as often as women in their twenties,

and ~~experience infant death~~ *their babies die* nearly twice as often as *babies of* mothers in

their twenties.

part of her revising process. She changed the order, combined and reworded sentences, and added more material. Sometimes revising requires more changes; sometimes, fewer.

All writers develop their own strategies at each stage of the revising process. Students, like professional writers, need to find out what works best for them as well as what does not. "I've always done it this way" doesn't mean that "this way" is the best. Even though you want to produce the best possible paper, you also want to learn a process that you can use for any paper. Trading information on revising practices with your classmates is a good way to pick up ideas that you might want to try.

Preparing to Revise

As you already know from revising short papers, revising can mean that an idea that was only partially developed in an early draft becomes clear; it can mean that new ways of thinking about your subject occur to you; it can mean that you refocus your topic. If you have allowed yourself an incubation period (as suggested in Chapter 7), your mind has unconsciously been at work on your paper. Revising, then, is not so much a matter of correcting what you have already written as it is a second stage of the writing process. If you leave wide margins and keep two or three spaces between the lines, you will be able to rearrange words and sentences easily. If you want to add a whole paragraph, or even a whole page, you can put it after the appropriate page and number it by adding a letter to the page number; for example, the page after page 2 would be page 2a. Make a note on your manuscript to show where page 2a is to be added when you recopy. Or if you want to take a paragraph out and insert it somewhere else, you can cut it out and place it where you want it, using transparent tape or staples. Some people like to use different colored paper for each draft so that they don't confuse one draft with another. You can use colored mimeograph paper, which is inexpensive, for separate drafts; or you can use plain white paper for one draft and yellow paper for another.

Revising with a Computer

Revising, or any stage of writing, is physically easier with the use of a computer or word processor. You can easily move parts of a manuscript from one place to another or omit them altogether by pressing a few keys. Such physical ease also benefits writers psychologically; all of us tend to do more of whatever is easier to do. In the revising process, computers are most helpful with the later stages of editing. Software is available to count the number of words in your sentences and to point out such structures as passive verbs and trite phrases, but only you can decide whether the changes are necessary. Availability of software varies according to the brand and type of computer you are using, but most computers can use programs to help you find spelling and typing errors.

When planning your revision with a word processor, print a copy of your paper before you start so that you can see more of your manuscript at one time. You can also make notes on your hard copy, or you can even cut and rearrange parts as you would with hand- or typewritten copy before you begin revising the file on your disk.

Following a Plan

Because you are re-viewing your entire paper, it's a good idea to make a plan for revision that focuses first on large elements—the paper's faithfulness to its purpose and to its organization—and then on smaller parts of the paper—paragraphs, sentences, individual words, and documentation. Too much early concern with the structure of sentences and the choice of words can waste your time if the paragraphs containing them are eventually enlarged, shortened, or eliminated altogether.

First Revising Stage:
Focusing on the Whole Paper

Listening to Your Paper

If possible, read your paper twice—once aloud and once silently. If you've written your paper on a computer, work from a printed copy. The first time you read it (or have someone read it to you), assume the role of your audience. Read the title first, as though you were hearing it for the first time, and then read your paper straight through. Just listen to the sound of it and make mental notes of your reactions. You can make notes on paper, too, but you don't want to be distracted right now with details. Do you have enough information? Do you have too much? Is the line of argument clear? Do you find yourself hesitating or stumbling over words or phrases? (These may be places that are difficult to understand.) Does the paper move clearly from one subject to the next and from one paragraph to the next, or do you find yourself trying to figure out your own meaning? Does the tone sound appropriate for the audience and is it consistently maintained? After hearing your paper, make a note of any changes you might want to make or any places that seemed unclear. You may not want to make these changes, however, until you have completed the second, silent, reading of your paper.

Making an Outline

Now read your paper once more, this time with a pad of paper and pen or pencil in hand, or work on a split screen on your computer. First read your thesis statement or summary sentence so that you have it clearly in mind as you start. Then read one paragraph at a time, and in a few words summarize what each one says. (As an alternative, you can write a summary sentence of each paragraph.) When you finish you will have a rough outline, which you can check against your original outline to see whether it corresponds. Where you find discrepancies, you may be able to see the reasons immediately and make the necessary changes. But it's a good idea to consciously check your paper for each of the following characteristics of a good paper to make sure that your paper contains them.

Check Your Paper's Unity.   Your paper has unity when everything in it is included in your thesis or summary statement. It has unity when every idea in your outline fits within your thesis statement. If you find in your outline something outside the scope of your original concept, you will have to either broaden your topic or eliminate the ideas that don't fit. If your summary statement is "Sex education programs in the schools have benefited teenage students," your outline should show only those benefits. However, if according to your outline, you have included some negative results and some needed improvements, you have more in your paper than you planned for. If you want to keep the negative results but show overall benefits, you should reword your summary statement to read: "Although sex education programs in the schools need some improvement, they have already resulted in important benefits to teenagers."

Check Your Paper's Organization. Make sure the order of your outline is logical. Try to identify the order: Have you used chronological order? Comparison and contrast? Order of importance? Order of size (large to small or small to large)? Or have you proceeded from problems to solutions? From causes to effects? From the general to the specific? Other kinds of order are possible, as well as combinations. After identifying the order you have used, make sure you have followed it throughout your paper. Also check the order of subheadings. If your summary sentence is "Although sex education in schools needs improvement, it has already resulted in substantial benefits for teenagers," you may have the following main headings:

Benefits of sex education in schools
    Reduction of the number of teenage pregnancies
    Other benefits
Some problems of sex education programs
Suggested reforms of current sex education programs

You have to decide whether this is the best order. You have three main topics: benefits, problems, and reforms. If benefits are most important, as indicated by the fact that you put them in your main clause in your summary statement, then you have a most-to-least-important organization. You also have chronological order: you start with current benefits, move to analysis of problems, and then suggest what can be done in the future.

Check Your Paper's Reasoning. Does everything in your paper support your thesis or your claim? Analyze your paper according to the Toulmin model for analyzing arguments (see Chapter 6). Have you adequate grounds for your claim? What warrants do you base your grounds on? Are they shared by your readers? If you are arguing, as one student did, that "the courts have been inconsistent in their decisions on cases involving affirmative action," you would have to cite the court cases, and possibly the statistics on the number of such cases, to prove your statement. One of your warrants would be that affirmative action is a desirable goal.

Check Your Paper's Coherence.   The links between points in your outline should be clear; the reader shouldn't be surprised when you shift to another subject. Such shifts or transitions are often prominently marked by the repetition of key words; by the use of transitional words such as *therefore, however, before,* and *for example;* or by the use of headings. Sometimes, however, transitions are more subtle; a time sequence, for example, may be enough to provide coherence between parts. Sometimes the visual break itself between sections or paragraphs is sufficient. If you add transitional words or phrases just because you think you should, rather than because logic or sense demands them, you may tell your readers what they already know. A common example is the use of *In conclusion* at the beginning of a concluding paragraph that obviously sums up what you have said. Putting yourself in the place of your readers will help you to discover where coherence is lacking.

First-Stage Revising Process: Student Examples

Wendy Cohen's Process: Limiting the Scope of the Paper.   Wendy Cohen started with what seemed to be a manageable topic: the care of pregnant women. After doing some preliminary reading, she had five main headings to help her direct her research:

1. Misconceptions and myths about pregnancy
2. Day-to-day care
3. Common problems
4. Problems of high-risk pregnant women
5. Diseases of pregnancy

She read eagerly and extensively because she was very interested in her subject. When she reached her deadline for ending her search for information, she knew she had a lot of material, but she didn't realize how much until she began to write it down. When she finished, she had more than seventy handwritten pages. Because she knew that revision in itself would be a sizable job, she decided that she could not meet her deadline unless she limited the scope of her paper.

First, Cohen made a detailed outline—a map to see where she was. Under "Day-to-day care" she listed "Nutrition, Effect of emotional health, Work, Sleep, Sex, Exercise, Clothing, and Travel." Under "Diseases of pregnancy," she listed "Rubella, Syphilis, Herpes, Gonorrhea, Rh disease, Diabetes, and Anemia." She seemed to be on her way to writing a book, but she didn't have time to write one. Obviously, she had to leave out something, but she didn't know what. In fact, she didn't really want to leave out anything; she wanted all the work she had done to show up on the pages of her paper. But Cohen finally decided to be realistic and limit her paper to the parts of her subject that she was most interested in—that is, to the care of women who were most likely to have problems in pregnancy and the diseases that caused some of those problems. She excluded the first three headings in her first outline. This was the final outline of her paper:

I. The importance of the prenatal period to mother and child [the introduction]
II. The risks of teenage pregnancy
III. The risks of pregnancy for women over 35 years of age
IV. The dangers of disease during pregnancy
   A. Rubella
   B. Toxemia—preeclampsia
   C. Rh disease
   D. Venereal disease
V. Recommended uses of drugs and vaccines in high-risk pregnancies

Cohen was now ready to write a second draft based on this outline. Because she had done so much research on her subject and knew it so well, she was able to write her second draft easily and confidently. By revising each section as she went along, she was able to complete her paper in three complete drafts—the minimum number for most writers.

Martha Cross's Process: Shaping and Focusing the Paper. Martha Cross wrote a paper on the criminal justice system. Her summary sentence was "The criminal justice system—consisting of law enforcement, judicial process, and corrections—does not adequately control crime." This was her working outline:

I. Law enforcement
II. The judicial process
   A. Attorneys
   B. Courts
III. Corrections
IV. Evaluation

After completing the first draft of her paper, she reread it paragraph by paragraph and made the following informal outline:

I. The police department
   A. Lack of emphasis on law enforcement
   B. Lack of sufficient staff and budget
II. The adversary system
   A. Use of inexperienced public defenders
   B. The greed of private lawyers

III. The courts
   A. Delayed hearings
   B. Inequities in sentencing
   C. Full dockets
   D. Overuse of plea-bargaining
IV. Correctional systems
   A. Overcrowded prisons
   B. Lack of sufficient staffing
   C. Lack of meaningful work
   D. Denial of simple amenities in order to punish
V. Lack of help for victims
VI. Evaluation and solutions

With her new outline in hand, she checked her paper for the following characteristics.

Unity. Here she noticed a problem. Heading V, "Lack of help for victims," did not fit into her summary statement. Her concern for victims had developed as she wrote her paper. At the beginning she had written:

> According to James Campbell, criminal justice means "effectively control-ling the increasing levels of deviant behavior in a manner consistent with our ideas of fair and humane treatment" (11). As a crime-controlling agent, our current criminal justice system does not work.

However, near the end of the paper she had written:

> Protection of victims should be a main concern of the justice system. Crim-inals have more rights than the victims. That is not justice! The offenders should pay restitution to the victims. The victims are the neglected ones, not the criminals.

Cross found that she had shifted the focus of her topic as she wrote—a common occurrence in writing a first draft. In the beginning she was writing about justice for criminals, and at the end she was writing about justice for victims. She had to decide whether she wanted to broaden the focus of her paper to include justice for both criminals and victims or to leave out an issue she felt strongly about—the rights of victims. Before making this decision, she thought she would wait until she had checked *all* four points.

Organization. Cross next checked the organization of her paper. It fol-lowed the chronological order of handling criminal cases—arrest, trial, and imprisonment. Each point she made fit into this order, except for one—"Overuse of plea-bargaining" under heading III. She began her discussion of plea-bargaining with this sentence: "The prosecuting and defense attorneys should not use plea-bargaining as freely as they do." Obviously she needed to move this idea to the section on the adversary system.

Reasoning. The issue of reasoning coincided with her unity problem. Her statement "Criminals have more rights than victims" was vehement and heartfelt, but she had given no evidence to prove it. In fact, she realized she would have trouble proving such a sweeping generalization. To add more details here would require more research and would change the whole focus of her paper; she would have to leave out much of what she had already written. Reluctantly, she decided to stay with the original design of her paper and leave out the section on lack of help for victims.

Coherence. Transitions occur between all elements of a paper—between sections, between paragraphs, and between sentences. Cross was looking now for transitions between sections. She had three major transition points: (a) between number I, "The police department," and number II, "The adversary system"; (b) between number II, "The adversary system," and number III, "The courts"; and (c) between number III, "The courts," and number IV, "Correctional systems." Major divisions of a paper are often like minipapers; hence, you can achieve a transitional effect by indicating the completion of the discussion of one subject and by using wording that looks forward to the next section or paragraph. Or the new section can look back by using a word or phrase that connects the two and shows their relationship.

Cross looked at her transitional sentences. This is the way sections II and III began (the transitional words are italicized):

The adversary system *also* needs to be modified.

The courts are *also* in need of radical changes.

In addition, she used the word *also* as a transitional word within sections: "The judges *also* create inequities within the court system." The transition to section IV had no transitional words at all:

There are many faults with the current system of corrections.

Obviously her transitions needed some attention. She needed some variety in her transitional words as well as different language to show the relationships between these sections. She changed the transition between sections II and III to the following sentence:

Although improvement in the adversary system would help to improve the justice system, changes in the courts are needed even more.

Then Cross rewrote the transition between sections III and IV (between the courts and correctional systems) in this way:

If these suggestions were followed, the improvement within the judicial process would be noticed within a year.

Thus she ended the section on the judicial process with an evaluation and a recommendation. The beginning of the section on correctional systems looked back at the first two sections and then focused on its own theme—corrections:

> However, the problems within police departments and the judicial process seem relatively easy to solve when compared with the problems of changing the offenders.

She was now ready for the second stage of revising.

Second Revising Stage:
Focusing on Parts of the Paper

Checking Paragraphs

Read each paragraph in your paper to make sure it is integrated, unified, complete, and coherent. The following examples show how students have rewritten paragraphs to improve them.

Improve Integration of Sources. Whether you summarize, paraphrase, quote, or use your own ideas, your writing should flow as though it came from one source—you. Your writing will be integrated if you make the information you collect part of your thinking rather than just copy from cards or articles. Here is a passage from the first draft of a paper on alcoholism.

> Studies have shown that family behavior patterns are often important in the transmission of alcoholism from parent to child. Some of these patterns are parental conflict about drinking, parental disagreement about drinking practices, and parental abuse of alcohol (3, p. 42). Scientists have claimed that problem drinking among males can be predicted just by looking at their age, socioeconomic class, ethnic origin, and religious affiliation (4, p. 163).

In rereading his paper, the writer noticed that the sentence beginning "Scientists have claimed" moved away from the subject of family behavior patterns and even contradicted what he had written in the first two sentences about family patterns as a primary cause of alcoholism. He had gotten the information for the first two sentences from one source and the information for the last sentence from another, and he hadn't integrated them. He rewrote the paragraph to show the relationship between these ideas and to clarify them. He also combined the first two sentences, with this result:

> In transmitting alcoholism from parent to child, such familial behavior patterns as parental conflict about drinking, parental disagreement about drinking practices, and parental abuse of alcohol have been important (3, p. 42). However, some scientists believe that alcoholism is more of a so-

cial phenomenon and claim to be able to predict problem drinking among males just by looking at their age, socioeconomic class, ethnic origin, and religious affiliation (4, p. 163).

Keep the Paragraph Unified.   The writer of a paragraph makes a promise to readers to explain something. Usually this promise is made in the first sentence (often called a *topic sentence*). Readers expect that everything in the paragraph will help to carry out the promise so that the paragraph will be unified. When the writer fails, readers are disappointed and confused. The following paragraph makes a clear promise but doesn't keep it.

> The real task for the black community and society as a whole is to develop incentives that will be more attractive to teenagers than having babies. Many people feel that teaching their child to say ''no'' to sex is the solution to the problem, but it is not. Saying ''no'' is an important part of solving the problem but not the solution in itself. According to Noel, parents must help teenage girls develop more self-confidence and improve their ability to make their own decisions (92). If they learn these skills, they are not so likely to succumb to peer pressure, not only in sexual matters but in other areas of their lives. Dr. Marion Howard, director of a teen services program, recommends the following guidelines for parents (Noel 94):
>
> Learn to listen.
> Try to avoid judging the child.
> [Etc.]

This paragraph promises to talk about the responsibility of society in dealing with the problem of teenage pregnancy. But it shifts to the problem of peer pressure and suggests ways for parents to help their child make decisions. The subject of this paragraph is really how improvement in the relationship between parents and child can help the child withstand the peer pressure that leads to pregnancy. This writer rewrote the beginning of the paragraph to make the promise match the content.

> As part of the solution to the problem of teenage pregnancy, professionals have suggested educating the parents so that they can communicate better with their children (Noel 92). Many parents feel that teaching their child to say ''no'' to sex is the solution to the problem; but, although saying ''no'' is part of the solution, it is not the solution itself. According to Noel, parents must help teen-age girls develop more self-confidence and improve their ability to make their own decisions (92). If they learn these skills, they are not so likely to succumb to peer pressure, not only in sexual matters but in other areas of their lives. Dr. Marion Howard, director of a teen services program, recommends the following guidelines for parents (Noel 94):
>
> Learn to listen.
> Try to avoid judging the child.
> [Etc.]

Now the paragaph is unified around the idea of what parents can do about this problem.

Sometimes the writer introduces an irrelevant idea into the middle of a paragraph.

> Since most of a prisoner's complaints are aired in prison disciplinary hearings, the organization of such hearings is interesting to examine. *In a correctional institution, administrators normally have several forms of enforcing discipline, such as the withdrawal of privileges afforded the average inmate. More severe discipline such as isolated confinement can be instituted for serious offenses.* In 1973 the Supreme Court determined that the state must provide twenty-four hours' written notice of charges, that prisoners have the right to call witnesses, and that an impartial body be chosen to consider the case. But prisoners are not allowed to cross-examine witnesses and there is no provision for legal counsel.

The italicized sentences introducing the idea of how administrators enforce discipline do not belong in this paragraph, which is about the organization of disciplinary hearings. The reasons for calling such hearings should be discussed in an earlier paragraph.

Include Enough Information. If a paragraph leaves unanswered questions in readers' minds, more information is probably needed. The first draft of a paper on subliminal advertising contained the following paragraph:

> As a result of Vance Packard's book *The Hidden Persuaders,* six state legislatures and the U.S. House of Representatives introduced legislation to ban subliminal techniques. In the 1960s, public discussion on the subject virtually disappeared; the proposed legislation was never enacted.

It was not the book but what Packard said in his book that led to the legislation. Readers are likely to wonder what that was. The writer rewrote the paragraph this way:

> As a result of Vance Packard's accusations in *The Hidden Persuaders* that advertisers practice the "psychoseduction" of consumers and "play on our subconscious," six state legislatures and the U.S. House of Representatives considered legislative action to ban subliminal techniques. . . .

Make the Paragraph Coherent. When a paragraph has coherence, each sentence fulfills the promise of the preceding sentence and in turn predicts what will follow. Thus each sentence is a link in the chain of sentences that forms the paragraph. This linkage allows readers to understand you easily and quickly. But when you set up readers' expectations and then don't fulfill them, the result is confusion. Readers may be able to sort out the order, but it will take some time. And they shouldn't have to do your job. A paragraph is like a conversation between the writer and readers, with the readers making mental responses or asking questions after each sentence and the writer setting up those responses or questions and then answering them.

In the following coherent paragraph, the reader's mental response is given in brackets so that you can see how each sentence satisfies the issue raised in the previous one:

> The main reason for the computer industry's vulnerability to microcomputer-assisted crime is that businesses do not want to spend money. [Reader: How does that encourage crime?] The necessary precautions are not being taken for a system whose usefulness relies heavily on security. [Reader: What precautions are not taken?] Businesses must have auditing systems so that they will know who is using their system. [What else?] They must keep back-up files to replace those that are erased and altered. [Anything else?] Finally, they must be willing to prosecute computer criminals, instead of refusing for fear of bad publicity. [The word *finally* signals the end of the paragraph.]

Because the expectation set up by each sentence is fulfilled by the succeeding sentence, readers can read the paragraph quickly, without confusion.

Checking Sentences and Words

Computer Editing Programs.   A number of computer programs are available to help you revise your paper. They can help you find such problems as use of linking verbs or passive voice, repetition of words or phrases, redundant expressions, and clichés. They can count the number of words in sentences; if you find too many short sentences or too many long ones, you can rewrite some of them. Computers can help you find errors in spelling, capitalization, and punctuation. But the computer has limitations; *you* have to decide whether to make any changes. Passive voice and linking verbs are frequently useful; and the computer can't distinguish words that are spelled correctly but are inappropriate in context such as *affect* for *effect* or *their* for *they're*. Still, these programs can be helpful.

Even if you don't use a computer, you should read your paper once again, focusing on the sound and meaning of the sentences. When a sentence seems unclear or when it does not flow easily and naturally, you may be able to see the problem immediately and correct it. But if you have trouble identifying the source of the difficulty, the following suggestions will help you improve your writing.

You'll notice that your sentences may need attention in more than one place because a breakdown in one place often causes breakdowns in others. A sentence with major problems needs more than the change of a word of two; it needs complete rewriting. Sometimes, too, your sentences may be free of errors but still need improvement.

The following suggestions show how you can improve the strength, unity, and coherence of your sentences by using strong verbs, by struc-

turing your sentences for emphasis and clarity, and by eliminating unnecessary words.

Use Strong Verbs. Writing conveys the energy of the writer, just as
the voice conveys the energy of a speaker. And, just as you soon find
your mind wandering from the words of a speaker who is dull or monotonous, you soon lose interest in reading sentences that lack vitality
and strength.

Verbs generate energy for your sentences and give your sentences
the life that keeps your readers reading. If you use too many weak
verbs, such as verbs in the passive voice (*was written*) or linking verbs
(forms of the verb *to be* such as *is, are, was,* and *were*), you make your
writing lifeless and dull. You can use a computer program to find such
verbs for you, but you still have to decide whether they are the best
choices. In general, you should use the passive voice only when the re-
ceiver of the action is more important than the doer or when you don't
know who the doer is. Linking verbs are useful, of course, but avoid
overusing them. The following examples show problem sentences that
students found in their papers, along with analyses and revised versions.

> **FIRST VERSION:** A decision was made by the president to begin the bomb-
> ing at once.

> **REVISION:** The president decided to begin the bombing at once.

Was made is in the passive voice. The real action in the sentence has
been weakened by putting it in the form of a noun—*decision*. To improve this sentence, the writer put the main action of the sentence into
a verb form—*decide*.

> **FIRST VERSION:** The adversary system is in need of improvement.

> **REVISION:** The adversary system needs improvement.

The linking verb *is* undermines the vitality of this sentence. The use
of the noun *need* instead of the verb form further weakens the sentence.

Revise Sentences That Are Too Long. The meaning of your sentences is conveyed partly by their structure. A sentence that is too long
can get monotonous and fail to emphasize anything. But counting the
number of words in a sentence won't tell you whether a sentence is too
long. A sentence is too long when it lacks a central, emphatic idea or
when the connections between words become so unclear that readers
can't follow the meaning to the end.

1. One remedy for a long, unwieldy sentence is to divide it, as the
following example shows.

> **FIRST VERSION:** According to Alvin Bronstein, the executive director of
> the ACLU's National Prison Project, "prisons were instituted in a Jackso-

nian hope that human improvement was possible if a criminal's unfortunate upbringing could be overcome in an antiseptic and healthy setting,'' but obviously today's prisons do not meet such standards.

REVISION: According to Alvin Bronstein, the executive director of the ACLU's National Prison Project, ''prisons were instituted in a Jacksonian hope that human improvement was possible if a criminal's unfortunate upbringing could be overcome in an antiseptic and healthy setting'' (19). Obviously today's prisons do not meet such standards.

None of the ideas in the first version stands out. To emphasize the last part of the sentence, the writer put it into a short simple sentence of its own. The contrast with the longer preceding sentence makes both sentences more effective.

2. Another remedy for a long sentence is to shorten it.

FIRST VERSION: Probably the greatest incentive that could lead the Soviets into a decision to invade the Gulf would be that it would be an ideal place from which to project power since currently their greatest logistical constraint is that they lack a warm water port, and the Middle East leads to everywhere in the world as the term used to describe it—''historical bridge between East and West''—implies.

REVISION: The Soviets might decide to invade Iran because such a move would give them a warm water port and a base of power in the Middle East—an area Kingston has called the ''historical bridge between East and West.''

In the first version the subordinate clauses follow one another (''that could lead . . . ,'' ''that it would be . . . ,'' ''that they lack . . . ,'') making it difficult for readers to keep track of the connections. Readers may lose interest. The verbs *could be* and *is* are weak. The writer found the main action word (the noun *decision*) and made it into the main verb of the sentence. The addition of the *because* clause shows the relationship of the other ideas to the main clause.

Combine Short Sentences by Using Subordination. A short, simple sentence is emphatic; it highlights one idea. When you have too many short sentences together, you are telling your readers that all the ideas in them are of equal importance. You are failing to show readers the relative importance of ideas and the relationships between those ideas, thus leaving them to figure out the relationships on their own. In addition, groups of short sentences usually repeat the same pattern (subject, verb, object) and repeat words, especially pronouns. Although, with care, use of one or two short sentences can be effective, too many of them make your writing monotonous and lifeless. Signs of sentences that might be improved by combining are successive short sentences, sentences that repeat words, and sentences that begin with pronouns. Notice the repetition of the same word (or a pronoun that refers to that word) at the beginning of each of the following sentences.

FIRST VERSION: The first law was known as the "28-hour law." It protected livestock shipped by rail. It stated that cattle had to be exercised in pens if their journey was to be longer than twenty-eight hours.

REVISION: The first law, passed in 1906 and known as the "28-hour law," required that livestock be shipped by rail and that they be exercised in pens if their trip was longer than 28 hours.

In the first version the word *law* and the pronoun *it* referring to *law* begin each sentence. In his revision the writer put the ideas he believed to be less important into subordinate (less important) structures. His revision is clearer and stronger.

Use Coordination to Show Equal Relationships.   Sometimes you want to show the equality of ideas; you want to coordinate rather than subordinate ideas. Joining two or three clauses of the same kind can be effective, as the following example illustrates.

FIRST VERSION: Many people believe that a child's sexual values develop slowly from observation, imitation, and guidance at home. Teaching sex education in school would only be a waste of time and energy because attitudes, values, and outlooks are already established at home.

REVISION: Many people believe that a child's sexual values develop slowly from observation, imitation, and guidance at home and that teaching sex education in school would only be a waste of time and money.

In the first version, some of the ideas in the two sentences are almost the same, so some can be eliminated. Since it seems clear that the second sentence is also part of what "many people feel," the writer combined and coordinated them.

Use Parallelism for Emphasis.   Parallelism is a form of coordination that uses repetition of structures and often words for emphasis. The writer sets up a pattern that gains its effectiveness from building to a climax, like Lincoln's conclusion to the Gettysburg Address: "that government of the people, by the people, and for the people, shall not perish from the earth." Here three prepositional phrases are linked and the word *people* is repeated. In Julius Caesar's famous statement about conquering Gaul (France)—"I came, I saw, I conquered"— three short clauses beginning with *I* build from the simple "I came" to the strong "I conquered." Use parallelism to create such emphasis when you can.

Problems can arise when you set up the pattern and do not follow it through. You must continue with the structure you started with (such as prepositional phrase, subordinate clause, noun, or adjective) and you must repeat the word, when there is one, that signals the parallelism. These structures are usually joined with coordinating conjunctions such as *and* or *but*. The examples show how a sentence can be strengthened by parallelism and how to remedy faulty parallelism.

FIRST VERSION: In the remedial reading clinic he learned how to coordinate his eye movements, how to scan for information, and how frequent reviewing for key ideas helps.

REVISION: In the remedial reading clinic he learned how to coordinate his eye movements, how to scan for information, and how to review for key ideas.

In the first version, *how* is repeated, but the pattern is the repetition of *how to*. The revision changes the final *how* clause to a clause beginning with *how to*.

FIRST VERSION: Other advantages [of the aircraft] include day or night operation in all types of weather, continued operation for 11 hours and twice as long if refueled in flight, and if systems malfunction, its computer switches all operations to back-up computer circuits.

REVISION: The aircraft can also operate in all types of weather, can fly for 11 hours (twice as long if refueled in flight), and, if systems malfunction, can switch to back-up computer circuits.

A long, complicated sentence like the first version needs the clarifying force of parallelism. First notice the use of a noun (*operation*) instead of a verb to carry the action in the first two elements and the use of a weak verb, *include*. In revising, the writer used strong verbs (*operate*, *fly*, *switch*). This example lends itself to more than one solution; the writer's choice depends to a great extent on what comes before and after this sentence.

Eliminate Unnecessary Words. Make every word count. When you add unnecessary words, you make your readers, who have to read them and disregard them, do your work for you.

FIRST VERSION: This illustration shows the financial impact with respect to FY83 salaries.

REVISION: This illustration shows the financial impact of FY83 salaries.

With respect to is one of many phrases, such as *with regard to* and *at this point in time* that can be shortened to one or two words.

Avoid Needless Repetition of Words. You can repeat words effectively for emphasis, but when you don't want to emphasize, the repetition is irritating. Needless repetition of words in successive sentences usually means that the sentences can be combined.

FIRST VERSION: They have fur which is a dense coat of underfur covered by longer guard hairs. This fur is shiny and varies in color from black to dark brown but may also have white-tipped hairs scattered throughout.

REVISION: Their dense, shiny coat of underfur, covered by longer guard hairs, varies from black to dark brown with scattered white-tipped hairs.

In the first version, the words *fur* and *is* are repeated; also the main verbs (*is*) are weak linking verbs. Notice also the unneeded phrase *in color.* If you read these sentences aloud, you will hear their deadness. In her revision the writer located the subject of the sentences and the main action word and then built a sentence around them. The subject is *coat of underfur,* and the main action word is *varies.* These form the core of the revised sentence.

Avoid Using Jargon.   Jargon is the language of a particular group, usually a professional group. Doctors, lawyers, teachers, computer programmers, truck drivers, musicians, and baseball players all use jargon among themselves. Jargon is the shorthand that makes it possible for the members of these groups to communicate more easily with each other. But jargon is also a way to show who belongs to the group and who doesn't. In the effort to prove membership, writers often use awkward constructions and unclear language. Overuse of the passive voice and linking verbs is common. Student writers can easily pick up this jargon as they read the sources used in writing their papers. In your paper you should use specialized terms only when clarity demands that you do, not to show that you know the language of a certain group. Now is the time to change any jargon you have used to plain English, as the following example illustrates.

FIRST VERSION: Similar experiments to those performed on nonhumans have yielded congruent results with humans.

REVISION: Experiments similar to those performed on nonhumans have shown the same results with humans.

The writer simplified the phrase *have yielded congruent results.*

Correcting Faulty Connections

Just as sections of your paper and paragraphs must be coherent, the parts of a sentence must be clearly connected. Each word in a sentence must link up with some word or words so that the sentence will read smoothly and make sense. The basic linkage is between subject and predicate or verb. Secondary linkages are between nouns and verbs, adjectives and nouns, and pronouns and nouns. Making these links correctly helps your readers understand your sentences more easily.

Make Subjects and Verbs Agree in Number.   The subject determines whether a verb is singular or plural. Most writers don't have trouble when the subject and verb are next to each other (*Jack is my brother*), but when the subject and verb are separated by a phrase or clause, it's easy to lose track.

FIRST VERSION: Many experts believe that specific *instructions* to prepare youngsters for the many responsibilities of marriage *is* now needed more than ever before.

REVISION: Many experts believe that specific *instructions* to prepare youngsters for the responsibilities of marriage *are* now needed more than ever before.

In the first version, the subject *instructions* is separated from the verb *is* by several words; although the word *marriage* comes immediately before the verb, the writer had to find the real subject and make the verb agree.

Connect Participles with Nouns or Pronouns.   Participles are verb forms used as adjectives; they must, then, link up with a noun. When this link is broken, a participle is said to be "dangling."

FIRST VERSION: After *studying* this definition, a *discrepancy* is immediately recognized.

REVISION: After studying this definition, I immediately recognized a problem.

When a participle (a verb form) appears in a phrase at the beginning of a sentence, readers expect it to modify or connect with the first noun in the main clause; that noun will explain who or what is doing the action. In the first version, *studying* is linked with *discrepancy,* a link that obviously doesn't make sense. In the revision the subject *I* links up with the participle *studying.* Note that the change results in another improvement: the verb becomes active instead of passive.

FIRST VERSION: So far, I am ahead of my research *deadline, making* the rest of my schedule relatively free of pressure.

REVISION: Because I am ahead of my research deadline, the rest of my schedule will be relatively free of pressure.

When the participial phrase comes at the end of a sentence, readers expect it to connect with the nearest noun. But in the first version, *making* seems to connect with the whole idea in the first clause. It's clearer to have a participle refer to a single word or to rewrite the sentence completely, as the writer did in the revision.

Make Pronouns Agree in Number with the Nouns They Refer to.   Because a pronoun represents a noun, it should be the same number (and also the same gender, if that's relevant) as the noun it's representing. The following examples show lack of such agreement.

FIRST VERSION: A *child* needs to be educated beginning at birth; teaching should not have to be delayed until *they* enter school.

REVISION: *Children* need to be educated beginning at birth; teaching should not have to be delayed until *they* enter school.

In the first version, the pronoun *they* refers back to *child*, but *they* is plural and *child* is singular. Either the noun or the pronoun could have been changed, and the writer chose to make the noun plural.

FIRST VERSION: The serious *runner* may alter his or her lifestyle considerably, because *he or she* begins to center *his or her* life around running. *One* must abstain from doing many things that *one* previously did.

REVISION: Serious *runners* may alter *their* lifestyles considerably, because *they* begin to center *their* lives around running. *They* must abstain from doing many things *they* previously did.

His or her and *he or she* are used in the first version to avoid sexism, but the repetition becomes awkward. To avoid this awkwardness, the writer shifted to *one* in the second sentence. The best solution here is to use the plural for both noun and pronouns.

Make Pronoun Reference Clear. Since pronouns are substitutes for nouns, readers must know which nouns the pronouns are replacing.

FIRST VERSION: Industrial recreation is a growing career opportunity. Because of *this*, I would like to learn more about *it*.

REVISION: Because *industrial recreation* offers many career opportunities, I would like to learn more about *it*.

In the first version, what does *this* refer to? What does *it* refer to? Industrial recreation? A career opportunity? Note that combining these sentences eliminates extra words and sharpens the meaning by subordinating the less important idea.

Maintaining Consistency

Keep the Same Person Throughout a Sentence. Sometimes the perspective of a sentence is shifted by changing the pronoun from first person (*I* or *we*) to second person (*you*) or to third person (*he, she,* or *it*). Of course you may want to refer to different people and use these different pronouns; but don't shift when you are referring to the same person or group.

FIRST VERSION: Many *people* lease cars because, compared to financing, the payments are much lower. The only drawback is that at the end of the leasing term *you* do not own the car.

REVISION: Many *people* lease cars because, compared to financing, the payments are much lower. The only drawback is that at the end of the leasing term *they* do not own the car.

The first sentence in the first version uses a noun in the third person, *people*. The second sentence uses a pronoun in the second person, *you*. The revision writes both sentences in the third person.

Keep the Same Point of View Throughout Your Paper.   Most research papers are written primarily in the third person. But the use of the first person (*I*) is no longer forbidden, as it once was. Of course, you do not want to overwhelm your readers with constant use of *I* and especially with the overuse of *I feel* or *I think*; and you also want to avoid using *we* as a polite form of *I*. But if you have conducted an experiment, for example, it is appropriate to use the first person in explaining it. James Watson and Francis Crick begin their article announcing their discovery of the structure of DNA with these words: "We wish to suggest a structure for the salt of deoxyribose nucleic acid (D.N.A.)." They continue to use *we* freely throughout the article.

If you are writing instructions, you should use the second person (*you*). Research papers are rarely how-to papers, but if you have written such a paper, make sure that you have not shifted from *you* to *one* or *they*.

Keep the Tense Consistent.   If you are talking about past events, use the past tense; if you are talking about the present, use the present tense. When you are referring to the contents of one of your written sources, use the present tense: "Young *concludes* that . . ." because what the writer has put into print still exists.

FIRST VERSION: The defendants *appealed* the decision, but the Court of Appeals *affirmed*. The Supreme Court, however, *reverses* the decision and *holds* that double-celling does not violate the Eighth Amendment.

REVISION: The defendants *appealed* the decision, but the Court of Appeals *affirmed*. The Supreme Court, however, *reversed* the decision and *held* that double-celling does not violate the Eighth Amendment.

The verbs in the first sentence of the first version are correctly in the past tense. But the first two verbs in the second sentence shift to the present tense. The third verb, *does,* is correctly in the present tense because it expresses something that is still true. The revision puts all verbs except the last in the past tense.

Changing Incorrect or Confusing Punctuation

Punctuation is part of the structure and meaning of your sentences. Periods and question marks define sentences; internal marks of punctuation such as commas and semicolons are crucial to the meaning and the sound within the sentence—they are not just decorative symbols. Try reading the following sentence using the marks of punctuation as sound clues. As you will gradually discover, the sound suggested by the punctuation doesn't fit the meaning.

> Although these definitions include groups such as the Hells Angels, who operate nationwide, engage in illegal activities and use violence to enforce their rules; and other organized outlaw groups, this paper will deal with the best-known organized criminal group, the Mafia.

Punctuated this way it is clearer:

> Although these definitions include groups such as the Hells Angels—an organization that operates nationwide, engages in illegal activities, and uses violence to enforce its rules—and other organized outlaw groups, this paper will deal only with the best-known organized criminal group: the Mafia.

Sometimes problems occur with a short sentence. Try to read this sentence aloud.

> His death was not the end however it was the beginning of a new medical era.

Now read these two versions of the sentence aloud to hear the difference.

> His death was not the end, however; it was the beginning of a new medical era.

> His death was not the end; however, it was the beginning of a new medical era.

The meaning changes with the punctuation. If you don't let your readers know, they will have to punctuate the sentence themselves.

When you construct your sentences, use the marks of punctuation with as much consideration of their meaning as you do your words. You will find detailed suggestions about punctuation in Chapter 9.

Focusing on Documentation

Check your documentation to make sure it is correct and complete. If you use the number system, you may have to renumber your parenthetical citations and the order of your references after you revise your paper. Detailed documentation conventions are given in Chapter 10 (author/page system), Chapter 11 (author/date system), and Chapter 12 (number system).

EXERCISES

1. Find two examples of passive voice in your paper and change the verbs to active voice. After observing the difference in effect, decide which voice you want to use.

2. Find two or three sentences in your paper that you think might sound better if they were combined. Decide first which idea is the most important. Then combine the sentences, putting the most important idea into the main clause and the other ideas into subordinate clauses or phrases. Assess the results and decide whether you made the best decision.

3. Rewrite the same sentences you worked with in Exercise 2, putting another idea in the main clause. Decide which version is best.

4. Read the sample paper ''Science Versus Human Dignity: The Controversy over the Repatriation of Indian Remains and Artifacts'' in Chapter 10. Then analyze it according to the Toulmin model for analyzing an argument (see Chapter 6). Discuss the results with your classmates.

5. **FOR YOUR SEARCH LOG**   Record your revising process in your search log. Evaluate your process and decide how you could make it more efficient.

6. **FOR PEER RESPONSE**   Form groups of three or four with your classmates and read the first few pages of your paper, depending on the amount of time you have, to the other members of the group; or have another member of the group read your paper to you. Read slowly. When you have finished, ask each member of the group to write a sentence summarizing what you have read. Read and compare the results, and then decide whether what you want to say in your paper is clear.

7. **FOR PEER RESPONSE**   Find a classroom partner. Interview each other about your revising processes (see the excerpts by the professional and student writers at the beginning of this chapter). If you have time, discuss the whole writing process starting with the first draft. When you have finished, report your discoveries to the class. Then, as a group, evaluate the most common revising practices and decide which ones might be improved.

8. **FOR PEER RESPONSE**   Number the paragraphs of your draft in the margin. Then exchange papers with a classmate. Read your partner's paper silently and, as you read, write on a separate sheet of paper the main idea of each paragraph.

   Return the paper to your partner. Reread carefully your own paper and your partner's list of the topics in your paragraphs. If any of the topics your partner has listed do not correspond to your own idea of what the paragraphs contain, consider rewriting the paragraphs to make them clearer.

Preparing Your Final Copy

After revising your first draft (following the suggestions in Chapter 8), you are now ready to complete your paper. Four steps remain:

1. A final revision to correct spelling, grammar, and mechanics
2. The preparation of preliminary elements (*front matter*)
3. The preparation of supplemental elements (*back matter*)
4. Typing and proofreading the final copy

Making Your Final Revision

After the extensive revision of your first draft, your copy is likely to be so messy that you will have trouble reading it. You will need a clean copy so that you can concentrate on details: checking your documentation to make sure you have the correct authors and page numbers; then, with the help of the suggestions on the following pages, checking spelling, grammar, and such mechanical elements as capitalization, abbreviations, and use of numbers.

Spelling and Usage

Spelling

Pay special attention to the correct spelling of homophones, words that sound the same but have different spellings and meanings (*their, there*; *led, lead*; *to, too, two*). A computer is no help in finding misuses of such words. If you are a chronic misspeller, your task will be easier if you have a list of words you frequently misspell to guide you (if you don't have such a list now, think of keeping one in the future). Reading your paper aloud will also help you to find misspellings. Consult your dictionary for any spellings you are uncertain of. If you are tempted to think that spelling is not important because your readers can figure out what you mean, remember that your readers should not have to assume a responsibility that is yours.

Word Usage

Use words accurately and idiomatically. Select the right preposition; words such as *by*, *for*, *in*, and *on* can be troublesome because their meanings are not easily defined and because dialects vary in their use of these words. Eliminate unnecessary words: use *off*, not *off of*; *result*, not *end result*; *green*, not *green in color*. Avoid vague words: instead of "I was involved in developing a data base . . . ," write "I developed . . ." or "I assisted in developing. . . ." When you aren't sure which word to use, consult a handbook or dictionary.

Mechanics

Abbreviations

The use of abbreviations varies according to the style you are using. Here are some general guidelines for use of abbreviations in your text. For illustrations of abbreviations with a specific style of documentation, see the sample paper in the chapter discussing the style you are using (Chapters 10, 11, 12).

Use abbreviations in the text of your paper in the following situations.

- When the abbreviation is commonly used as a word itself: *A.D. 200* or *AD 200* (anno Domini, in the year of the Lord, or since the beginning of the Christian era); *a.m., p.m.* or *A.M., P.M. (ante meridiem,* before noon; *post meridiem,* after noon); *IQ* (intelligence quotient); *UN* or *U.N.* (United Nations).
- After spelling out the complete term the first time it is used and giving the abbreviation. This convention applies especially to terms that may be frequently used in your text: *Rapid Deployment Force (RDF); Department of Transportation (DOT); miles per hour (mph).*
- For personal and professional titles: *George Brown, Ph.D.; Mark Stevens, Jr.; Prof. Julia Lawson.*

- In technical or scientific writing for units of measurement when they are accompanied by numerical values (usually without punctuation): *20 mm* (millimeters), *50 l* (liters).

Note: A recent dictionary may list abbreviations in alphabetical order as it does words or it may present a list of abbreviations in a separate section—and it will also indicate whether the abbreviation should contain periods.

Do not abbreviate the following elements in the text of your paper.

- Latin terms, except when they are used in parenthetical material: *for example*, not *e.g.*; *that is*, not *i.e.*; *and so forth*, not *etc.*; *versus* or *against*, not *vs*.
- Personal titles preceding the surname only: *Governor Cuomo*; but: *Gov. Mario Cuomo*.
- Names of countries, states, counties, cities, and the like (except *USSR*): *the United States*; *Annapolis, Maryland* (in addresses in correspondence use abbreviations).
- Geographical words such as *street, avenue, drive, road,* and the like (remember to capitalize them when they are part of a name): *Rodeo Drive, Lorcom Lane*.

Capitalization

When you capitalize a word, you give it special distinction. To preserve this distinction, capitalize as sparingly as possible. You already know that the first letter of a sentence is capitalized, including the first letter of a quotation that is a complete sentence. Listed here are other frequent instances of capitalization (but note that documentation systems often follow different capitalization conventions).

Capitalize the following elements in the text of your paper.

- The first, last, and all principal words of book titles. Do not capitalize articles (*a, an,* and *the*), prepositions (such as *in, by, of, before*), and coordinating conjunctions (such as *and, or, but, nor, for*), unless they are the first or last words of a title: "He was reading *Of Time and the River*." Note that the divisions of a book or literary work are not always capitalized when referred to in the text: *preface, introduction, appendix, chapter 4, act 1, stanza 3*.
- Periodical, journal, and newspaper titles. Do not capitalize the introductory definite article unless it is part of the name: the *New York Times,* but *The New Yorker*.
- Most derivatives of proper names: *Freudian slip*; but *china doll, roman numerals*.
- Regions of the country: *Hemingway and Fitzgerald both grew up in the Middle West*; but not directions such as north, south, east, and west: *Americans went west in large numbers during the Gold Rush*.

- Titles preceding personal names: *Professor Rosabeth March*; but not titles following names: *Rosabeth March, professor of history*.
- Titles of college courses: *He taught History of the American Revolution*; but not names of subjects unless they are proper nouns: *She changed her major from French to biology*.

Documentation

Check your parenthetical or endnote documentation carefully against your note cards to make sure authors, titles, and page numbers are correct. Details about documentation are given in Chapters 10, 11, and 12.

Numbers

For the use of numbers in parenthetical citations, see Chapter 7. For the use of numbers in reference lists, see the chapter discussing the documentation system you are using (Chapter 10, 11, or 12); the list of references or works cited at the end of each sample paper illustrates the principles you will read about. The conventions or style for numbers within the text varies from one discipline to another and even from one organization to another. Newspapers, businesses, and government agencies often have their own conventions. Conventions used by the three main academic divisions—humanities, social sciences, and applied sciences—are given here for the most common situations.

Numbers in the Humanities and Social Sciences. General rule: Use words for whole numbers from one through nine and numerals for all other numbers. However, when a number over nine occurs at the beginning of a sentence, spell out the number. If a sentence begins with a number requiring several words, it's best to recast the sentence:

FIRST VERSION: 1,039 new employees were hired during the past week.

REVISION: During the past week, 1,039 new employees were hired.

Use numerals for the following elements.

- Numbers over nine: *29, 138, 2,986*.
- Dates: *June 19, 1950*.
- Street addresses, decimals, fractions, percentages, and times of day: *312 Perkins Lane, $20.18, 3-1/2, 5%, 8 a.m.*
- A series of numbers: *8 days, 4 hours, and 30 minutes*.
- References to pages and other parts of literary works: *page 42, chapter 3, act 1, lines 295–98*.

Use a combination of words and numerals for the following.

- Large numbers: *3.2 billion*.
- Consecutive modifying numbers: *three 2-way radios*.

Note: A comma is usually placed in large figures after every third digit, counting from the right: *2,098* and *3,229,894*. Exceptions are address numbers: *2100 Vacation Lane;* four-digit years: *1986*; and page numbers: *page 2389*.

Numbers in the Earth and Applied Sciences.   There is wide disparity in style and format among the sciences, partly because of the different kinds of measurements that are used in the different branches of science. The most commonly used conventions for numbers (given here) should be adequate for most college papers. If you wish to publish your paper, you should follow the style of the publication you plan to send your manuscript to.

General rule: For numbers one through nine, use words; for all others, use numerals (as in the humanities and social sciences). Note the following distinctive uses of numbers in science papers.

- Numbers with four digits have no punctuation and no spaces: *3597*.
- Numbers over four digits contain a space between each group of three, beginning with the decimal point and going in either direction: *14 583* and *500 243 489*.
- A number preceding a unit of measurement is given in numerals: *3 mm*.
- Dates are written without punctuation: *9 June 1983*; *12 January*.
- Time is expressed in the 24-hour system: *0830* and *2259*.
- Measurements are given in the metric system, and the decimal system is usually used instead of fractions (except in equations).

Punctuation

Punctuation is a matter of convention. If we are to talk to each other on paper, we must agree on what these marks mean or what sounds they create in pitch and rhythm. For example, if you know the different sounds created by the use of a comma and a semicolon, you will be able to hear the difference in meaning between the following sentences:

> I am not passing judgment on the conduct of the war, rather I wish to explain the reasons for continuing it.

> I am not passing judgment on the conduct of the war; rather I wish to explain the reasons for continuing it.

Notice that as you read the first sentence, your voice dropped only a little after *war* because you were expecting an added-on phrase, perhaps like the pattern in this sentence: "Let's go by train, rather than by plane." However, as you read the second sentence, your voice probably dropped more after *war* and there was a greater pause because of the signal given by the semicolon; then you moved on to the second clause of the sentence. In contrast, the first sentence misled you. You may have had to read part of the second clause of the sentence before you realized that the comma did not signal the addition of a minor sentence structure, such as a phrase. If so, you had to quickly reread the sentence in order to understand it. Writers must follow the conventions of punctuation to avoid confusing readers.

The following guidelines are intended to help you understand how marks of punctuation are used to create sound and meaning. But because these guidelines are attempts to describe what experienced writers do most of the time, they cannot make allowances for all of the variations that are possible. Therefore, your ultimate objective should be to develop a sense of how marks of punctuation make your sentences sound, so that instead of consulting a rule when you punctuate, you can listen to the meaning the punctuation gives to your sentence.

Apostrophe.   Use an apostrophe

- To form the possessive: *the boat's rudder* (singular); *the boats' rudders* (plural); *Mr. Jones's house* (singular ending in *s*). *Note:* Do not use an apostrophe in the possessive pronouns *its, hers,* or *theirs: The house lost its roof in the storm.*
- To indicate an omitted letter in a contraction: *can't, it's* (meaning *cannot* and *it is*). Be sure to place the apostrophe where the omission occurs. *Note:* An occasional contraction in a research paper can be the right word choice, but too many contractions detract from the serious tone that you want to maintain throughout your paper.

Brackets.   Use brackets

- To insert explanatory material or editorial comment into a quotation: *James Fenimore Cooper wrote, ''The class to which he [the gentleman] belongs is the natural repository . . . of the principles of a country.''*
- To enclose *sic,* a Latin word meaning *thus,* placed after an error in a quotation to indicate that the error was in the original: *He wrote that ''President Crater's [sic] administration was marred by numerous errors.''*

Other uses of brackets with quotations are discussed in Chapter 7.

Colon.   Use a colon

- To introduce items in a series when the words introducing the series form a complete clause: *A business letter must have the following parts: return address, inside address, greeting, body, and complimentary close.* Notice that the word before the colon (*parts*) identifies the kind of items that will be listed. Notice, too, that a significant pause follows the word just before the colon. If you incorrectly use a colon between a verb and its object or between a preposition and its object, you cause an unnecessary break in your sentence: *The courses offered in literature included: Eighteenth-Century Poets, Victorian Novel, and American Short Story.*

A colon here causes an undesirable break between the two main parts of the sentence—the verb and its objects.

- To separate titles from subtitles: *Eight American Authors: A Review of Research and Criticism.*
- To separate two main clauses when the second explains the first: *I knew the man who answered the door: he was my father.*

For use of the colon with quotations, see Chapter 7.

Comma.   Insert a comma

- After a long introductory clause or phrase: *Because he has fought for a lost cause, he serves as a symbol for Adam's ancestors.*
- Before *and, but, or, for, nor, so,* and *yet* (coordinating conjunctions) when they connect two independent clauses (clauses that can stand alone as sentences): *Hospital costs have risen 170 percent, and physicians' fees have risen 60 percent.*
- Between coordinate adjectives: *The long, dry, dusty climb up the canyon wall exhausted the hikers.*
- After words introducing or following direct quotations: *"Most people favor presidential primaries," he reported.*

For use of the comma with quotations, see Chapter 7.

Use a pair of commas

- To separate clauses or phrases that are not essential to the meaning of the sentence (nonrestrictive elements): *The idea of property rights, especially the rights to possession of land, can be traced to Locke.* But do not use commas to set off elements of a sentence that are essential to its meaning (restrictive elements): *The two candidates who received the most votes ran in the run-off election.*
- To set off a contrasting phrase: *Carson City, not Reno, is the capital of Nevada.*

Dashes.   You can use dashes

- To indicate an interruption or a shift in direction at the end of a sentence: *The president restrained his anger until the end of the meeting—well, almost until the end.*
- In pairs to set off words and phrases from the rest of the sentence. Dashes differ from comma pairs and parentheses, which de-emphasize what they enclose, by emphasizing the words they set off: *He had one reservation—and it was a big one—about the decisions they had to make.*

Note: When typing dashes, use two hyphens with no space before or after.

Ellipsis Points.   Insert ellipsis points (spaced dots)

- To indicate an omission in a quotation: *Thoreau wrote in* Walden: *"It would be some advantage to live a primitive and frontier life . . . if only to learn what are the gross necessaries. . . . "* When omitted words come at the end of a sentence, four dots are used—a period and the three ellipsis points. Unless confusion would result from not using them, ellipsis points are usually not needed when words are omitted at the beginning of a quotation: *John Kennedy called courage "that most admirable of human virtues."*

Other uses of ellipsis points are explained in Chapter 7.

Hyphen.   Insert a hyphen

- To divide a word at the end of a line. Avoid breaking a word at all, if possible. When necessary, divide a word between syllables: *syl-lables.* Use your dictionary if you are in doubt. Do not leave one letter alone at the end of a line: *a-lone.* Do not leave only one or two letters to begin a new line: *lone-ly.*
- To join words: *self-evident.* Divide hyphenated words only at the hyphen: not *self-ev-ident.* It's not always easy to tell when a word should be written as a compound (*per-cent*), as one word (*percent*), or as two words (*per cent*) because some words that used to be two words are now hyphenated or written as one. (*Percent* is now the most common spelling.) Your dictionary can help you. However, you should join words with a hyphen in the following cases: (a) When an adjective that is created by joining two or more words precedes the noun it modifies, as the following examples illustrate. A noun and participle: *death-defying leap*; an adjective and noun: *a low-percentage risk*; a number and a noun: *a four-way stop*; a phrase of three or more words: *a once-in-a-lifetime chance.* But do not hyphenate two modifiers when the first is an adverb ending in *-ly*: *a heavily wooded site.* (b) When a noun is created from a verb and a preposition: *My car needs a tune-up.* Do not use a hyphen when you use a verb followed by a preposition: *The mechanic agreed to tune up my car.*

Parentheses.   Use parentheses to separate less important information from the rest of the sentence so that the flow of the sentence is disrupted as little as possible, as in the following circumstances.

- When citing sources in your text: *(Adams 105).*
- When adding explanatory material: *He was elected president of the OAS (Organization of American States).*
- When enclosing figures or letters that introduce sequential elements: *Leasing a car has three advantages over buying: (1) you need only a small down payment; (2) you can buy the car at a depreciated price at the end of*

the leasing term; and (3) your insurance premiums are lower. Note: This use of numbers to introduce the clauses signals their beginning and emphasizes them. But the numbers also interrupt the flow of the sentence, so use them sparingly.

Period.   Use a period

- At the end of a sentence that makes a statement. In a sentence ending with a quotation, even if it is only a single word, always place the period *before* the quotation marks: *He closed his concert with Beethoven's "Moonlight Sonata."*
- After most abbreviations: *Ms., p.m.* Omit the period after abbreviations of some organizations known better by their initials: *UN, IRS, NBC.*
- After numbers or letters introducing items in a list when these are stacked, as in an outline:

> A. To benefit employees
>   1. By improving mental health

Parentheses usually enclose numbers used to itemize elements within a sentence: *He made the following decisions:* (*1*) *to . . . and* (*2*) *to. . . .*

Question Mark.   Use a question mark

- After a direct question: *What causes soil erosion?* Do not use a question mark after an indirect question: *He wanted to find out what causes inflation.* Place the question mark within quotation marks when the quotation is a question: *I couldn't answer the question "Who wrote* Rabbit, Run?" Place the question mark outside the quotation marks when the whole sentence is a question: *When are you going to say "I quit"?*

Quotation Marks.   Use double quotation marks

- To enclose direct quotations: *"Who are you, anyway?" he demanded.*
- To enclose titles of short pieces (poems, short stories, articles, parts of books, short pieces of music, and speeches).

Use single quotation marks

- To enclose quoted words within another quotation: *The speaker began: "Ladies and gentlemen, let us recall Patrick Henry's words 'Give me liberty or give me death.'"*

Punctuation of quotations in the text of your paper is discussed fully in Chapter 7.

Semicolon.   Insert a semicolon

- Between two independent clauses not linked by a coordinating conjunction. Remember that *however* and *therefore* can't take the place of coordinating conjunctions; therefore (as in this sentence), a semicolon is needed when either introduces the second independent clause.
- When two independent clauses linked by a coordinating conjunction contain internal punctuation: *The politician of the earlier novels was controlled by the money of the businessman—he was a hireling; but here he has become a big businessman himself.*
- Between items in a series when there are commas within the items: *The following cities recorded temperatures below zero for the period studied: Butte, Montana; Bismarck, North Dakota; Boise, Idaho; and Escanaba, Michigan.*

For use of the semicolon with quotations, see Chapter 7.

Slash (or Virgule).   Use the slash

- To indicate the end of a line of poetry when it is run in with the text: *Hamlet's speech beginning "O, that this too too sullied flesh would melt, / Thaw, and resolve itself into a dew!" is often cited as an indication of his despair.*
- To indicate a choice: *The best sellers in recent months have been in science fiction and/or romance.* The use of the slash in *and/or* can easily be overdone—usually you should use either *and* or *or*. Sometimes it sounds better to repeat *or*: *I may decide to major in science or math or both.*
- To separate the numerator from the denominator in a fraction: *2/3.*

Note: There is no space before or after the slash except when it is used to separate lines of poetry run in to your text.

Underlining.   Underlining in typewritten copy appears as italics in print. Use underlining

- To indicate titles of separate publications, such as books, plays, newspapers, pamphlets, and periodicals, as well as nonprint titles, such as the names of television and radio programs, records, films, musical compositions, paintings, sculpture, ships, and planes.
- To distinguish words being discussed from words that are part of the text: *He doesn't seem to know what monophobia means.*
- To show emphasis: *"I said I did not want to go."*
- To distinguish foreign words not yet anglicized: *He explained to the class the use of the deus ex machina in Greek and Roman plays.* Words that have been anglicized shouldn't be underlined: *The main item on the menu was quiche.*

Front Matter

Title Page

A short paper (up to ten pages) does not usually need a separate title page. If your paper is longer, if it is a technical report, if it has front matter, or if your instructor prefers, use a title page. It should contain, on separate lines, the title of your paper, your name, the instructor's name, the course title, and the date. Although you can use any attractive format, the most common and probably the easiest is centering these items beginning a little above the middle of the page. Only the first letter of each important word of the title should be capitalized; the words should not be underlined. If your title is long, use two lines and divide it where a pause seems natural (see the title page of the sample paper on page 259).

If you do not use a title page, leave a one-inch margin at the top of the first page and then place your name, the name of the professor, the course title, and the date in the upper left corner, using double-spacing. After another double-space, center the title; then double-space and begin your text (see the sample paper on page 278).

Abstract

Place your abstract on a separate page with the heading Abstract centered. Capitalize only the first letter of the heading (unless you are writing a technical report, in which case you would usually capitalize all letters). Double-space your abstract (see Chapter 7 for an explanation of writing an abstract).

Table of Contents

A table of contents (TOC) is often part of a technical report or a research paper prepared for education, business, or government organizations or for private research groups. Each audience may have different interests and needs. Employees or the public may want to learn what research has been done at an institution; managers may want a general view of the research on the subject presented in the report; experts may want to find out the details of a research project. The table of contents, which is really an outline in a different format, provides readers with a detailed summary of the report as well as page numbers, so that readers can locate specific subjects quickly and easily. The headings used in the TOC make reading and understanding the text of the report easier.

You can easily transfer the headings and subheadings of your outline to the TOC, although you don't need to include any subheadings below the third level. Every heading or subheading that you list in your

TOC must appear word-for-word as in the report. The numbers or letters that you use with the headings in your outline are usually not included in the TOC; instead, typography or indenting indicates the different levels of headings. (For suggestions on typography in headings, see Chapter 11.) If you do include numbers and letters with the headings in the body of your paper, they should also appear in the TOC.

You can prepare the TOC after typing the final copy of your paper so that you can insert the correct page numbers. An alternative would be to type it at the beginning and insert the page numbers later. (Note that the front matter should be numbered with lowercase roman numerals.)

Although the order, contents, and typography of a formal report can vary, the form for the table of contents described here will be acceptable in most cases. If possible, confirm this form with the person for whom you are writing the report.

In main headings of the TOC, the first letters of main words are usually typed in capital letters. Main headings begin at the left margin; subheadings are indented and usually only the first letter of the first word is capitalized. Spaced periods often connect these headings to the page numbers at the right margin; but some writers, preferring a less cluttered look, do not use the periods. Double- or triple-space headings to make them easier to read. If you use an outline numbering system, use it only for the body of the paper, not for the front or back matter.

See page 324 for an example of a table of contents in a research paper.

List of Illustrations

If your paper includes both figures and tables (any graphic that is not a table is considered and labeled a figure), combine them in one list called List of Illustrations or simply Illustrations and subdivide that list into parts labeled Figures and Tables. If you have only one kind, title it accordingly—List of Figures or List of Tables. A list of three or fewer illustrations can be placed on the same page as the table of contents, just below the contents. If you have more, list them on a separate page (see the list for the sample paper on page 325).

Outline

An introductory outline is optional. You do not need an outline if you have either an abstract or a table of contents. If your instructor wishes you to submit an outline, place the word Outline at the center of the page as your heading. (See Chapter 6 for guidelines for the spacing and punctuation of outlines.) The outline you prepared for your first revision (see Chapter 8) will probably need no changes; however, if you have made changes in the order or content of your text, adjust your outline to reflect them. Proofread it carefully to ensure that the headings are parallel and that the mechanics (capitalization, punctuation, and use of numbers and symbols) are correct.

Back Matter

Appendixes

The appendix or appendixes contain information that isn't necessary to the body of your paper and may be difficult to integrate into your text but that is important and helpful to your readers. Any of the following might appear in an appendix: sample questionnaires, maps, worksheets for feasibility studies, excerpts from documents, interview questions, correspondence, photocopies of documents, details of an experiment, lengthy tables or lists of statistics. An appendix is useless, however, unless readers know it's there; when you are discussing a point amplified in an appendix, refer to it: (*see appendix, p. 19*). You may number appendixes as a continuation of your text (with arabic numerals) or, if the appendix is the last section of your paper, you may use a separate numbering system consisting of capital letters to identify the main groups of information and arabic numerals to identify the separate items of those groups; for example, A1, A2 (for two questionnaires used) and B1, B2 (for statistics and calculations based on the questionnaires). Peter DeGress included worksheets in the appendix of his feasibility study on solar heating (see Figure 9.1).

Content or Explanatory Notes

Writers who use parenthetical documentation rather than endnotes may still use content or explanatory notes to amplify or explain information they have given in the text. You can use content notes to cite further sources of information on a subject, to give details or statistics that may be interesting but are not essential to your paper, to explain procedures you have used, to acknowledge contrary evidence, or to mention the names of those persons or organizations that provided you with special help. Such notes should be used sparingly; if the information is not important enough to be included in your text, you may not need it at all.

If you use a content note, type a superscript number in the text ([1]) to refer readers to the note. The note itself may be positioned in any of the following places, depending on the citation style you are using.

1. In the author/page style, notes are placed on a page titled Notes, following the body of the manuscript.

FIGURE 9.1 A Sample Appendix

```
Appendix 1.  Project Data Sheet.

WORKSHEET A--PROJECT DATA
```
PROJECT *Drain Down DHW System*

Location *Washington, D.C.*   Latitude   = *40°*

Building Heating and/or (Hot Water Load)

    Design Heat Loss Rate, q_d = *N/A* Btu/h

    Winter Design Temperature (97-1/2%), t_w = *N/A* °F

    Average Hot Water Consumption   = *60* gal/day
    (may vary on a monthly basis)

    Average Cold Water Supply (main) Temp., t_m = *55* °F

    Hot Water Supply Temp., t_s = *140* °F

2. In the author/date style, notes are also placed on a page following the body of the manuscript, but they are titled Endnotes.
3. In the number style, footnotes are positioned at the bottom of the page on which the superscript number or symbol is given.

It's likely that any of these styles will be acceptable in a college class unless your instructor has a preference. For the first two styles, center the title (Notes or Endnotes) on the page following the text. Double-space before beginning the first note. Indent the number for each note five spaces and raise it one half-space above the line. Double-space throughout—both within entries and between entries. A content note for the MLA and number styles would look like this (for the author/date style, do not leave a space after the superscript number):

    [1]However, in his introduction to the American edition of <u>Fabian Essays</u>, Bellamy states that he favored not only government ownership of the productive mechanism but also equal distribution of the product.

Footnotes or Endnotes

Although most writers find it easier to document their papers by putting brief citations in parentheses within the text and a list of references at the end, some writers, especially those in the humanities, prefer to use footnotes or endnotes either with or without a separate list of references. This system of documentation is explained in Appendix 2.

Glossary

If you are writing a technical or scientific paper for an audience that includes nonexperts, you will probably need a glossary—a list of technical or scientific words and their definitions. Two or three technical words can easily be defined within your paper by putting each definition in parentheses following the term. But too many of these will clutter your paper and can annoy those readers who are already familiar with the terms.

In compiling a glossary, you will have to assess carefully the knowledge of your audience to decide which words or terms to include. Then you will have to define those terms—that is, translate them into words that your audience will understand. The first time you use a word defined in your glossary, highlight it with italics or underlining, boldface type, or capital letters. Then refer your reader to the glossary in a footnote or in parentheses:

```
An asthmatic reaction always includes a bronchospasm in the lower

respiratory tract (underlined terms are defined in the glossary).
```

Many glossaries consist entirely of nouns to be defined, but glossaries may also contain verbs, adjectives, and adverbs. Each definition should be cast in the same part of speech as the word being defined. In other words, if the word being defined is a noun, the definition should begin with a noun giving the class to which the item belongs and a qualifying clause or phrase; if it is a verb, the definition should consist of an infinitive with possibly a modifying clause or phrase; if it is an adjective, it should be defined with an adjective or perhaps an adjectival phrase. The following examples illustrate incorrect and correct ways to define terms.

DEFINING A NOUN
Incorrect: software: computer programs. [Incomplete.]
Correct: software: programs used to direct the operation of computers.

DEFINING AN ADJECTIVE
Incorrect: panchromatic: imagery in all colors. [*Panchromatic* is an adjective; *imagery* is a noun.]
Correct: panchromatic: sensitive to light of all colors.

DEFINING A VERB
Incorrect: digitize: the process of converting measured data into digits readable by computer. [*Digitize* is a verb and *process* is a noun.]

Correct: digitize: to translate measured data into digits readable by a computer.

Definitions in a glossary can be brief because the reader has the advantage of seeing the word in context, which further defines it. Avoid using such unnecessary phrases as "a word which means" or "a term which is used to." Definitions in a glossary can also be complete sentences, but most consist of phrases. The two structures should not be mixed.

The glossary is usually placed in the back matter but sometimes appears as part of the front matter. Figure 9.2 shows an excerpt from a glossary for a report comparing two computer programs.

List of References

At the end of your paper, on a separate page, place the list of the sources you have cited. You can label this list Works Cited (used by writers following the author/page system) or References (used by those following either the author/year system or the number system). These lists contain only the works cited in the text of your paper. In an alternate style, the list can be labeled Bibliography and can include background sources as well as sources cited. Some writers even use two lists—Works Cited and Works Consulted.

Your list of references should include all sources: books, articles, chapters of books, pamphlets, unpublished writing, and nonprint sources, such as radio and television programs, paintings, and com-

---

FIGURE 9.2   Excerpt from a Glossary

GLOSSARY

add-in board: an electronic component that provides additional
    functions to the computer system.

compiler: a computer program that converts programs written in a
    high-level language into a code that is understandable to a
    computer.

database: a comprehensive collection of related data organized for
    access electronically.

hard disk: a rigid disk coated with magnetic material on which in-
    formation can be stored.

modem: an electronic device that makes it possible to transmit
    data to or from computers by telephone.

---

puter databases. Chapter 10 explains the author/page reference system; Chapter 11, the author/date system; and Chapter 12, the number system.

Typing Your Final Copy

Your final copy will usually contain these elements in the following order (remember that your paper may not contain all of these and that some styles of documentation may recommend a different order of elements).

Front matter (or preliminary elements)

Title page (explained in this chapter, p. 226)
Abstract (see Chapter 7, p. 180)
Table of contents (explained in this chapter, p. 226)
List of illustrations (explained in this chapter, p. 227)
Outline (see Chapter 6, p. 141)

Text of your paper
Back matter (or supplementary elements)

Appendixes (explained in this chapter, p. 228)
Content notes (explained in this chapter, p. 228)
Endnotes (explained in Appendix 2, p. 387)
Glossary (explained in this chapter, p. 230)
List of references (see Chapter 10, 11, or 12 for the appropriate documentation style)
Bibliography

A preface is usually unnecessary in a college paper. If you want to acknowledge special help, use a content note. If someone has provided you with information orally, use the proper citation format for your documentation style.

Computer Help

As you prepare your final copy, use your computer to help you complete the following formatting tasks.

- Number your pages.
- Insert a header in the upper right corner containing your last name and the page number.
- Set the margins you want, according to the guidelines for your documentation system. Also adjust the right margin so that it's justified or unjustified (ragged right). Most writers prefer a ragged right margin for this kind of document because it promotes easier reading

and eliminates the awkward spacing of words that sometimes results with justified margins.

- Set the spacing to double-space.
- Set paragraph indentation to five space or one-half inch.
- Select a suitable type size. The best type size for a paper like this is 10- or 12-point.
- Select a suitable typeface. Avoid exotic typefaces such as Times Outline, Times Shadow, or any of the script typefaces. Choose one of the commonly used typefaces with serifs (small cross strokes at the top or bottom of the letters) such as Schoolbook or Courier; these are easier for the eye to follow. However, if you want a cleaner, more modern look, use a typeface without serifs (sans serif) such as Helvetica.

Computer programs are available to format your notes, your parenthetical documentation, and your reference lists according to the documentation system you are using.

Materials

If your paper is typed, use 8½-by-11-inch white paper of good quality and a new black ribbon. Most instructors prefer that you avoid using onionskin or erasable paper. Erasable paper smudges easily and does not photocopy well. If your instructor will accept a good-quality photocopy, you can use white correction fluid or correction tape to correct errors without having to retype your paper. Handwritten manuscripts, if your instructor will accept them, should be legibly written with black or blue-black ink on lined paper with margins. (Be sure to observe the same margins on all sides, including the bottom, as you would use when typing. See the next section, on typing format.) Always write or type on only one side of the paper.

If you use a computer, use a letter-quality printer rather than a dot matrix printer, unless it is near letter quality. The forming of the words by dots makes the readers' eyes work harder; in addition, some letters, such as q's and g's, are difficult to distinguish.

Format

Margins vary according to the documentation format you are using. Please see details in the chapter illustrating your format—Chapter 10, 11, or 12. Double-space the text of your paper, including indented quotations. Indent the first line of each paragraph five spaces. Number pages consecutively throughout the paper, using arabic numerals without punctuation (use lowercase roman numerals for front matter). Place numbers in the upper right corner. Page headings vary according to the documentation system you are using.

Proofreading and Duplicating

After your paper has been printed or typed, read it again. Read it aloud, if possible, to force yourself to slow down and recognize typographical and spelling errors. If you have lengthy tables or other groups of figures in your paper, try to find a friend to check your figures as you read them aloud. Open your computer file and make the necessary corrections.

Make corrections on the typewriter by using correction tape or white correction fluid. Make brief last-minute insertions by typing or by neatly writing in ink just above the space where you want to add the word or brief phrase. If you have more than two or three corrections on a page, you should retype the page.

Be sure to make a photocopy of your paper for yourself before handing it in. You may be able to submit a good-quality photocopy of your paper, but check with your instructor before doing so.

Cover and Binding

Most short student papers need no special cover or binding. A blank sheet of paper before the title page and after the final page helps keep your paper neat. You can secure the pages with a paper clip in the upper left corner. However, if you are writing a formal report or a long paper, you may want to use a cover. Use a lightweight cardboard cover that will lie flat when it's opened. Fasten a label on the cover on which you have typed your name and the title of your paper. Avoid plastic covers with removable spines; they often fall apart when opened.

EXERCISES

1. **FOR YOUR SEARCH LOG**   As your last entry in your search log, record your final thoughts on this project. What have you learned about your subject that is important to you? What have you learned about the process of writing a paper that you will be able to use when you write future papers? What parts of your process will you repeat? How will you improve your process next time?

2. **FOR PEER RESPONSE**   In this exercise you will proofread a classmate's finished paper. Proofreading is different from editing. When you proofread, you will look only for minor errors in spelling and typing and for small punctuation errors. If you are proofreading the day the paper is due, it is too late to make larger changes. For

this exercise, exchange papers with the person next to you, or follow the directions of your instructor for redistributing papers.

FOR READERS   Use a pencil and write lightly so you do not mar the appearance of the paper.

a. Write your last name in the top right-hand corner of the first page.
b. Read your classmate's paper carefully and slowly. Focus on individual words. Do not read primarily for meaning, as you normally do, because such reading causes you to read words in groups and to see the words and spelling that you expect to see. When you find an error or an omission, put a light pencil mark in the margin. *Do not make any changes in the paper.*
c. Confer with the writer and explain your findings. The writer may not agree with you. It is up to the writer to decide whether to make the changes you suggest.

FOR WRITERS

a. Note the comments of your reader and decide what changes you want to make.
b. If the paper is to be handed in during class, make changes neatly only with dark ink. Write extra words above the line and use a caret ($\wedge$) to show where they should be inserted. Draw a line through words to be omitted. If there is room, insert the correct punctuation.
c. Erase your reader's pencil marks.
d. If there are too many errors, or if there are major errors, recopy your paper (with your instructor's permission).

PART III

Writing Papers Across the Curriculum

DOCUMENTATION SYSTEMS

Writing a Paper in the Humanities: The Author/Page Style

The suggestions for format and documentation given here and in the sample papers that follow use the guidelines recommended in the *MLA Handbook for Writers of Research Papers* (3rd ed., 1988). Parenthetical citations are given in the text of the papers, and a list of works cited is placed at the end.

Parts of the Manuscript

A paper in the humanities usually places its emphasis on the text of the paper itself. Therefore, most papers have only two parts: the text and the list of works cited. However, the following list shows the possible elements of such a paper. Your instructor will help you decide how many of these you need.

Title page (optional)
Outline (optional)
Text of paper
Content notes
Works cited

Format

Title Page

You do not need a title page with your paper unless you include an outline at the beginning of the paper. If you do use a title page, center the following information on the page, using a separate line for each element: the title of the paper, your name, instructor, course name, and date. Capitalize the first word, the last word, and all important words in your title. Do not underline or use other punctuation marks unless your title contains a quotation or another title (1). Use a colon to separate the title from the subtitle (2).

(1)   Critics' Changing Views of Troilus and Cressida

(2)   "In the Beginning":

        A Discussion of Metaphors in the Creation Story

Use spacing between the elements on the title page to make the page attractive.

Margins and Spacing

Leave one-inch margins on all sides of the text, including the top and bottom. Indent paragraphs five spaces. Use double-spacing in the text; in all long quotations, which should be indented ten spaces from the left margin; and in all other parts of your paper including the outline, the works cited section, and notes, if you use them.

Page Numbers

Place page numbers half an inch from the top of the page and one inch from the right. Use arabic numerals without punctuation. Number all pages (except the title page if you include one) and place your last name before each number beginning with page 2 to identify your paper in case pages are separated. If you use a title page and outline, number the pages of the outline with small roman numerals, starting with page ii (the title page is counted as page i but is not numbered).

Headings

Papers in the humanities usually do not have headings within the text. You should have a heading at the beginning of each of these parts of your paper: the outline (if you have one), the text, notes, and works cited. Start each of these on a new page and center the title one inch from the top of the page. Capitalize the first letter of each word; do not underline or use other marks of punctuation.

Outline

If you include an outline, it should come after your title page. Center the heading Outline one inch below the top of the page. Double-space and begin your outline. (See Chapter 6 for the format of outlines.)

First Page

If your paper does not have a title page, place your name, instructor's name, course title, and date (double-spaced) in the upper left corner on the first page half an inch below the page number and one inch from the top. Double-space and center the title of your paper. Then double-space and begin your text.

If you are using a title page, you need repeat only the title of your paper on the first page of the text. Place it one inch below the top of the page (half an inch below the page number). Double-space and begin your text.

Content Notes

Content notes can be used with parenthetical documentation to explain something not important enough to interrupt your text. You may not need to include them, but if you do, avoid lengthy discussions and limit them to brief explanations or bibliographic comments. Use the same format as for endnotes. For further information on these notes and examples, see Chapter 9.

Documentation

Parenthetical Citation

Give the sources of your information in parentheses as close as possible to the material you are documenting—at a natural pause or at the end of a sentence. Your parenthetical citation must give enough information to identify a source in your list of works cited; it must also give the page number on which you found the information. The sample papers in this chapter show how these citations are used.

The following examples illustrate the most common types of parenthetical references.

ENTIRE WORK

You might refer in your text to a whole work; in that case you wouldn't need a parenthetical citation. Be sure to include the name of the author in your text also.

In The Politics of Non-Violent Action, Sharp outlines the long

history of successful nonviolent struggle.

WORK BY ONE AUTHOR

If you use the author's name as part of your sentence, put only the page number in parentheses.

```
Wyman mentions that German miners in the sixteenth century used
dowsing to find silver, copper, and lead (47).
```

If you give neither the name nor the page number in the sentence, then you must give both in parentheses with no punctuation between them.

```
German miners in the sixteenth century used dowsing to find silver,
copper, and lead (Wyman 47).
```

Follow the same format for citing the work of an editor, a translator, or compiler. Do not include abbreviations indicating the role of a person: *Smith, ed.* This role will be identified in the list of works cited.

TWO OR MORE WORKS BY THE SAME AUTHOR

If you have included more than one work by an author in your list of works cited, you must include a brief title in your text or in your parenthetical citation.

```
In fact, Adams admitted that he unwittingly benefited from corrupt
political practices (Education 49).
```

The complete title of the book cited is *The Education of Henry Adams.* Note that there is no punctuation between the title and the page number.

If you name both the author and the work in your text, you need only the page number in parentheses.

```
In fact, Adams admitted in his Education that he unwittingly bene-
fited from corrupt political practices (49).
```

If you name neither the author nor the title in the text, include both in the parenthetical citation. Note that a comma separates the author from the title.

```
He unwittingly benefited from corrupt political practices (Adams,
Education 49).
```

WORK BY TWO OR THREE AUTHORS

If your source has two or three authors, cite all of them either in your text or in parentheses, as you would a single author.

```
As Friedman and McLaughlin point out, a poem is "a mirror of the
conventions . . . of the period in which it was written" (3).
A poem is "a mirror of the conventions . . . of the period in
which it was written" (Friedman and McLaughlin 3).
```

WORK BY MORE THAN THREE AUTHORS

If your source has more than three authors, give the name of the first author listed in Works Cited, followed by *et al.* (not underlined), the Latin abbreviation for *et alii*, meaning ''and others.'' There is no punctuation between the name of the first author and the abbreviation.

> According to Spiller et al., America was the embodiment of a long-
> held European dream (192).

> America was the embodiment of a long-held European dream (Spiller
> et al. 192).

CORPORATE AUTHOR

Give the name of a corporate author (government agency, association, or research organization) in the text or in a parenthetical reference, as you would with a personal author. If the group is known by its abbreviation, give its abbreviation with the first citation and then abbreviate it in subsequent citations. For example, the first citation:

> In a recent study of freshman writing, the National Council of
> Teachers of English (NCTE) found that students think of revising as
> nothing more than correcting grammar and punctuation (58).

The subsequent reference:

> The study recommended that . . . (NCTE 92).

When the name of a corporate author is long, it is probably best to include it in the text rather than interrupt the text with a long parenthetical reference.

WORK WITHOUT AN AUTHOR

Give in your citation enough of the title to enable your readers to find it in your list of works cited; usually one, two, or three words are enough (including the first word or two of the title as it is listed in Works Cited). For a pamphlet entitled *Marriages of the Dead*:

> The ceremonial life is not open to everyone (Marriages 71).

If you include the title in your sentence, put the page number in the parenthetical reference.

> In Marriages of the Dead the reader is warned that the ceremonial
> life is not open to everyone (71).

MULTIVOLUME WORK

In citing one volume of a multivolume work, use the following format. Note that the volume number is followed by a colon and then by the page number.

> Cardenal tells the group that "in the Old Testament the messianic
> era had often been described as an epoch of great abundance of
> wine" (1: 154).

If you include the author's name in the parenthetical reference, use the following format. Do not use a comma between the author and the volume number.

```
"In the Old Testament the messianic era had often been described
as an epoch of great abundance of wine" (Cardenal 1: 154).
```

The next two examples show how to cite an entire volume. A comma separates the author's name from the abbreviation for volume.

```
Volume 1 gradually introduces the Solentiname group through their
interpretations of the stories (Cardenal).
The Solentiname group is gradually introduced through their inter-
pretations of the stories (Cardenal, vol. 1).
```

If you have included only one volume of a multivolume work in your list of works cited, you do not need the volume number in parenthetical citations.

INDIRECT SOURCE

It is best to cite the original source, but if that source is unavailable to you, use the abbreviation *qtd. in* for "quoted in" to indicate that you have used an indirect source for the information.

```
Dodd ascertained that in 1814 "there were 1,733 croppers in Leeds,
all in full employment" (qtd. in Thompson 551).
```

You can include a content note giving the full publication information for the original source, as cited in the indirect source.

TWO OR MORE WORKS BY DIFFERENT AUTHORS IN THE SAME CITATION

When citing two or more authors within the same parentheses, cite each as you normally would but separate the citations with semicolons.

```
It was generally believed that the soldiers acted under a solemn
oath and that disobedience to the general's orders was punished
with death (Carroll 67-70; Lee and Hammonds 261-65).
```

If the citation is long, include it in the text or in a bibliographic content note to avoid interrupting the text.

Literary Works.   For literary prose works that might be published in different editions, give the page number first, followed by a semicolon, and then include other identifying information such as book or chapter (328; bk. 3). For classic poems and plays, omit the page number and include the act, scene, or line in the parenthetical reference. This information will enable readers to find the material in different editions.

When you use the title of a literary work several times in your text, write it out the first time and give its abbreviation in parentheses. You can use the abbreviation you find in your source, or create your own from the first letters of the main words: The Winter's Tale (WT).

NOVEL OR OTHER PROSE WORK

In Babbitt, Sinclair Lewis portrays a businessman who was "no more

conscious of his children than of the buttons on his coat-sleeves"

(227; ch. 18).

VERSE PLAY

Omit page numbers; instead, include the act, scene, and line numbers, with the divisions separated by periods. Use arabic numerals rather than roman numerals unless your instructor asks you to do otherwise.

In Hamlet's famous lines about acting, he says that the purpose of

playing is "to hold, as 'twere, the mirror up to nature" (Hamlet

3.2.23).

You can include the title of the play in your text.

According to Shakespeare in Hamlet, the purpose of the theater is

"to hold, as 'twere, the mirror up to nature" (3.2.23).

POETRY

Do not use the abbreviations *l.* or *ll.* for "lines" because these can be confused with numbers. Include identifying information (book, canto, or part) followed by the line numbers in a parenthetical citation.

Tennyson's In Memoriam reveals his cautious optimism: "I can but

trust that good shall fall / At last . . ." (44.14-15).

If you are citing only lines, use the word *line* or *lines* in your first reference and in subsequent references cite the numbers only, as in these two examples from Edgar Allan Poe's "Annabel Lee." The first reference:

"That the wind came out of the cloud, chilling / And killing my

Annabel Lee" (lines 25-26).

The subsequent reference:

"In her tomb by the side of the sea" (41).

ONE-PAGE ARTICLES AND WORKS ARRANGED ALPHABETICALLY

In citing a one-page article from a periodical or an article from a work arranged alphabetically (an encyclopedia or a dictionary, for example), include the author's name in the text or in a parenthetical reference and omit the page number. If an encyclopedia or dictionary article is long, give the page number.

```
"Although folk belief accepts the skills of dowsers, their suc-
cesses in finding water are no more frequent than those gained by
other methods" (Middleton).
```

If the article is not signed, include a brief title in the text or in a parenthetical citation.

```
He was almost forty years old before his first volume of poetry was
published ("Frost").
```

List of Works Cited

The Works Cited page follows the content notes, if there are any. Center the heading one inch from the top of the page. Number the page as you have numbered the other pages. Arrange the entries alphabetically according to the last name of the author or, if no author is given, by the first word in the title, except for *A*, *An*, or *The*. Arrange the information for each entry in this order (omitting items that do not apply): author's name, title of part of book, title of book, name of editor or translator, edition, number of volumes, series name, place of publication, name of publisher, and date of publication. This information is usually found on the title and copyright pages. If the publisher or publication date is not given, use the abbreviation *n.p.* or *n.d.* in its place.

Begin the first line of each entry at the left margin and indent all other lines five spaces. Double-space throughout—between items and between lines in each item.

Books. Here are examples of the most commonly used entries.

ONE AUTHOR

The last name of the author is first, with periods after the author's name, the title, and the date. The title is underlined. A colon follows the place of publication, and a comma is placed after the publisher.

```
Faulkner, William.  A Fable.  New York: Random, 1954.
```

TWO OR MORE BOOKS BY THE SAME AUTHOR

Put the titles in alphabetical order. Instead of repeating the author's name, type three hyphens followed by a period.

```
---.  The Reivers: A Reminiscence.  New York: Random, 1962.
```

Note: If the author of one book is coauthor of another book, do not use three hyphens. Give the full name as coauthor.

TWO AUTHORS

The last name of the first author is first; the second author's name is in regular order. Give the names in the order in which they appear on the title page.

Kunitz, Stanley J., and Howard Haycraft. American Authors, 1600-
  1900. New York: Wilson, 1938.

THREE AUTHORS

Parsons, Talcott, Robert F. Bales, and Edward A. Shils. Working
  Papers in the Theory of Action. Glencoe: Free, 1953.

MORE THAN THREE AUTHORS

Note the comma between the first author and the abbreviation *et al.* because the order of the name has been reversed.

Hubbell, Jay B., et al. Eight American Authors: A Review of
  Research and Criticism. New York: Norton, 1963.

CORPORATE AUTHOR

Life Sciences Research Office. Evaluation of the Health Aspects
  of Caffeine. Bethesda: Federation of American Societies for
  Experimental Biology, 1978.

GOVERNMENT PUBLICATIONS

When the name of the author is not known, give the government agency as author. Then give the title of the publication, identifying information such as bill or document numbers, and publication information (place, publisher, and date).

United States. Cong. Senate. Senator Riegle Speaking for Kennedy's
  Health Plan. 96th Cong., 1st sess. S. Doc. 1720. Washington: GPO, 1979.

This is a Senate document. Like most government documents, it was published by the Government Printing Office (GPO). Other types of congressional publications are House documents (H. Doc. 976), bills (S 45; HR 52), resolutions (S. Res. 101; H. Res. 45), and reports (S. Rept. 32; H. Rept. 3).

When the name of the author is known, follow the format for a book or periodical (see "Periodicals," p. 252).

Hile, Joseph P. "Proposed Exemption of Required Label Statements
  on Food Containers with Separate Lids." Dept. of Health and

> Human Services. Food and Drug Administration. 21 CFR Part
>
> 101. <u>Federal Register</u> 50 (249): 52937-38.

For references to the *Congressional Record*, you need only the abbreviated title of the publication, date, and page numbers.

> Cong. Rec. 6 Dec. 1985: S17128.

Note: House and Senate sections are paged separately, so be sure to give the identifying letter (H or S).

TWO OR MORE PUBLICATIONS BY THE SAME GOVERNMENT

For consecutive works by the same government agency, in entries following the first entry use three hyphens and a period in place of the government and agency names common to the initial entry. In the following example, the two sets of hyphens replace "United States" and "Cong."

> United States. Cong. House. Subcommittee on General Oversight
>
> and Investigations of the Committee on Interior and Insular
>
> Affairs. <u>The Destruction of America's Architectural Heritage</u>:
>
> <u>Looting and Vandalism of Indian Archaeological Sites in the</u>
>
> <u>Four Corners States of the Southwest</u>. 100th Cong., 2nd sess.
>
> Washington: GPO, 1988.
>
> ---. ---. Senate. Select Committee on Indian Affairs. <u>Hearing</u>
>
> <u>on the Native American Museum Claims Commission Act</u>. 100th
>
> Cong., 2nd sess. Washington: GPO, 1988.

Four sets of hyphens replace "United States," "Cong.," "House," and the name of the committee.

> United States. Cong. House. Committee on Energy and Commerce.
>
> Subcommittee on Health and the Environment. <u>Acid Rain</u>
>
> <u>Control Proposals</u>. 101st Cong., 1st sess. Washington: GPO,
>
> 1989.
>
> ---. ---. ---. ---. Subcommittee on Energy and Power. <u>Acid</u>
>
> <u>Rain Oversight</u>. 100th Cong., 2nd sess. Washington: GPO,
>
> 1989.

ANONYMOUS AUTHOR

When the author's name is not given on the title page, the entry begins with the title of the book.

Solid for Mulhooly. New York: Carleton, 1881.

PSEUDONYMOUS AUTHOR

The author's real name is placed in brackets.

Blot, Thomas [William Simpson]. The Man from Mars. San Francisco: Bacon, 1891.

EDITOR OF AN ANTHOLOGY

Keene, Donald, ed. Anthology of Japanese Literature. New York:
Grove, 1955.

EDITOR

If the focus of your paper is on the work or its author, cite the author
first.

Melville, Herman. Moby-Dick or, the Whale. Ed. Alfred Kazin.
Boston: Houghton, 1956.

If your paper emphasizes the editor or the edition used, cite the editor
first.

Kazin, Alfred, ed. Moby-Dick or, the Whale. By Herman Melville.
Boston: Houghton, 1956.

TRANSLATOR

If the focus of your paper is on the work or its author, cite the author
first.

Dante. The Inferno. Trans. John Ciardi. New York: NAL, 1954.

If your paper emphasizes the translation used, cite the translator first.

Ciardi, John, trans. The Inferno. By Dante. New York: NAL, 1954.

WORK IN A SERIES

After the author and title of the individual work, include the series
name and number, if any, and a period. Do not underline the name of
the series or enclose it in quotation marks.

Meinert, Charles W. Time Shortened Degrees. ERIC/Higher Education Research Rept. 8. Washington: American Assn. for Higher
Educ., 1974.

WORK IN SEVERAL VOLUMES

Use this format to cite one volume when each volume has a separate title:

```
Parrington, Vernon L.  1800-1920: The Romantic Revolution in
     America.  Vol. 2 of Main Currents in American Thought.
     3 vols.  New York: Harcourt, 1920.
```

Use this format if all volumes are listed under one title:

```
Morison, Samuel Eliot, and Henry Steele Commager.  The Growth of
     the American Republic.  2 vols.  New York: Oxford UP, 1941.
```

WORK IN A COLLECTION OF WRITINGS BY THE SAME AUTHOR

For an essay, short story, or poem, place the title of the work in quotation marks and include the page numbers on which it appears in the collection.

```
Orwell, George.  "Shooting an Elephant."  A Collection of Es-
     says.  Garden City: Anchor-Doubleday, 1954.  154-62.
```

WORK IN A COLLECTION OF WRITINGS BY DIFFERENT AUTHORS

Besides the title of the work and page numbers, also identify the collection's editor as given on the title page of the book.

```
Hearn, Lafcadio.  "Mosquitoes."  Mentor Book of Modern Asian
     Literature.  Ed. Dorothy Blair Shimer.  New York: NAL, 1969.
     236-38.
```

For a novel or play, underline the title of the work.

```
Rizal, Jose.  Noli me Tangere.  Mentor Book of Modern Asian Lit-
     erature.  Ed. Dorothy Blair Shimer.  New York: NAL, 1969.
     251-74.
```

In citing a work in a collection of previously published pieces, give the complete information for the original publication if you can and then add *Rpt. in* (for ''reprinted in''), and give publication information for the collection.

```
Oates, Joyce Carol.  "Where Are You Going, Where Have You Been?"
     The Wheel of Love.  New York: Vanguard, 1970.  Rpt. in The
     Story and Its Writer.  Ed. Ann Charters.  New York: Bedford,
     1983.  1081-94.
```

Cross-references: If you are citing two or more works from the same collection, you can list the entire collection in one entry and then list individual works by referring to the collection. Give the author and title of the piece, followed by the last name of the collection's editor and the page number of the individual piece.

Swansea, Charlene, and Barbara Campbell, eds. Love Stories by New
     Women. Charlotte: Red Clay, 1978.

Thompson, Jean. "The People of Color." Swansea and Campbell
     11-30.

Vreuls, Diane. "The Seller of Watches." Swansea and Campbell
     141-49.

INTRODUCTION, PREFACE, FOREWORD, OR AFTERWORD

Use the format in the following example if you are citing only the introduction, preface, foreword, or afterword. If the author of that element is also the author of the book, give only the last name of the author after "By." If you are citing the whole book, use the regular author format and omit the citation for the introduction, preface, foreword, or afterword and the page numbers.

Elliott, Osborn. Preface. The Negro Revolution in America. By
     William Brink and Louis Harris. New York: Simon, 1964.
     11-17.

REVISED EDITION

Use the designation given in the book on the title page or the copyright page: *Rev. ed., 1st ed., 1985 ed.*

Curti, Merle. The Growth of American Thought. 2nd ed. New York:
     Harper, 1951.

REPRINT OF OLDER EDITION

Give the date of the original edition before the publication information of the edition you're using.

Pater, Walter. Marius the Epicurean. 1885. London: Macmillan,
     1927.

PUBLISHER'S IMPRINT

Give the name of the imprint followed by a hyphen and the name of the publisher.

Hitching, Francis. Dowsing: The Psi Connection. Garden City:
     Anchor-Doubleday, 1978.

THE BIBLE

No bibliographic listing is necessary if you use the King James version and if your reference is to chapters or verses in the Bible. Give the book, chapter, and verse citation parenthetically in your text: (John 5.3–6). Abbreviate parenthetical references to books of the Bible when they contain five or more letters (Gen. for Genesis, Chron. for Chronicles). Spell them in full in the text. If your reference is to commentary or notes in a particular edition of the King James version or to another translation, give bibliographic information as you would for any book. Use this format for other editions or other translations of the Bible.

```
The New English Bible.  New York: Oxford UP, 1972.
```

Encyclopedias and Dictionaries.   For encyclopedias, dictionaries, and similar reference works that are regularly updated and reissued, you do not need to supply the editor, publisher, or place of publication. Give the author's name first if the article is signed. If only the author's initials are given, find the full name in the list of authors. Give the title of the article, the name of the reference work, and the edition. Volume and page numbers are unnecessary when the work is arranged alphabetically.

UNSIGNED ARTICLE

```
"Pornography."  Encyclopaedia Britannica: Micropaedia.  1990 ed.
```

Note the British spelling of the title.

SIGNED ARTICLE

```
Bender, Paul.  "Obscenity."  Encyclopedia Americana.  1981 ed.
```

Periodicals.   For all periodicals, you will need to supply the author's name, the title of the article, and the name of the publication. For professional journals you will also need the volume number (and sometimes the issue number), year of publication, and inclusive page numbers. For magazines, which are usually published weekly, biweekly, or monthly, you will need the complete date, instead of volume and issue numbers, as well as the page numbers.

ARTICLE IN JOURNAL WITH CONTINUOUS PAGINATION

Most professional journals use continuous pagination throughout the year. That is, the second and subsequent issues do not begin with page 1 but with the page number that follows the last page number of the previous issue. When bound yearly, the continuous pagination provides easy reference. In your citation, give volume number, year, and inclusive page numbers.

Holzman, Michael. "Writing as Technique." College English 44

(1982): 129-34.

ARTICLE IN JOURNAL WITH SEPARATE PAGINATION

The issue number (1 in the example) appears after the volume number (30 in the example) so that the article can be located when the issues are bound. An alternative is to add the month or season in parentheses before the year: 30 (Jan. 1982). When a journal uses only an issue number, put the issue number in place of the volume number.

Moskey, Stephen T. "College Instructors as Writing Consultants."

Technical Communication 30.1 (1983): 12-13.

SIGNED ARTICLE IN WEEKLY MAGAZINE

Give the complete date, beginning with the day, and abbreviate all months except May, June, and July.

Dyson, Freeman. "Reflections (Nuclear Weapons--Part IV)." New

Yorker 27 Feb. 1984: 54-103.

SIGNED ARTICLE IN MONTHLY MAGAZINE

Starbird, Ethel A. "The Bonanza Bean Coffee." National Geo-

graphic Mar. 1981: 388-405.

UNSIGNED ARTICLE IN MAGAZINE

Alphabetize according to the first word of the title, not including *A*, *An*, or *The*.

"Are You a Caffeine Addict?" Saturday Evening Post May-June 1982:

50-53.

SIGNED, TITLED REVIEW

De Mott, Benjamin. "Tocqueville Meets Narcissus." Rev. of

American Journey, by Richard Reeves. Psychology

Today May 1982: 79+.

Use a plus sign (+) instead of an ending page number when pages are not consecutive.

PUBLISHED INTERVIEW

Scarr, Sandra. "What's a Parent to Do?" Interview. Psychology

Today May 1984: 58-63.

Newspaper Articles. For the author's name and article title, use the same format as for other periodicals. In giving the name of the newspaper, omit any introductory article. Then give the day, month, year, and page numbers, including the section number if each section starts with 1. If an edition appears on the masthead, show it before the page number.

SIGNED ARTICLE

Brody, Jane. "Weaning the Body from Dependence on Caffeine." New
    York Times 21 Apr. 1982: C6.

UNSIGNED ARTICLE

"Gene's Protein Apparently Aids the Onset of Leukemia." Washing-
    ton Post 20 July 1984: A5.

SIGNED EDITORIAL

Immel, A. Richard. "Ralph Nader's Shoddy Product." Editorial.
    Wall Street Journal 2 Nov. 1971, eastern ed.: 10.

UNSIGNED EDITORIAL

"Lebanon for the Lebanese." Editorial. Times [London] 13 July
    1984: 15.

LETTER TO THE EDITOR

Fallon, James. Letter. Boston Globe 25 July 1985: 23.

Other Written Sources. Here are some examples of citations for other written sources.

UNPUBLISHED DISSERTATION

Cox, James Melville. "Mark Twain: A Study in Nostalgia." Diss.
    Indiana U, 1955.

For a published dissertation, use the same format as you would for a book.

MANUSCRIPT OR TYPESCRIPT

The order should be author, description of material (or a title if it has one), form of material (*ms.* for manuscript, *ts.* for typescript), identifying number and name of institution, if any, and location. This example cites privately owned and stored papers.

Ostby, Vivian. Journal, ms. Private papers. Arlington, VA.

MONOGRAPH

Dale, Richard S., and Richard P. Mattione. <u>Managing Global Debt</u>:
<u>A Staff Paper</u>. Washington: Brookings Inst., 1982.

PAMPHLET

Pamphlets are treated like books.

Potter, Joseph C., and Edward H. Robinson III. <u>Parent-Teacher</u>
<u>Conferencing</u>. Washington: NEA, 1982.

PUBLISHED PROCEEDINGS OF A CONFERENCE

Kleimann, Susan, Eric Rice, and Mary Scheltema, eds. <u>Proceedings</u>
<u>of the Third Maryland Composition Conference</u>. 15 Mar. 1985.
College Park: Maryland U, 1985.

LEGAL DOCUMENT

Legal citations are varied. For documents not illustrated here, see *A Uniform System of Citation* published by the Harvard Law Review Association (1986). In referring to the United States Code, give the title number, US Code or USC, section number, and date. Alphabetize under ''US code.''

29 US Code. Sec. 65. 1976.

For court cases, give the name of the case, volume, name and page of the report cited, name of the court that decided the case, and year. The following case, for example, was decided by the U.S. Court of Appeals for the District of Columbia in 1965. It can be found in volume 350 of the *Federal Reporter*, second series, page 445.

Williams v. Walker-Thomas Furniture Co. 350 F 2d 445. DC Cir. Ct.
1965.

PERSONAL LETTER

Earnest, Dorothy. Letter to the author. 21 July 1982.

Nonprint Sources. In your research some of your sources may not be in printed form. Here are examples of bibliographic entries for nonprint sources.

ART

In a museum:

Bernini, Gianlorenzo. <u>Neptune and Triton</u>. Victoria and Albert
Museum, London.

Reproduction in a book or periodical:

Mondrian, Piet. Composition. Albright-Knox Gallery, Buffalo, NY.

   Illus. in Dictionary of Arts and Artists. By Peter and Linda

   Murray. New York: Praeger, 1965.

INTERVIEW

In person:

Van Valkenburgh, Willard. President, Federal Investment Co. Per-

   sonal interview. 12 Oct. 1990.

By telephone:

Ebb, Carmel. Telephone interview. 2 July 1989.

FILM

For a film give the title, director, distributor, and date. Include any other information pertinent to your paper such as writer, performers, producer, and length of film.

Another Country. Dir. Marek Kanievska. Orion, 1984.

If you are citing a person connected with the film, give that name first.

Kanievska, Marek, dir. Another Country. Orion, 1984.

LECTURE

At a professional conference:

Peterson, Jane E. "Valuing Teaching: Assumptions, Questions, and

   Possibilities." Address. Opening General Sess. Conference

   on College Composition and Communication. Chicago, 22 Mar.

   1990.

For a lecture in a college class, give the name of the lecturer, the subject or title of the lecture, the course title, the name of the college, and the date.

DRAMATIC PERFORMANCE

If you wish to cite the performance, give the playwright and title first. If you wish to cite the director, put his or her name first.

Pinter, Harold. The Homecoming. Dir. Peter Hall. Music Box The-

   ater, New York. 5 Jan. 1967.

Hall, Peter, dir. The Homecoming. By Harold Pinter. Music Box

   Theater, New York. 5 Jan. 1967.

MUSICAL PERFORMANCE

Woodside, Lyndon, dir. War Requiem. By Benjamin Britten. Orato-
    rio Soc. of New York. Carnegie Hall, New York. 10 May 1984.

If you wish to cite the composer, put his or her name first.

Britten, Benjamin. War Requiem. Dir. Lyndon Woodside. Oratorio
    Soc. of New York. Carnegie Hall, New York. 10 May 1984.

DANCE PERFORMANCE

To cite the ballet company, put its name first. To cite the music, put
it first.

American Ballet Theatre. Swan Lake. By Igor Stravinsky. Metro-
    politan Opera House, New York. 15 June 1984.

Fancy Free. By Leonard Bernstein. Chor. Jerome Robbins with John
    Gardner and Ricardo Bustamante. Cond. Jack Everly. American
    Ballet Theatre. John F. Kennedy Center for the Performing
    Arts, Washington. 27 Mar. 1990.

If you are citing the composer or the performance of a particular
person, begin with that person's name.

RECORDING

Give the name of the person you are citing, the title of the record or
tape, artists if you wish, manufacturer, catalog number, and year of issue (if unknown, use *n.d.*). After the name of a cited orchestra conduc-
tor, give the name of the orchestra. In the following entry, the date of
recording is given in addition to the much later date of issue.

Ellington, Duke, cond. Duke Ellington Orch. Duke Ellington at
    Fargo, 1940. Rec. 7 Nov. 1940. Book-of-the-Month Records,
    30-5622-F, 1978.

TELEVISION OR RADIO PROGRAM

Give the title of the program, actors' or other pertinent names, network, local station and city, and broadcast date.

Brideshead Revisited, Episode 4. With Anthony Andrews and Jeremy
    Irons. PBS. WETA, Washington. 24 July 1984.

VIDEOTAPE

Romeo and Juliet. Videocassette. Bolshoi Ballet. MGM, 1976. 109
    min.

MGM is the distributor. Include any other information important to your paper, such as director, producer, or main performers.

MUSICAL COMPOSITION

Give the composer's name, title (underlined only if identified by name, such as the *Moonlight Sonata*) or form, number, key, and opus number. Here the sonata cited is not identified by name, and it has no number.

```
Beethoven, Ludwig van.  Violin sonata in A major, op. 12.
```

INFORMATION OBTAINED THROUGH A COMPUTER DATABASE

Use the same format as you would for a printed reference; then add the name of the vendor and the identifying numbers.

```
Whitehall, J.  "Loopholes for Child Pornography."  Medical Jour-
     nal of Australia 1980.  Dialog file 12, item 1109-1110.
```

Two Sample Research Papers
Using the Author/Page Style

The author/page system of documentation used in the following two papers is recommended in the *MLA Handbook for Writers of Research Papers* (3rd ed., 1988). This system is used by writers in literature and other disciplines in the humanities. In the author/page system, brief parenthetical citations in the text refer to a list of works cited, which is placed at the end of the paper. In the first paper, an argument for the return of Native American remains, the writer provides a title page because he includes a formal outline with the paper. In the second paper, a literary research paper on the changing reputation of Robert Frost, the text begins on page 1, following a brief heading and the title of the paper.

Science Versus Human Dignity:

The Controversy over the Repatriation

of Native American Remains and Artifacts

by

George Forte

If you are handing in an outline with your paper, include a title page. Center the title of your paper (not underlined or enclosed in quotation marks) and type your name, your instructor's name, the course name, and the date below it. If you are not handing in an outline, type identifying information on the first page of the text. (See the sample paper on Robert Frost in this chapter.)

Professor Eunice Miller

English 231

December 12, 199-

Forte ii

Outline follows title page and begins on p. ii (title page is counted but not numbered). Last name used before page number for identification.

Thesis states what the paper attempts to prove.

Outline

Thesis: Religious artifacts and ancestral remains should be returned to Native Americans, and burial and archaeological sites should be protected from further destruction. In addition, a substantial public education program should be undertaken to change the long-held image of Native Americans as subhuman savages.

Topic outline. You could also use a sentence outline.

I. Origins of the controversy

   A. Location of Native American remains and artifacts

   B. The anger and pain of Native Americans

   C. Attitudes and philosophy of early explorers and settlers

II. Actions needed to recognize the rights of Native Americans

III. Three groups who have opposed the proposals of Native Americans

   A. The collectors

   B. The museums

   C. The scientists

   D. The root problem: a basic difference in values

IV. Beginnings of change

   A. Changing attitudes of museums and scientists: the return of some museum holdings

   B. Congressional hearings

V. Future needs

   A. Passage of legislation

   B. Public education on Native American culture

Forte 1

Science Versus Human Dignity:

The Controversy over the Repatriation

of Native American Remains and Artifacts

Center title: double space to text.

The words "Rest in Peace" appear on many tomb-
stones in the United States. But the skeletal remains
of thousands of Native Americans[1] are not resting in
peace. They have been dug up from graves by archaeologists and anthropologists,[2] who examine and study them,
and by relic hunters, who sell them. They have been
collected from battlefields by soldiers and have ended
up as curios--skulls have been fancied as candleholders.
They have been picked up from fields by farmers, and
they have surfaced during the excavations for roads and
dams.

Superscript numbers refer to content notes giving additional information at end of paper.

Writer starts paper with background information.

In addition to human remains, Native American artifacts of all kinds--from weapons and religious objects
to the pipes and pots of everyday use--have been found.
These have ended up in public or private museums, where
they are displayed or studied, or in the possession of
private collectors, who can sell some of them for thousands of dollars at collectors' shows (Arden 92). Other
artifacts and human remains--still underground on public
and private land--could be dug up and appropriated by
virtually anyone with the time and the money to do so.

Citation appears at the end of the sentence, before the period.

Native Americans believe these objects are theirs,
and, despite the attempts of museums, scientists, and
collectors to justify their holdings, Native Americans
seem to have logic on their side. But there is another,
perhaps more fundamental issue in this controversy: the
lack of respect for the human remains and sacred objects
of Native Americans, an attitude that translates into a
lack of respect for Native Americans themselves as well
as for their culture.

Forte 2

It is not surprising, then, that Native Americans
are angry and hurt. Douglas Preston, a former writer
and editor at the American Museum of History in New
York, supports them. He believes that Native Americans
still feel the humiliation of losing their land and,
further, that the looting of their graves and the keeping of their remains is just one more aspect of this
conquest (67).

Native Americans, with considerable justification,
view as racist the interest of museums and curio collectors in the remains and religious objects of their
ancestors. Walter Echo-Hawk, staff attorney for the
Native American Rights Fund, has described the prevailing attitude of Americans this way: "You desecrate
a white grave and you end up sitting in prison. But
desecrate an Indian grave, and you get a Ph.D." (Brower
43). At a Senate committee hearing in 1988 on a bill
to provide protection for Native American remains, he
expressed the viewpoint of many Native Americans
(Senate, Select Committee, Hearing): "Historically
. . . the Native people have been subjected to a systematic national expropriation of their dead by private, by State, and by Federal agencies and entities"
(86).

Another Native American, Suzan Shown Harjo, executive director of the National Congress of American Indians, sums up views of her people this way: "It comes
down to whether Indians are human. . . . The fact that
the Smithsonian has 19,000 of our people is one of the
last vestiges of colonialism, dehumanization, and racism
against our people" (Molotsky A14).

Many historians would agree with them. When the

*Author's name is in
text, so only page
number appears in
citation.*

*Quotation shorter
than three lines is
integrated into the
text.*

*Writer quotes
authorities to back his
assertion.*

Forte 3

European explorers and conquerors came to this country, the morality of appropriating Indian lands was debated by philosophers and theologians. One of the doctrines supporting the rights of conquest in this country held that the Indians were barbarians and heathens and that "By divine law the Christian imperial nations were superior and had the right to dominion and rule over non-Christian inhabitants and their territories" (Parker 3).

Writer provides evidence of racist attitudes and behaviors toward Native Americans.

Paraphrase, summary, and quotation combined.

All of the arguments of Europeans justifying the taking of Indian lands led to the same comforting conclusion--that, as Timothy Christian, dean of law at the University of Atlanta puts it, "European occupation was lawful according to the law of nations" (ix). But, he adds, "the law of nations . . . was little more than a self-serving, crystallization of state practice." The crux of the matter is that the colonists did not regard Native Americans as human: "As subhumans they were incapable of possessing rights--legal, natural, or divine" (xiii).

Writer paraphrases source as a transition between two quotations.

This attitude that Native Americans were less than human lasted well past colonial days. One of the most gruesome examples of this subhuman treatment occurred in the American Museum of Natural History in New York in 1896. The explorer Robert F. Peary brought six Eskimos from Greenland to visit New York. Franz Boas, an anthropologist, and his colleague Aleš Hrdlička wanted to study them and arranged to house them on the museum's fifth floor. The Eskimos had colds when they came and, because of their lack of immunity, four of them developed tuberculosis and died. Preston tells what happened next:

Writer uses an example to support his assertion.

Forte 4

*Quotation of more
than four lines is
indented ten spaces
from the left margin
and double-spaced.
No quotation marks.*

Hrdlička and Boas quickly went to work. Here
was a splendid, unparalleled opportunity to
add postmortem data to their Eskimo file.
Hrdlička directed that all four be macerated,
boiled, and reduced to skeletons at the College of Physicians and Surgeons of Columbia
University. He then installed the skeletons
in the museum's collection, where he could
study them at leisure. (71)

*Citation in
parentheses two spaces
after end punctuation.*

Native Americans are pressing for some acknowledgment of their rights and redress of their grievances.

*After defining the
problem, writer
discusses the
controversy
caused by it.*

They want the bones of their ancestors returned so they
can be reburied with appropriate ceremonies. For some
tribes this reflects not only a desire for respect and
ownership but a fulfillment of religious obligations.
Many tribes, like the Lakota, believe that the spirit
remains after death and must be taken care of. If it is
disturbed, it wanders until it is reburied (Preston 73).
Native Americans also believe that the return of remains
and artifacts would help them reestablish their native
culture and would reduce the "cultural despair" that is
leading to alcoholism and high suicide rates among Native Americans (Preston 73).

How would these goals be implemented? Native Amer-

*Writer cites the
proposals of Native
Americans.*

icans would like Congress to pass a bill requiring museums to return skeletal remains and religious artifacts
to Native Americans. Such a bill would provide legal
remedies to solve disputes between those who possess the
remains and relics and Indian tribes. They would also
like a bill passed to make further excavations stopped
or at least conducted with tribal cooperation or permission. The passage of these bills would seem a small

Forte 5

enough way to compensate these people for the treatment they have received. Yet such bills have not yet been passed.

The interests of three main groups--museums, scientists (archaeologists and anthropologists), and private collectors--conflict with the interests of Native Americans. Among these three groups, the interests of the museums and the scientists are closely allied: the scientists, who want to study the remains, depend on the museums to house the items, and the museums depend on the scientists to provide them with material to display and information to explain the displays to the public. They claim that they need museum holdings to study past cultures; for example, scientists have discovered traces of certain proteins that remain in human bones many years after death. By analyzing these they believe they will be able to track the spread and evolution of certain diseases and perhaps help wipe them out (Preston 72).

Writer summariz arguments of museums, scienti and collectors . .

The collectors, on the other hand, are private individuals who look on the artifacts and remains as the property of the owners of the land where they are found. They believe they are entitled to dig on private land when they have permission of the landowner. Many of them think of themselves, like the scientists and museums, as preservers of the articles they collect.

Native Americans can make good cases against each of these groups. First of all, they do not agree that the museums own the Indian artifacts they have. Many of the artifacts, they believe, were stolen or dug up without consideration for the descendants. In addition, they find it difficult to understand why museums need so

. . . Nati rebu argu

Forte 6

many specimens. The American Museum of Natural History
in New York has about 25,000; the Smithsonian Institution in Washington, D.C., 18,500; Harvard's Peabody Museum, 5,000; and the National Park Service, 20,000.
Other museums, universities, and private collectors have
an estimated 600,000 (Preston 67). Native Americans
don't think it should take that many specimens to find
information on tribal life.

As for the collectors, it's fairly easy to make a
case against them. Native Americans claim that collectors have no respect for them or their culture, that
they just want to make money. Though some may be sin-
cere in their declarations of respect for these ancient
artifacts, most of them seem to be primarily interested
in profit. One clay pipe in the shape of a human head
brought a collector $4,500 (Arden 376). Scientists, who
call collectors "looters," complain that collectors
destroy historical evidence by digging without care and
without making records of what they find and where they
find it. George Stuart of the National Geographic gives
an example of the damage they have done:

> In New Mexico virtually every site of the
> Mimbres--a people of the Mogollon culture--has
> been wrecked by looters seeking their deli-
> cately painted black-on-white bowls. In North
> Carolina the strata of 7,000 years of human
> occupation lie in a jumble, destroyed in a
> matter of days by seekers of a few "collect-
> ible" stone spearpoints and scrapers.
>
> As an archaeologist I deplore the ongoing
> destruction, for my profession literally de-

*No indentation for
first line of a
quotation that does not
begin a paragraph in
the source.*

Forte 7

pends on the excavation of in situ material—
remains of the past in the precise place where
they were left by those who made and used
them. The artifact out of context is, for the
most part, of as little use as the beached
plank of a wrecked ship. (393)

Perhaps the most notorious of these digs occurred
on Slack Farm in Kentucky. In 1987, ten men paid a
farmer $10,000 to open more than 650 gravesites on his
farm (Arden 381) to collect bones and artifacts presum-
ably for resale to collectors. Because the disturbing
of graves is against the law in Kentucky, these men were
charged with "'desecration of a venerated object'"
(Arden 378). But the damage had been done.

Of course, these groups counter with their own
arguments. To the argument that museums have far more
remains than they need for study, the museums respond
that scientists need large numbers of individual specimens to be able to draw general conclusions. Still, it
hardly seems possible that the museums would be able to
examine the thousands of specimens they have on their
shelves.

*Writer presents
groups' arguments.*

Dr. William Boyd, president of the Field Museum of
Natural History in Chicago, sees public education as the
main value of these remains. He explained his view of
the controversy in a radio interview (Indian Artifacts I):

*Writer gives
credentials to establish
source's authority.*

I don't think we should view this debate as
only one between Native Americans [on one
side] and insensitive faceless museums on the
other because what is involved here is the

*Writer places brackets
around words inserted
to clarify a quotation.*

Forte 8

enlightenment and understanding of millions of
Americans who come each year to museums to be
educated and to learn about each other.

*Writer quotes, then
disputes, the source.*

However, thousands of museum remains and artifacts have
never been moved from the shelves and are likely to remain there. Education, like scientific study, could be
accomplished even if some of the remains were returned.

The museums' reluctance to return Native American
burial remains and artifacts has been reinforced and
supported by anthropologists and archaeologists, who
consider such holdings as their "data base" (Preston
67). Besides using current remains for study, archaeologists continue to conduct digs, but they are careful to
mark and catalog everything they find. In many cases,
they rebury items they have found.

Like the museums, scientists see themselves as
preservers of the Native American culture, not de-
stroyers of it, and believe their work is beneficial not
only to the general public but to Native Americans themselves. From the artifacts and religious objects,
Native Americans have been able to revive past cultural
beliefs and practices. Before 1930, when much of Native American culture was being destroyed, the scientists collected artifacts and observed and recorded
rituals that were being lost. Now they find it ironic
that they are being attacked by those whose cultural
heritage they have been preserving. They fear that the
return of many of these items may result in their loss
or their sale to collectors.

The strength of such feelings compelled an anthropologist at San Jose State University to call Stanford's
return of its remains "'scientifically indefensible'"

Forte 9

(Gross A6); he seemed to be implying that the scientists' professional code of honor requires them to keep
their collections.

Despite the claims of scientists that their interests reinforce those of Native Americans, the evidence
clearly suggests that there is a basic value difference
between the two. Scientists seem interested primarily
in scientific discoveries, preservation of artifacts,
and study; human sensibilities are not usually considered. A book by two Missouri archaeologists, Indians
and Archaeology of Missouri, illustrates this scientific point of view. The book, written for the inexperienced archaeologist, contains directions for collecting and digging for artifacts. They advise new
archaeologists to first get a map of the area they want
to survey, locate the house nearest the area, and get
permission from the owner to do a survey. They explain
what to look for in the way of artifacts, how and where
to dig, and how to record those they collect (Chapman
and Chapman 144).

Though they caution archaeologists to keep careful
records, they make no mention of consulting living Native Americans (the last tribes living in Missouri moved
to Kansas and Oklahoma in 1823 and ceded their land to
the United States) (117). The authors don't say whether
any archaeologists in Missouri have tried to make any
connections with these tribes. They aren't thinking in
those terms at all. It's hard to imagine them digging
up the graves of other Americans' ancestors in this
cold, objective way.

The museums, the scientists, and the Native Americans all bring compelling arguments to justify their

*Writer asserts that
conflict between
scientists and Native
Americans stems from
a value difference.*

Summary of source.

*Writer interprets
evidence; he doesn't
just report it.*

Forte 10

actions, beliefs, and feelings. But the museums and
scientists on the one hand and the Native Americans on
the other see this issue in a different framework: museums see themselves as preservers of a culture and their
collections as data banks of information for future
generations; scientists, besides agreeing with museums
about the holding of collections, see unopened graves as
undiscovered riches to be added to their data banks.
Still, many Native Americans see museums and researchers
primarily as desecrators of ancestral remains and tor-
mentors of their spirits and even as holders of stolen
or illegally acquired property.

At least these have been the prevailing views. The
attitudes of scientists and museums toward the Native
Americans seem to be slowly changing. Some of this
change is due no doubt to the efforts of Native Americans to have laws passed that would require museums and
others to return burial remains and artifacts. Museums
may hope that by returning some items they can forestall
the passage of laws that would require all to be returned.

Whatever the reason, many museums are moving toward
repatriation. The Smithsonian Institution will return
Native American remains to any Indian tribe that can
provide "'reasonable certainty'" of an ancestral link
("Sensible Compromise"). The Museum of the American
Indian in New York is returning the skeletal remains
that it has; and Stanford University agreed last year to
return over 500 remains of Ohlone Indians to their descendants (Brower 41). The University of South Dakota
followed by returning remains of Sioux in their possession to be reburied at Wounded Knee, where more than 200

Writer summarizes the arguments of the groups involved in the debate.

Writer introduces a central theme— changing attitudes.

Writer makes claim and provides evidence to support it.

Forte 11

Sioux were massacred by U.S. cavalry (Brower 44). A few
states have passed laws governing museum holdings: a
Nebraska law requires that all state museums return
Indian remains and burial artifacts when requested.
Alaska, Iowa, and Massachusetts have laws supporting
repatriation of human remains. In Kentucky, desecration
of any graves has for some time been considered a fel-
ony.

The archaeologists have also softened their position somewhat. Cheryl Ann Munson spoke for the Society
for American Archaeology in 1988 at the Hearings of the
Senate Select Committee on Indian Affairs at a hearing
on Native American Museum claims. Munson agreed that
human remains should be returned if they have no scientific value or if "direct lineal relationships" can be
established (64). But in all other cases they should be
kept, she said, and disputes should be "resolved on a
case-by-case basis" (63-64). Like the museum officials, society members do not want a law passed requiring the return of remains. They prefer to operate
voluntarily.

These concessions have not completely satisfied
Native Americans. Because they don't believe that vol-
untary repatriation will be sufficient, they want the
protection of a law <u>requiring</u> repatriation--a
law that would cover both private and public institutions as well as individuals. Senate Bill 1980, the
Native American Grave Protection and Repatriation Act,
has been proposed by the Select Committee on Indian
Affairs. It requires museums receiving federal aid to
inventory their Native American holdings, to notify the
tribe about items that may belong to it, and to return

*Writer presents
counterviews of Native
Americans.*

*Past tense (has been
proposed) indicates
past action; present
tense (requires) used
for information in
print.*

Forte 12

any items requested. It further requires that any excavation or removal of remains and "objects of Native
American cultural patrimony" is forbidden without legal

*Writer summarizes
the Senate bill he is
discussing.*

permission (10). Finally, anyone who buys or sells human remains or objects of a Native American without the
"right of possession" may be fined or imprisoned (13).
This bill would regulate the activities of all groups
opposing Native Americans: museums, scientists, and
collectors.

The passage of Senate Bill 1980 would make it unnecessary for Native Americans to apply pressure to each
individual museum and to lobby individual states to

*Writer recommends
one option and
justifies his choice.*

enact laws. In addition they would not have to provide
museums with proof of ownership for repatriation of
remains they hold; the burden of proof of relationship
would be on the museums. The bill would also protect
Native Americans from further desecration of their burial sites on federal, tribal, and private lands and
would stop the profiting from sales of artifacts. At
the same time, museums would be able to keep a considerable number of their holdings because many of the remains would probably go unclaimed.

*Writer summarizes
current status of the
controversy.*

The people of the United States are inching their
way slowly and somewhat reluctantly toward doing justice
to the Native American. Museums and scientists are so
far cooperating to some extent in redressing the com-
plaints of Native Americans even without a law. One law
is already on the books: the Archaeological Resources
Protection Act (ARPA), which prohibits digging on public
lands and Indian lands without permission. But Senate
Bill 1980 needs to be passed. Vandalism on private
lands, which is still legal unless state laws prohibit

Forte 13

it, is merely getting worse as laws preventing looting on public lands are strengthened. We lag behind other countries in these matters. According to a report issued by the House Subcommittee on General Oversight and Investigations,

> In many other nations prehistoric objects are considered public property regardless of whether they are on public or private lands. In the United States, private landowners are free to do anything they want to archaeological resources on their lands. (66)

But passing laws may not be enough. Some museum directors and scientists are beginning to see that the problem requires a change in attitude and a reordering of values. Secretary Adams of the Smithsonian agrees on the one hand with scientists that the skeletons in the museums can tell us much about the past and can provide future benefits. But he also realizes that "'when you face a collision between human rights and scientific study, then scientific values have to take second place'" (Molotsky A14). In a similar vein anthropologists at Stanford, acknowledging the dilemma between "'the sensitivities . . . of living Native Americans . . . and our obligation to the future scientific community,'" decided "'to give more weight to the first than the second'" (Gross A1).

Scientists and museums are beginning to recognize that we need to change the way we think about Native Americans if we are to live together with mutual respect. The stereotypes of the old western movies, which picture Indians as cruel, subhuman enemies brandishing tomahawks as they ride across the plains, won't do any-

Writer ends by proposing a long-term solution for the problem.

Integration of quotations in the sentence.

Writer concludes by proposing that we change how we think about Native Americans.

Forte 14

more. To help abolish those stereotypes, the House subcommittee has suggested "an extensive public education,
interpretation, and advertising program to educate citizens" (70) about the importance of preserving the cultural treasures of Native Americans. By acquiring an
appreciation of the value of Indian culture, we might
come to realize that Native Americans are human beings
like other Americans and that they are entitled to the
same respect and legal protection.

Forte 15

Notes

[1] The term "Native American" refers to those living in what is now the United States, including Alaska and Hawaii. Following the definitions given in Senate Bill 1980, the Native American Grave Protection and Repatriation Act, the word "Indian" is also sometimes used here to refer to a member of an Indian tribe--a group of Native Americans joined by organization or common lineage in the United States. The term "Alaska Native," though not used in this paper, is defined in the bill as an Eskimo, Aleut, or Alaska Indian. Similarly, the term "Native Hawaiian" is defined as a descendant of those living in Hawaii before the coming of the Europeans in 1778.

[2] Anthropologists study people, especially their social relationships and customs. Archaeologists study and interpret ancient cultures by means of artifacts and other remains often found through excavation. Archaeologists studying Native American culture are usually trained in anthropology as well as archaeology.

Forte 16

Works Cited

Sources arranged alphabetically by authors' last names.

First line is flush left; rest of citation is indented five spaces.

Arden, Harvey. "Who Owns Our Past?" National Geographic
    Mar. 1989: 376-93.

Brower, Montgomery. "Walter Echo-Hawk Fights for His
    People's Right to Rest in Peace--Not in Museums."
    People 4 Sept. 1989: 42-44.

Book.

Chapman, Carl H., and Eleanor F. Chapman. Indians and
    Archaeology of Missouri. Columbia: Missouri UP,
    1983.

Christian, Timothy J. Introduction. The Law of Nations
    and the New World. By L. C. Green and Olive P.
    Dickason. Edmonton: Alberta UP, 1989. vii-xiii.

Newspaper article; when pages are not consecutive, put beginning page and "+."

Gross, Jane. "Stanford Agrees to Return Ancient Bones
    to Indians." New York Times 24 June 1989: A1+.

Radio broadcast.

Indian Artifacts I. Rept. Rebecca Clay. NPR. WAMU,
    Washington. 30 July 1990.

Molotsky, Irvin. "Smithsonian to Give Up Indian Re-
    mains." New York Times 1 Sept. 1989, natl. ed.:
    A14.

Parker, Linda S. Native American Estate: The Struggle
    over Indian and Hawaiian Lands. Honolulu: U of
    Hawaii P, 1989.

Preston, Douglas J. "Skeletons in Our Museums'
    Closets." Harper's Feb. 1989: 66-75.

Monthly magazine.

Anonymous article listed alphabetically by title.

"A Sensible Compromise on Indian Bones." Editorial.
    New York Times 26 Aug. 1989: A22.

Stuart, George E. "The Battle to Save Our Past." Na-
    tional Geographic Mar. 1989: 392-93.

United States. Cong. House. Subcommittee on General
    Oversight and Investigations of the Committee on
    Interior and Insular Affairs. The Destruction of

Forte 17

America's Archaeological Heritage: Looking and
Vandalism of Indian Archaeological Sites in the
Four Corners States of the Southwest. 100th Cong.,
2nd sess. Washington: GPO, 1988.

---. ---. Senate. Select Committee on Indian Affairs.
Hearing on the Native American Museum Claims Com-
mission Act. 100th Cong., 2nd sess. Washington:
GPO, 1988.

---. ---. ---. ---. S. 1980: The Native American
Grave Protection and Repatriation Act. 101st
Cong., 2nd sess. Approved in Committee. 1990.

*Consecutive
government
publications.*

use this form

1

Format for paper without a title page: heading is typed flush left and double-spaced; title is centered; text begins two spaces below the title.

Chris Schaffer

Professor Marjorie Lyman

English 101

May 10, 199-

The Changing Reputation of Robert Frost

The Complete Poems of Robert Frost opens with "The Pasture," a poem inviting readers to join the speaker as he is "going out to clean the pasture spring" and "going out to fetch the little calf" (3). With its rural setting, simple diction, and clear subject, this poem firmly establishes the image of its author as a poet-farmer. This was the image that Frost himself cultivated and the image that many of his critics and readers praised. As Gerber explains:

Quotation longer than four lines indented ten spaces and double-spaced.

> To his great public Frost was the epitome of the benevolent farmer-sage, a type of ideal regional figure whose communion with nature purified him and raised him to the status of a seer, but whose total humility rendered him

Short title used because two books by Gerber appear in Works Cited.

> approachable to all. (Robert Frost 19)

The popular image of Frost was challenged by a few critics early on and by others late in the poet's career. These critics focused on a different Frost, one whose sense of the grim and tragic aspects of life pervades his poetry. Another group of critics attacked Frost in the middle of his career as a poet of sentiment and nostalgia--a poet out of touch with the major issues of his time. A study of the critical reception to Frost

Thesis states what the paper will demonstrate.

throughout his career reveals him to be a complex man and poet whose work has provoked a strong and lasting critical debate. Frost is a poet whose reputation in American literature is still evolving more than twenty years after his death.

Schaffer 2

In a career that covered much of this century (he lived from 1874 to 1963), Frost worked hard to be recognized by critics and accepted by readers (Thompson xv-xix). He was almost forty years old before his first volume of poetry, A Boy's Will, was published. Although Frost received mixed reviews in England, where this book first came out, he was championed in America by important literary figures including William Dean Howells and Ezra Pound (Cox 4). Another early supporter, Amy Lowell, gave Frost's second book, North of Boston, a favorable review in the New Republic and then devoted a chapter to Frost in her Tendencies in Modern American Poetry. Lowell was one of the few early critics to focus on what she characterized as Frost's grimly ironic vision: "Mr. Frost's book reveals a disease which is eating into the vitals of our New England life, at least in its rural communities" (81). In discussing the characters in Frost's poems, she called them "the leftovers of the old stock, morbid, pursued by phantoms, slowly sinking to insanity" (81).

Other early critics like Edward Garnett recognized Frost's psychological insight and his ability to respond to both tragic and humorous situations (39-41), but many commentators glossed over the more disturbing images and strains in Frost's poetry. As Gerber explains, Lowell's view of Frost was not echoed by the majority of commentators in the early part of the twentieth century:

> In writing of Frost's tragic sense (which she felt to be overly obsessive) and the quality of disillusionment that touched so much of his work, Miss Lowell introduced topics that would not be dealt with easily by other commentators for decades to come. (Robert Frost 151)

Schaffer 3

The more common view was expressed by Sylvester Baxter, who talked about Frost's "winsome personality" and about the homesickness the poet felt for his New England farm while Frost was in England (29). An anonymous critic in the Philadelphia Public Ledger summed up the popular image of the poet at this time: "Mr. Frost has windblown cheeks and clear blue eyes. He's a Yankee of yankees and glad of it . . ." ("Of Axe-Handles" 48). Frost himself contributed to this impression. According to Wayne Tefs, Frost "labored diligently to promote himself as a kindly, diffident rural sage: as he confided to one of his early correspondents, he wanted to be perceived as 'Yankier and Yankier'" (224).

Single quotation marks used for quotation within a quotation.

Soon after the publication of his first two books, Frost became recognized as one of the most important new poets in America. His works were anthologized in influential collections of poetry such as Louis Untermeyer's Modern American Poetry (1919) and Harriet Monroe's The New Poetry (1917), and he began making reading tours of college and university campuses across the country (Gerber, Critical Essays 5-6). The next few decades were filled with such achievement that one of his biographers, Lawrance Thompson, wrote a book about that period in Frost's life called The Years of Triumph: 1915-1938. Literary prizes and honorary degrees became ordinary events for Frost. By the time he published A Witness Tree in 1943, he had received four Pulitzer Prizes, among other awards; he had been elected to the National Institute of Arts and Letters; and he had held distinguished academic positions at Amherst, Harvard, and the University of Michigan at Ann Arbor (Cox 199-201).

Citation for author, short title, and page numbers.

Writer summarizes information found in a chronology of important dates in Frost's life.

Yet even after Frost was in his fifties, not every-

Schaffer 4

one was willing to recognize his mastery as a poet.
Certain critics attacked Frost for not writing directly
about the important political and social issues of his
time. In reviewing Collected Poems in 1930, Granville
Hicks claimed that Frost "cannot give us the sense of
belonging in the industrial, scientific, Freudian world
in which we find ourselves. . . . That is why no one
would think of maintaining that he is one of the great
poets of the ages" (78). Ivor Winters complained that
Frost was a "spiritual drifter," and Harold H. Watts
joined Winters in concluding that Frost had not adequately explored the relationship between the individual
and society (Gerber, Robert Frost 160).

For some critics, Frost simply seemed unsophisticated, or worse, politically conservative. Malcolm
Cowley, in "Frost: A Dissenting Opinion," complained
that Frost had become the symbol of those espousing a
narrow nationalism who demanded that "American literature should be affirmative, optimistic, uncritical and
'truly of this nation'" (312). In the second part of
his series, "The Case Against Mr. Frost: II," Cowley
condemned Frost himself for being opposed to "innova-
tions in art, ethics, science, industry or politics"
(345), and for setting limits on the exploration of
himself and "on almost every other human activity"
(346). In his final assessment of Frost, Cowley called
him "a poet who celebrates the diminished but prosper-
ous and self-respecting New England of the tourist home
and the antique shop in the abandoned gristmill" (347).

The attacks on Frost were met with strong defenses
of the poet's work. Bernard DeVoto claimed that Frost
was a poet with authority: "Frost's poetry is a new

*Writer combines
quotation and
paraphrase to
represent other critical
perspectives.*

Schaffer 5

assertion of eternal things--that, whether in tragedy or
in fulfillment, life counts, is worthy, can be trusted,
has dignity. . . . It is the only major affirmation
that modern American literature has made" (109). Others agreed with DeVoto, among them George Whicher of
Amherst, who praised Frost for maintaining "during a
time of general disillusionment" his faith in democracy
(Cook 21).

Ellipses points indicate that something was omitted from the original.

As Gerber recounts in his history of critical response to Robert Frost, the poet survived the attacks of
the 1930s and early 40s to find his public reputation
secure and growing (Robert Frost 159). Though the negative criticism did not disappear, it was overshadowed by
praise and analysis of Frost's later work and by Frost's
great popularity with readers and audiences across the
country. When Frost turned seventy-five, the United
States Senate passed a resolution honoring Frost for
writing poems that "have helped to guide American
thought with humor and wisdom, setting forth to our
minds a reliable representation of ourselves and of all
men . . ." (qtd. in Thompson and Winnick 186).

Qtd. in ("quoted in") indicates that statement came from secondary source.

But the prevalent view of Frost as the optimistic
voice of American values and hopes was disturbed once
again, however, at a public celebration of Frost's
eighty-fifth birthday given by his publishers, Henry
Holt and Company. Lionel Trilling, who was the speaker
at the dinner, later wrote of the event because his
speech upset many of those present and many who later
heard about the speech. Trilling wanted to know why his
remarks about Frost nearly "approached a scandal"
(151). The provocation in Trilling's speech was his
point that "the manifest America of Mr. Frost's poems

Schaffer 6

may be pastoral; the actual America is terrifying."
About the characters in Frost's poems, Trilling wondered: "when ever have people been so isolated, so
lightning-blasted, so tried down and calcined by life,
so reduced, each in his own way, to some last irreduc-
ible core of being" (157). Trilling ended by comparing
the poet to Sophocles and by calling Frost a poet "who
could make plain the terrible things" (158). Trilling
did not mean to discredit Frost by focusing on the
darker aspects of his poetry, but to a large group of
his critics and readers, this focus was unacceptable.
J. Donald Adams reprinted parts of the speech and
blasted Trilling for it in the New York Times Book
Review. As Trilling reports in his account of the
event, his speech was taken as an "affront to some
part of American opinion. It was a very deep affront
if I can judge by the letters, published in the Book
Review of April 26th, which applauded Mr. Adams for
his reply to me" (151-52). Trilling's speech polarized
critics to some degree; more importantly, it highlighted again the complexity of Frost's vision of
experience.

    Because Frost was such a public figure, up until
his death it was difficult to consider the poetry apart
from the poet and his public image. And after his
death, memoirs of Frost published by friends, collections of his letters, and the three-volume biography of
Frost written by Lawrance Thompson provided a great deal
of new and controversial material for the debate about
this complex man and artist. The question of whether
Frost was a benevolent poet-farmer or a terrifying
tragic poet was complicated by the new image of Frost

Trilling is quoted rather than paraphrased because his words are striking and evocative.

Writer interprets Trilling's intentions and analyzes the effect of the event.

Chronological order of paper is useful for illustrating the evolution of Frost's reputation.

Schaffer 7

that emerged from the letters and from Thompson's biography. Tefs summarizes what was revealed:

> Frost often referred to the "scatteration" of his family and felt profound guilt about his relations with his children. He was a difficult husband and father: as his public stature grew, his household increasingly felt the strain of his intense and stubborn personality. Probably because he was himself so insecure, Frost was often bitingly cruel to colleagues, friends, and family. (227)

It seems that Frost's understanding of isolation and despair, which was noted by Amy Lowell early on and highlighted by Trilling, was rooted in his own personal experience as well as in his observations of life in New England and elsewhere.

Conclusion does not resolve the debate, since studies are ongoing. Instead, writer summarizes agreed-upon strengths of Frost's poetry.

Recent critics are now trying to sift through all the evidence to understand Frost, his poetry, and his place in American literature. The debate about Frost will not be easily resolved. The poet who expresses the simple values of rural America is the same poet who, acquainted with the night himself, shows us the darkness of night and solitude and reveals to us our own fears. But as Tefs remarks, the poetry itself stands as a triumph over these fears. For many of Frost's critics and for the great majority of his readers, "the enduring appeal of his poetry springs from his transcendence of the fears overshadowing him through formal structures which testify to the strength and endurance of the human will" (228-29).

Schaffer 8

Works Cited

Baxter, Sylvester. "New England's New Poet." American
Review of Reviews Apr. 1915: 432-34. Rpt. in Gerber, Critical Essays 26-30.

Cook, Reginald. "The Critics and Robert Frost."
Frost: Centennial Essays. Comp. Committee on the
Frost Centennial of the U of Southern Mississippi.
Jackson: U Press of Mississippi, 1974. 15-30.

Cowley, Malcolm. "The Case Against Mr. Frost: II."
New Republic 18 Sept. 1944: 345-47. Pt. 2 of a
series begun on 11 Sept. 1944.

---. "Frost: A Dissenting Opinion." New Republic 11
Sept. 1944: 312-13. Pt. 1 of a series.

Cox, James M., ed. Robert Frost: A Collection of
Critical Essays. Englewood Cliffs: Prentice, 1962.

DeVoto, Bernard. "The Critics and Robert Frost." Saturday Review of Literature 1 Jan. 1938. Rpt. in
Gerber, Critical Essays 104-111.

Frost, Robert. Complete Poems of Robert Frost. New
York: Holt, 1967.

Garnett, Edward. "A New American Poet." Atlantic
Monthly Aug. 1915. Rpt. in Gerber, Critical Essays
35-42.

Gerber, Philip L., ed. Critical Essays on Robert Frost.
Boston: Hall, 1982.

---. Robert Frost. Rev. ed. Twayne's United States
Authors Series. Boston: Twayne, 1982.

Hicks, Granville. "The World of Robert Frost." Rev.
of Collected Poems, by Robert Frost. New Republic
3 Dec. 1930: 77-78.

Lowell, Amy. Rev. of North of Boston, by Robert Frost.
New Republic 20 Feb. 1915: 81-82.

List of works cited, alphabetically arranged, begins new page.

Article reprinted in a collection of essays.

Serialized article.

Three hyphens followed by a period for second work by an author.

Book review in a weekly magazine.

Schaffer 9

Anonymous author, alphabetized by title.

"Of Axe-Handles and Guide-Book Poetry." Philadelphia
Public Ledger 4 Apr. 1916. Rpt. in Gerber, Critical Essays 48-50.

Journal with continuous pagination.

Tefs, Wayne. "The Faces of Robert Frost." Canadian
Review of American Studies 13 (1982): 223-29.

Thompson, Lawrance. Robert Frost: The Years of Triumph,
1915-1938. Vol. 2 of Robert Frost. 3 vols. New
York: Holt, 1970.

Each volume in Thompson's three-volume biography has a separate subtitle. The third has a coauthor.

Thompson, Lawrance, and R. H. Winnick. Robert Frost:
The Later Years, 1938-1963. Vol. 3 of Robert
Frost. 3 vols. New York: Holt, 1976.

Trilling, Lionel. "A Speech on Robert Frost: A Cultural Episode." Partisan Review 26 (1959): 445-
52. Rpt. in Cox 151-58.

C H A P T E R   11

Writing a Paper in the Social Sciences: The Author/Date Style

Many writers in anthropology, biology, business, education, economics, psychology, political science, and other social sciences follow the system of documentation known as the author/date style, explained in the *Publication Manual of the American Psychological Association* (3rd ed., 1984). These writers give the author and date in the text because this information is important to readers. Because the APA *Manual* applies primarily to manuscripts that will be submitted for publication, not to college papers or dissertations, many of the suggestions, such as margins and spacing, are designed for the convenience of editors and printers; the authors suggest that students adapt these to their use. Therefore, the following guidelines give priority to the needs of student writers of "final-copy" manuscripts in these disciplines. If you plan to publish your article in a journal, you will find most of these guidelines compatible with your purpose; however, for some formatting details, you should consult the APA *Manual*. Jean Carroll's paper in this chapter uses the APA's author/date style.

Parts of the Manuscript

**FOR ORIGINAL RESEARCH
PAPERS**
Title page
Abstract
Table of contents

FOR THEORETICAL PAPERS
Title page
Abstract
Table of contents

FOR ORIGINAL RESEARCH PAPERS	FOR THEORETICAL PAPERS
List of tables and figures	List of tables and figures
Introduction	Introduction
Method	Body with headings
Results	————
Discussion	————
Content notes, if used	Content notes, if used
References	References
Appendixes	Appendixes

Consult your instructor for the parts that you need for your paper. For example, you many not need a title page, table of contents, or appendixes. Use extra spacing to improve readability, especially before and after headings.

Format

Title Page

On the title page place the title of your paper, your name, and any other information your instructor prefers, such as course number, instructor's name, and date. Center your title on the page, capitalizing the first letter of all important words; don't underline the title or place it in quotation marks. Place each of the other items on a separate line below your title, beginning with your name; double-space between items. You don't need a number on this page, but it should be counted as small roman numeral i. (If you are preparing a manuscript for publication, you should place an arabic numeral 1 in the upper right corner and number succeeding pages consecutively with arabic numerals.)

Margins and Spacing

Leave margins of 1½ inches on all sides. Double-space throughout the manuscript including the abstract and long indented quotations. The reference list may be single-spaced within entries (double-space between them) if you will not be submitting your paper for publication. Indent the first word of each paragraph five spaces. Indent long quotations (more than forty words) five spaces from the left margin. For long quotations of more than one paragraph, indent the first line of subsequent paragraphs five additional spaces.

Page Numbers

In a student paper use small roman numerals for preliminary pages (ii, iii); in papers for publication, use arabic numbers for all pages. Beginning with the introduction, number the pages in the body of your paper consecutively with arabic numerals placed in the upper right corner, two spaces below a shortened title of your paper. Although the APA *Manual* recommends that the title rather than your name be placed at the top of the page for the sake of blind review of your paper for journal publication, your instructor may prefer your last name there for identification.

Abstract

The abstract is a one-paragraph summary of your paper: an appropriate length is from 100 to 150 words for a primary research paper, from 75 to 100 words for a theoretical paper. It gives the purpose and content of your paper but does not evaluate or comment on the content. For more information on writing abstracts, see Chapter 9. As part of the front matter of your paper, the abstract should be numbered with small roman numerals; if you use a title page, give the abstract page the number ii in the upper right corner below the short title.

Place the title Abstract at the center of the page two spaces below the page number. Unlike other paragraphs, the text of the abstract begins at the left margin.

Headings

Headings serve the purpose of an outline. Some papers contain as many as five levels of headings. A student paper, however, is unlikely to contain more than two or three levels. For clarity, you should make these headings typographically distinct. For two levels, use the following format for a theoretical paper:

Water Erosion
[Level one, centered]

Rainsplash Erosion
[Level two, at left margin and underlined]

A two-level heading system for a primary research paper would look like this:

Method
[Level one]

Procedure
[Level two]

If you have three levels of headings, use this system for theoretical papers.

Production
[Level one, centered]

Cost and Efficiency
[Level two, at left margin and underlined]

Larger areas in production.
[Level three, indented five spaces and underlined; initial capital letter only; text follows on same line]

For a primary source paper, the headings would be Method at level one, Observation at level two, and Setting at level three.

First Page

Type the number 1 under the short title in the upper right corner of the page. Center the title two to four spaces below the page number, capitalizing the first letter of each important word. Double-space and begin typing the text.

Introduction

The first paragraphs of the paper introduce readers to the problem being studied, the reasons for the study, and previous work done and literature written on the subject. It may also summarize the research that was done for this particular study. The APA *Manual* recommends that the introduction have no label or heading because its position shows that it is an introduction, but a heading is used in some journals. Chapter 7 gives several examples of introductions.

Content Notes

Content notes provide supplementary information not essential to the main text of the paper; they should be used sparingly. They may be placed at the bottom of the page containing the material they refer to or on a separate page following the body of the paper. Superscript numbers should be placed in the text after the material to be footnoted. If you place the notes on a separate page, use the heading Footnotes at the top of the page two spaces below the page number; double-space and begin with the superscript number of the first footnote. Indent the first line of each footnote five spaces and double-space between lines. The same format should be used for footnotes at the bottom of the page, except that the heading is omitted and the first footnote begins two spaces below the last line of the text.

Documentation

Parenthetical Citation

To indicate the source of the information you use, give the author and the year of publication either as part of your text or in parentheses as near as possible to the cited information. Some writers also include the page number: (Jones, 1984, p. 36). Page numbers must be given with quotations.

WORK BY ONE AUTHOR

If you use the author's name as part of your sentence, place only the date of publication in parentheses.

```
Olson (1984) first reported the results in a recent study.
```

If you give both date and author in your sentence, you do not need a citation.

```
In a 1984 study at Stanford, Olson addressed this problem.
```

If you give neither in your sentence, you must give both in parentheses.

```
A recent study at Stanford (Olson, 1984) addressed this problem.
```

WORK BY TWO AUTHORS

Give the names of both authors every time the work is cited.

```
Barlow and Seidner (1983) contend that . . .
```

WORK BY THREE, FOUR, OR FIVE AUTHORS

Give the names of all authors the first time the work is cited. When the names are given in parentheses, use an ampersand (&) instead of *and*.

In later citations, give only the name of the first author, followed by *et al*.

```
According to Hewitt, Smith, and Larson (1984) . . .

Recent research (Hewitt, Smith, & Larson, 1984) has shown . . .

The researchers (Hewitt et al., 1984) further hypothesized . . .
```

WORK BY SIX OR MORE AUTHORS

Give only the last name of the first author followed by *et al*. A work written by Wilson, Miles, James, Wylie, Masters, and Flower would be cited as follows:

```
According to Wilson et al. (1982) . . .

A recent study of phobics (Wilson et al., 1982) showed . . .
```

CORPORATE AUTHOR

Give the full name of a corporate author (government agency, association, or research organization) each time it occurs in the text. However, if the group is well known by its abbreviation, give its abbreviation with the first citation and use the abbreviation in subsequent references.

```
In a recent television series on mental health (National Broad-
casting Company [NBC], 1985) . . .
In the first of its series, NBC (1985) . . .
Schizophrenia was shown (NBC, 1985) . . .
```

WORK WITHOUT AN AUTHOR

In your citation give enough of the title to enable your readers to find it in your reference list; usually two or three words are enough. For example, an article titled ''Power Conflict in Groups'' would be cited as: (''Power Conflict,'' 1980).

TWO OR MORE AUTHORS WITH SAME LAST NAME

If you have used as sources two or more authors with the same last name, you must give their initials each time you refer to their work.

```
According to C. R. Lewis (1984) and L. M. Lewis (1985) . . .
```

TWO OR MORE WORKS BY THE SAME AUTHOR

Give the name followed by the dates of the works.

```
Research shows (Hallam, 1979, 1984) . . .
```

If the works were published in the same year, use the alphabetical suffixes you assign to the works in the reference list.

```
(Marston, 1979a, 1979b)
```

TWO OR MORE WORKS BY DIFFERENT AUTHORS

When citing two or more authors within the same parentheses, give them in alphabetical order and separate the entries with semicolons.

```
(Jones, 1983; Mower & Rhodes, 1984)
```

PART OF A SOURCE

You may want to cite a page, chapter, illustration, or other specific part of a source. When you use a quotation, you must always give the page number.

```
(Rogers & Martin, 1979, chap. 4)
(see Figure 4 in Lorenzo, 1975, p. 45)
```

PERSONAL COMMUNICATION

When you refer to letters, interviews, or telephone conversations, give the citation in your text only. Don't include it in your reference list because it cannot be found by anyone else. Give the initials as well as the last name.

```
According to J. R. Davis (personal communication, March 4,
1985) . . .
```

LEGAL DOCUMENTS

For court cases mentioned in the text, give the name of the case, underlined, and the date in parentheses.

```
United States v. Castillo (1975)
```

If the reference is a parenthetical citation, the entire reference is in parentheses.

```
(United States v. Castillo, 1975)
```

For statutes, give the name of the act and year.

```
Equal Employment Opportunity Act (1972)
```

or

```
Equal Employment Opportunity Act of 1972
```

For other kinds of legal citations, see *A Uniform System of Citation* published by the Harvard Law Review Association (1986).

Reference List

Center the heading References at the top of the page and number the page with the number that continues the numbering of the text. For example, if the text of your paper ends on page 12, the content notes page (if there is one) would be numbered 13, and the list of references would be numbered 14.

Begin each reference at the left margin and indent subsequent lines of the entry three spaces. If you are writing for publication, double-space within and between entries, but if you're writing a final-copy paper (the usual college paper), you can save space by single-spacing within items. Always double-space between items.

Arrange references in alphabetical order according to the last name of the first author. If more than one reference is by the same author, give the author's name each time and arrange the entries in chronological order of publication.

```
Flavell, J. H. (1963).
Flavell, J. H. (1977).
```

If you have entries with the same first author and different second or third authors, the entry with one author precedes multiple-author entries. Then arrange entries alphabetically in order of the subsequent authors.

```
Leakey, R. E. F. (1976).
Leakey, R. E. F., & Lewin, R. (1977).
Leakey, R. E. F., & Walker, A. C. (1976).
```

When two works by the same author are published in the same year, arrange the works alphabetically by title and distinguish them by using lowercase letters—a, b, c—after the date.

```
Chomsky, N. (1976a).
Chomsky, N. (1976b).
```

The next sections illustrate formats for references appropriate for most college papers using the author/date system. You'll find an example of a reference list at the end of Jean Carroll's paper (p. 313).

Books. Here are some examples of entries for books in the APA author/date system.

ONE AUTHOR

Give last name of author first, followed by initials only. The date of publication (in parentheses) is followed by a period. Underline the title of the book and capitalize only the first letter in the first word of the title as well as the first letter of the subtitle, if any. Give the city of publication and, if necessary for clarity, the state or country. Use a short title of the publishing company as long as it's intelligible, but give names of university presses in full.

```
Goodwin, D. W. (1983). Phobia: The facts. New York: Oxford Uni-
     versity Press.
```

TWO OR MORE AUTHORS

Include all names, no matter how many. (Note that in-text citations use a different format with multiple authors.) Use commas to separate all names; use an ampersand (&) instead of *and* before the last name. Invert all authors' names.

```
Blake, R. R., & Mouton, J. S. (1964). The managerial grid. Hous-
     ton: Gulf.
```

CORPORATE AUTHOR

Alphabetize corporate authors by the first significant word. When the author and publisher are the same, use *Author* for the name of the publisher.

National Broadcasting Company. <u>Why sales come in curves</u>. New
    York: Author, 1954.

BOOK WITHOUT AN AUTHOR OR EDITOR

Alphabetize a book with no author by the first significant word in
the title; in this case, *uniform*.

<u>A uniform system of citation</u>. (1986). Cambridge, MA: Harvard Law
    Review Association.

REVISED EDITION

McIlwain, H. (1972). <u>Biochemistry and the central nervous system</u>
    (rev. ed.). New York: Churchill.

ONE VOLUME IN MULTIVOLUME WORK

Use the U.S. Postal Service abbreviation for the state when the location of the city is not well known or if it might be confused with another
city of the same name.

Stouffer, S. A., Suchman, E. A., DeVinney, L. C., Star, S. A., &
    Williams, R. M., Jr. (1949). <u>Studies in social psychology in</u>
    <u>World War II: Vol. 1.</u> <u>The American soldier: Adjustment during</u>
    <u>army life</u>. Manhattan, KS: Military Affairs/Aerospace Histo-
    rian.

ENGLISH TRANSLATION OF A BOOK

Bringuier, J. (1980). <u>Conversations with Jean Piaget</u> (B. M. Gu-
    lati, Trans.). Chicago: University of Chicago Press. (Original
    work published 1977)

In your text, use this citation: (Bringuier, 1977/1980).

CHAPTER OR ARTICLE IN EDITED REPRINT OF A BOOK

Do not invert the editor's name when it is not in the author position.

Price, H. H. (1976). The causal theory. In R. J. Swartz (Ed.),
    <u>Perceiving, sensing, and knowing</u> (pp. 395-437). Berkeley: Uni-
    versity of California Press. (Original work published 1965)

For a reprinted work, use this citation in your text: (Price, 1965/1976).

Periodicals. Here are some typical periodical articles in a reference list.

JOURNAL ARTICLE: ONE AUTHOR

For the article title, capitalize only the first word, any proper nouns,
and the first word of the subtitle, if any. Do not underline the title and
do not put it in quotation marks. For the periodical title, capitalize the

first letter of each main word and underline the title; also underline the volume number and follow it with a comma; give beginning and ending page numbers for the article. Use *p.* or *pp.* before page numbers in references to magazine and newspaper articles but not in references to journal articles.

> Brotsky, S. (1968). Classic conditioning of the galvanic skin response to verbal concepts. Journal of Experimental Psychology, 70, 244-253.

JOURNAL ARTICLE: TWO AUTHORS

Give last names of both authors first; use an ampersand (&) between them.

> Barlow, D. H., & Seidner, A. L. (1983). Treatment of adolescent agoraphobics: Effects on parent-adolescent relations. Behavioral Research and Therapy, 21, 519-525.

JOURNAL ARTICLE: THREE OR MORE AUTHORS

Give names of all authors in the list of references regardless of how many; use an ampersand before the last name. Underline the volume number and follow it with a comma. In the text, however, when there are more than five authors, give only the name of the first, followed by *et al.* (not underlined).

> Telch, M. J., Tearnan, B. H., & Taylor, C. B. (1983). Antidepressant medication in the treatment of agoraphobia: A critical review. Behavioral Research and Therapy, 21, 505-516.

ARTICLE IN JOURNAL WITH SEPARATE PAGINATION

Place the number of the issue in parentheses after the volume number without a space between them.

> Bunney, W. E., Jr. (1976). Acute behavioral effects of lithium carbonate. Neurosciences Research Program Bulletin, 14(2), 124-131.

MAGAZINE ARTICLES

The month follows the year. Use the abbreviations *p.* for "page" and *pp.* for "pages."

> Casson, L. (1985, June). Breakthrough at the first think tank. Smithsonian, pp. 158-168.

SIGNED NEWSPAPER ARTICLE

Give the year first, followed by the month and day. Give section number, if any, followed by page number. Place a comma between numbers when pages are discontinuous.

Mansfield, S. (1981, October 25). For 30 years she was a prisoner
    of fear. Washington Post, sec. G, pp. 1, 3.

UNSIGNED NEWSPAPER ARTICLE

When an article has no author, alphabetize the entry by the first significant word of the title.

Grey area of surrogate mother and child. (1985, January 13).
    Manchester Guardian, p. 1.

LETTER TO THE EDITOR

Hammer, A. (1985, July 26). We have to find domestic fuel solu-
    tions [Letter to the editor]. New York Times, sec. A, p. 26.

Other Printed Material.   Here are some examples of references for
other kinds of printed material.

TECHNICAL OR RESEARCH REPORT

Give identifying information or the report number in parentheses
following the title of the report.

Trivett, D. A. (1975). Academic credit for prior off-campus
    learning (ERIC/Higher Education Research Report No. 2). Wash-
    ington, DC: American Association for Higher Education.

Congressional Budget Office. (1982). Financing social security:
    Issues and options for the long run (S/N 052-070-05787-4).
    Washington, DC: U.S. Government Printing Office.

LEGAL DOCUMENT

This court case was decided by the U.S. Court of Appeals for the
District of Columbia in 1965. It can be found in volume 350 of the *Federal Reporter*, second series, page 445.

Williams v. Walker-Thomas Furniture Co., 350 F.2d 445 (D.C. Cir.
    1965).

The following act was codified in title 29 of the *United States Code* in
section 65. For legal references, the symbol for *section* (§) if you have it
on your typewriter or computer, is preferred to the abbreviation *Sec.*
given here.

Occupational Safety and Health Act, 29 U.S.C. Sec. 65 (1976).

PROCEEDINGS OF A MEETING

Austin, J. L. (1956). Ifs and cans. Proceedings of the British
    Academy, 42, 109-132.

UNPUBLISHED MANUSCRIPT

Meyer, P. (1974). Assessing life/work experience: A rationale
    for faculty-based models. Unpublished manuscript, Florida In-
    ternational University, Miami.

Nonprint Sources.   The APA *Manual* recommends these formats for
nonprint sources.

FILM

Give the name and role of the principal contributors or originators
first, with their function in parentheses. After the date and title, give
the medium in brackets. Finally, give the location and name of the distributor or museum (in the case of a work of art). You can use this format for other nonprint media, such as videotapes, slides, and artwork.

Turple, J. (Producer). (1981). Acid rain: Requiem or recovery
    [Film]. New York: National Film Board of Canada.

CASSETTE RECORDING

If you have a number for the recording, give that in parentheses in
place of the name of the medium in brackets. For example: (*Cassette Recording No. 192*) instead of [*Cassette recording*].

Kellogg, P. P., & Allen, A. A. (Producers), & Peterson, R. T. (Col-
    laborator). (1982). A field guide to bird songs [Cassette
    recording]. Boston: Houghton Mifflin.

Sample Research Paper
Using the Author/Date Style

In the following paper Jean Carroll has used the author/date system
recommended in the *Publication Manual of the American Psychological Association*. Because the *Manual* is intended to be used primarily by those
who are preparing manuscripts for publication in professional journals, the APA advises writers of undergraduate or graduate papers to
modify the guidelines to conform to their own department's or instructor's requirements. Accordingly, Carroll has adapted the *Manual* suggestions to suit a paper she wrote for an undergraduate course. (Note
that she has chosen the option of including page numbers in her citation.) The style used here should be acceptable in most college classes
in which the author/date documentation system is recommended.

The Causes and Treatment of Agoraphobia

Jean M. Carroll

Valley State College

May 15, 198-

Title, writer's name, and any other information specified by instructor.

Agoraphobia

ii

Abstract

Agoraphobia, or "fear of the marketplace," is a fear of fear; those who are afflicted are unable to leave their homes. Recent studies have shown three causes: psychological problems, a single spontaneous attack that is then repeated, or biological problems. The most common treatments are psychotherapy, various kinds of behavioral therapy, and drugs. The best results seem to come from behavior therapy. Clearly, agoraphobics can now receive help and learn to lead normal lives.

Agoraphobia

The Causes and Treatment of Agoraphobia

Fear helps us react to danger in order to protect ourselves. When we recognize danger, our bodies release extra energy so that we will be ready to do what is necessary to respond. Our hearts begin to beat more rapidly; we tense our muscles; we feel hot or cold; we breathe faster. As a result we are ready to yell, run, jump, or use force. Some people, though, have these symptoms even when there is no danger; they may feel faint or nauseous when they cross a bridge, see a snake, fly in planes, or ride in elevators. Psychologists call these victims of irrational, excessive, or uncontrollable fears "phobics."

Goodwin (1983, p. 25) identifies three classes of phobias: simple, social, and agoraphobic. A simple phobia is a fear of objects or situations, such as animals, heights, or illness. A social phobia is a fear of being seen; common social phobias are the fear of public speaking, of blushing, or of eating in public. Agoraphobia (literally "fear of the marketplace") is more than a fear of a single external object or of an activity; it is a fear of leaving a safe place (a home or a room) or the companionship of a trusted person. Thus the fears of agoraphobics make it almost impossible for them to function outside the home. Because agoraphobia is a fear not of the known, but of the unknown, it is "the most disabling of all the phobias" (Whitehead, 1983, p. 31).

Almost two million Americans are afflicted by agoraphobia and most of these are believed to be women, although some researchers think that the statistics may

Text page 1; title is centered, using first-level heading.

Introduction is not labeled.

Page number must be given for direct quotation.

Agoraphobia

2

Short title used for a work with no author.

"reflect in part the willingness of women to be more open about problems" ("The Fight," 1984, p. 71). But more women may be agoraphobic because it is easier for them to stay home without questions from others (Weekes, 1972, p. 12). Agoraphobia in men usually appears as a

Superscript number refers to content note at end of paper.

reluctance to leave their town.[1] Although most agoraphobics are adults, some children and adolescents have also sought treatment (Barlow & Seidner, 1983, p. 519).

The amount of anxiety that accompanies these fears or the extent of the inconvenience they cause determines whether the person decides to seek help. A person who has a panic attack at the sight of a mouse may be able to avoid mice most of the time. But a person who has the same symptoms crossing a bridge or riding an elevator to get to work is severely handicapped. As a result such a person will usually seek help.

First-level heading format.

Publication date placed close to author's name.

Symptoms of Agoraphobia

Sheehan (1983) believes that agoraphobia is not a single phobia but is the name given to a group of phobias that are acquired over a period of time: "as far as acquiring phobias are concerned, the agoraphobia stage is the end of the line" (p. 68). He explains:

Quotation of more than forty words is indented five spaces from the left margin and double-spaced.

> When the condition was named, "agoraphobia" was chosen from the cluster of phobias as being one of the most representative or typical of all the many fears the patient has at this point. Curiously,

Brackets enclose material not in original.

> the literal symptom of agoraphobia [fear of the marketplace or fear of crowded places] is not the most common or even central fear shared by patients with the anxiety disease. More common and central

Agoraphobia

3

is a fear that might be called "phobiaphobia"--a
fear of having another spontaneous panic attack.
It is usually this fear that is the most intense
and guides their behavior more than any other fear.
(p. 68)

*Page number in
parentheses after the
period.*

Marjorie Goff, a 64-year-old woman who recovered
from agoraphobia, explained her experience in an interview in the Washington Post (Mansfield, 1981). Her
problem began one Saturday in 1946 when, as a successful
young career woman, she went to the beauty shop where
she regularly had her hair done. She described what
happened:

*Specific case shows
how symptoms
develop.*

I was sitting under the dryer, and all of a sudden
this feeling swept over me. I'm losing my mind, I
thought. I'm going crazy. My heart started beat-
ing fast. My legs felt weak. My body trembled.
It was the most incredible feeling of fear. I
wanted to scream, to run out of there. I got up
with all the pins in my hair, slapped a 5-dollar
bill on the counter and ran all the way home. I
was white, I felt that everyone was looking at me,
that everyone knew. I didn't know what was wrong
with me. (sec. G, p. 1)

Other panic attacks followed--at work, on buses, in the
grocery store, and in elevators. By 1949, Goff's fears
forced her to stay inside her apartment, living on $300
a month sent to her by her father.

*Newspaper section
number when each
section begins page 1.*

Like most other phobics, Goff realized that her
phobia was irrational, but acknowledging the irrational-
ity of the fear was not enough to overcome it. For many
phobics the stress caused by the bewilderment and fear

*Writer makes useful
generalization from a
specific case.*

Agoraphobia

4

that accompany their condition so intensifies the problem that they may become depressed. They become caught in a vicious circle in which fear creates fear.

Causes of Agoraphobia

Stress is generally considered the immediate cause of the panic attacks that lead to agoraphobia, but there is little agreement on what causes the stress or on why the stress develops into agoraphobia. In general, theories about the causes of agoraphobia fall into three groups: psychological, behavioral, and biological or genetic causes.

Organization of the section is outlined.

Second-level heading.

Psychological Causes

Theorists who favor the idea that agoraphobia results from psychological causes claim that panic attacks result from unconscious fears that express themselves symbolically. An unconscious conflict over separation from a close friend or relative, for example,

Source either in parentheses or as part of text.

may cause the initial attack (Lehman, 1985). Whitehead (1983), on the other hand, suggests that agoraphobic anxiety may be a result of clinical depression. According to this theory, agoraphobia can be a way of avoiding a deeper problem. Melville (1977), agreeing with this theory, suggests that agoraphobia is a "subconscious safeguard against a fear of failure" (p. 17) such as a fear of facing marriage, battle, or a job.

Behavioral Causes

Some experts believe that the anxiety attack occurs spontaneously as a result of a single frightening experience, which is then reinforced by similar later experiences. According to Wolpe (1981), panic attacks tend to occur with people "who, because of an early fearful experience, will be more vulnerable to the later devel-

Agoraphobia

5

opment of severe fears arising from similar experiences" (p. 31).

Although Wolpe (1981) believes that agoraphobics
have an unexpected attack, associate it with the place
where it occurred, and then repeat it, Neuman (1985)
maintains that they learn anxious behavior from "parents who are themselves, one or both of them phobic to
some degree" (p. 15). He believes that parents "communicate a frightened feeling to their children" by constantly warning them about possible dangers. "After a
while the children see the world as a threatening
place" (p. 16).

Writer summarizes contrasting theories.

Biological or Genetic Causes

Many researchers believe that agoraphobia is either
a genetic defect passed on from generation to generation
or a defect in one of the systems of the phobic's body,
such as an "overactivity of certain parts of the brain"
(Lehman, 1985, p. 43). Studies of twins have shown that
identical twins are more likely than nonidentical twins
to develop agoraphobia (Sheehan, 1983, p. 91). Since
the family environment of both kinds of twins would be
the same, the fact that agoraphobia occurs more often in
identical twins suggests to Sheehan that "a genetic
weakness could give rise to biochemical abnormalities"
which in turn would lead to anxiety attacks (p. 91).

Quoted phrases integrated with writer's words.

Other researchers are less certain about the origins of agoraphobia. Goodwin (1983), for example, is
forced to conclude: "The cause of phobias remains unknown" (p. 89).

Treatment

The treatment advocated for agoraphobia is based
primarily on the therapist's or doctor's theory as to

Treatment section organized in relation to the causes section.

the cause. That is, those who believe in psychological
causes will advocate some type of psychotherapy; those
who believe that it is learned behavior will recommend
behavioral therapy; and those who believe it has a biological or physiological cause will prescribe drugs.
Many therapists and doctors use a combination of these
treatments.

Psychotherapy

　　　Psychotherapy is seen as the most effective treatment by those who believe that the causes of agoraphobia
are largely psychological or emotional. The psychother-
apist or psychologist helps the patient to identify the
cause of the stress or depression that has finally led
to anxiety attacks and agoraphobia. The patient may
have to search the experiences of childhood to find the
cause. One disadvantage of this method is that it is
very time-consuming and consequently very expensive. In
addition, it has a poor success rate (Goodwin, 1983).

Behavioral Therapy

　　　Behavioral techniques are used by those who believe
that, because anxiety attacks are learned behavior,
"treatment is a process of education" (Neuman, 1985, p.
27) or, really, re-education. In behavioral therapy, the
patient is exposed to the situation that brings on the
phobic attack and gradually learns to respond to it
without fear. Wolpe, in Psychotherapy by Reciprocal Inhibition (1958), is generally given the credit for
initiating this type of treatment. He recommends that
therapists abandon the search for underlying causes of
anxiety and attempt to confront their patients' fears
directly. The most common techniques used by therapists

*Book title underlined
in text.*

Agoraphobia

7

in this relearning process are systematic desensitization, flooding, cognitive therapy, and group therapy.
Relaxation techniques are usually taught along with
these.

Systematic desensitization (or graded exposure).

Third-level heading.

With systematic desensitization, patients are first
taught to relax, then to imagine the situation or object
that produces the least anxiety for them. Gradually
they are led to imagine fear-producing situations of
greater and greater intensity, until their sense of
control within this special, supportive environment
helps them to face the most terrifying scenes without
anxiety. At this point, they can begin to practice in
real life what they have visualized in the therapist's
office.

*Writer has given a
brief but full
description of each
method of treatment.*

Flooding or ungraded exposure. Flooding skips the

slow desensitization process and instead exposes patients immediately to the situation that terrifies them.
The therapist relies on the fact that terror cannot be
sustained indefinitely. Little by little the anxiety
subsides. Flooding can be used either by having patients imagine the feared situation or by putting them
into the real-life setting that they fear. If the patient is afraid of the grocery store, the therapist may
take her to the grocery store and stay with her there
until her anxiety peaks and then wait with her there
until it subsides. She would thus learn that the attack
has limits and that she can control it. Repeated trips
would reinforce the learning.

*Common knowledge;
writer does not have to
cite specific source on
flooding.*

In imaginary flooding the therapist might ask the
patient to visualize herself going into the grocery

Agoraphobia

8

store during a very busy time when the lines to the check-out counters are long. She would imagine going through the aisles and then waiting in line. As with real-life flooding, the visualization would be repeated until anxiety is reduced.

Flooding can obtain results much faster than other methods. However, it works best with simple phobias, such as fear of bridges, elevators, or animals. For the agoraphobic, it carries the risk of making the anxiety more severe, and attacks often recur (Sheehan, 1983, p. 160). Besides, such a technique requires the cooperation of the patient; and some patients do not want to experience again the situation that has caused them so much pain (Goodwin, 1983, p. 111). Younger patients, especially, have trouble with this method; Barlow and Seidner (1983) have shown that it does not work with adolescents.

Writer integrates three different sources.

Cognitive therapy. First developed by Aaron Beck and described by him in Cognitive Therapy and the Emotional Disorders (1976), this method relies more on changing behavior through altering thought processes than on changing behavior directly. Many agoraphobics engage in negative thinking ("I won't be able to breathe" or "Everyone will be watching me and will think I am crazy"). The therapist helps the patient identify these thoughts and recognize that they can be the real cause of an anxiety attack. With this realization patients can learn to substitute more positive thoughts.

Effective transition made by contrasting cognitive therapy with other methods.

Group therapy. Treating agoraphobics in groups has become widely used among behavioral therapists. Neuman (1985) has described in Fight Fear how group therapy,

Agoraphobia

9

along with exposure therapy, has helped phobics in the
eight-week program at the White Plains Phobia Clinic, of
which he is the associate director. In groups, he
points out, phobics "encourage each other and learn
from each other" (p. 185).

Group therapy allows for the use of such techniques
as behavior rehearsal, role-playing, relaxation training, and social skills and assertiveness training (Lazarus, 1981). Therapists using these methods usually
assemble groups consisting of four to ten members, which
meet for an hour or two once or twice a week. A series
of such meetings commonly lasts from eight to twelve
weeks.

Drug Use. Drugs are used most often by therapists
who believe that the panic attacks of agoraphobics are
caused by chemical imbalances in the body. Sheehan
(1983), an advocate of using drugs, considers the group
of drugs called "MAO inhibitors" (monoamine oxidase
inhibitors) "the single most effective drugs overall"
(p. 131). However, a study by Telch, Tearnan, and Taylor
(1983) concludes that "the enthusiasm by advocates of
drug treatments (for example, Sheehan, 1983) seems un-
warranted." They cite the following reasons: (a) "patients' reluctance and in some cases unwillingness to
take the medication"; (b) the undermining of positive
results of drugs because of side effects; and (c) "re-
lapse following withdrawal of the medication" (p. 516).
Often drugs are used as the first step in treatment with
psychotherapy.

Success Rates

Most therapists use a combination of these techniques and, of course, claim success for their methods.

Writer gives credentials to establish source's authority.

Unfamiliar abbreviation spelled out at first use.

Quotations combined with paraphrase.

Agoraphobia

10

Precise recovery figures are difficult to find, partly because recovery can be difficult to measure. However, the treatment that seems to be reported most often as effective is one or more of the behavioral techniques in combination with other treatment. Dr. T. Byram Karasu, Chair of the American Psychiatric Association's Commission on Treatment of Psychiatric Disorders, claims that drugs used with behavior therapy succeed for 78% of patients (Lehman, 1985). Dr. Arthur B. Hardy (1984) in a workshop at the Fifth Annual National Phobia Conference, discussed his success with psychotherapy plus group therapy at his treatment center in Menlo Park, California. He claimed that 40% of his patients recover in six months and that an additional 40% show improvement in two to three years. The rest drop out early in the treatment. Hardy speculated that these patients are not ready and added that some come back later.

In a study by Doctor, Gaer, and Wright (1983), over 94% of patients in their therapy program using a variety of behavioral techniques reported continuing improvement one year after treatment. Doctor et al. also cite "data from other studies . . . indicating that three quarters of those who have been in another type of therapy made no change or actually got worse as a result of the treatment" (p. 3). In addition they point out the disadvantages of drug treatment: "inevitable slipback or regression" (p. 8) when antidepressant drugs are withdrawn and, among a large percentage of those taking drugs, unacceptable side effects.

The case of Marjorie Goff, related earlier, shows that even a person who has spent thirty years in her

Statistics used as evidence.

Symbol for percent used only when preceded by a numeral.

Names of all three authors are given the first time. After that, last name of first author is given, followed by et al. *and the year.*

Subsequent reference in the same paragraph does not need date.

Account of successful treatment of agoraphobic provides satisfying conclusion.

Agoraphobia

11

apartment can recover from agoraphobia. Goff was discovered, alone in her apartment, by a volunteer from a
senior citizens' group. She entered a 20-week program
of desensitization and group therapy. Slowly she expanded the length of her trips outside her apartment--
from the mailbox on the corner to a two-block distance
and then to a store. She was able to celebrate Christmas by eating in a restaurant and eventually was able to
return to the beauty shop where her problem began.

Clearly, agoraphobia and other phobias can now be
treated successfully. A good therapist will select the
treatment best suited to the individual patient. The
existence of the Phobia Society of America, which holds
annual conferences, is only one indication of the growth
of knowledge about this affliction.[2] The first and
simplest step agoraphobics can take is to see their
family doctor. Treatment is available, and agoraphobics
can learn to lead normal lives.

*Ending summarizes
findings and points to
hopeful future.*

Agoraphobia

12

Content notes give information not essential to paper but helpful to readers.

Footnotes

[1]Whitehead (1983) has suggested that there may be as many agoraphobic men as women, but they may be "much less willing to reveal their problem to anyone because they fear they will be looked upon as 'sissys'" (p. 31). Most experts, however, still believe that more women than men suffer from the disease. There is little agreement on why this is true.

No space between superscript number and first word.

[2]Information about this organization can be obtained by writing to the Phobia Society of America, 6181 Executive Boulevard, Rockville, MD 20852.

References

Barlow, D. H., & Seidner, A. L. (1983). Treatment of adolescent agoraphobics: Effects on parent-adolescent relations. Behavioral Research and Therapy, 21, 519-525.

Beck, A. (1976). Cognitive therapy and the emotional disorders. New York: International Universities Press.

Doctor, R. M., Gaer, T., & Wright, M. (1983). Success at one year follow-up for agoraphobia treatment. Paper presented at the Fourth Annual National Phobia Conference, White Plains, NY.

The fight to conquer fear. (1984, April 23). Newsweek, pp. 66-72.

Goodwin, D. W. (1983). Phobia: The facts. New York: Oxford University Press.

Hardy, A. B. (1984). Basic evaluation and treatment procedures effective for agoraphobia. Paper presented at the Fifth Annual National Phobia Conference, Washington, DC.

Lazarus, A. A. (1981). The practice of multimodal therapy. New York: McGraw-Hill.

Lehman, B. (1985, June 3). Holding fear of fear at bay. Boston Globe, pp. 41, 43.

Mansfield, S. (1981, October 25). For 30 years she was a prisoner of fear. Washington Post, sec. G, pp. 1, 3.

Melville, J. (1977). Phobias and obsessions. New York: Coward, McCann & Geoghegan.

Neuman, F. (1985). Fight fear: An eight-week guide to treating your own phobia. New York: Macmillan.

Sheehan, D. V. (1983). The anxiety disease. New York: Scribner's.

Telch, M. J., Tearnan, B. H., & Taylor, C. B. (1983). Antidepressant medication in the treatment of agoraphobia: A critical review. Behavioral Research and Therapy, 21, 505-516.

Usually, only works cited in text are listed as references. Give last names first, followed by initials.

Journal with continuous pagination.

Book.

Paper presented at a conference.

Magazine article with no author given.

Signed newspaper article; newspaper sections numbered separately.

Journal article by multiple authors.

Agoraphobia

14

Weekes, C. (1972). Peace from nervous suffering. New
    York: Hawthorne.

Whitehead, T. (1983). Fears and phobias. New York:
    Arco.

Wolpe, J. (1958). Psychotherapy by reciprocal
    inhibition. Palo Alto: Stanford University Press.

Wolpe, J. (1981). Our useless fears. Boston: Houghton
    Mifflin.

References with the same author are ordered by date of publication, earliest first.

C H A P T E R 12

Writing a Paper in Science or Technology: The Number System

Those who use the number system of citing sources—that is, placing only a number after the information cited in the text—prefer it because its brevity disturbs readers less than other systems. Some form of the number system is usually followed by writers in chemistry, physics, biology, mathematics, engineering, medicine, nursing, and computer science. Many writers of technical reports also use the number system. Among writers using the number system, there are several variations in format. Therefore, writers planning to publish should follow the style of the journal they plan to submit their writing to. The number system explained here is one of the most frequently used in science and technology.

Parts of the Manuscript

The elements of a scientific or technical paper vary according to the contents and the purpose for which it is written. Three possible formats appear here. Consult your instructor about the parts you will need in your paper.

FOR ORIGINAL RESEARCH PAPERS	FOR THEORETICAL PAPERS OR REVIEWS	FOR TECHNICAL REPORTS
Title page	Title page	Title page
Abstract	Abstract	Abstract
Introduction	Introduction	Table of contents

FOR ORIGINAL RESEARCH PAPERS	FOR THEORETICAL PAPERS OR REVIEWS	FOR TECHNICAL REPORTS
Subjects, materials, and method	Headings, as needed	List of illustrations (optional)
Results	Text	Headings, as needed
Discussion	Text	Text
References	References	References
Tables	Tables	Tables usually included in text
Glossary (optional)	Glossary (optional)	Glossary (optional)
Appendix (optional)	Appendix (optional)	Appendix (optional)

Format

Title Page

On the title page put the title, your name, and any other identifying information you and your instructor might wish, such as instructor's name, course number, and date. The title page doesn't usually carry a number but is always counted. If you plan to publish, you may be required to put a running head on the title page as well as on other pages.

Margins and Spacing

Type your manuscript on 8½-by-11-inch paper. Use double-spacing throughout. Leave margins of one inch on all sides of the page. Indent each paragraph five spaces.

Page Numbers

Number all pages consecutively with arabic numerals beginning with the title page, unless you use front matter other than the abstract (see next paragraph). Place the page number in the upper right corner. If you have only a title page and an abstract, count the title page as page 1 and number the abstract page 2; your text then begins on page 3.

When you have front matter and a table of contents, number all pages before the beginning of the text with small roman numerals (ii, iii, etc.). You do not need to place a number on the title page, but you should count it in the numbering. A running head, a brief form of the title placed before the page number, is sometimes used for papers written for publication so that initial evaluators won't be able to identify the author. Such headings are helpful in any paper because pages may be misplaced. In a college paper, however, you can place your last name instead of the title before the page number.

Abstract

Begin your abstract on a separate page and number it as you would any other page. Abstracts should be concise; usually they are between 125 and 250 words. Give your objectives; the methods, materials, and techniques you have used; and any hypotheses you are testing. If you are not using primary research for your main information source, explain your purpose, the problem studied, or questions being explored. Use abbreviations and symbols sparingly. (See Chapter 7 for more information on writing an abstract.)

Illustrations

You may include a list of illustrations in the front part of a technical report if you have more than three or four. Illustrations for a manuscript submitted for publication should be grouped at the end of the manuscript. In a college paper they should be placed in the text near their text reference.

You should identify the source of your information at the bottom of each illustration. If information for a figure comes from several sources, put a superscript lowercase letter after the data cited and give the sources in corresponding footnotes at the bottom of the figure. Superscript letters are used instead of numbers to avoid confusion with the numbers in the illustration.

Headings

To help your readers grasp the structure and the content of your paper, use headings derived from your outline. Avoid using the heading Introduction for your first section. Two or three levels of headings are common. For three levels, the following format is often used in technical writing (for two levels, eliminate the third level).

DISEASES
[First level, centered. Use all
capitals or capitalize first letter
of each word.]

<u>Melioidosis</u>
[Second level, flush with left margin and underlined.]

    <u>Skin Infections</u>.
    [Third level, run in at the beginning of a paragraph
of text and underlined.]

First Page

Place the page number and running head in the upper right corner at least one-half inch from the top of the page. Double-space twice and type the title of your paper, centered, in capital letters. Double-space and begin your introduction.

Introduction

The introduction usually doesn't have a heading; its place in the paper is self-explanatory. You should make clear here what your purpose is or what problem you are studying or trying to solve. However, avoid writing "My purpose in this paper is. . . ." If you are doing original research, you should briefly review the relevant writing on the subject so that your readers know the background of your study.

Footnotes

Use footnotes sparingly to add explanatory material when its inclusion in the text would be disruptive. Place a symbol such as an asterisk or dagger after the material to be explained and place a corresponding superscript symbol at the bottom of the page to introduce the footnote. Indent the first line of each footnote five spaces.

Documentation

Textual Citation

Although a few scientific writers give references at the bottom of the page (footnotes) and some use the author/date system, most use a form of the number system. Writers in the sciences tend to prefer this system because scientific sources often have multiple authors; the use of numbers saves space and disrupts the text less than giving authors' names, especially when several articles are cited for the same information. In the number system, sources in the list of references are assigned numbers that are then used in the text to refer readers to the list. Some writers use superscript numbers, others put the numbers in parentheses or brackets, and a few underline the numbers in parentheses. With any of these systems, the number follows the information documented. Superscript numbers, if used, are placed after all marks of punctuation, including periods, without spacing. Parenthetical numbers are placed before all marks of punctuation, with a space before the first parenthesis. Here are some examples.

```
Hayes has proposed several solutions.[1]
Hayes has proposed several solutions (1).
Although Mason has disagreed,[1] Morris maintains . . .
Although Mason has disagreed (1), Morris maintains . . .
```

If you are citing more than one source in the same place, use a comma between the numbers, with no space after the comma.

```
Recent research2,5 has shown . . .

Recent research (2,5) has shown . . .
```

Reference List

Title your list of sources References, References Cited, Works Cited, or a similar term, and number your entries in one of the following ways:

In the order in which they are mentioned in the text. If you mention a source more than once, use the originally assigned number at each reference in the text.

In alphabetical order. Order your list alphabetically and then number the items. If you use this system, the citations in your text won't be in numerical order.

You can punctuate the numbers of the entries in your list of references with parentheses, (1); with a period, 1.; or with a superscript number, 1. Whichever you choose, be sure to be consistent. If you are writing for publication, use the style of the journal you wish to publish in. For a college paper, any of these is satisfactory.

The following examples, illustrating a list of references using numbers followed by periods, are based on the *CBE Style Manual* (1983), published by the Council of Biology Editors. Other examples appear in the References section at the end of the sample research paper (page 339).

BOOK WITH ONE AUTHOR

Use last name and initials of author. Capitalize only the first word of the title, unless it includes a proper noun. Use a semicolon after publisher's name. Second and subsequent lines of an entry are indented in line with the first letter of the first line. The periods following the numbers should be in line vertically.

```
1.  Restak, R. M.  The brain: the last frontier.  New York: Warner
    Books; 1976.
```

BOOK WITH TWO OR MORE AUTHORS

Give names of all authors, with semicolons between them, regardless of the number.

```
2.  Penfield, W.; Roberts, L.  Speech and brain mechanisms.
    Princeton, NJ: Princeton Univ. Press; 1959.
```

CORPORATE AUTHOR

3. Institute of Electrical and Electronics Engineers. Automating intelligent behavior applications and frontiers. Silver Spring, MD: IEEE Computer Society Press; 1983.

BOOK WITH EDITOR

4. Bronfenbrenner, U., editor. Influences on human development. Hinsdale, IL: Dryden; 1972.

CHAPTER OR SELECTION IN EDITED ANTHOLOGY

5. Ransom, C. J.; Hoffee, L. H. The orbits of Venus. In: Talbott, S. L., ed. Velikovsky reconsidered. New York: Warner Books; 1977:140-147.

ARTICLE IN JOURNAL WITH CONTINUOUS PAGINATION

Capitalize only the first letter of the title of the article (don't capitalize the first letter of the subtitle) and all important words of the journal title. Titles of journals are usually abbreviated following recommendations of the *American National Standard for Abbreviations of Titles of Periodicals*, but some journals don't use such abbreviations in their articles. If you don't know the accepted abbreviation of a journal title, it's better to write it out. After the title of the journal, give both the volume number and the page numbers in arabic numerals, followed by a semicolon and the year.

6. Brown, M.; Stewart, J. B.; Garrett, C. J. Melioidosis: a report on ten cases. Quarterly Journal of Medicine 153:115-125; 1970.

ARTICLE IN JOURNAL PAGINATED BY ISSUE

When the first page of each issue is numbered 1, place the issue number in arabic numerals in parentheses following the volume number.

7. Keeping up with cholesterol. Harvard Medical School Health Letter 10(8):3-5; 1984.

NEWSPAPER ARTICLE

Follow the date with a colon, section and page number, and, in parentheses, column number.

8. Green, H. P. Why E.P.A. supervision is needed. The New York Times. 1984 July 15:A2 (col. 3).

MAGAZINE ARTICLE

Put the date in place of the volume number.

9. Bernard, J. Looking at lasers. Radio-Electronics. 1986
    June:39-42.

DISSERTATION

10. Berkman, L. F. Social networks, host resistance and mortal-
     ity: a follow-up study of Alameda county residents. Berke-
     ley: Univ. of California; 1977. Dissertation.

Sample Research Paper
Using the Number System

The number system of documentation used in the following paper is one of the number documentation styles suggested in the *CBE Style Manual* (1983), published by the Council of Biology Editors. References are numbered in the order in which they are mentioned in the text, and the list of references at the end of the paper is then arranged in numerical order. When a source is referred to more than once in the text, the original number assigned to it is repeated. Page numbers are given in the text along with the reference number only when the article referred to is lengthy or when a quotation is given.

Although the subject of the paper and many of the articles cited are technical, Margaret Little translated technical terms into language understandable to a general, rather than a primarily professional, audience. She believes that caffeine consumption is of interest to most adults.

CBE style requires title page and abstract. Do not use a number on the title page but count it in the numbering.

THE EFFECTS OF CAFFEINE CONSUMPTION

by

Margaret A. Little

The title page, abstract, and table of contents make the paper accessible to a varied audience.

Professor Cline

Nutrition 270

November 13, 199-

Effects of Caffeine ii

ABSTRACT

Studies have shown that the ingestion of caffeine, a widely consumed substance in all age groups, has a harmful effect on the body. It increases heart rate, stimulates gastric secretions, and causes headaches, nervousness, and insomnia in healthy people. Coffee drinkers who consume five or more cups per day can become unknowingly addicted to caffeine. Those with psychological disorders can regress when they consume excessive caffeine. Children are particularly sensitive to the effects of caffeine. Studies also show that pregnant women who drink coffee have a greater risk of problems at delivery, and their children may be born with abnormalities. Whether these effects are permanent has yet to be determined. Even though caffeine has some benefits, people would be well advised to avoid it or use it sparingly.

Use small roman numerals for any front matter and arabic numbers for all pages in the body of the text.

An informative abstract summarizes the paper's contents. Complete details and statistics are not included.

Effects of Caffeine iii

TABLE OF CONTENTS

Table of contents (not required for CBE style) derived from outline is used in technical report. First-level headings are typed flush left; second-level headings are indented five spaces; third-level headings, ten spaces.

Page numbers for third-level headings in paper are optional in table of contents.

Dots connecting heading to page number are optional.

Effects of Caffeine iv

LIST OF ILLUSTRATIONS

Page

List of illustrations included because there are more than three figures and tables.

Brief title before the page number.

First-level heading.

(1) indicates source of information; it refers to the first item in the reference list.

First part of paper introduces the subject, gives background information, and ends with a summary statement.

Page numbers will help reader locate information. Page numbers are always given for quotations.

Effects of Caffeine 1

THE HISTORY OF CAFFEINE

The use of caffeine as a stimulant dates back thousands of years. Ethiopians chewed coffee beans before battle, the ancient Chinese drank tea, and the Mayan Indians drank chocolate made from cocoa beans. Other common sources of caffeine are the kola nut, the ilex plant (used for making a Brazilian beverage called maté), tea leaves, and the cassina or Christmas berry tree (1).

Coffee, the most popular source of caffeine, appears in recorded history as early as 1000 A.D., when Arab Muslims included it as part of their daily ritual. Later, when the Islamic faith was accepted by people in Turkey, so was coffee. In 1615, Venetian traders began to fill their boats with coffee in Constantinople; by 1750, most of Western Europe was drinking coffee.

Meanwhile, as the English began to bring back tea from the East, tea drinking became a custom in England and its colonies. England's heavy taxes on colonists' tea, which led to the Boston Tea Party, forced Americans to change from tea to coffee (2, pp. 388, 394, 405). Today, according to a report by the Life Sciences Research Office, 62% of Americans drink coffee every day (3, p. 9) and many people who don't drink coffee consume caffeine in other forms. The results afflict people of all ages.

CAFFEINE CONSUMPTION

In the United States 80% of adults are coffee drinkers, with the average consumption 3-1/2 cups a day (4). More people in the 40- and 50-year-old group drink 3 to 5 cups of coffee a day than do those in other groups (figure 1, p. 2). But much of the caffeine con-

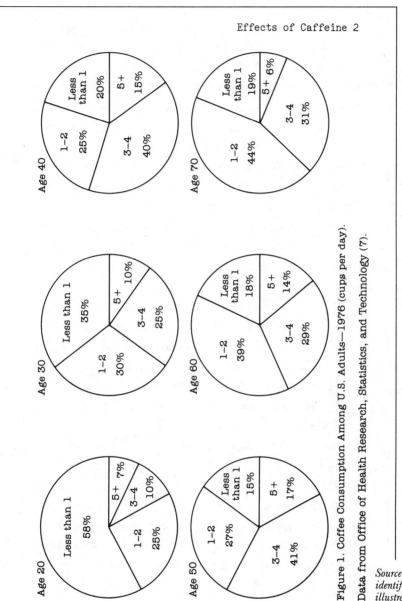

Figure 1. Coffee Consumption Among U.S. Adults—1976 (cups per day).
Data from Office of Health Research, Statistics, and Technology (7).

Source of information identified at bottom of illustration.

Effects of Caffeine 3

References to figures and tables for sources of data. Statistics are interpreted and related to the discussion.

sumed by all groups comes from sources other than coffee, such as tea, chocolate, soft drinks, and over-the-counter medications. (Tables 1 and 2, pp. 4-5, show the caffeine content in these sources.) Many consumers of these products are children. In fact, children between the ages of 1 and 5 consume more caffeine by body weight from soft drinks than do people in any other age group (figure 2, p. 6). Sources of caffeine for children also include iced tea and chocolate products. Even nursing infants consume caffeine--the equivalent of the

Detailed information establishes Little's point about caffeine consumption.

caffeine in 2/3 cup of coffee daily--from breast milk and from soft drinks, which are sometimes used to treat colic.

While coffee and tea contain caffeine naturally, the substance is added to soft drinks, the most heavily consumed caffeinated beverage in the United States (5).

Superscript symbol refers to footnote adding explanatory material.

It's no secret that colas are caffeinated,* but it may be surprising that three drinks without "cola" in their names (Mountain Dew, Mellow Yellow, and Sunkist Orange) contain more caffeine than many so-called colas (see Table 1, p. 4). Many consumers believe that soft drink manufacturers add caffeine to their products to cause children to become addicted to the caffeine in them (6).

Although people consume less tea than either coffee or soft drinks, tea is still an important source of caffeine. The amount of caffeine in tea depends greatly on the length of time it is brewed as well as on the

* Because caffeine is a natural element of the kola nuts used to flavor these sodas, the Food and Drug Administration requires that colas contain caffeine (5).

Effects of Caffeine 4

Table 1. Common sources of caffeine.

NONPRESCRIPTION DRUGS, one tablet	Milligrams of Caffeine
Anacin	32[a]
Aspirin	0
Excedrin	65[a]
Midol (regular)	0
NoDoz	100
Vanquish	33[a]
Vivarin	200

SOFT DRINKS, 12 fl oz	
Coca-Cola	46[b]
Diet Pepsi	36[b]
Mountain Dew	54[b]
Mr. Pibb	40[b]
Orange Sunkist	40
Orange Sunkist-Diet	40
Pepsi-Cola	38[b]
Pepsi Light	36[b]
RC Cola	36[b]
RC 100	0
7-Up	0

In scientific papers, measurements are abbreviated without a period.

COFFEE, 6 fl oz	
Brewed	103[b]
Instant	57[b]
Instant decaffeinated	2[b]

CHOCOLATE	
Chocolate milk (8 fl oz)	8[b]
Hot cocoa (6 fl oz)	4[b]
Baker's Semisweet (1 oz square)	13[b]

[a] Data from Physicians' Desk Reference (8).

[b] Data from Bowes (9).

Effects of Caffeine 5

Table 2. Caffeine in teas (in milligrams)

HOT TEA--Domestic   Strength*

Brand Name	Type	Weak	Medium	Strong
Red Rose	bag	45	62	90
Salada	bag	25	60	78
Lipton	bag	25	53	70
Tetley	bag	18	48	70

HOT TEA--Imported   Strength*

Brand Name	Type	Weak	Medium	Strong
English Breakfast	bag	26	78	107
(Twinings)	loose	39	84	90
Darjeeling	bag	39	74	91
(Twinings)				
Formosa Oolong	loose	42	65	78
(Jacksons)				

INSTANT TEA (prepared according to package directions)

Lipton		62
Nestea		48
Lipton with sugar and lemon	76	
Nestea with sugar and lemon	67	

* Determined by color intensity in 6 oz hot water.

Data from Groisser (10).

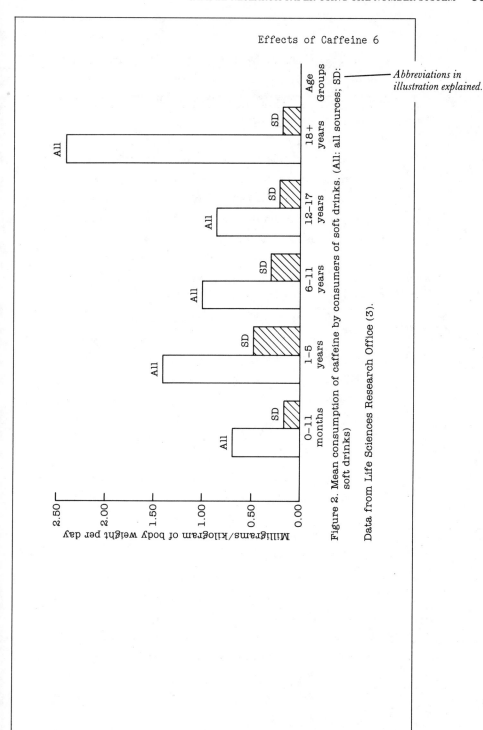

Figure 2. Mean consumption of caffeine by consumers of soft drinks. (All: all sources; SD: soft drinks)

Data from Life Sciences Research Office (3).

Effects of Caffeine 7

brand used. (Table 2, p. 5, lists the caffeine content
of teas according to brand and brewing time.)

EFFECTS OF CAFFEINE ON ADULTS

Second-level heading. Descriptive headings aid the reader in finding particular sections of the paper.

Effects on normal body processes

Caffeine, a white, needle-shaped methylxanthine
compound, is a drug that stimulates the central nervous
system (CNS). According to the Food and Drug Administration (FDA) (11, p. 69829), it is the only ingredient
added to food at levels that will achieve its pharmaco-
logical effect, that is, the stimulation of the CNS. As
a result, the FDA has proposed that caffeine be removed
from the Generally Recognized As Safe (GRAS) List to an
interim category until it has been further tested (12).

At first use, technical term is spelled out and followed by its abbreviation; the abbreviation is used from then on.

One of the major effects of caffeine on the body is
the dilation of the heart's blood vessels. Caffeine
relaxes smooth muscles in vessel walls so that the heart
rate increases. At the same time, caffeine stimulates a
section of the brain to decrease heart rate. These
antithetical effects result in an overall increase in
heart rate. If the brain did not slow the heart, the
increase in heart rate would be greater.

Caffeine also decreases the blood flow in the brain
by constricting its blood vessels, decreases blood glu-
cose and pancreatic insulin output, increases urine
output, stimulates gastric secretion, and increases
basal metabolic rate (13).

"Restless legs syndrome" can afflict some coffee
drinkers. In his study of this condition, Lutz (14)

Lutz, an authority, is quoted because his words provide the most accurate description of symptoms. Source is given after author, page reference is given after quotation.

describes the symptoms as "unpleasant, creeping sensations in the lower legs between the knee and ankle"
(p. 693), as well as restlessness in the arms and shoulders. Those who spend much of their time in sedentary

Effects of Caffeine 8

occupations or pastimes are most often afflicted, and
their discomfort usually occurs in the evening and at
night. Once the sensations start, those who suffer from
the syndrome find it impossible to keep their legs still
and feel the need to get up and walk. All of Lutz's 62
patients with "restless legs syndrome" had consumed
methylxanthine stimulants equivalent to at least 1 cup
of coffee daily.

Disease states worsened by caffeine

Ulcers. Scientists have known for many years that
caffeine and other methylxanthines stimulate secretion
of two digestive juices, hydrochloric acid and pepsin,
increasing the chances of developing ulcers. A University of California study of 25 000 college students
found that those who drank 2 or more cups of coffee per
day had a 70% greater chance of developing ulcers later
in life than their classmates who consumed no coffee
(15). Other studies of humans and animals have shown
that caffeine significantly stimulates secretion of
gastric juices (3, p. 64).

Heart disease. Although a 200 mg dose of caffeine
causes the heart to pump faster, correlations between
caffeine and heart disease are difficult to make. Kannel and Dawber (3) found "no relation between coffee
consumption and myocardial infarction [damaged heart
muscle or heart attack]" (p. 63). But they did find
that the heart rate and blood pressure of fasting, non-coffee drinkers increased 1 hour after ingestion of 250
mg caffeine--a result suggesting that persons prone to
dysrhythmias (abnormal heart beats) should restrict
their caffeine consumption (p. 31). Dobmeyer et al.
(16) concluded that patients who show arrhythmic symp-

Third-level heading. Section discusses general effects first, then disease-related effects.

In scientific papers, a space instead of a comma separates numbers of five or more digits.

Place additions that aren't part of the quotation in brackets.

Use et al. to cite reference to more than two authors.

Effects of Caffeine 9

toms (irregular heart beats) after caffeine administration "should avoid caffeine" (p. 815). A study by the
Boston Drug Surveillance Program (15) found that persons
drinking 5 cups of coffee daily had a 50% greater risk
of heart attack than coffee nondrinkers. Those drinking
6 or more cups increased their chances of heart attack
by 100%.

In scientific or technical papers, use numerals, not words, for numbers over ten or for statistics. Use %, not percent.

Fibrocystic breast disease. A surgeon at Ohio
State University, John Minton, studied 88 women with
fibrocystic breast disease (benign breast lumps). After
their condition was diagnosed, 45 of these women gave up
caffeine entirely. Minton reported that, of the 45,
"37 experienced total disappearance of breast lumps,
and 7 reported some disappearance" (6, p. 20). Of the
88 women, 15 continued consuming their usual amount of
caffeine. Only 2 of those women reported that their
breast lumps disappeared spontaneously. Boyle et al.
corroborated some of Minton's findings (17). However,
Heyden and Muhlbaier (18) were unable to report similar
dramatic results in their study of the same disease.
They concluded that it is difficult to relate the amount
of methylxanthine consumption to fibrocystic breast
disease because the condition itself is so variable (it
has such a high degree of waxing and waning with or
without treatment). They recommend greater experimental
controls in future testing.

When a source has more than two authors, give the first author followed by et al.

Little reports differing results. Researchers, especially in science, should include conflicting data.

Cancer. Studies have not demonstrated a cause-
and-effect relationship between coffee drinking and
cancer, though James and Stirling found "a relatively
strong relationship" between cancer of the pancreas and
coffee drinking (19). The FDA has claimed that bladder
cancer is more prevalent among coffee drinkers than
noncoffee drinkers, and a correlation between deaths

Effects of Caffeine 10

from renal cancer and coffee consumption has been observed (11, p. 69828).

Caffeine addiction

Most people who consume 5 or more cups of coffee per day (about 500 mg) have caffeinism, an addiction to caffeine (5). As figure 1 (p. 2) shows, 17% of U.S. adults, age 50, qualify as addicts.

Coffee drinkers can detect caffeinism by curbing caffeine intake for 1 to 2 days and checking for the following symptoms: sensations of fullness in the head, drowsiness, euphoria, nausea, excessive yawning, constant runny nose, and throbbing headache made worse by bending over and exercising. Withdrawal symptoms can last up to two weeks. A person can alleviate the pain of withdrawal by gradually decreasing caffeine consumption. For example, a coffee drinker can blend decaffeinated coffee with regular coffee, gradually increasing the ratio of decaffeinated to regular over a 2- to 3-week period (20).

Smooth transition made by repeating caffeinism *and by moving from a generalization about the number of addicts to specific symptoms.*

Aggravation of mental and emotional disorders

Heading signals shift in focus.

Mentally retarded and emotionally disturbed persons are particularly susceptible to the effects of caffeine. Podboy and Mallory (21) observed fifteen severely retarded women accustomed to drinking 4 to 15 cups of coffee per day (mean consumption was 7.1 cups). These women often kicked other patients and, waking at night, yelled and walked about. When decaffeinated coffee was given to them, the average number of aggressive outbursts per week decreased from 14.78 to 6.35 during the last 2 weeks of the 6-week treatment period. The women also drank their decaffeinated coffee more slowly and asked for fewer refills.

Clear, effective summary of procedures and results of two studies.

In another study, Bezchlebnyk and Jeffries (22)

Effects of Caffeine 11

observed the coffee-drinking habits of psychiatric patients in a Canadian institution. The patients were
offered coffee or tea 6 times a day, and they consumed
as many as 1000 mg of caffeine daily. Doctors at the
institution noticed that patients consuming over 250 mg
per day were more anxious, depressed, and likely to be
diagnosed psychotic; caffeine also worsened schizo-
phrenic symptoms among these patients. When 14 in-
patients were covertly switched to decaffeinated coffee
for 3 weeks, their hostility, suspiciousness, anxiety,
and irritability diminished. Only the originally diagnosed levels of psychiatric disorders remained.

EFFECTS OF CAFFEINE ON PREGNANT WOMEN AND NEWBORNS

In a 1977 study (23), P. S. Weathersbee found evidence of abnormal deliveries among pregnant women who
drank coffee. "Of 16 women who drank 8 or more cups of
coffee per day (600+ mg) during pregnancy," he reported, "only one had an uncomplicated delivery of a
normal term infant" (p. 160). On the other hand, 72%
of 104 women who drank no more than 45 mg of caffeine
daily had normal deliveries. Evidence of birth defects
from caffeine was found by the FDA in a 1980 study (5)
in which rats were fed the equivalent of 2 cups of coffee per day. The result was a delay in the skeletal
development of the offspring.

Still, the links between pregnancy and caffeine are
not completely proven. Weathersbee was unable to establish a firm cause-and-effect relationship between caffeine ingestion and abnormal deliveries, and researchers
at Boston University and Howard University (20) could
not duplicate the correlation between coffee and birth
defects in their similar studies. They also found it
difficult to interpret results of studies with rats

Little moves from effects of caffeine on adults to a special case. Heading is worded as it was in the table of contents.

Direct quotation and paraphrase are combined.

The word Still *makes a smooth transition to a paragraph that qualifies Weathersbee's findings.*

Effects of Caffeine 12

because of the differences in the way rats and humans
metabolize caffeine. Nevertheless, the FDA recommends
that women avoid caffeine during pregnancy because any
drug crossing the placenta, especially during the first
3 months, can be dangerous to the fetus (5).

Infants may be exposed to caffeine immediately
after birth. Horning et al. (3, p. 13) analyzed human
breast milk and found it to contain 1.3 to 6.9 mg caffeine per liter. An infant consuming 150 ml breast milk
per kg (of infant weight) has a daily caffeine intake of
1.2 mg per kg, the equivalent of the consumption of 1
cup of perked coffee per day by a 154 lb adult. Horning
also confirmed that infants are exposed to caffeine
before birth; urine samples of 100 newborn infants whose
mothers consumed caffeine all contained caffeine.

Writer uses an analogy to clarify her point.

BENEFICIAL EFFECTS OF CAFFEINE

Although most of the evidence suggests that caffeine consumption is harmful to human health, there are
some beneficial effects of the drug. According to
Stephenson (13), caffeine consumption relieves respira-
tory failure caused by morphine and codeine overdoses,
energizes elderly persons who have brain damage and
atherosclerosis, and improves interest and lessens irritability in severely regressed psychiatric patients. In
addition, caffeine has been found to enhance the speed
and accuracy of those performing physical tasks such as
typing (3); it also increases endurance during exercise
by reducing carbohydrate oxidation and increasing fat
metabolism (24).

Little incorporates contradictory evidence showing that caffeine can be beneficial.

CONCLUSION

Research into the effects of caffeine on human
health has increased greatly in the last 5 years. Because many studies have found caffeine to be harmful and

Little summarizes her findings and makes a recommendation.

Effects of Caffeine 13

because caffeine consumers themselves have observed harmful effects of the drug, the public has become more wary of ingesting products with caffeine in them. Industries have responded to these worries by developing caffeine-free, cola-flavored soft drinks and decaffeinated coffees and teas.

Little strikes a balance between contradictory evidence.

Still, scientists have been unable to prove that these harmful effects cause permanent health damage among healthy adults. Insomnia, nervousness, and rapid heart rate disappear soon after caffeine is removed from the body. The effects on infants, young children, and people prone to heart disease may be less benign, but the evidence, though strongly suggestive of permanent damage, is not yet conclusive. The FDA has encouraged further research on this subject.

Paper ends with quotation from two authorities to support the point about the dangers of caffeine.

Despite the lack of conclusive evidence, adults, children, and especially pregnant women would do well to decrease their consumption of caffeine. Within the next few years, scientists should be able to state with more certainty correlations between caffeine and various health disorders. Already, as James and Stirling point out, "growing numbers of authorities are voicing their alarm and recommending moderation in the use of this drug" (19, p. 255).

Effects of Caffeine 14

REFERENCES

1. Graham, D. M. Caffeine--its identity, dietary
    sources, intake and biological effects. Nutrition
    Reviews 36:97-102; 1978.

2. Starbird, E. Z. The bonanza bean coffee. National
    Geographic. 1981 Mar.:388-405.

3. Life Sciences Research Office. Evaluation of the
    health aspects of caffeine. Bethesda, MD: Federa-
    tion of American Societies for Experimental Biol-
    ogy; 1978.

4. Is caffeine bad for you? Newsweek. 1982 July 19:
    62-64.

5. Burros, M. Caffeine controversy. The New York
    Times. 1982 April 21:C1 (col. 5), C6 (col. 1).

6. The caffeine catch. Family Health. 1981 Apr.:
    20-21.

7. Office of Health Research, Statistics, and Technol-
    ogy. Use habits among adults of cigarettes, coffee,
    aspirin, and sleeping pills. Hyattsville, MD:
    National Center for Health Statistics; 1978.

8. Physicians' desk reference for nonprescription
    drugs. Oradell, NJ: Medical Economics Co.; 1990.

9. Bowes, Anna De Planter. Bowes and Church's food
    values of portions commonly used. 15th ed. rev. by
    Jean A. T. Pennington 1989.

10. Groisser, Daniel S. A study of caffeine in tea.
     American Journal of Clinical Nutrition 31:1729;
     1978.

11. Department of Health and Human Services. Soda
     water: amendment to standard. Federal Register
     45:69816-69838; 1980.

Begin new page, center heading, and double-space throughout.

Author's initials follow last name.

Corporate author given first as for an individual author.

For a weekly magazine, give date instead of volume and issue number.

Newspaper article with separate pagination. When page numbers are discontinuous, use a comma between them.

For personal communications, give source, affiliation, type of communication, and date.

12. Lin, L., Consumer Safety Officer, Division of Toxicology, Food and Drug Administration, interview, 1982 Feb. 9.

13. Stephenson, P. E. Psychologic and psychotropic effects of caffeine on man. Journal of the American Dietetic Association 71:242-245; 1977.

14. Lutz, E. G. Restless legs, anxiety, and caffeinism. Journal of Clinical Psychology 39:693-696; 1978.

For a magazine, give date of issue instead of volume number.

15. Are you a caffeine addict? Saturday Evening Post. 1982 May/June:50-53.

16. Dobmeyer, D. J.; Stine, R. A.; Leier, C. V.; Greenberg, R.; Schaal, S. F. The arrhythmogenic effects of caffeine in human beings. New England Journal of Medicine 308:814-816; 1983.

17. Boyle, C. A.; Berkowitz, G. S.; LiVolsi, V. A.; Ort, S.; Merino, M. J.; White, C.; Kelsey, J. L. Caffeine consumption and fibrocystic breast disease: a case-control epidemiologic study. Journal of the National Cancer Institute 72:1015-1019; 1984.

18. Heyden, S.; Mulhbaier, L. H. Prospective study of "fibrocystic breast disease" and caffeine consumption. Surgery 96:479-483; 1984.

19. James, J. E.; Stirling, K. P. Caffeine: a survey of some of the known suspected deleterious effects of habitual use. British Journal of Addiction 78:251-258; 1983.

20. Brody, J. Weaning the body from dependence on caffeine. The New York Times. 1982 April 21:C6.

21. Podboy, J. W.; Mallory, W. A. Caffeine reduction and behavior change in the severely retarded. Mental Retardation 15:40; 1977.

Effects of Caffeine 16

22. Bezchlebnyk, K.; Jeffries, J. Should psychiatric
    patients drink coffee? Canadian Medical Associa-
    tion Journal 124:357-358; 1981.

23. Caffeine, cigarette smoke: effects on the unborn
    child. Hospital Practice 15 (Oct.):160, 164; 1980.

24. Costell, D. L.; Dalsky, G. P.; Fink, W. J. Effects
    of caffeine ingestion on metabolism and exercise
    performance. Medicine and Science in Sports
    10:155-158; 1978.

APPENDIX 1

Annotated List
of References

This guide to reference sources provides you with a short cut in your search for information by listing many of the books and journals that contain titles of specific books and articles about your subject. In your catalog search you will be able to go directly to the specific works that you identify in this list. The list is arranged from the most general levels of sources to the most specific; you can start your search at the level that suits your situation best. In general, the less you know about a subject, the more you will benefit from a wider initial view. However, some of the general sources, such as *Ulrich's International Periodicals Director* or the *Vertical File Index*, can be helpful whatever your level of knowledge. The annotations accompanying each entry will help you decide whether a source will be useful.

The first group of books, General Sources, provides the names of bibliographies or general books as well as indexes on a range of subjects, directories of periodicals, sources of biographies, and books containing specific data or facts. At the next level, you will find sources in three primary disciplinary groups: the humanities, the social sciences, and science and technology. Many students find that using the books in one of these groups is a good way to start.

Finally, you will find specific reference books for more than twenty-five subjects arranged alphabetically within each subject. The standard encyclopedia or dictionary references can help you focus a topic by providing brief definitions, giving background information, and suggesting a few related citations with which you can begin your search. For most subjects, you will also find a guide to the literature describing research methodology in the subject area and providing relevant reference sources. For each subject, indexes, collections of abstracts, computer databases (when they exist), and at least three primary journals are provided. Notice that the title is listed first for sources better known by their titles than by their authors or editors (for example, the *Readers' Guide to Periodical Literature*).

When you consult any of these reference sources, be sure to read the explanatory material at the beginning of the book to find out how it is organized, what information is provided, and what the abbreviations and symbols mean.

Brief Contents of Appendix

General Sources

Guides to Reference Works

Armstrong, C. J., and J. A. Large. *Manual of Online Search Strategies*. Boston: Hall, 1988.

A brief introduction to searching strategies that apply to most subjects. The manual is intended primarily for searchers who have some knowledge of online searching. Appendixes include a list of all databases mentioned in the volume and a bibliography of reference works and directories related to online searching.

Cuadra Associates. *Directory of Online Databases*. Santa Monica: Cuadra, 1979–. Quarterly.

Provides up-to-date information on available online databases. More than 4,000 databases are listed in the 1989 directories. Each directory is arranged in alphabetical order with several indexes, including a subject index.

Katz, William. *Introduction to Reference Work*. 5th ed. 2 vols. New York: McGraw-Hill, 1987.

A more comprehensive and sophisticated guide than *Your Library: A Reference Guide* (the next entry). The second volume of this work covers online searching and computer databases.

Katz, William. *Your Library: A Reference Guide*. 2nd ed. New York: Holt, Rinehart and Winston, 1984.

A handbook on the use of libraries for the beginning researcher. Discusses ways to familiarize yourself with library facilities and collections. A chapter is included on finding sources for a research paper. Following chapters on general reference books, a final section describes the best reference books to use in different subject disciplines according to the type of information you are looking for.

Sheehy, Eugene P. *Guide to Reference Books*. 10th ed. Chicago: American Library Assn., 1986.

Identifies reference books in all subjects published or printed in the United States. Annotated entries are arranged by subject; this guide includes an index arranged by title.

Walford, A. J. *Walford's Guide to Reference Material*. 4th ed. London: The Library Assn., 1980–(in progress).

An international guide to bibliographies and reference books. Volume 1 (1980) covers science and technology; volume 2 (1982) covers social sciences, history, religion, and philosophy; volume 3 (1987) covers general sources, languages and literature, and the arts. The reference works are grouped by subject. Each entry gives a complete citation and critical description of the work. The focus is on British reference works. Walford's *Concise Guide to Reference Material* (1 vol., 1981) covers all subjects.

Bibliographies and Book Catalogs

Bibliographic Index: A Cumulative Bibliography of Bibliographies. New York: Wilson, 1938–. Published three times a year; third issue is cumulative.

Arranged alphabetically by subject, this listing includes bibliographies published in books and periodicals as well as bibliographies published separately.

Books in Print. New York: Bowker, 1948–. Annually, with midyear supplements since 1975.

A multivolume guide to books of all types, including textbooks, paperbacks, and children's books, that are currently in print. Separate volumes list books by authors, titles, and subjects, and information is given for purchasing the books. One volume contains an alphabetical listing of publishers, with their addresses. The 1989–90 edition includes, for the first time, a volume that lists out-of-print and out-of-stock books. Available online and on CD-ROM.

Indexes

Biography Index. See entry under Biographical Reference Sources.

Book Review Digest. New York: Wilson, 1905–. Monthly, except February and July, with quarterly and annual cumulations.

Includes excerpts from selected book reviews. Nonfiction works are included if they have been reviewed at least twice and fiction works if they have been reviewed at least four times. Reviews indexed are from general and scholarly journals.

Book Review Index. Detroit: Gale, 1965–.

Indexes reviews from 470 publications, including popular magazines like the *Atlantic* as well as scholarly and professional journals. Entries are listed alphabetically according to the name of the author reviewed. The listings do not include excerpts of reviews, but they do include the reviewer's name and the date and place of publication of the review. Available online and on CD-ROM.

Dissertation Abstracts International. Ann Arbor: University Microfilms International, 1938–. Monthly.

Includes abstracts of doctoral dissertations from universities in the United States and Canada. Since 1966, the abstracts have been divided into two sections: humanities and social sciences, and sciences and engineering. The abstracts are divided by subject categories outlined in the table of contents. The author and keyword indexes at the end of each listing cumulate annually in the *Comprehensive Dissertation Index* (same publisher). Copies of dissertations included in *Dissertation Abstracts International* are available from the publisher in hard copy or on microfilm. Available online and on CD-ROM.

Essay and General Literature Index. New York: Wilson, 1900–. Annually, with five-year cumulations.

An aid to locating essays, primarily in the humanities and social sciences, that are part of collections not otherwise easily located. Access is by author and by subject; essays written by authors can be found as well as essays about them and their individual works. Available online and on CD-ROM.

InfoTrac. San Mateo: Information Access Company, 1985–.

A computer reference system that provides access to several database indexes, including Academic Index, General Periodicals, Index Backfile Databases, Government Publications Index, Health Index, LegalTrac, Magazine Index/Plus, and National Newspaper Index. Institutions can subscribe to all or some of the databases. References are arranged in one alphabetical listing of subject headings, names, author names, geographic place names, and titles of books and movies about which articles have been written. More useful for references to magazine sources than to journal sources. The system is available on CD-ROM.

Magazine Index. Belmont, CA: Information Access, 1959-.

A microfilm index to more than 435 general-interest magazines. Information is listed for the preceding four years by subject, author, and product name; book, movie, play, and restaurant reviews are included. Microfilm is updated monthly. Indexes for the previous years are available on microfiche. Available online and on CD-ROM.

National Newspaper Index. Belmont, CA: Information Access, 1979-. Monthly. This guide (on microfilm and microfiche) indexes articles from five newspapers: the *Christian Science Monitor*, *Los Angeles Times*, *New York Times*, *Wall Street Journal*, and *Washington Post*. Available online and on CD-ROM.

New York Times Index. New York: New York Times, 1913–. Semimonthly, with annual cumulations. Available online.

Because a short summary is given for each entry instead of a title, this index can be used to answer questions about dates and sequences of events. Abbreviations (S, M, L) indicate the length of the original article. The *Personal Name Index to the New York Times Index* (25 vols.), by Byron J. Falk, Jr., and Valerie R. Falk (Verdi, NV: Roxbury Data Interface) indexes names appearing in the *New York Times* from 1851 to 1979. A full text version of the *New York Times* from 1980 to the present is available online.

Readers' Guide to Periodical Literature. New York: Wilson, 1900–. Semimonthly, with quarterly and annual cumulations.

An index, arranged by author and subject, to articles in more than 195 general, nontechnical magazines; also includes entries for reviews of books, motion pictures, television shows, and plays. Available online and on CD-ROM.

Vertical File Index. New York: Wilson, 1935–. Monthly, except August, with annual cumulations.

A subject and title index to pamphlets. Complete bibliographic and ordering information is given for each pamphlet. Brief summaries or descriptions are included for most entries. Arrangement is by subject; there is also a title index. Available online.

Directories of Periodicals

Gale Directory of Publications: An Annual Guide to Newspapers, Magazines, Journals, and Related Publications. Detroit: Gale, 1869–. Annually.

A geographical listing providing basic information about nearly 25,000 newspapers, magazines, journals, and similar publications in the United States and Canada. Information includes title, publisher, address, description, and subscription and advertising information.

Katz, William. *Magazines for Libraries*. 6th ed. New York: Bowker, 1989.

A selective, annotated listing of more than 6,000 periodicals grouped by subject. Bibliographic information and subscription rate and frequency are given. Annotations describe the contents and specific features of each periodical and give a recommendation of the value of the periodical for different types of libraries.

Ulrich's International Periodicals Directory. New York: Bowker, 1932–. Annually, with quarterly updates.

Describes more than 145,000 serial publications: international magazines, newsletters, and general-interest publications published regularly as well as annuals, continuations, conference proceedings, and other serials published at least once every three years. Periodicals are arranged by subject with cross-references to related subjects. Complete bibliographic information for each title, including address, subscription price, frequency of publication, date of original publication, and a list of indexes and abstracting services that include the journal (if it is indexed). A list of serials available online and an online vendor listing is included. Available online and on CD-ROM.

Union List of Serials in Libraries of the United States and Canada. 3rd ed. 5 vols. New York: Bowker, 1965.

Useful in locating a particular periodical, this is an alphabetical listing of more than 155,000 serial titles held by 956 libraries in the United States and Canada. Entries give the beginning and ending dates of publication (or indicate if the serial is still currently published), selected locations, and any name changes the serial has had. Entries indicate which issues of a serial a particular library has. The *Union List* is supplemented by *New Serial Titles*, which lists serials published after 1949. There is a subject guide to *New Serial Titles*.

Biographical Reference Sources

Biography and Genealogy Master Index. Ed. Miranda C. Herbert and Barbara McNeil. 2nd ed. Detroit: Gale, 1980. Annual supplements.

A master index to more than 350 biographical dictionaries and subject encyclopedias, such as *Who's Who in America*, the *Dictionary of American Biography*, and the *Oxford Companion to English Literature*. Entries in the alphabetical listing of names give birth and death dates and indicate which reference books include further biographical information. Available online.

Biography Index: A Cumulative Index to Biographical Material in Books and Magazines. New York: Wilson, 1946–. Quarterly, with annual and three-year cumulations.

An important index to biographical information published in English-language books and periodicals. Works cited include memoirs, journals, obituaries, and collective biographies as well as works that are strictly biographical. Each issue includes an index by profession. Available online and on CD-ROM.

Current Biography. New York: Wilson, 1940–. Monthly, with annual cumulations.

Contains lengthy biographical sketches of men and women currently in the news. Entries include references to additional sources of information. Each issue has an index classified by profession and obituaries.

Dictionary of American Biography. 11 vols., with index and supplements. New York: Scribner's, 1928–1937.

Consists of long scholarly articles about American men and women who were not living at the time the *Dictionary* was published. Bibliographies are included at the end of each entry. Indexes are arranged by place of birth, college, and profession.

McGraw-Hill Encyclopedia of World Biography. 12 vols. New York: McGraw-Hill, 1973.

Contains short biographies of approximately 5,000 world figures. Entries include suggestions for further reading. The illustrations are a valuable feature. The index volume provides access by name and by subject.

Notable American Women, 1607–1950: A Biographical Dictionary. 3 vols. Cambridge: Belknap–Harvard University Press, 1971.

Presents scholarly articles (patterned after the *Dictionary of American Biography*) about American women living between 1607 and 1950 who made contributions to American society. Articles include bibliographies. Volume 3 lists names by profession. *Notable American Women: The Modern Period* (Cambridge: Belknap–Harvard University Press, 1980) gives biographical sketches for American women who died between 1951 and 1975.

Who's Who in America. Chicago: Marquis Who's Who, 1899–. Biennially.

The standard biographical dictionary on living Americans. Biographical information is given in concise form. Besides *Who's Who in America*, a number of more specific biographical dictionaries, such as *Who's Who in the Midwest*, *Who's Who in American Politics*, *Who's Who among Black Americans*, and *Who's Who in France*, focus on a particular geographic area or group.

Yearbooks and Almanacs

Facts on File. New York: Facts on File, 1941–. Weekly, with annual cumulations.

A weekly summary in looseleaf format of U.S. and world news events as covered in more than 50 U.S. and international documents, government publications, and news releases. Every two weeks a new index gives access to specific news items. At the end of the year a cumulated *Facts on File Yearbook* replaces the loose-leaf binder. *Facts on File* is particularly useful for verifying dates and tracing the sequence of events.

World Almanac and Book of Facts. New York: Newspaper Enterprise Assn., 1868–. Annual.
A comprehensive source of statistics, geographical and historical data, and current events information. The *World Almanac* includes information ranging from color illustrations of the flags of the world to a chronology of the events of the previous year. Sources are given for each set of facts. A general subject index is located in the front of the volume.

Government Documents

American Statistical Index. Washington, DC: Congressional Information Service, 1971–. Monthly, with annual cumulations.
Indexes all U.S. government statistical publications by subject, place or agency name, program name, and personal name. Summaries are given in the Abstract volume, and the actual documents are available on microfiche.

Congressional Information Service. *CIS Annual*. Washington, DC: Congressional Information Service, 1970–. Monthly, with annual cumulations.
Indexes all congressional publications, including hearings, committee reports, and publications of congressional offices, such as the Congressional Budget Office. Publications are indexed by subject and name as well as by bill number, document number, Senate hearing number, and committee chair. Summaries of the publications (which also include SuDoc numbers) can be found in the companion volumes. Available online and on CD-ROM.

Guide to U.S. Government Publications. Ed. John L. Andriot. McLean, VA: Documents Index, 1973–.
Annual annotated two-part guide to government materials. Part 1 contains series and periodicals published by U.S. government agencies, and part 2 lists the Superintendent of Documents classification numbers issued to date.

United States Department of Commerce, Bureau of the Census. *Statistical Abstract of the United States*. Washington, DC: GPO. Annually.
Summarizes statistical information on economic, social, and political subjects for the United States. Some international statistics are included. Statistics are grouped by general subject, such as foreign commerce and aid or agriculture, with a detailed index. Each graph or table has a citation to the government document from which it was taken.

United States Superintendent of Documents. *Monthly Catalog of United States Government Publications*. Washington, DC: GPO, 1895–. Monthly, with quarterly cumulations and semiannual index cumulations.
Lists government publications published each month. Entries are arranged alphabetically by issuing agency and are indexed by author, title, subject

(using Library of Congress subject headings), report, contract number, and the title key word. Entries marked with a black dot are available at federal depository libraries. Available online and on CD-ROM.

Sources in Primary Disciplinary Groups

Humanities

Arts and Humanities Citation Index (AHCI). Philadelphia: Institute for Scientific Information, 1978–. Bimonthly, with annual cumulations.
A multidisciplinary index composed of three separate indexes to about 1,300 periodicals in the arts and humanities: the *Source Index*, *Citation Index*, and *Permuterm Subject Index*. For format and directions for use, see the discussion of the *Social Sciences Citation Index*, Chapter 3, p. 68. Available online and on CD-ROM.

Blazek, Ron, and Elizabeth S. Versa. *The Humanities: A Selective Guide to Information Sources*. 3rd ed. Littleton, CO: Libraries Unlimited, 1988.
A guide to the literature of the humanities covering information sources in philosophy and religion, visual arts, performing arts, and language and literature. For each subject, a chapter explains how to obtain information in that field and a chapter lists the major reference works and periodicals. Evaluative annotations that explain coverage, arrangements, and most appropriate use accompany each citation.

Current Contents: Arts and Humanities. Philadelphia: Institute for Scientific Information, 1979–. Weekly.
A weekly compilation of the tables of contents of more than 1,300 humanities periodicals arranged in eight general subject categories. This publication provides the most current access to the content of these journals through a title key word (subject) index and an author index. Available online.

Humanities Index. New York: Wilson, 1974–. Quarterly, with annual cumulations. Supersedes *Social Sciences and Humanities Index*, 1965–1974, and *International Index to Periodicals*, 1907–1965.
Provides access by subject and author to more than 290 core periodicals in the classics, archaeology, language, literature and literary criticism, folklore, religion and philosophy, area studies, history, theater, and film. Book reviews are included alphabetically by author in a separate listing at the end of the volume. Available online and on CD-ROM.

Index to Book Reviews in the Humanities. Williamston, MI: Phillip Thomson, 1960–. Annually.
A comprehensive index to book reviews included in several hundred general and scholarly humanities periodicals. Through 1970 the subject coverage included history and some social sciences; since 1971 coverage has been confined to the arts and humanities. Access is by author's name.

Social Sciences

Book Review Index to Social Science Periodicals. Ed. Arnold M. Rzpecki. Ann Arbor: Pierian, 1964–1974.

Indexes book reviews by the name of the author in approximately 300 social science periodicals published from 1964 to 1974. Since 1970, history journals have been included. Book reviews published after 1974 can be found in the *Social Sciences Index*.

Current Contents: Social and Behavioral Sciences. Philadelphia: Institute for Scientific Information, 1974 –. Weekly.

A compilation of the tables of contents of more than 1,300 social and behavioral science periodicals arranged by thirteen subject disciplines. Provides the most current access to the contents of these journals through a title key word (subject) index and an author index. Available online.

International Encyclopedia of the Social Sciences. Ed. David L. Sills. 18 vols. New York: Macmillan, 1968.

Contains signed scholarly articles on the concepts, methods, major persons, and theories in anthropology and psychiatry, sociology, and statistics. Articles are arranged alphabetically by topic with additional access provided by a detailed index (volume 17) and cross-references. Each article has a bibliography of references. Volume 18 (1980) provides a biographical supplement. This encyclopedia updates but does not replace the classic *Encyclopedia of the Social Sciences* (New York: Macmillan, 1930–1935).

Public Affairs Information Service Bulletin (PAIS). New York: Public Affairs Information Service, 1915–. Semimonthly, with quarterly and annual cumulations.

Provides access by subject and author to periodical articles, government documents, books, and reports in public policy. Subject areas covered include economics, public administration, international relations, demographics, law, journalism, and politics. Available online and on CD-ROM.

Social Sciences Citation Index (SSCI). Philadelphia: Institute for Scientific Information, 1969–. Bimonthly, with annual cumulations.

Indexes more than 1,400 periodicals in the behavioral and social sciences. Following the same plan as ISI's other citation indexes, this *Index* has three separate ways of finding information in the indexed periodicals: the Citation Index, Source Index, and Permuterm Index. (See *Social Sciences Citation Index*, Chapter 3.) Available online and on CD-ROM.

Social Sciences Index. New York: Wilson, 1974–. Quarterly, with annual cumulations. Supersedes *Social Sciences and Humanities Index*, 1965–1974, and *International Index to Periodicals*, 1907–1965.

Provides access by subject and author to the major English-language periodicals in political science, sociology, economics, anthropology, psychology, planning and public affairs, environmental sciences, law, criminology, and behavioral sciences. Book reviews are listed alphabetically by author at the end of each volume. Available online and on CD-ROM.

Webb, William H., and Associates. *Sources of Information in the Social Sciences: A Guide to the Literature*. 3rd ed. Chicago: American Library Assn., 1986.

The standard guide to the social sciences, with sections on social science literature in general, history, geography, economics, business administration, sociology, anthropology, psychology, education, and political science. For each discipline there is an essay reviewing the basic works and methodologies in that field and an annotated guide to abstracts, periodicals, current and retrospective bibliographies, dictionaries, handbooks, and other reference works.

Science and Technology

American Men and Women of Science: Physical and Behavioral Sciences. Ed. Jaques Cattell Press. 17th ed. 8 vols. New York: Bowker, 1989–1990.
A biographical directory of more than 130,000 living American scientists. Arranged alphabetically, the entries include data on age, educational background, professional experience and memberships, mailing address, and area of research. Behavioral and social scientists were included in the first 13 editions. Available online.

Chen, Ching-Chih. 2nd ed. *Scientific and Technical Information*. Cambridge: MIT Press, 1987.
An annotated guide to reference books in all areas of science and technology except medicine. The book is arranged by type of reference book (dictionaries, handbooks, abstracts) and by subject within each category.

Current Contents: Life Sciences. Philadelphia: Institute for Scientific Information, 1958–. Weekly.
A weekly compilation of the tables of contents of more than 1,100 life science periodicals arranged in eleven subject groups. This publication provides current access to the contents of these journals by subject (through a title key word index) and by author. ISI publishes similar publications in other areas of science: *Current Contents: Agriculture, Biology and Environmental Sciences*; *Current Contents: Physical, Chemical, and Earth Sciences*; *Current Contents: Engineering, Technology and Applied Sciences*; and *Current Contents: Clinical Practice*. Available online.

General Science Index. New York: Wilson, 1978–. Quarterly, with annual cumulations.
Provides subject access to approximately 110 core science periodicals in the fields of biology, medicine, environmental science, mathematics, chemistry, geology, astronomy, meteorology, physics, and general science. Includes a separate listing of book reviews arranged alphabetically by author. Available online and on CD-ROM.

McGraw-Hill Dictionary of Scientific and Technical Terms. 4th ed. New York: McGraw-Hill, 1988.
Designed to supplement general dictionaries by providing brief and up-to-date definitions of specialized scientific and technical words. Line drawings illustrate some of the definitions.

McGraw-Hill Encyclopedia of Science and Technology. 6th ed. 20 vols. New York: McGraw-Hill, 1987.
Covers all areas of science and technology, including medicine. With emphasis on recent advances, the articles include both broad surveys as well as discussions of more specific, technical concepts. Articles are arranged al-

phabetically by topic with cross-references to the text and bibliographies in-cluded for most articles. Volume 20, the Index, includes both an analytical index (every concept, person, and term) and a topical index (grouping all articles under 78 general subject headings). The encyclopedia is updated by the *McGraw-Hill Yearbook of Science and Technology*.

Primack, Alice Lifler. *Finding Answers in Science and Technology*. New York: Van Nostrand Reinhold, 1984.

A guide to sources of scientific information for beginning researchers. Two initial chapters explain search strategy and give information on libraries and computer searching; the arrangement of the rest of the book is by sub-ject discipline. Each chapter discusses the reference works used in a specific discipline from general introductory works to specialized indexes.

Science Citation Index (SCI). Philadelphia: Institute for Scientific Information, 1955-. Bimonthly, with annual cumulations.

Indexes more than 1,000 periodicals and monographic serials in science, technology, medicine, agriculture, and the behavioral sciences. It does not include book reviews except those published in *Science* and *Nature*. It follows the same plan as ISI's other indexes. (See *Social Sciences Citation Index*, Chap-ter 3.) Available online and on CD-ROM.

Technical Book Review Index. Pittsburgh: JAAD, 1935-. Monthly, with annual cumulations.

Identifies book reviews in English-language journals in all areas of science, medicine, and technology. The reviews are arranged alphabetically by au-thor within broad subject groups. An author index is located at the end of each annual cumulation. Short excerpts from the reviews are included.

Sources in Specific Academic Disciplines

Accounting.   See Business, Accounting, and Economics.

Agriculture.   See Biology and Agriculture.

Anthropology and Archaeology

Abstracts in Anthropology. Farmingdale, NY: Baywood, 1970-. Quarterly.
Consists of abstracts in the fields of archaeology, cultural and physical an-thropology, and linguistics; the abstracts are grouped in a classified ar-rangement, with author and subject indexes.

The Cambridge Encyclopedia of Archaeology. Ed. Andrew Sherratt. New York: Cambridge University Press, 1980.
Instead of being arranged alphabetically by subject, the chapters are ar-ranged in three groups. Chapters 1–7 deal with the development of modern archaeology. Chapters 8–61 cover different archaeological periods and re-gions. The final chapters discuss methodology and provide a chronological

atlas. A bibliography, organized by the chapter divisions, and a detailed subject index conclude the volume.

Encyclopedia of Anthropology. Ed. David E. Hunter and Phillip Whitten. New York: Harper and Row, 1976.
Short, signed articles arranged alphabetically on concepts, methodology, and major anthropologists; some articles include bibliographies.

Frantz, Charles. *The Student Anthropologist's Handbook: A Guide to Research, Training and Careers*. Cambridge, MA: Schenkman, 1972.
A guide to the history and nature of anthropology and to research in the field and in the library; the final chapter discusses the profession.

Heizer, Robert F., et al. *Archaeology: A Bibliographical Guide to the Basic Literature*. New York: Garland, 1980.
A guide to the literature on the history and methodology of archaeology. The final chapter lists bibliographies, dictionaries, and atlases. The detailed table of contents provides access by subject and an author index is included.

JOURNALS

American Anthropologist. Washington, DC: American Anthropology Assn., 1888–. Quarterly.
Contains scholarly articles and research reports covering all areas of anthropology. The section Commentaries provides a forum for discussion of previous research; the journal contains an extensive bibliography of book and film reviews arranged by subject.

American Journal of Archaeology. Bryn Mawr: Archaeological Institute of America, 1885–. Quarterly.
Publishes research articles on the archaeology and art history of the Mediterranean region with some articles on neighboring areas. It also includes notes, grant information, and book reviews.

Anthropological Quarterly. Washington, DC: Catholic University of America Press, 1928–. Quarterly.
Contains three or four scholarly articles per issue as well as lengthy book reviews.

Archaeology. Boston: Archaeological Institute of America, 1948–. Bimonthly.
Intended for lay readers as well as scholars, articles report results of archaeological research in all regions of the world. It includes book reviews and information on exhibitions, new books, tours, and excavations.

Art and Architecture

Architectural Periodicals Index. London: British Architectural Library, 1972–.
Indexes more than 450 journals in architecture and allied arts, construction techniques, design, environmental studies, and planning. Arranged by class with a name index and a topographical and building name index. Available online.

ARTbibliographies Modern. Santa Barbara: ABC-Clio, 1974–.
Provides access to the literature on modern art and design found in books, periodicals, dissertations, and exhibition catalogs. Online only.

Art Index. New York: Wilson, 1929–. Quarterly, with annual cumulations.
An index by author and subject to approximately 200 international periodicals, yearbooks, and museum bulletins on art and related subjects, such as aesthetics, design, film, and photography. Available online and on CD-ROM.

Ehresmann, Donald. *Fine Arts: A Bibliographic Guide to Basic Reference Works, Histories, and Handbooks.* 3rd ed. Littleton, CO: Libraries Unlimited, 1987.
An annotated guide to the literature of painting, sculpture, and architecture. The first part covers bibliographies, library catalogs, indexes, and dictionaries as well as references on iconography. The second part provides references to histories and handbooks on historic periods in a chronological arrangement. An author/title/subject index is included for the whole volume.

Encyclopedia of World Art. 15 vols., with supplements. New York: McGraw-Hill, 1968.
Presents lengthy articles arranged alphabetically on concepts, artists, periods, and geographic regions. Each article is signed and gives a bibliography of further references. Volume 15 is an index to the rest of the volumes.

Information Sources in Architecture. Ed. Valerie J. Bradfield. London: Butterworths, 1983.
Designed for the researcher and professional architect, the book covers information sources for each step of the construction process. Contributed chapters cover libraries, information retrieval techniques, trade literature, government publications, design, and office management. Includes an index.

Jones, Lois Swan. *Art Research Methods and Resources: A Guide to Finding Art Information.* 2nd ed. Dubuque: Kendall/Hunt, 1984.
An introduction and detailed guide to researching art for both students and specialists.

Oxford Companion to Art. Ed. Harold Osborne. Oxford: Clarendon, 1970.
Contains brief, general information on the visual arts and artists and extensive bibliographies. The articles cover all time periods and geographical regions.

JOURNALS

Art Bulletin. New York: College Art Assn. of America, 1912–. Quarterly.
Prints scholarly articles about art and art history, often grouped by related subjects, with each issue covering several topics. The articles include research notes and lengthy book reviews.

Art in America. New York: Art in America, 1913–. Monthly.
Consists of review articles and commentary on art and artists of all historical periods. The emphasis is on contemporary American art, but non-American work is also covered. It also publishes book reviews and reviews of exhibitions.

Art Journal. New York: College Art Assn. of America, 1941–. Quarterly.
Includes scholarly articles on art and artists from all countries and periods as well as book reviews and museum news.

Burlington Magazine. London: Burlington Magazine Publications, 1903–. Monthly.

Publishes two or three scholarly articles per issue on individual artists, works of art, schools, and periods of art history. It also contains short research articles, extended book reviews, and exhibition reviews.

Journal of the Society of Architectural Historians. Philadelphia: Society of Architectural Historians. 1940–. Quarterly.

Publishes architectural criticism, book reviews, and articles on architectural history.

Progressive Architecture. Stamford, CT: Reinhold, 1920–. Monthly.

Covers the international scene in architecture with emphasis on the United States. It is written for the professional and deals with all aspects of architecture, with two special sections each month, one of design and one of building technology.

Astronomy and Space Science

Astronomy and Astrophysics Abstracts. New York: Springer-Verlag, 1969–. Semi-annually.

A classified subject index with international coverage of astronomy and astrophysics. Each volume includes a subject and author index.

The Cambridge Encyclopedia of Astronomy. Ed. Simon Milton. New York: Crown, 1977.

A broad-based survey of astronomy prepared by astronomers, intended for both amateurs and professionals. It includes an index and a star atlas.

International Aerospace Abstracts. Phillipsburg, NJ: American Institute of Aeronautics and Astronautics, 1961–. Semimonthly.

An index to published literature in periodicals and books, meeting papers, and conference proceedings in space sciences and aeronautics. It includes separate indexes by subject, author, contract number, meeting paper and report number, and accession number. Semiannual and annual cumulations. Available online.

Seal, Robert A. *A Guide to the Literature of Astronomy*. Littleton, CO: Libraries Unlimited, 1977.

An introduction to the literature of astronomy.

JOURNALS

Astronomy and Aeronomics. New York: American Institute of Aeronautics and Astronautics, 1932–. 11 issues per year.

Covers recent trends and developments in space flight, hydronautics, and rocketry.

Astrophysical Journal. Chicago: University of Chicago Press, 1895–. Semimonthly.

Reports original observations and research at national and academic institutions. Each issue comes in two parts: part 1 contains full-length research papers and part 2 contains shorter reports.

Aviation Week and Space Technology. New York: McGraw-Hill, 1916–. Weekly.

Covers current trends and events affecting scientific as well as business aspects of aviation and aerospace. It also contains occasional in-depth reports and some directory-type information.

Sky and Telescope. Cambridge: Sky, 1941–. Monthly.
Publishes popular and semitechnical articles on all aspects of astronomy. It includes a celestial calendar, sky chart, and news notes.

Biology and Agriculture

Bibliography of Agriculture. Phoenix: Oryx, 1942–. Monthly, with annual cumulations.
Provides access by subject and author to the world literature on agriculture and related fields, such as food and nutrition. It includes periodicals, books, government documents, and conference proceedings. Available online and on CD-ROM.

Bibliography of Bioethics. Detroit: Gale, 1975–. Annually.
A subject index to magazine and newspaper articles, audiovisual materials, books, and government documents in bioethics. The subject headings used are listed in the thesaurus in volume 1; each volume also contains an author and title index. Available online.

Biological Abstracts. Philadelphia: BioSciences Information Service, 1926–. Semimonthly, with semiannual cumulations.
Covers international research literature in all the life sciences except clinical medicine. Five indexes provide access to the abstracts: author, subject, generic (organism name), biosystematic, and concept. The subject index lists key words from the titles of the articles. The concept index indexes the articles by one of 500 major concepts. Available online and on CD-ROM.

Biological and Agricultural Index. New York: Wilson, 1916–. Monthly, with annual cumulations. Formerly *Agricultural Index*, 1916–August 1964.
Provides subject indexing to more than 200 periodicals in the life sciences and agriculture. Book reviews arranged alphabetically by author are included in each annual volume. Available online and on CD-ROM.

Encyclopedia of Bioethics. Ed. Warren T. Reich. 4 vols. New York: Macmillan/ Free Press, 1978.
Contains lengthy scholarly articles on moral and ethical aspects of the life sciences, such as euthanasia, drug use, ethical use of technology, and behavior control. Extensive cross-references and bibliographies are included.

Gray, Peter, ed. *The Encyclopedia of the Biological Sciences.* 2nd ed. New York: Van Nostrand Reinhold, 1970.
Consists of signed articles on major biologists and concepts that cover all areas of the life sciences. The arrangement is alphabetical and most articles contain bibliographies.

Guide to Sources on Agricultural and Biological Research. Ed. J. Richard Blanchard and Lois Farrell. Berkeley: University of California Press, 1980.
An annotated guide to research tools in agriculture and the life sciences. The introduction explains the communication process used in science. Following a chapter on general information sources in the life sciences, chapters describe reference works in the plant sciences, animal sciences, physi-

cal sciences, food sciences and nutrition, environmental sciences, and the relevant social sciences. The final chapter discusses computerized databases.

Smith, Roger C., et al. *Smith's Guide to the Literature of the Life Sciences.* 9th ed. Minneapolis: Burgess, 1980.

A guide to research in the life sciences. After an introductory section on research and libraries, this guide is arranged by class of research tool, such as indexes, primary research journals, ready reference works, and taxonomic literature. The book also includes chapters on research methods and scientific writing.

Tootill, Elizabeth. *The Facts on File Dictionary of Biology.* Rev. ed. New York: Facts on File, 1988.

Gives brief definitions of biological terms, concepts, processes, and descriptions of organisms. Diagrams and charts illustrate such concepts as the carbon cycle and the geological time scale.

JOURNALS

American Journal of Botany. Columbus, OH: Botanical Society of America, 1914–. 10 issues per year.

Presents original research articles in all areas of botany, including economic botany and paleobotany.

American Zoologist. Thousand Oaks, CA: American Society of Zoologists, 1961–. Quarterly.

Includes original research and review articles as well as symposium papers on specific zoological topics. It also contains information on the society and occasional book reviews.

BioScience. Arlington, VA: American Institute of Biological Sciences, 1950–. Monthly.

Covers the entire range of current topics in biology and is suitable for both specialists and lay readers.

Business, Accounting, and Economics

ABI/Inform. UMI/Data Courier, 1970–. Updated weekly.

A database that indexes and abstracts more than 800 international periodicals in business and management. Available online and on CD-ROM.

Accountant's Index. New York: American Institute of Certified Public Accountants, 1921–. Quarterly, with annual cumulations.

Comprehensive index to English-language books, pamphlets, government documents, and articles on accounting and related fields. Listing is by author and title as well as by subject. Available online.

Daniells, Lorna M. *Business Information Sources.* Rev. ed. Berkeley: University of California Press, 1985.

The first eight chapters cover business reference sources, bibliographies, indexes and abstracts, directories, statistical sources, investment sources, and data on current business and economic trends. The second part of the book discusses management resources in accounting, information systems, banking, insurance, marketing, personnel management, and related fields. The last chapter lists important reference books for a small office library. Entries are annotated and a subject, author, and title index is included.

The Encyclopedia of Management. Ed. Carl Heyel. 3rd ed. New York: Van Nostrand Reinhold, 1982.

Contains signed articles on management concepts and techniques, accounting, labor relations, and related subjects. Most articles give additional sources of information; an outline of core subject readings can be used to guide a reading program.

Journal of Economic Literature. Nashville: American Economic Assn., 1963–. Quarterly.

Each issue includes an annotated list of new books, classified by subject, a subject index of articles in current periodicals with abstracts for the most significant articles, and tables of contents for current economics journals. Critical book reviews are at the beginning of each volume. Available online.

Ness, Dan, Jr. *Fast Facts Online: Search Strategies for Finding Business Information.* Homewood, IL: Dow Jones–Irwin, 1986.

A practical introduction to business databases and their use. A chapter on overall search strategy and detailed information on a variety of databases are included.

Predicasts F & S Index United States. Cleveland: Predicasts, 1968–. Monthly, with quarterly and annual cumulations.

A good index to use when looking for current information about U.S. companies and industries. The index covers more than 750 business, industrial, and financial periodicals. It is divided into two sections: the white pages list articles by company name and the colored pages are arranged by 7-digit industry codes and by basic economic indicators. Major articles are designated with a black dot. Available online.

Rosenberg, Jerry M. *Dictionary of Business and Management.* 2nd ed. New York: Wiley, 1983.

Contains brief definitions for more than 10,000 terms. Appendixes include tables for forms of measurement and interest, a list of graduate programs in business and management, and a summary of major economic events in U.S. history.

Wall Street Journal Index. New York: Dow Jones, 1958–. Monthly, with annual cumulations.

Indexes the final eastern edition of the *Wall Street Journal* and *Barron's* (since 1981). The index to *Barron's* (the green pages at the end of the volume) includes entries by subject and corporate name; the rest of the index is divided into two sections: general and corporate. Entries give a citation and brief summary of the contents of each article.

JOURNALS

American Economic Review. Nashville: American Economic Assn., 1911–. Quarterly.

Includes lengthy articles and short papers on economic topics as well as commentary and notes.

Harvard Business Review. Cambridge: Harvard University, 1922–. Bimonthly.
Contains articles on management issues, problems, and theories. Ideas for
Action section has brief articles reporting developments and trends. Occa-
sional book reviews are included.

Journal of Accountancy. New York: American Institute of Certified Public Accountants, 1905–. Monthly.
Provides three or four major articles per issue discussing issues, developments, and practical applications in accounting, as well as brief news reports; professional news; book reports; and brief notes on articles of interest in other periodicals.

Journal of Business. Chicago: University of Chicago Press, 1928–. Quarterly.
Contains empirical and theoretical studies of business and economics topics; lists of books received; and news of appointments, grants, retirements,
and dissertations.

Quarterly Journal of Economics. New York: Wiley, 1886–. Quarterly.
A highly regarded journal, and the oldest English-language journal of economics. Articles are geared to economists, professors, and students and are
highly theoretical.

Chemistry and Physics

Applied Science and Technology Index. See entry under Engineering and Electronics.

Besancon, Robert M. *The Encyclopedia of Physics*. 3rd ed. New York: Van Nostrand Reinhold, 1985.
A one-volume encyclopedia with signed scholarly articles. Articles on major topics are less technical for general readers, while specific articles are
more advanced.

Chemical Abstracts. Columbus, OH: American Chemical Society, 1907–.
Weekly, with semiannual cumulations.
Provides access to the world's chemical and chemical engineering research
literature. Besides a general subject index that uses a controlled vocabulary, it includes a chemical substance index, a formula index, an index of
ring systems, a patent index, and an author index. All of these indexes provide access to the weekly abstracts, which are arranged by subject classifications. Available online.

CRC Handbook of Chemistry and Physics. 70th ed. Boca Raton: Chemical Rubber
Co., 1989.
A compilation of formulas, tables, and charts presenting data of use to
chemists, researchers in the physical sciences, and mathematicians. Information is grouped in six broad categories with a subject index included at
the end of the volume.

Kirk-Othmer Encyclopedia of Chemical Technology. 3rd ed. 24 vols., with supplement and index. New York: Wiley, 1978.
Consists of background articles on chemical technology and related issues,
such as energy and toxicology. Approximately half of the articles discuss
chemical substances and describe chemical properties and the manufactur-
ing process; a separate index provides subject access to the entire set.

Malinowsky, H. Robert, and Jeanne M. Richardson. *Science and Engineering Literature*. See entry under Engineering and Electronics.

Physics Abstracts. Surrey, England: Institution of Electrical Engineers, 1898–. Twice monthly, with cumulative subject and author indexes every six months.
> Publishes abstracts for English-language journals, books, reports, dissertations, and conference proceedings on physics. Abstracts are grouped in ten major subject classifications with subdivisions. A detailed summary of the classification system as well as a subject index is given at the beginning of each issue. Each set of six months' cumulated index volumes contains the following indexes: subject, author, bibliography, conference, and corporate author. Available online.

JOURNALS

American Chemical Society Journal. Washington, DC: American Chemical Society, 1879–. Biweekly.
> Publishes research articles; brief articles discussing, correcting, or amending earlier research; and book reviews.

American Journal of Physics. New York: American Institute of Physics, 1933–. Monthly. Formerly *American Physics Teacher*, 1933–1940.
> Contains technical research and review articles on physical science, particularly the instructional and social aspects; short reports on new apparatus or new techniques; and book reviews.

Chemical Reviews. Washington, DC: American Chemical Society, 1924–. Bimonthly.
> Reports research in chemistry and allied fields.

Physics Today. New York: American Institute of Physics, 1948–. Monthly.
> Provides research and review articles; occasional articles on special topics such as neutron scattering; book reviews and reports on new products; and institute news.

Communications (Radio, Television, Speech, Journalism)

Blum, Eleanor. *Basic Books in the Mass Media*. 2nd ed. Urbana: University of Illinois Press, 1980.
> An annotated bibliography of reference books and other sources of information on mass communications, book publishing, broadcasting, film, magazines, and advertising. Titles are arranged by broad subject categories with access by subject and author-title indexes.

Communications Abstracts. Beverly Hills: Sage, 1978–. Quarterly.
> Abstracts articles from more than 150 journals as well as research reports and books in communication theory, mass communications, journalism, broadcasting, advertising, speech, and radio and television. Subject and author indexes appear in each issue and cumulate in each year's final issue.

International Encyclopedia of Communications. 4 vols. Philadelphia: Annenberg School of Communications; New York: Oxford University Press, 1989.

Publishes signed articles covering communications. Articles range from historical treatment of communication techniques to the psychological, sociological, and anthropological treatments of communication processes. Most articles are followed with a brief bibliography. The back of volume 4 contains a topical guide to the contents and an index.

Longman's Dictionary of Mass Media and Communication. Ed. Tracy Daniel Connors. New York: Longman, 1982.

Gives brief definitions of terms and acronyms used in broadcasting, advertising, journalism, marketing, publishing, and other communications-related fields.

Paneth, Donald. *The Encyclopedia of American Journalism.* New York: Facts on File, 1983.

Attempts to cover all aspects of American journalism: the gathering, evaluating, and dissemination of news and information, fact, and opinion. It looks at each form of journalism from print to electronic media and the history and technology of each form. Cross-references and bibliographies are included, as is a subject index at the back of the volume.

JOURNALS

Columbia Journalism Review. New York: Columbia University, 1962–. Bimonthly.

Publishes articles for lay readers and professionals analyzing issues in journalism. The Briefings section gives short reviews of symposia, books, and media productions. Book reviews are included.

Communications Quarterly. University Park, PA: Eastern Communication Assn., 1953–. Quarterly. Continues *Today's Speech.*

Contains scholarly articles on all aspects of communication, including public speaking, nonverbal communication, and interpersonal communication, as well as lengthy book reviews.

Journal of Broadcasting and Electronic Media. Washington, DC: Broadcast Education Assn., 1956–. Quarterly.

Publishes research articles on issues in broadcasting; some shorter research reports and industry commentary; and lengthy book reviews.

Journal of Communication. Philadelphia: Annenberg Press, 1951–. Quarterly.

Covers communication theory and practice. In addition to research articles, each issue focuses on a specific review topic, such as the international flow of information. The Intercom section provides professional news, book reviews, and commentary.

Journalism Quarterly (JQ). Columbia, SC: Assn. for Education in Journalism and Mass Communications, 1924–. Quarterly.

Presents scholarly articles reporting research in mass communications and journalism; brief research reports; book reviews; and annotated bibliographies of articles on mass communications.

Quarterly Journal of Speech. Annandale, VA: Speech Communication Assn., 1915–. Quarterly.

A scholarly journal concentrating on speech research and education at the college or university level. Articles focus on historical, critical, empirical, and theoretical issues; a section of book reviews is included.

Computer Science and Mathematics

ACM Guide to Computing Literature. New York: Assn. for Computing Machinery, 1977–. Annually. Continues *Bibliography of Current Computing Literature*.

Contains seven sections: bibliographic listing, author index, key word index, category index, proper noun subject index, *Computing Reviews* (a reviewer index), and source index. Covers the literature of computer science, including papers from conferences and the major journals of computer science.

Computer Abstracts. London: Technical Information Co., 1957–. Monthly, with annual author and subject indexes.

Abstracts of books, journal articles, proceedings, and government documents in classified arrangement with monthly author and patent indexes.

Computer Literature Index. Phoenix: Applied Computer Research, 1980–. Continues *Quarterly Bibliography of Computers and Data Processing*, 1968–1979. Quarterly.

A comprehensive index to the professional literature, covering periodicals, books, conference proceedings, trade journals, and technical reports. Entries are arranged by subject classifications and cover computer hardware, software, and applications; brief abstracts are given for most entries.

Dictionary of Computing. 2nd ed. Oxford: Oxford University Press, 1986.

Briefly defines technical terms, concepts, and acronyms related to computer science.

Encyclopedia of Computer Science and Engineering. Ed. Anthony Ralston. 2nd ed. New York: Van Nostrand Reinhold, 1983.

Contains signed articles on computer hardware and software, information systems management, theory and methodology of computing, and computer applications. Articles are arranged alphabetically, with a general classification system described in the front of the volume to guide reading on general subject areas; some articles have bibliographies. Appendixes provide helpful information in the form of acronym lists, lists of journals and of universities offering Ph.D. programs in computer science, and a glossary of major terms in five languages.

Hildebrandt, Darlene Myers, ed. *Computing Information Directory: A Comprehensive Guide to the Literature*. 3rd ed. Federal Way, WA: Pedaro, 1986.

A guide to reference books in all areas of computer science and data processing. In addition to a bibliography of important computer books published during the 1970s, the text covers journals, technical reports, indexes and abstracts, dictionaries, directories, newsletters, software resources, and programming languages. An appendix includes information on careers and salary trends, publishers, and a master index.

Mathematical Reviews. Providence: American Mathematical Society, 1940–. Monthly, with semiannual cumulation.

Contains comprehensive coverage of pure and applied mathematics literature. Abstracts are arranged according to a classification system with semiannual author and subject indexes. Available online and on CD-ROM.

Schaeger, Barbara Kirsch. *Using the Mathematical Literature: A Practical Guide*. New York: Dekker, 1979.

Written for students, teachers, and practitioners of mathematics. This guide provides an introduction to the different types of mathematical literature.

JOURNALS

ACM Communications. New York: Assn. for Computing Machinery, 1958–. Monthly.
Presents research and review articles on the design and applications of computers. Occasional issues focus on topics such as computer science education and professional news.

American Mathematical Monthly. Washington, DC: Mathematical Assn. of America, 1894–. 10 issues per year.
Publishes expository and review articles directed at a college-level mathematics education. Issues include book reviews and a section on "elementary and advanced problems."

American Mathematical Society Bulletin. Providence: American Mathematical Society, 1894–. Quarterly.
Includes detailed articles on current issues of interest to mathematicians. This journal publishes practical and theoretical articles and covers all areas of mathematics.

Association for Computing Machinery Journal. New York: Assn. for Computing Machinery, 1954–. Quarterly.
Includes technical articles on programming languages, system analysis, computing theory, and artificial intelligence.

Byte: The Small Systems Journal. Peterborough, NH: McGraw-Hill, 1975–. Monthly.
Contains 12–18 feature articles per issue as well as reviews of books, software, hardware, and computer languages. Selected programs, computer news, and an international calendar of events are presented.

Computers and People. Newtonville, MA: Berkeley Enterprises, 1951–. Bi-monthly. Continues *Computers and Automation*, 1952–1974.
Publishes review articles on computers, computer applications, artificial intelligence, social implications of computers, and computer games.

Datamation. New York: Technical Publishing Co., 1957–. Twice monthly.
Contains news and review articles on developments in computer hardware and software along with descriptive reviews of hardware and software.

Criminal Justice.   See Law and Criminal Justice.

Drama

Breed, Paul F., and Florence M. Sniderman, eds. *Dramatic Criticism Index*. Detroit: Gale, 1972.
A bibliography of books and articles on modern American and foreign playwrights. Citations are arranged alphabetically by playwright and by name of play; indexes of play titles and critics are included.

McGraw-Hill Encyclopedia of World Drama. 2nd ed. 5 vols. New York: McGraw-Hill, 1984.

Provides articles on dramatists, directors, national, regional, and ethnic dramas, as well as on aspects of performance, such as makeup and costume. Articles on major dramatists give biographical and critical information, bibliographies, and plot summaries for the plays. Volume 5 includes a glossary with definitions of concepts and terms, a play title list giving authors' names, and an author/title/subject index.

The New York Times Theater Reviews. New York: New York Times, 1971–.
A chronological reproduction of theater reviews appearing in the *New York Times* from 1920 to 1970. Volumes 9 and 10 have indexes by title, by production company, and by personal name; volume 9 also has an appendix listing theater awards and prizes and summaries of productions and runs by season.

Whalon, Marion K. *Performing Arts Research: A Guide to Information Sources.* Detroit: Gale, 1976.
Annotated bibliography of sources on theater dance, musical theater, and motion pictures. The reference sources, arranged by type, include guides, dictionaries and handbooks, directories, play indexes, review sources, bibliographies and indexes, and picture and audiovisual sources. An author/title/subject index is provided.

JOURNALS

Drama: The Quarterly Theatre Review. London: British Theatre Assn., 1919–. Quarterly.
Prints reviews of British drama, interviews with directors and actors, and book reviews.

The Drama Review. Cambridge: MIT Press, 1955–. Continues the *Tulane Drama Review.* Quarterly.
Covers the international avant-garde in performance art and theater. Each issue contains 6–10 articles focusing on a single topic, such as French theater. TDR also includes short descriptive reports on contemporary works, short plays, and book reviews and is well illustrated with photos.

Theatre Journal (TJ). Washington, DC: University and College Theatre Assn., 1949–. Quarterly. Continues *Educational Theatre Journal.*
Contains 5 or 6 scholarly articles per issue; theater review and book review sections; and a list of recent books, arranged by subject.

Theatre Research International. Oxford: Oxford University Press, 1958. 3 issues per year. Continues *Theatre Research.*
Provides scholarly historical and critical articles on drama along with lengthy book reviews.

Earth Sciences.   See Environmental and Earth Sciences.

Economics.   See Business, Accounting, and Economics.

Education

Berry, Dorothea M. *A Bibliographic Guide to Educational Research.* 2nd ed. Metuchen, NJ: Scarecrow, 1980.

A guide to research sources in education. The book is an annotated bibliography arranged by type of information source, such as bibliographies, indexes, research studies, government documents, nonprint materials, and reference books. These categories are subdivided by area of education, such as special education, curriculum, international education, and educational technology. The final chapter focuses on guides to research. The guide also includes an author/editor index, a title index, and a subject index.

Education Index. New York: Wilson, 1929–. 10 times a year, with annual cumulations.

A subject and author index to English-language periodicals, monographs, and yearbooks in educational administration; teaching from preschool through adult; and curriculum and teaching methods in all subject fields. From 1961 to 1969, author indexing and book reviews were omitted; since 1969, book reviews have been included. Available online and on CD-ROM.

The Encyclopedia of Education. Ed. Lee C. Deighton. 10 vols. New York: Macmillan, 1971.

Contains 1,000 articles on educational history, philosophy, theory, and practice, concerned mainly with education in America. Entries are signed and have bibliographies. Volume 10 has a directory of contributors, a guide to articles (grouped by subject area and giving cross-references), and a subject index.

ERIC (Educational Resources Information Center). *Current Index to Journals in Education* (*CIJE*). Phoenix: Oryx, 1969–. Monthly, with semiannual cumulations.

A subject index to almost 800 journals; access is through a controlled vocabulary, the Thesaurus of ERIC Descriptors. Each citation includes a list of assigned descriptors and an abstract. An author index and a journal contents index are also included. Available online and on CD-ROM.

ERIC (Educational Resources Information Center). *Resources in Education* (*RIE*). Phoenix: Oryx, 1969–. Monthly, with semiannual cumulations.

A companion to *CIJE*, RIE indexes educational research reports, books, government publications, conference papers, and unpublished manuscripts. Documents are available on microfiche or in hard copy through the ERIC Document Reproduction Service. An abstract is given for each document. Available online and on CD-ROM.

Good, Carter V., ed. *Dictionary of Education.* 3rd ed. New York: McGraw-Hill, 1973.

Gives brief definitions for specialized terms and concepts in all areas of education; personal and institution names are not included.

JOURNALS

American Educational Research Journal. Washington, DC: American Educational Research Assn., 1964–. Quarterly.

Contains empirical research articles on issues in education.

American Journal of Education. Chicago: University of Chicago Press, 1893–. Quarterly. Continues *School Review*, 1893–1979.

Presents research and review articles and book reviews. Some issues focus on a specific topic such as the development of literacy in American schools.

Harvard Educational Review. Cambridge: Harvard University, 1931–. Quarterly. Continues *Harvard Teachers Record*.
Publishes scholarly articles reporting research and opinion on educational topics as well as both extended and brief book reviews. Special issues treat topics such as education and the threat of nuclear war.

Journal of Educational Psychology. Washington, DC: American Psychological Assn., 1910–. Bimonthly.
Presents original research on psychological aspects of learning.

Engineering and Electronics

Applied Science and Technology Index. New York: Wilson, 1958–. Continues *Industrial Arts Index*. Quarterly, with annual cumulations.
Subject index to more than 300 English-language journals in engineering, earth sciences, food technology, textile production, energy, computer science, petroleum, metallurgy, physics, electronics, and other related fields. Book reviews are listed by author in a separate section. Available online and on CD-ROM.

Engineering Index. New York: Engineering Information, 1884–. Monthly, with annual cumulations.
Provides abstracts for the world's literature in engineering sciences taken from journals, technical reports, books, and conference proceedings; the abstracts are arranged by subject with additional access through an author index and an author affiliation index. Available online and on CD-ROM.

IEEE Standard Dictionary of Electrical and Electronics Terms. 4th ed. New York: Institute of Electrical and Electronics Engineers, 1988.
Each entry in this alphabetical list has a number that keys it to a source in the back of the book. There is also a separate list of abbreviations, symbols, code names, project names, and acronyms.

McGraw-Hill Dictionary of Engineering. Ed. Sybil P. Parker. New York: McGraw-Hill, 1984.
Presents the specialized vocabularies of 13 different engineering disciplines, including civil, mechanical, aerospace, and systems engineering; does not include chemical, electrical, or food engineering terms.

Malinowsky, H. Robert, and Jeanne M. Richardson. *Science and Engineering Literature*. 3rd ed. Littleton, CO: Libraries Unlimited, 1980.
Contains introductory chapters on scientific literature and the methods of locating this literature, followed by a section on multidisciplinary reference tools and sections on each scientific discipline. The physical sciences covered are mathematics, astronomy, physics, chemistry, geoscience, energy, and engineering; each of these chapters is divided by type of reference tool. A bibliography on science librarianship and an author/title/subject index are also provided.

JOURNALS

Electronics Week. New York: McGraw-Hill, 1930–. Weekly. Continues *Electronics*.
Contains articles on new developments in technology and news of the electronics industry; one section covers previews of new products.

IEEE Spectrum. New York: Institute of Electrical and Electronics Engineers, 1964-. Monthly.

Prints technical articles on new technological developments and their applications; articles on systems and analysis of specific problems; and book reviews.

Mechanical Engineering. New York: American Society of Mechanical Engineers, 1906-. Monthly.

Reviews developments in mechanical engineering; contains sections on computer applications, information on new products, society news, and book reviews.

Environmental and Earth Sciences

Ecology Abstracts. Bethesda: Cambridge Scientific Abstracts, 1975-. Monthly.

Includes abstracts of articles from approximately 5,000 journals on topics related to ecology. Abstracts are grouped into 56 subject categories with more specific access through a subject index that can be searched through the Life Sciences Collection database (Cambridge Scientific Abstracts, 1978-). Available online.

Environmental Periodicals Bibliography. Santa Barbara: Environmental Studies Institute, 1972-. 6 issues per year, with annual cumulative index.

Contains the tables of contents of journals dealing with environmental topics. Journals are grouped by general subject with access to specific subjects through a key word index. Available online.

Geological Society of America. *Bibliography and Index of Geology.* Alexandria, VA: American Geological Institute, 1933-. Monthly, with annual cumulations.

Indexes the world's literature (books, periodicals, reports, maps, and North American theses and dissertations) on geology. Each month the Field of Interest section gives bibliographic citations for all documents covered, grouping the citations by subject category and then by document type; each issue also contains subject and author indexes. In the annual cumulation, citations in the Fields of Interest section are in alphabetical order. Available online.

Grzimek's Encyclopedia of Ecology. Ed. Bernhard Grzimek. New York: Van Nostrand Reinhold, 1976.

Publishes background articles on ecology grouped in two categories: environment of animals and environment of humans. A detailed table of contents and an index identify specific topics.

McGraw-Hill Encyclopedia of Environmental Science. 2nd ed. New York: McGraw-Hill, 1980.

Consists of signed scholarly articles of some length on subjects related to the environment, including meteorology, public health, agriculture, and geology; articles include bibliographies. Besides the general articles arranged alphabetically, major essays in the beginning of the volume discuss topics such as urban planning and environmental analysis.

McGraw-Hill Encyclopedia of Geological Sciences. 2nd ed. New York: McGraw-Hill, 1988.

Contains signed background articles on geology, the earth sciences, and related subjects in oceanography and meteorology. Except for brief entries, most articles have bibliographies.

Smith's Guide to the Literature of the Life Sciences. See entry under Biology and Agriculture.

Ward, Dederick C., Marjorie W. Wheeler, and Robert A. Bier. *Geologic Reference Sources.* 2nd ed. Metuchen, NJ: Scarecrow, 1981.

Annotated entries are divided into general reference sources (indexes, directories, encyclopedias); a subject section that describes sources for earth science, meteorology, oceanography, geology, mineralogy, soil science, petrology, paleontology, environmental geology, and other related subjects; and a regional section. There are subject and geographic indexes.

JOURNALS

Earth Science Reviews. Amsterdam, 1966–. Quarterly.

Articles in English from many countries on current developments and research. Each issue contains two long articles with extensive bibliographies. An especially valuable news supplement to each issue, Atlas, lists the contents of selected other geological journals and contains 8–10 book reviews.

Ecology. Tempe: Ecological Society of America, 1920–. Bimonthly.

Concerned with the study of organisms in relation to the environment, this journal contains research articles (about 25 per issue), a notes and comments section, and lengthy book reviews. *Ecological Monographs* (same publisher) is a quarterly journal for longer articles (more than 20 pages).

Environment. Washington, DC: Helen Dwight Reid Educational Foundation and the Scientists' Institute for Public Information, 1958–. 10 issues per year.

Contains technical articles (about three per issue) on environmental problems and solutions as well as abstracts for these articles in the table of contents. Also included are short book reviews and an overview of current environmental topics.

Environmental Geology and Water Sciences. New York: Springer-Verlag, 1975–. Quarterly.

Prints international research articles on natural and human pollution in the geological environment; also includes environmental impact studies.

Journal of Geology. Chicago: University of Chicago Press, 1893–. Bimonthly.

Contains 4–6 research articles, with abstracts, on all aspects of theoretical and applied geology; a section titled Geological Notes; and book reviews of varying lengths. Occasional issues are devoted to particular subjects.

Film

Film Literature Index. Albany, NY: Film and Television Documentation Center, 1973–. Quarterly, with annual cumulations.

A subject and author index to the world's periodical literature on film covering more than 200 magazines and newspapers. Citations indicate whether the articles include screen credits, biographical information, interviews, or illustrations.

New York Times Film Reviews. New York: Times Books, 1913–1968. Biennial supplements.

A collection of film reviews from the *New York Times* arranged chronologically and including films made since 1913. Entries are reproductions of the actual signed reviews and include the credits and photographs (if any accompanied the original review); indexes by title, personal name, and corporate name are included.

The Oxford Companion to Film. Ed. Liz-Anne Bawden. New York: Oxford University Press, 1976.

Publishes short unsigned articles on all aspects of cinema, including film production, actors, directors, and movies. Lists of films by specific actors or directors are not necessarily comprehensive; cross-references to related articles are included.

Whalon, Marion K. *Performing Arts Research: A Guide to Information Sources*. See entry under Drama.

JOURNALS

Film Comment. New York: Film Society of Lincoln Center, 1962–. Bimonthly.

Each issue has 3 or 4 extended articles and several brief articles on films, directors, and actors.

Film Quarterly. Berkeley: University of California Press, 1945–. Quarterly.

Contains articles for nonspecialists and specialists on film, film production, and specific movies; articles and interviews with directors and actors; book reviews and film reviews on foreign and domestic films, documentaries, and experimental films.

Sight and Sound: The International Film Quarterly. London: British Film Institute, 1932–. Quarterly.

Presents articles about film and film production worldwide with emphasis on Great Britain; has film and book reviews.

Folklore

Abstracts of Folklore Studies. Austin, TX: American Folklore Society, 1963–1975. Quarterly.

Contains abstracts from approximately 40 international folklore periodicals arranged alphabetically by name of periodical; no index.

Brunvand, Jan Harold. *Folklore: A Study and Research Guide*. New York: St. Martin's, 1976.

A research guide consisting of essays that place the study of folklore in context, discuss reference tools for folklore study, and explain the methodology for writing research papers; glossary and author index are included.

Jobes, Gertrude. *Dictionary of Mythology, Folklore, and Symbols*. 3 vols. New York: Scarecrow, 1961.

Volumes 1 and 2 contain alphabetically arranged explanations of mythological and folklore characters and symbols. Volume 3 is an index to the first two volumes with entries grouped in two tables: deities, heroes, and personalities, and mythological affiliations.

Mythology of All Races. Ed. Louis H. Gray. 13 vols. New York: Cooper Square, 1964.

Publishes scholarly descriptions of the mythology of the world. Each volume covers one area's mythology, including Roman and Greek, Teutonic, Celtic and Slavic, Finno-Ugric and Siberian, Semitic, Indian and Persian, Armenian and African, Chinese and Japanese, Malayo-Polynesian and Australian, Egyptian, and North and South American Indian. Each volume has its own bibliography, and volume 13 is an index to the whole set.

JOURNALS

Folklore. London: Folklore Society, 1978–. Semiannually. Continues *Folklore Record* and *Folklore Journal*.

Publishes scholarly articles on folk culture, folk music, and the oral tradition of literature as well as society news and book reviews.

Journal of American Culture. Bowling Green: Bowling Green State University, 1978–. Quarterly.

Prints scholarly articles on American culture with an emphasis on popular culture; special issues are devoted to specific topics, such as Chicano culture or television and society.

Journal of American Folklore. Washington, DC: American Folklore Society, 1888–. Quarterly.

Publishes 3 or 4 articles per issue on folk culture, folklore, and folk music. The Notes section includes shorter discussion and review articles. Lengthy book, record, and film reviews are included.

Southern Folklore. Lexington: University of Kentucky, 1937–. 3 issues per year.

Presents scholarly historical and comparative studies of American and international folk cultures; book reviews are included.

Geography

Geo Abstracts, A-G. Norwich, England: Geo Abstracts, 1972–. Bimonthly.

The major abstracting source in geography, *Geo Abstracts* consists of seven parts covering landforms, climatology and hydrology, economic geography, social and historical geography, sedimentology, regional and community planning, and remote sensing and cartography. Each part is published separately and has a classified arrangement described in a table of contents; the final issue each year has author and regional indexes. Available online.

A Guide to Information Sources in the Geographical Sciences. Ed. Stephen Goddard. Totowa, NJ: Barnes and Noble, 1983.

Divided into three sections. Written by librarians and academics this guide provides bibliographic reviews of the field of geography, regional information, and tools for the geographer. There is no index.

Longman Dictionary of Geography: Human and Physical. Ed. Audrey N. Clark. London: Longman, 1986.

Consists of short entries arranged alphabetically defining geographic terms, describing geographic locations, and giving biographical information on explorers. The dictionary also includes various lists, such as a ranking of countries by size, and chronologies of explorers and earthquakes. An appendix gives a selective bibliography.

The New York Times Atlas of the World. 2nd rev. ed. New York: Times Books in collaboration with the Times of London, 1987.

Includes, in addition to maps of the world, an introduction on the origin and geology of the earth, its resources, and its physical nature. Human settlement and population patterns, trade, and industry are also considered.

JOURNALS

Association of American Geographers Annals. Washington, DC: Assn. of American Geographers, 1911–. Quarterly.

Publishes scholarly research reports in all aspects of geography; includes papers from the association's meetings, commentary, and book reviews.

Geographical Review. New York: American Geographical Society, 1916–. Quarterly.

Contains scholarly research and review articles, brief reports in Geographical Record, and book reviews.

Journal of Historical Geography. London: Academic Press, 1975–. Quarterly.

Prints research and review articles on historical geography and related subjects, such as agriculture, archaeology, and anthropology; includes an extensive book review section.

Geology. See Environmental and Earth Sciences.

Government. See Political Science and Government.

History

America: History and Life. Santa Barbara: ABC-Clio, 1955–.

A bibliography with abstracts of the historical literature of North America (Canada and the United States); abstracts are arranged chronologically within geographic groups. Also includes an index to book reviews (Part B), a section on American history bibliography containing books and dissertations (Part C), and an annual subject and author index (Part D). Available online.

American Historical Association. *Guide to Historical Literature.* New York: Macmillan, 1963.

Assists in historical research for all areas of the world. Following a section on general works and references, the book is divided geographically and then chronologically. Within each section, sources are arranged by form: bibliographies, reference works, geographies, anthropological and demographic studies, histories, biographies, government publications, and periodicals. Evaluative annotations are particularly helpful.

C.R.I.S.: The Combined Retrospective Index Set to Journals in History, 1838–1974. 11 vols. Washington, DC: Carrollton, 1977.

A comprehensive key word index for 243 periodicals covering all historical periods and geographic areas. The first nine volumes are subject indexes grouped geographically (with four volumes for world history and five for American history); volumes 10 and 11 are author indexes.

Dictionary of American History. Rev. ed. 8 vols. New York: Scribner's, 1976.
A collection of articles arranged alphabetically on all aspects of American history and life. Articles are signed and each has at least one bibliographical reference.

Freidel, Frank, ed. *Harvard Guide to American History*. Rev. ed. Cambridge: Belknap–Harvard University Press, 1974.
Volume 1 contains background articles and bibliographies on research methods and materials, biographies, comprehensive and regional histories, and histories of special subjects, such as economics, immigration, and education. The bibliographies in volume 2 are arranged chronologically; volume 2 also contains a subject index and an index of names to both volumes.

Historical Abstracts. Santa Barbara: ABC-Clio, 1955–.
A bibliography with abstracts of the research literature on world history except the history of the United States and Canada. It consists of two parts: Modern History Abstracts, 1450–1914 and Twentieth Century Abstracts, 1914–; subject and author indexes are included. Available online.

Langer, William L., ed. *The New Illustrated Encyclopedia of World History*. 2 vols. New York: Abrams, 1975.
A comprehensive encyclopedia covering prehistory to space exploration. Arranged chronologically, the articles are supplemented by approximately 2,000 illustrations, maps, and chronological tables; volume 2 has an index to both volumes.

The New Cambridge Modern History. Ed. G. R. Potter. 14 vols. Cambridge: Cambridge University Press, 1957.
The classic scholarly history of the Western world from the Renaissance through World War II. Each volume has its own subject index; volume 14 is a historical atlas. The *Cambridge Ancient History* and the *Cambridge Medieval History* cover prehistoric time through the 15th century.

JOURNALS

American Historical Review. Washington, DC: American Historical Assn., 1895–. 5 issues a year.
Contains 4 or 5 scholarly articles per issue as well as research notes, an extensive book review section subdivided by geographic region and period, and a section listing documents and bibliographies.

English Historical Review. Harlow, England: Longman, 1886–. Quarterly.
Publishes scholarly articles covering all fields of history; also includes research notes, book reviews, and an extensive section of short notices.

Journal of American History. Bloomington, IN: Organization of American Historians, 1914–. Quarterly. Continues *Mississippi Valley Historical Review*.
Prints research articles on American history; also extensive book reviews, a bibliography of articles and dissertations, and lists of bibliographies and archive acquisitions.

Journal of Modern History. Chicago: University of Chicago Press, 1929–. Quarterly.
Publishes research and review articles on modern European history since the Renaissance and lengthy book reviews. Special issues focus on topics such as political practice in the French Revolution.

Law and Criminal Justice

Black's Law Dictionary. 5th ed. St. Paul: West, 1979.
Standard law dictionary for ready reference.

Cohen, Morris L. *Legal Research in a Nutshell.* 4th ed. St. Paul: West, 1985.
Intended to provide students with a brief introduction to the main areas of legal literature. Appendixes list state research guides, loose-leaf services, official state reporters, and titles in the national reporter system.

Criminal Justice Abstracts. Hackensack: National Council on Crime and Delinquency, 1977–. Quarterly. Continues *Crime and Delinquency Literature,* 1968–1976.
Contains in-depth abstracts of current books, journal articles, dissertations, and reports published worldwide. Many issues include a review or bibliographic essay on a current issue in criminal justice. This is a classified index with a separate subject index.

Criminal Justice Periodical Index. Ann Arbor: University Microfilms, 1975–. 3 issues per year with annual cumulations.
Indexes more than 100 English-language periodicals in criminal justice. Includes both author and subject index.

Encyclopedia of Crime and Justice. 4 vols. Ed. Sanford H. Kadish. New York: Free Press, 1983.
Covers the nature and cause of criminal behavior, crime prevention, punishment and treatment of criminals, administration of criminal justice systems, law that defines criminal behavior, and the application of criminal law. Articles are signed, with bibliographies. Volume 4 contains an index.

Index to Legal Periodicals. New York: Wilson, 1908–. Monthly, with annual cumulation.
Subject and author index to English-language periodical literature on legal topics. Includes a table of cases and a book review index. Available online and on CD-ROM.

JOURNALS

American Bar Association Journal. Chicago: American Bar Association, 1915–. Monthly.
This official journal of the membership of the American Bar Association contains articles of interest to legal practitioners and the public. Special columns include What's New, Supreme Court Report, and Computer Corner. Book reviews are included.

Crime and Delinquency. Beverly Hills: Sage, 1955–. Quarterly.
Publishes articles on all aspects of crime and the administration of justice.

Harvard Law Review. Cambridge: Gannett House, 1887–. 8 issues per year.
Contains lengthy articles on all aspects of law.

Journal of Criminal Justice. Elmsford, NY: Pergamon, 1973–. Bimonthly.
Written for professionals and academics, this scholarly journal covers all aspects of the criminal justice system. A regular feature publishes short descriptive abstracts of recently published books.

Literature

Abstracts of English Studies. Calgary, Alberta: University of Calgary Press, 1958-. Quarterly.

Contains abstracts of articles from more than 700 journals concerned with English-language, English, and American literature and world literature published in English. Abstracts are grouped in four broad classes and are then arranged either chronologically or geographically. Each issue has its own index; the fourth issue of the year has an annual cumulative index.

American Women Writers: A Critical Reference Guide from Colonial Times to the Present. Ed. Lina Mainiero. 4 vols. New York: Ungar, 1979-82.

Contains biographical data, critical assessments, and bibliograpical lists for 1,000 women writers. Volume 4 contains an index to names and subjects.

Black American Writers: Bibliographical Essays. Ed. M. Thomas Inge, Maurice Duke, and Jackson R. Bryer. 2 vols. New York: St. Martin's, 1978.

A good preliminary source for the study of black writers, these volumes evaluate biographical and critical writings about selected black authors and offer suggestions for further study. Essays are organized by topic, such as slave narratives and the Harlem Renaissance, as well as by individual author.

Contemporary Authors. Detroit: Gale, 1972-.

Records biographic information about living international authors writing in all subject areas. Each entry includes biographic information, a list of works published, and works in progress. Because entries are often updated and revised, check the most recent cumulative index to find complete listings.

Encyclopedia of World Literature in the 20th Century. 2nd ed. 5 vols. New York: Ungar, 1981-1985.

Contains short articles (1-2 pages) on authors who have produced their major works in the 20th century and on national literatures, genres, and movements. Articles on authors give brief biographical information, discuss and list their major works, and supply further references.

Hart, James D. *The Oxford Companion to American Literature.* 5th ed. New York: Oxford University Press, 1983.

A one-volume encyclopedia with brief articles on American authors, (including biographic information and bibliographies), literary works, and allusions as well as persons and events important in social and cultural history. Articles on individual literary works give summaries of the works and include verse form for poems. A chronological index lists a parallel chronology of American literary history and social history.

Harvey, Paul. *Oxford Companion to Classical Literature.* Oxford: Clarendon, 1937.

Provides articles and descriptions of classical Greek and Roman authors, works of literature, mythology, genres, and social and historical events relevant to the literature.

Humanities Index. See entry under Humanities.

Literary History of the United States. Ed. Robert E. Spiller et al. 4th ed. 2 vols. New York: Macmillan, 1974.

Volume 1 contains scholarly essays tracing the social and cultural history of American literature from colonial times through the 1960s with a bibliography for further reading. Volume 2 is a guide to literary resources and bibliographies on American literature and culture that include listings on literary periods (arranged by genre), American cultural background, language, folklore, popular culture, literary movements and influences, and individual authors. Bibliographies on individual authors provide evaluative comments on editions of their works and on biography and criticism of the authors.

The MLA International Bibliography of Books and Articles on the Modern Languages and Literature. New York: Modern Language Assn., 1921–. Annual.

A classified list of international periodical articles, *Festschriften*, books, and dissertations on modern languages, literature, and folklore. Citations are grouped by national literature and then chronologically. For details on using this index, see p. 66. Available online and on CD-ROM.

New Cambridge Bibliography of English Literature. Ed. George Watson. 5 vols. Cambridge: Cambridge University Press, 1974.

A comprehensive bibliography of English literature from A.D. 600 through 1950. Arranged chronologically, each section lists general works and genre studies and then individual authors. For each author, bibliographies and information on special collections or location of manuscripts are given; collections are listed chronologically. Also included is a comprehensive international bibliography of criticism. Besides the index in each volume, volume 5 contains an index to the whole set.

The Oxford Companion to English Literature. Ed. Margaret Drabble. 5th ed. Oxford: Clarendon, 1985.

A one-volume encyclopedia with brief articles on English authors (some American authors are included), literary works, literary societies, characters, and allusions. Facts about each author's life and a list of major works with dates are given.

Patterson, Margaret. *Literary Research Guide.* 2nd ed. New York: Modern Language Assn., 1983.

Annotated bibliography of reference books in literature. The guide first discusses general research tools, such as national and annual bibliographies, indexes and abstracts, sources on specific genres, and periodicals. The main section is divided by national literature and arranged chronologically with general sources discussed first; most major national literatures and classical literature are included. A final section covers literature-related subjects such as autobiographies, book collecting, film, folklore, linguistics, textual criticism, and women's studies. A glossary of bibliography terms is included; a particularly helpful feature is the Short-Title Table of Contents.

JOURNALS

American Literature: A Journal of Literary History, Criticism, and Bibliography. Durham: Duke University Press, 1929–. Quarterly.

Publishes scholarly historical and critical articles on American authors; includes 20–25 lengthy book reviews per issue with an additional section

(Brief Mention) of short book reviews. Each issue also contains a selected annotated bibliography on American literature.

ELH (English Literary History). Baltimore: Johns Hopkins University Press, 1931–. Quarterly.
Provides about 10 lengthy critical articles on British literature in each issue.

Modern Fiction Studies. West Lafayette: Purdue University, 1955–. Quarterly.
Publishes literary criticism and bibliographic articles on modern (post-1880) fiction together with lengthy book reviews; two issues each year focus on one writer or on a special topic, such as modern war fiction.

Modern Poetry Studies. Buffalo: Media Study/Buffalo, 1970–. 3 issues per year.
Prints critical studies of modern poets and poetry as well as original poetry.

PMLA (Publication of the Modern Language Association). New York: Modern Language Assn., 1884–. 6 issues per year.
Contains scholarly articles on themes, critical approaches, and other aspects of modern languages and literature along with association news and commentary.

Mathematics.   See Computer Science and Mathematics.

Medicine and Nursing

Cumulative Index to Nursing and Allied Health Literature. Glendale, CA: Glendale Adventist Medical Center, 1977–. Continues *Cumulative Index to Nursing Literature*, 1956–1976. Bimonthly, with annual cumulations.
Indexes approximately 300 English-language journals in nursing, health, and health care–related fields; pamphlets, audiovisual materials, and book reviews are included. A list of subject headings (organized in a hierarchical structure) is used to assign terms for a subject index. Available online and on CD-ROM.

Harrison's Principles of Internal Medicine. Ed. Eugene Braunwald et al. 11th ed. 2 vols. New York: McGraw-Hill, 1987.
This textbook on internal medicine is used in most libraries as a major source of background information on health concerns. After an introductory section on clinical medicine, two volumes are divided into sections on disease: the clinical manifestations, biological aspects, biological and environmental causes, and organ systems. The section on each disorder includes a definition and background information, description of symptoms, complications, diagnosis and treatment, and additional references. An index at the end of each volume provides access by specific disease or disorder.

Index Medicus. Bethesda: National Library of Medicine, 1960–. Monthly, with annual cumulations. Continues *Quarterly Cumulative Index Medicus*, 1928–1959, and *Index Medicus*, 1879–1927.
Indexes periodical literature in medicine worldwide; subject access is through headings assigned from *Medical Subject Headings (MeSH)*, which arranges terms from general concepts to specific terms. There is also an Au-

thor section (all authors are cross-referenced) and a Medical Reviews section. Available online and on CD-ROM.

Roper, Fred W., and Jo Anne Boorkman. *Introduction to Reference Sources in the Health Sciences.* 2nd ed. Chicago: Medical Library Assn., 1984.
A guide to research in the health sciences divided into two main sections: bibliographic sources and information sources. Bibliographic sources discuss reference books used to locate books, periodical articles, government documents, conference proceedings, and reviews. Information sources describe sources for medical terminology, handbooks, statistics, biographical and historical information, audiovisual resources, drug information, grant sources, and health legislation sources.

JOURNALS

American Journal of Human Genetics. Chicago: American Society for Human Genetics, 1949–. Bimonthly.
Publishes research and review articles on heredity and genetic applications in sociology, anthropology, and medicine; book reviews and society news.

American Journal of Nursing. New York: American Journal of Nursing, 1900–. Monthly.
Publishes articles reporting developments in techniques and treatment in clinical medicine as well as brief clinical news reports and professional news.

JAMA: Journal of the American Medical Association. Chicago: American Medical Assn., 1848–. Weekly.
Contains brief reports on medical news; original research articles and case studies in clinical medicine and related areas; association news; and book reviews.

Journal of Nutrition. Rockville, MD: American Institute of Nutrition, 1928–. Monthly.
Contains scholarly articles reporting original research on the physiology of nutrition.

New England Journal of Medicine. Boston: Massachusetts Medical Society, 1812–. Weekly.
Prints articles reporting original research and case studies, editorials, commentary, correspondence, and occasional book reviews.

Music

Duckles, Vincent. *Music Reference and Research Materials.* 4th ed. New York: Free Press/Macmillan, 1988.
An annotated guide to references for music and musicology divided by type of reference book, such as dictionaries, histories, bibliographies, and discographies. Indexes provide access by subject, title, and author/editor/reviewer.

The Music Index. Detroit: Information Coordinators, 1949–. Monthly, with annual cumulations.
An index by subject, author, and title of work to periodicals on music and dance. Book reviews are listed alphabetically by author; reviews of per-

formers and music are listed under the performer's or composer's name, and record reviews are listed under Recordings.

The New Grove Dictionary of Music and Musicians. Ed. Stanley Sadie. 6th ed. 20 vols. London: Macmillan, 1980.
A scholarly encyclopedia on all aspects of music. Entries cover terminology, performers, theory, instruments, composers, history, music of all regions of the world, and folk music. Many articles include bibliographies and lists of works. A glossary of terms used in non-Western music is included in volume 20.

JOURNALS

Acta Musicologica. Basel: International Musicological Society, 1928–. 2 issues per year.
Publishes articles by international scholars on musicology.

American Musicological Society Journal. Philadelphia: American Musicological Society, 1948–. 3 issues per year.
Prints scholarly articles on musicology; issues contain lengthy book reviews and lists of publications received.

Journal of Music Theory. New Haven: Yale School of Music, 1957–. 2 issues per year.
Contains scholarly articles on music theory, lengthy book reviews, and bibliographies of books and articles on music theory.

Nursing.   See Medicine and Nursing.

Nutrition.   See Medicine and Nursing.

Philosophy and Religion

Adams, Charles J. *A Reader's Guide to the Great Religions.* 2nd ed. New York: Macmillan/Free Press, 1977.
Contains bibliographic essays describing resources for research on primitive religions; religions of the ancient world, Mexico, and China; Hinduism, Buddhism, Sikhism, Jainism; religions of Japan; early, classical, medieval, and modern Judaism; Christianity; and Islam. Author and subject indexes are given.

Brandon, S. G. F., ed. *A Dictionary of Comparative Religion.* New York: Scribner's, 1970.
Provides brief descriptive entries on all aspects of world religions, including deities, religious leaders, concepts, sects, geographic locations, rites, and rituals. Many articles have bibliographies.

DeGeorge, Richard T. *The Philosopher's Guide to Sources, Research Tools, Professional Life, and Related Fields.* Lawrence: Regents Press of Kansas, 1980.
An annotated guide to the literature of philosophy that includes a guide to research tools and a bibliography of sources on the history of philosophy and the various branches, schools, and national philosophies. The bibliography also includes a section on philosophical periodicals and professional

issues, such as publishing, associations, and research centers. An index by author, title, and subject is provided.

Encyclopedia Judaica. 16 vols. New York: Macmillan, 1972.
Contains signed scholarly articles as well as brief descriptions of topics in all areas of Jewish history, religion, and culture; most articles have short bibliographies. Volume 1 indexes the entire set.

The Encyclopedia of Philosophy. Ed. Paul Edwards. 8 vols. New York: Macmillan, 1967.
Publishes scholarly articles on Eastern and Western philosophy and on philosophers, concepts, and theories from ancient to modern times; bibliographies are given at the end of each article. Volume 8 includes a subject index.

Encyclopedia of Religion. Ed. Mircea Eliade. 16 vols. New York: Macmillan, 1986.
Covers important ideas, beliefs, rituals, myths, symbols, and persons that have played a role in religious history from paleolithic times to the present. Articles are signed and include bibliographies. Volume 16 is an index.

Encyclopedia of Religion and Ethics. Ed. James Hastings. 13 vols. New York: Scribner's, 1908–1926.
A classic encyclopedia covering world religions and ethical systems as well as related subjects such as psychology, anthropology, and folklore. Articles are signed and most have extensive bibliographies. Volume 13 is a detailed subject index.

Nelson's Complete Concordance to the Revised Standard Version Bible. Ed. John Ellison. 2nd ed. New York: Thomas Nelson, 1984.
Arranged alphabetically, this reference gives the context and location of nearly every word in the RSV Bible. Nelson also publishes *Young's Analytical Concordance to the King James Version of the Bible* (rev. ed., 1982), which gives the context, location, and Hebrew and Greek words from which the English was translated. *Young's* contains a Universal Subject Guide to the Bible.

The Philosopher's Index. Bowling Green: Philosophy Documentation Center, 1967–. Quarterly, with annual cumulations.
Indexes all English-language philosophy books and English, French, German, Spanish, and Italian philosophy journals as well as some journals in related fields. Abstracts are provided for many of the citations in the author index. Also included are a subject index and a book review index. Available online.

Religion Index One: Periodicals. Chicago: American Theological Assn., 1977–. Continues *Index to Religious Periodical Literature*, 1949–1976.
Indexes more than 300 journals in religion and theology. Abstracts are included for many of the citations in the author index. A subject index and Scripture index are also provided. This index can be searched using the Religion Index database (1975–). Book reviews were included until 1985 and are now indexed in a separate publication, *Index to Book Reviews in Religion*. A companion of this set is *Religion Index Two: Multi-Author Work*, which indexes composite works by author and subject. Available online and on CD-ROM.

JOURNALS

Ethics: An International Journal of Social, Political, and Legal Philosophy. Chicago: University of Chicago Press, 1890–. Quarterly.
Publishes scholarly articles on the social, ethical, and legal aspects of philosophy; book reviews and book notes; short discussions; survey articles; and reviews.

Journal of Biblical Literature. Chico, CA: Society of Biblical Literature, 1882–. Quarterly.
Contains scholarly papers on the Old and New Testaments, lengthy book reviews, a section on essay collections, and a list of books received.

Journal of Philosophy. New York: Journal of Philosophy, 1904–. Monthly.
Presents scholarly papers in all areas of philosophy; some issues include papers from various symposia as well as comments and criticism.

Journal of Religion. Chicago: University of Chicago Press, 1882–. Quarterly.
Publishes critical, scholarly articles on theology and related religious studies, review articles, and book reviews.

Journal of Symbolic Logic. Providence: Assn. for Symbolic Logic, 1936–. Quarterly.
Publishes technical articles on symbolic logic and related fields, such as mathematics and philosophy; includes book reviews and association news.

Physical Education and Sports

Encyclopedia of Physical Education, Fitness and Sports. Ed. Thomas K. Cureton, Jr. 3 vols. Salt Lake City: Brighton, 1980.
Each volume covers one area of physical education in detail and has its own table of contents, index, and biographical directory. Volume 1 covers the philosophy and history of physical education and programs for schools, the armed forces, and the handicapped. Volume 2 has sections on training and conditioning, nutrition, and fitness for children and adults. Volume 3 contains articles on types of sports, dance, and related physical activities.

Physical Education Index. Cape Girardeau, MO: Ben Oak, 1978–. Quarterly.
Indexes English-language periodicals covering physical education, physical therapy, health, dance, recreation, sports, and sports medicine. Entries include research reports, legislation, biographies, and reports from associations; a book review listing is given.

JOURNALS

American Journal of Sports Medicine. Baltimore: American Orthopaedic Society for Sports Medicine, 1972–. Bimonthly.
Publishes review and research articles on the medical aspects of sports and sports injuries, society news, book reviews, and an annual bibliography on sports medicine.

Journal of Physical Education, Recreation, and Dance. Reston, VA: American Alliance for Health, Physical Education, Recreation, and Dance, 1896–. Monthly except July.
Contains brief news and research reports, review articles on issues and

techniques in sports and physical education, and book reviews. Issues occasionally focus on one topic, such as gymnastics.

The Physical Educator. Indianapolis: Phi Epsilon Kappa Fraternity, 1940–. Quarterly.
Publishes articles on the history, theory, and philosophy of sports and physical education. Each issue focuses on one of four themes: special populations, program development, foundations, or human performance.

Research Quarterly for Exercise and Sport. Reston, VA: American Alliance for Health, Physical Education, Recreation, and Dance, 1930–. Quarterly.
Presents lengthy, scholarly articles reporting the results of empirical research and short articles reporting research in progress.

Physics.   See Chemistry and Physics.

Political Science and Government

ABC Pol Sci: Advanced Bibliography of Contents, Political Science and Government. Santa Barbara: ABC-Clio, 1969–. Bimonthly.
A subject index and an author index provide access to the tables of contents of more than 300 U.S. and international journals in political science and related subjects, such as area studies and sociology.

Holler, Frederick L. *Information Sources of Political Sciences.* 4th ed. Santa Barbara: ABC-Clio, 1986.
A detailed, annotated guide to research resources. Holler begins with a general section on political science research and then discusses specific tools classified as general reference sources, social sciences, American government and politics, international relations, political theory, and public administration. It contains indexes by subject, author, title, comparative and area studies, and typology.

International Encyclopedia of the Social Sciences. See entry under Social Sciences.

Kalvelage, Carl, Albert P. Melone, and Morley Segal. *Bridges to Knowledge in Political Science: A Handbook for Research.* Pacific Palisades: Palisades, 1984.
A practical guide for students of political science organized around the process of writing a term paper. It includes annotated bibliography of political science reference materials.

Lacquer, Walter. *A Dictionary of Politics.* Rev. ed. New York: Macmillan, 1974.
Contains brief entries arranged alphabetically that explain terms and give biographical, geographical, and historical information about contemporary politics; events included date mainly from 1933 to the publication date.

Public Affairs Information Service Bulletin. See entry under Social Sciences.

United States Political Science Documents. Pittsburgh: University of Pittsburgh, 1975–. Annual.
Published by the University of Pittsburgh's University Center for International Studies in conjunction with the American Political Science Association. Indexes more than 120 American journals in the political, social, and policy sciences. Each year's volume is published in two parts. Part 1 con-

tains five indexes: author/contributor, subject, geographic area, proper name, and journal. Part 2 has 100- to 200-word abstracts for each citation. Available online.

JOURNALS

American Journal of Political Science. Austin: University of Texas Press, 1957–. Quarterly.

Published for the Midwest Political Science Assn. Articles are concerned mainly with American politics, but some deal with international affairs.

American Political Science Review. Washington, DC: American Political Science Assn., 1906–. Quarterly.

Presents scholarly papers on American government, political science, and related fields, such as area studies, law, and economics. It also contains extensive book reviews and review essays grouped by subject.

Foreign Affairs. New York: Council on Foreign Relations, 1922–. 5 issues per year.

Publishes articles expressing opinions and discussing issues in international relations, occasionally written by national and international political leaders. Includes brief book reviews and bibliographies of relevant government documents and other related publications.

Journal of Politics. Gainesville: Southern Political Science Assn., 1939–. Quarterly.

Publishes scholarly articles on political science, research notes, book reviews (including review essays), and association news.

Psychology

Encyclopedia of Psychology. Ed. Raymond J. Corsini. 4 vols. New York: Wiley, 1984.

Includes signed background articles on all aspects of psychology and biographical articles on important psychologists. Some articles have bibliographies, and all references mentioned in the articles are listed in complete form in a single bibliography in volume 4. Volume 4 also includes a name index (persons and titles) and a subject index.

Psychological Abstracts. Arlington, VA: American Psychological Assn., 1927–. Monthly, with semiannual cumulations.

A bibliography with abstracts of the world's literature in psychology and related fields. Entries include journal articles, books, technical reports, and dissertations. Abstracts are grouped in 16 subject classifications with more specific access through subject and author indexes. Available online and on CD-ROM.

Reed, Jeffrey G., and Pam M. Baxter. *Library Use: A Handbook for Psychology.* Washington, DC: American Psychological Assn., 1983.

A guide to library research in psychology. It begins with topic selection and works through the research process for writing a paper. Detailed instructions for using sources such as *Psychological Abstracts* and citation indexes are provided.

JOURNALS

American Psychologist. Washington, DC: American Psychological Assn., 1946–. Monthly.

Issues contain review articles and articles reporting empirical research, a section titled Psychology in the Public Forum, association news, and a commentary section.

Journal of Counseling Psychology. Washington, DC: American Psychological Assn., 1954–. Quarterly.

Publishes research articles on counseling arranged by subject: counseling process and outcomes, counseling assessment, career development, group intervention, special populations and setting, professional issues and training, and research methodology. There are also brief research reports and a comments section.

Journal of Personality and Social Psychology. Washington, DC: American Psychological Assn., 1965–. Monthly.

Publishes scholarly articles covering empirical and theoretical studies grouped in three sections: attitudes and social cognition, interpersonal relations and group processes, and personality processes and individual differences.

Psychological Bulletin. Washington, DC: American Psychological Assn., 1904–. Bimonthly.

Presents review articles evaluating and synthesizing research and methodological studies in psychology as well as articles on quantitative methods in psychology.

Religion.   See Philosophy and Religion.

Space Science.   See Astronomy and Space Science.

Sociology

Book Review Index to Social Science Periodicals. See entry under Social Sciences.

C.R.I.S.: The Combined Retrospective Index Set to Journals in Sociology, 1895–1974. 6 vols. Washington, DC: Carrollton, 1978.

A comprehensive index to journals in sociology and related fields, such as anthropology, covering the literature since 1895. Articles are arranged in the first five volumes by subject key word within 86 subject categories. Volume 6 is an author index.

International Encyclopedia of the Social Sciences. See entry under Social Sciences.

Social Sciences Index. See entry under Social Sciences.

Sociological Abstracts. San Diego: Sociological Abstracts, 1952–. 5 issues per year.

A bibliography with abstracts of the periodicals in sociology and related fields, such as education and anthropology. The abstracts are grouped in 13 subject classifications. Available online and on CD-ROM.

Women Studies Abstracts. Rush, NY: Rush, 1972–. Quarterly.

Indexes general magazines and scholarly journals concerned with all phases of women's studies, from literature and sports to women in developing countries. Citations are grouped by broad subject with abstracts provided for some of the entries. A subject index is included in each issue; a cumulative index is included at the end of the year.

JOURNALS

American Journal of Sociology. Chicago: University of Chicago Press, 1895–. Bimonthly.

Publishes articles reporting empirical and theoretical research in sociology and related fields, such as social psychology. It also includes research notes, review essays, discussion, and lengthy book reviews.

American Sociological Review. Washington, DC: American Sociological Assn., 1936–. Bimonthly.

Contains scholarly papers on research and theoretical methodological developments in sociology. Research notes, comments, and articles on professional issues are included.

Sociology and Social Research: An International Journal. Los Angeles: University of Southern California, 1916–. Quarterly.

Presents research and review articles on sociology and related fields, such as urban sociology, sociology of education, and family studies; also contains book reviews.

Sports.   See Physical Education and Sports.

APPENDIX 2

Using Footnotes
or Endnotes
to Document Your Paper

The system of using notes at the bottom of each page or at the end of the paper (called footnotes, endnotes, or notes) is often called the Chicago Style or the Harvard system. However, this system of citation, formerly widely used in the humanities, the arts, and some social sciences, has been replaced in many periodicals by the author/date system. Even the *Chicago Manual of Style* (13th ed., 1982) recommends the author/date system over either the footnote system or the number system because it saves time for scholars and saves money for publishers. Still, many writers and publishers in the humanities, especially in the fine arts, prefer to use the note system.

Although this system uses numbers to refer to the sources, it differs from the number system. The number system (see Chapter 12) requires a list of references that are assigned numbers (the list is organized either alphabetically or according to order of reference in the text of the paper). A number is repeated as many times as the source is used. In the note system, a note is used each time a source is referred to; accordingly, though numbers are not repeated, a source is repeated as many times as it is used. The notes themselves usually serve as the list of references or bibliography.

In-text Citations

If you use the note system, refer to the source of your information by placing a number in the text either half a space above the line or in parentheses on the line. Put the number outside all marks of punctuation except the dash. Try to place numbers at the end of a sentence or at a break in structure or meaning. Here are some examples:

```
The Indian Vedas[1] are a collection of theories about the origins

of the cosmos and mankind.
```

(The Babylonians also taught Sumerian in their schools.)[2]

Hinduism combines religion, cultural tradition, and social structure[3]--it is a complex philosophy.

The corresponding note is placed either at the bottom of the page on which the number appears or in a list at the end of the paper or book. A bibliography is often supplied in addition to the notes, but if full citation is given in the notes, a bibliography is not necessary. Occasionally a bibliography is added to give additional related sources not specifically cited.

Notes

Spacing of notes varies greatly from one book or journal to another. For a student paper, the best format is to indent the first line of each note three or five spaces. Single-space within each note if it is at the bottom of the page; double-space between notes placed at the end of the paper. Number footnotes consecutively throughout the paper. If you place your notes at the end of your paper, begin them on a separate page following the body of the paper with the heading Notes or Endnotes. The first reference to a source should give the complete citation, even though the author or title is given in the text. For subsequent references, give the last name of the author, followed by a page number.

1. Nancy Ruyter, Reformers and Visionaries (New York: Dance Horizons, 1979), 90.

2. Ruyter, 95.

If the note refers to the same source as the immediately preceding note, some writers use the abbreviation Ibid., for *ibidem*, meaning "in the same place."

3. Kenneth Clark, Feminine Beauty (New York: Rizzoli International Publications, 1980), 65.

4. Ibid., 42.

If the whole citation, including the page number, is the same as the preceding reference, you can use just the abbreviation.

5. Ibid.

More and more writers and journals are dropping the use of all Latin abbreviations in footnotes and endnotes. The abbreviations Loc. cit. and Op. cit. are no longer recommended by the *Chicago Manual of Style*, and Ibid. is only reluctantly included as an option.

Repeat the title as well as the author's name when you have cited more than one title by the same author. When you repeat a source with a long title— either a book or an article—use a shortened title consisting of key words from the title (do not change word order).

FULL TITLE: The American Writer and the European Tradition

SHORT TITLE: American Writer

Here are some commonly used footnote or endnote forms.

BOOK WITH ONE AUTHOR

6. Janet Wolff, The Social Production of Art (New York: St. Martin's Press, 1981), 19.

BOOK WITH TWO AUTHORS

7. Harry Dichter and Elliott Shapiro, Handbook of Early American Sheet Music: 1768-1889 (New York: Dover Publications, 1977), 68-69.

BOOK WITH MORE THAN THREE AUTHORS

8. Robert E. Spiller et al., Literary History of the United States, vol. 1 (New York: Macmillan, 1948), 75.

BOOK WITH ANONYMOUS AUTHOR

9. Wild Animals of North America (Washington, D.C.: National Geographic Society, 1960), 21.

Begin the reference with the title of the book or article. Do not use Anonymous or Anon.

EDITOR OR TRANSLATOR

10. Jacob Simon, ed., Handel: A Celebration of His Life and Times (London: National Portrait Gallery, 1985), 32.

11. Mohan Singh, "Evening," in Mentor Book of Modern Asian Literature, ed. Dorothy Blair Shimer (New York: New American Library, 1969), 44-45.

12. Gustave Flaubert, Madame Bovary, trans. Paul De Man (New York: W. W. Norton, 1965), 121.

JOURNAL ARTICLE

13. Gabrielle M. Patty, "Foreign-Language Study for Graduate English Majors," College English 51 (Nov. 1989): 689.

The volume number precedes the date; only the page or pages of the portion cited in the text are provided. Inclusive page numbers for the entire article would be provided in a bibliography.

MAGAZINE ARTICLE

14. Bennett Schiff, "The World According to Joseph Wright," Smithsonian, Sept. 1990, 53.

In a note for a periodical, only the specific page cited is given; in a bibliography, the inclusive pages of the article are given.

NEWSPAPER ARTICLE FROM A COMPUTER SERVICE

More and more complete texts are available online, on CD-ROM, and on microfiche, from which they can be printed out. The document in the following example was obtained from a combination of these; the article was located through an index in a Newsbank CD-ROM file and printed out from a copy of the article on microfiche.

Notice that for information from a full-text computer database, you give the original source first, as you would for any entry. Then in parentheses provide the vendor or news service. Follow this with another set of parentheses containing the database, identifying information such as number or date, and the storage format of the text: online, CD-ROM, microfilm, or microfiche.

15. Elizabeth Mehren, "New Aids Research Under Fire," Los Angeles Times, 8 Mar. 1988, sec. C, 6. (Newsbank) (Health file, vol. 19, Mar. 1988, microfiche).

BOOK REVIEW IN A NEWSPAPER

16. William W. Warner, "The Call of the Running Tide," review of Looking for a Ship, by John McPhee, Washington Post, 9 Sept. 1990, Book World section, 1.

The word *section* is spelled out when it is not followed by a number or letter; the abbreviation *p.* or *pp.* is not necessary.

GOVERNMENT PUBLICATION

17. Senate Select Committee to Study Governmental Operations with Respect to Intelligence Activities, Alleged Assassination Plots Involving Foreign Leaders, 94th Cong., 1st sess., 1975, S. Rept. 94-465, 22.

In a note, the country need not be given because it can usually be inferred from the context. It would be given in a bibliography.

ENCYCLOPEDIA

18. Encyclopaedia Britannica, 4th ed., s.v. "English horn."

The abbreviation "s.v." stands for *sub verbo*, meaning "under the word." Topics are organized alphabetically in the reference work, so no other information is needed.

BOOK WITHOUT PUBLICATION INFORMATION

If the publisher or place is not given, use the abbreviation *n. p.* for each. If no date is given use *n. d.*

19. Clark Wissler, Indians of the United States (New York: n.p., 1940), 42.

Bibliography

A bibliography is sometimes used with notes, especially if it contains works of general interest on the subject in addition to the works cited in the notes. In a bibliography the works are listed alphabetically by the last names of the authors. The punctuation is also different, as the following examples show.

Notes

1. Shirley Brice Heath, Ways with Words (Cambridge: Cambridge University Press, 1873), 25.

2. Roger Warner, "After Centuries of Neglect, Angkor's Temples Need More Than a Face-lift," Smithsonian, May 1990, 38.

Bibliography

Heath, Shirley Brice. Ways with Words. Cambridge: Cambridge University Press, 1873.

Warner, Roger. "After Centuries of Neglect, Angkor's Temples Need More Than a Face-lift." Smithsonian (May 1990): 36-50.

APPENDIX 3

Style Manuals and Handbooks in Various Disciplines

Any one of the four documentation styles explained in this book and illustrated in Chapters 10, 11, 12, and in Appendix 2 can be used in most of the papers written by college students. The style manuals and handbooks listed in this appendix are useful especially for those wishing to publish in a specific discipline. They contain detailed information about bibliographic format and about such matters as punctuating and spelling scientific terminology. Some of them contain suggestions on the process of research and writing in particular subject areas.

Agronomy

American Society of Agronomy. *Publication Handbook and Style Manual*. Madison, WI: American Society of Agronomy, 1988.

Art

Barnet, Sylvan. *A Short Guide to Writing About Art*. Glenview: HarperCollins, 1989.

Biochemistry

The Practical Handbook of Biochemistry and Molecular Biology. Ed. Gerald D. Fasman. Boca Raton: CRC Press, 1989. Series of multivolume handbooks in four areas.

Biology

CBE Style Manual Committee. *CBE Style Manual: A Guide for Authors, Editors, and Publishers in the Biological Sciences*. 6th ed. Chicago: 1992.

McMillan, Victoria E. *Writing Papers in the Biological Sciences*. New York: Bedford/St. Martin's, 1988.

Business.   See also Economics.

Smith, Charles B. *A Guide to Business Research: Developing, Conducting, and Writing Research Projects*. Chicago: Nelson-Hall, 1991.

Chemistry

Dodd, Janet S. *The American Chemical Society Style Guide*. Washington, DC: American Chemical Society, 1985.

Handbook for AOAC Members. 6th ed. Washington, DC: Association of Official Analytical Chemists, 1989.

Earth Science, Geology

Bates, Robert. *Writing in Earth Science*. Alexandria: American Geological Institute, 1988.

Economics.   See also Business.

Officer, Lawrence H., Daniel H. Sachs, and Judith A. Saks. *So You Have to Write an Economics Term Paper*. East Lansing: Michigan State University Press, 1981.

Education

Katz, Sidney B., Jerome T. Kapes, and Percy A. Zirkel. *Resources for Writing for Publication in Education*. New York: Teachers College Press, Columbia University, 1980.

Engineering

Michaelson, Herbert B. *How to Write and Publish Engineering Papers and Reports*. 3rd ed. Phoenix: The Oryx Press, 1990.

Film

Corrigan, Timothy J. *A Short Guide to Writing About Film*. Glenview: HarperCollins, 1989.

Geography

Lounsbury, John F., and L. Lloyd Haring. *Introduction to Scientific Geographic Research*. 3rd ed. Dubuque: William C. Brown, 1982.

History

McCoy, Florence N. *Researching and Writing in History: A Practical Handbook for Students*. Berkeley: University of California Press, 1974.

Marius, Richard, Marcia Stubbs, and Sylvan Barnet. *A Short Guide to Writing About History*. Glenview: HarperCollins, 1989.

Law

The Columbia Law Review, et al. *A Uniform System of Citation*. 15th ed. Cambridge: Harvard Law Review Association, 1991.

Linguistics

Linguistic Society of America. "LSA Style Sheet." *LSA Bulletin*. December 1990. Annually.

Literature

Gibaldi, Joseph, and Walter S. Achtert. *MLA Handbook for Writers of Research Papers*. 3rd ed. New York: Modern Language Association, 1988.

Mathematics

American Mathematical Society. *A Manual for Authors of Mathematical Papers*. 9th ed. Providence: American Mathematical Society, 1990.

Swanson, Ellen. *Mathematics into Type*. Providence: American Mathematical Society, 1987.

Medicine

Huth, Edward J. *How to Write and Publish Papers in the Medical Sciences*. Baltimore: Williams & Wilkins, 1990.

Modern Languages.   See Literature.

Music

Helm, Ernest Eugene, and Albert T. Luper. *Words and Music: Form and Procedure in Theses, Dissertations, Research Papers, Book Reports, Programs, and Theses in Composition*. Valley Forge: European American Music, 1982.

Physical Therapy

American Physical Therapy Association. *Style Manual: Physical Therapy*. 8th ed. Alexandria: Journal of the American Physical Therapy Association, 1989.

Physics

American Institute of Physics. *Style Manual*. 4th ed. New York: American Institute of Physics, 1990.

Political Science

Goehlert, Robert U. *Political Science Research Guide*. Monticello, IL: Vance Bibliographies, 1982.

Stoffle, Carla J., Simon Karter, and Samuel Pernacciaro. *Materials and Methods for Political Science Research*. New York: Neal-Schuman, 1979.

Psychology

American Psychological Association. *Publication Manual of the American Psychological Association*. 3rd ed. Washington, DC: American Psychological Association, 1983.

Religion

Sayre, John L. *A Manual of Forms for Research Papers and D. Min. [Doctor of Ministry] Field Project Reports*. 5th ed. Enid, OK: Seminary Press, 1991.

Science—General

American National Standard for the Preparation of Scientific Papers for Written or Oral Presentation. New York: American National Standards Institute, 1979.

CBE Committee on Graduate Training in Scientific Writing. *Scientific Writing for Graduate Students: A Manual on the Teaching of Scientific Writing*. Chicago: Council of Biology Editors, 1968.

Day, Robert A. *How to Write and Publish a Scientific Paper*. 3rd ed. Phoenix: The Oryx Press, 1990.

Social Work

National Association of Social Workers. *Writing for NASW*. 2nd ed. Silver Spring, MD: NASW, 1992.

Sociology

Cuba, Lee J. *A Short Guide to Writing About Social Science*. Glenview: HarperCollins, 1988.

Gruber, James, and Judith Pryor. *Materials and Methods for Sociology Research*. New York: Neal-Schuman, 1980.

Sociology Writing Group. *A Guide to Writing Sociology Papers*. 2nd ed. New York: St. Martin's, 1990.

Acknowledgments (continued from p. vi)

Jane E. Brody, from "Weaning the Body from Dependence on Caffeine" in *The New York Times*, April 21, 1982. Copyright © 1982 by The New York Times Company. Reprinted by permission.

Truman Capote, from *Writers at Work*, George Plimpton, editor. New York: Penguin, 1981.

Choice, from M. Silverman's review of *A Software Law Primer* by Frederic William Neitzke. Copyright © 1985 by the American Library Association. Reprinted with permission from CHOICE, a publication of the American Library Association.

Congressional Information Service Annual, from *Abstracts of Congressional Publications*, January–December 1988. Copyright © 1989 by the Congressional Information Service. Reprinted with permission of Congressional Information Service (Bethesda, MD). All rights reserved.

Consumer Reports, from "Soaping Up." Copyright © 1990 by Consumers Union of United States, Inc., Yonkers, NY 10703. Excerpted by permission from *Consumer Reports*, October 1990.

Encyclopaedia Britannica, 15th edition, from the *Propaedia, Macropaedia, Micropaedia,* and *Index*. Copyright © 1989 by Encyclopaedia Britannica, Inc. Reprinted with permission of Encyclopaedia Britannica, Inc.

Encyclopedia Americana, "Pirandello, Luigi" entry. Copyright © 1988 by *Encyclopedia Americana*. Reprinted with permission of Grolier, Inc.

Essay and General Literature Index, from "Atwood, Margaret" entry. *Essay and General Literature Index*, 1985 to 1989. Copyright © 1985, 1986, 1987, 1988, and 1989 by The H. W. Wilson Company. Material reproduced with permission of the publisher.

Robert Frost, from "The Pasture," in *The Poetry of Robert Frost*, edited by Edward Connery Lathem. Copyright 1939, © 1967, 1969, by Holt, Rinehart and Winston. Reprinted by permission of Henry Holt and Company, Inc.

William Gass, from *Writers at Work*, George Plimpton, editor. New York: Penguin, 1981.

Daniel S. Grossier, from "A Study of Caffeine in Tea" in *American Journal of Clinical Nutrition* 31. Copyright © 1978 by the *American Journal of Clinical Nutrition*. Reprinted by permission of the American Society for Clinical Nutrition.

Humanities Index, "Browning, Robert" entry. *Humanities Index*, April 1989–March 1990. Copyright © 1989, 1990 by The H. W. Wilson Company. Material reproduced with permission of the publisher.

Bill Katz and Berry G. Richards, from *Magazines for Libraries*, 3rd edition. Copyright © 1978 by Reed Publishing (U.S.A.) Inc. Reprinted by permission of R. R. Bowker/Martindale-Hubbell.

Library of Congress Subject Headings, 13th edition, from vol. 2, "Solar energy" entry.

The Literary Essays of Thomas Merton, edited by Brother Patrick Hart, from copyright page. Copyright © 1981 by the Trustees of the Merton Legacy Trust and Our Lady of Gethsemani Monastery. Reprinted by permission of New Directions Publishing Corp.

MLA International Bibliography of Books and Articles on the Modern Languages and Literatures, 1988, from Subject Index and Classified Listings with Author Index. Copyright © 1989 by the Modern Language Association. Reprinted by permission of the Modern Language Association.

Ogden Nash, "Song of the Open Road," from *Verses from 1929 On* by Ogden Nash. Copyright © 1932 by Ogden Nash. First appeared in *The New Yorker*. Reprinted by permission of Little, Brown and Company (Inc.).

Elizabeth A. Nist, from "Tattle's Well's Faire: English Women Authors of the Sixteenth Century" by Elizabeth A. Nist in *College English* 46.7 (November 1984). Reprinted by permission of the National Council of Teachers of English.

The Oxford English Dictionary, 2nd edition, definition of "educate." Prepared by J. A. Simpson and E. S. C. Weiner. Copyright © 1989 by Oxford University Press. Reprinted by permission of Oxford University Press.

Miriam Polster and Erving Polster, *International Encyclopedia of Psychiatry, Psychology, Psychoanalysis, and Neurology*, from vol. 5, and "Gestalt Therapy" entries edited by Benjamin B. Wolman. Copyright © 1977 by Aesculapius Publishers, Inc., New York. Reprinted by permission of Aesculapius Publishers, Inc.

Index

Directory to Documentation Models

AUTHOR/PAGE STYLE (MLA)